JOHN CALVIN AN
THEOLOGY:
Legacy and Prospect

JOHN CALVIN AND EVANGELICAL THEOLOGY: Legacy and Prospect

In Celebration of the Quincentenary of John Calvin

Edited by Sung Wook Chung

WESTMINSTER
JOHN KNOX PRESS
LOUISVILLE · KENTUCKY

© 2009 Sung Wook Chung

First published in 2009 by Paternoster
Paternoster is an imprint of Authentic Media
9 Holdom Avenue, Bletchley, Milton Keynes, Bucks, MK1 1QR
1820 Jet Stream Drive, Colorado Springs, CO 80921, USA
OM Authentic Media, Medchal Road, Jeedimetla Village,
Secunderabad 500 055, A.P., India
www.loveauthentic.com

1st edition
Published by Westminster John Knox Press
Louisville, Kentucky

09 10 11 12 13 14 15 16 17 18—10 9 8 7 6 5 4 3 2 1

Book design by Lugovallum
Cover design by Pam Poll Design

Library of Congress Cataloging-in-Publication Data

John Calvin and evangelical theology: legacy and prospect: in celebration of the quincentenary of John Calvin
/ ed. by Sung Wook Chung. — 1st ed.
p. cm.
 Includes bibliographical references.
 ISBN 978-0-664-23346-4 (alk. paper)
 1. Calvin, Jean, 1509-1564. 2. Reformed Church—Doctrines. 3. Evangelicalism. I. Chung, Sung Wook, 1966–
BX9418.J6134 2009
230'.42—dc22

2009028338

PRINTED IN THE UNITED STATES OF AMERICA

♾ The paper used in this publication meets the minimum requirements of the American National Standard for Information Sciences—Permanence of Paper for Printed Library Materials, ANSI Z39.48-1992

Westminster John Knox Press advocates the responsible use of our natural resources.
The text paper of this book is made from 30% post-consumer waste.

Contents

Contributors

Antonio Carlos Barro is President and Professor of Mission, South American Theological Seminary, Londrina, Brazil. He has researched and published widely on mission studies and systematic theology.

Henri Blocher is Professor of Systematic Theology at the Faculté Libre de Théologie Evangélique in Vaux-sur-Seine, Paris, France. His most recent books include *Evil and the Cross: An Analytical Look at the Problem of Pain* (2005).

John Bolt is Professor of Systematic Theology, Calvin Theological Seminary, Grand Rapids, Michigan. His most recent books include *A Free Church, a Holy Nation: Abraham Kuyper's American Public Theology* (2001).

J. Lanier Burns is Research Professor of Theological Studies, Senior Professor of Systematic Theology, Dallas Theological Seminary, Dallas, Texas. He is the author of numerous books and articles.

Sung Wook Chung is Associate Professor of Theology, Denver Seminary, Littleton, Colorado. His most recent books include *A Case for Historic Premillennialism: An Alternative to "Left Behind" Eschatology* (2009).

Oliver D. Crisp is Reader in Theology, University of Bristol, Bristol, UK. His most recent books include *Divinity and Humanity: The Incarnation Reconsidered* (2007).

Elias Dantas is Director of the Doctoral Program at Alliance Theological Seminary, in Nyack, New York. He is the author of numerous books and articles in both English and Brazilian Portuguese.

Gabriel Fackre is Abbot Professor of Christian Theology Emeritus, Andover Newton Theological School, Massachusetts. His most recent books include *The Church: Signs of the Spirit and Signs of the Times* (2007).

Michael S. Horton is J. Gresham Machen Professor of Systematic Theology and Apologetics at Westminster Seminary California, Escondido, California. His most recent books include *People and Place: A Covenant Ecclesiology* (2008).

Veli-Matti Kärkkäinen is Professor of Systematic Theology, Fuller Theological Seminary, Pasadena, California. His most recent books include *Trinity and Religious Pluralism: The Doctrine of the Trinity in Christian Theology of Religions* (2004).

Jung-Sook Lee is the Dean and Associate Professor of Church History, Torch Trinity Graduate School of Theology, Seoul, Korea. She has researched and published widely on John Calvin and Reformation history.

Dieumeme Noelliste is Professor of Theological Ethics; Director of the Grounds Institute of Public Ethics, Denver Seminary, Littleton, Colorado. He has researched and published widely on Caribbean evangelical theology and Christian social ethics.

Kurt Anders Richardson is Professor in the Faculty of Theology, McMaster University, Ontario, Canada. His most recent books include *Reading Karl Barth: New Directions for North American Theology* (2004).

Mark D. Thompson is Academic Dean and Head of Theology, Moore Theological College, Australia. His most recent books include *A Clear and Present Word: The Clarity of Scripture* (2006).

Foreword

Why Contemporary Evangelicalism Needs to Heed John Calvin

Alister E. McGrath

Why do we need to listen to John Calvin? Why take a voice from the past with such seriousness when there are so many challenges and concerns in the present? Isn't reading and reflecting on Calvin simply a scholarly luxury, which is out of place in today's culture? While I understand and respect the concerns being expressed here, I have long believed that engaging with Calvin could help evangelicalism deepen its self-understanding, its grasp of the gospel, and above all its sense of connection with Christian history. I am not for one moment suggesting that evangelicals should replicate what they find in Calvin's works. After all, evangelicals are those who ground themselves in the Bible, seeing all interpretations of the biblical texts as being secondary to its supreme authority. Rather, I am suggesting that Calvin can be both a stimulus and a guide to contemporary evangelicalism as it wrestles with questions of interpretation and application. Let me explain what I mean.

Evangelicalism celebrates and proclaims the supreme spiritual, moral, and theological authority of Scripture. At the Diet of Worms (18 April 1521), Martin Luther famously declared: "My conscience is captive to the word of God." This powerful and bold statement resonates throughout evangelical history—a principled intention to listen attentively and obediently to Scripture, and to respond faithfully in our beliefs and actions. Yet evangelicals are aware that an emphasis upon the authority of Scripture cannot be uncoupled from the question of its proper interpretation. One of the major theological weaknesses of the "Battle for the Bible" within American evangelicalism during the 1980s was an apparent reluctance to accept that an infallible text was open to fallible interpretation. To assert the supreme authority of Scripture does not resolve how it is to be understood.

This familiar problem is often cited as the Achilles' heel of contemporary evangelicalism. How can the validity of competing interpretations of Scripture be determined without appealing to some ground of authority that ultimately lies beyond Scripture itself? Evangelicalism, having affirmed the supreme authority of Scripture, finds itself without any meta-authority by which the correct interpretation of Scripture can be determined. This question is usually resolved politically, rather than theologically, by committees or organizations laying down how certain texts are to be interpreted. Yet this is not a new problem, nor one that is unique to evangelicalism. It has been an issue for the Protestant theological tradition as a whole. How can conflict over biblical interpretation be resolved without ultimately acknowledging certain criteria or agencies as standing *above* Scripture? To place any means of adjudication above Scripture is ultimately to compromise its unique authority. This realization has led to a growing appreciation of the role that engagement with the past might play in contemporary evangelical biblical interpretation and systematic theology. This naturally leads us to reflect on the role that Calvin can play in this respect for contemporary evangelicalism.

Calvin speaks to us as one who shares evangelicalism's emphasis upon the supreme authority of Scripture, yet who recognizes that the affirmation of this authority does not close down the question of how it is to be interpreted. Calvin's biblical commentaries and his *Institutes* are models of excellence in the comparative evaluation of scriptural interpretations. Although I do not always agree with Calvin, I constantly find myself delighted and excited by the clarity of his biblical exposition, and the rigorous analysis that leads him to his theological conclusions. To use the language of J.I. Packer, Calvin has a *ministerial*, rather than a *magisterial*, authority within evangelicalism. Packer's point is that evangelicalism recognizes no authority above Scripture; nevertheless, it welcomes wisdom and insight as it seeks to understand Scripture. And, as these essays indicate so clearly, Calvin offers us a rigorous theological analysis of the core themes of the Christian faith, constantly grounding them in the biblical text. Calvin represents a landmark, a benchmark of theological excellence, which is both a resource and a challenge to our own biblical interpretation and theological system-building.

There is another point to be made. Calvin himself constantly referred to and engaged earlier interpreters of Scripture—theologians such as Augustine and Chrysostom, to name only two obvious examples. Why? Because, as Calvin made clear at the Disputation of Lausanne (1536), evangelicalism valued and honored the Christian witness of the past, and sought to weave its insights appropriately into its own renderings of Scripture. While Calvin was not prepared to endorse the theological opinions of the fathers uncritically, he nevertheless emphasized their stabilizing and ministerial role for evangelical theology, and the importance of critical and respectful engagement with their ideas. "We do not exalt their authority in such a way as to debase the dignity of the word of our Lord, to which alone total obedience is due within the church of Christ." For Calvin, the Christian tradition was a providential aid to the interpretation of Scripture. Calvin thus offers a double motivation for serious engagement with the past, in that he himself has now become a valued part of the "great tradition" of faith.

Evangelical theology seems to be coming to appreciate the theological heritage of the past as a resource and stimulus for its own reflections. The potential significance of this development for the stabilization and enrichment of evangelicalism is enormous. The rise of interest in "paleo-orthodoxy" within contemporary evangelicalism is a sure sign of this trend. Calvin himself is one of the treasures of this "great tradition"; this volume will surely encourage further reflection and discussion of his significance. I commend it warmly, valuing both its historical and contemporary significance. I note with particular pleasure how so many of the contributors seek to apply the past to the present, so that we might learn *from* the past, not simply learn about it. This will unquestionably lead to a better understanding and appreciation of Calvin. Yet, more importantly, it could also lead to a theologically enriched and spiritually alert evangelicalism.

Alister E. McGrath
King's College, London

Preface

The year 2009 marks the five-hundredth anniversary of John Calvin's birth. It is almost axiomatic that Calvin has been one of the most influential theologians for evangelicalism and its theology for the past 500 years. It is a scholarly consensus that Calvin has made an indelible and incalculable impact not only upon Reformed tradition but also upon other evangelical traditions within the global evangelical movement. Many evangelical historians, including Alister E. McGrath, Mark Noll, George Marsden, and David Bebbington, regard Calvin as one of the foremost founding fathers of the modern evangelical movement. Furthermore, many contemporary evangelical theologians acknowledge that their theological works are deeply indebted to Calvin's theological thought.

On the basis of this insight, this book aims to explore the legacy and prospect of Calvin's theology for evangelical theology in the twenty-first century. As many scholars have argued, the centers of Christianity have already moved to Africa, Asia, and Latin America, and Christianity of the global South has demonstrated a more evangelical slant in its beliefs and practices. As a result, Calvin's influence has been expanding greatly over the whole globe, penetrating into African, Asian, and Latin American Christianity. For example, evangelical Christianity in Korea has been considerably influenced by Calvin's theological thought and insights. As a consequence, most Korean evangelicals today belong to the Reformed and Presbyterian tradition. In addition, evangelical Christianity in Brazil and other Latin American countries has been appropriating valuable lessons from Calvin's Reformed and evangelical theological ideas. In this context, it is significant and meaningful for us to attempt to reappropriate creatively Calvin's theological thought through an assessment of his theological legacy and prospect for the future of global evangelical theology.

It is one of the most significant features of this book that contributors are from various traditions within the global evangelical movement, traditions such as Dutch neo-Calvinism, the French Reformed tradition, Scottish-American Presbyterianism, Anglicanism, Congregationalism, the Baptist tradition, Calvinist Dispensationalism, the Asian Reformed tradition, and Latin American evangelicalism.

In addition, another important feature of this book is that it deals with a variety of evangelical doctrines and theological themes upon which Calvin made a significant impact. By examining the legacy and prospect of John Calvin's theology for the future of global evangelical theology, this book will provide evangelical Christians and theologians with an invaluable opportunity to celebrate the dynamics and maturity of global evangelicalism and its theology.

Special thanks go to my wife, In-Kyung, for her editorial help.

Sung Wook Chung

1

Knowing God: Calvin's Understanding of Revelation

Michael Horton

Although Calvin's goal in writing the *Institutes* was to provide a defense of the evangelical faith and a basic summary for pastors, especially for persecuted refugees flocking to Geneva, this remarkable work was not a systematic theology. Furthermore, we are used to genitive theologies in the modern era: Theology of Crisis, Theology of Revelation, Theology of Correlation, and the like. Unlike many modern theologians, Calvin did not think that he was developing a "system" bearing his own special imprint, but firmly believed that he was simply teaching Scripture, following traditional interpretations wherever possible and departing where he thought necessary. Regardless of our own evaluation, Calvin did not regard himself as an original thinker.[1]

Although we cannot develop a dogmatic construal of something like "Calvin's doctrine of revelation" or "Scripture," there are crucial presuppositions, arguments, and motifs that he inherited and modified, which can be brought together to reveal a definite pattern. Other motifs could be included and there are many other ways of summarizing them, but I will point up three distinctive emphases that characterize Calvin's treatment of revelation: God's incomprehensibility, God's condescension, and God's speech.

---

[1] Richard A. Muller, *The Unaccommodated Calvin: Studies in the Foundation of a Theological Tradition* (New York: Oxford University Press, 2000), 7, 182–3.

1 God's incomprehensibility

Given the positive ontological difference (incomprehensible majesty) and the negative ethical opposition of God and fallen humanity, we dare not attempt to ascend to heaven by our own reason, will, and works, but must meet God where he has promised to descend to us, meeting us in grace. This is the covenant of grace, with Christ's mediation as the only basis for a safe conduct into God's presence. The Reformers therefore contrasted the *theology of glory* with the *theology of the cross*. Instead of striving as masters of reality to behold God in his archetypal majesty, we must take our place as unfaithful servants and be addressed by him on his own terms, in judgment and grace.

It was Martin Luther who, in his Heidelberg Disputation (1518), first coined this contrast between a theology of glory and a theology of the cross.[2] While the theology of the cross proclaims God's descent in the flesh to sinners, by grace alone in Christ alone, theologies of glory represent human attempts to ascend away from the flesh to union with God through mysticism, merit, and philosophical speculation. However, God's majesty is not benign. When Moses asked to see God's glory, Yahweh allowed his "backside"—that is, his goodness and grace—to pass by while he sheltered the prophet behind a rock. "'But,' [God] said, 'you cannot see my face, for man shall not see me and live'" (Ex. 33:20, ESV). All that we know—or think we know—about God already within ourselves is a revelation of God's law, which we have distorted and suppressed in order to justify ourselves as we attempt to ascend to heaven. We must learn to receive God's revelation and redemption where he has condescended to us, in the lowliness of a manger, on the cross, and in the baseness of ordinary human language.

Similarly, Calvin explained that the attributes of God are set forth in Scripture. "Thereupon his powers are mentioned, by which he is shown to us *not as he is in himself, but as he is toward us*: so that this recognition of him consists *more in living experience than in vain and high-flown speculation*."[3] Knowing God as he is in himself has been the familiar refrain of

---

[2] See Walther von Loewenich, *Luther's Theology of the Cross*, tr. Herbert J.A. Bouman (Minneapolis: Augsburg Publishing House, 1976); A.E. McGrath, *Luther's Theology of the Cross: Martin Luther's Theological Breakthrough* (Oxford: Basil Blackwell, 1985); B.A. Gerrish, "To the Unknown God: Luther and Calvin on the Hiddenness of God," *Journal of Religion*, 53 (1973), 263–92.

[3] John Calvin, *Institutes of the Christian Religion*, ed. John T. McNeill, tr. Ford Lewis Battles, The Library of Christian Classics, vol. XX (Philadelphia: Westminster Press, 1960 (1559)), I.10.2 (emphasis added). (Henceforth, references to the *Institutes* will be indicated in the text by book, chapter and section.)

mystics and other enthusiasts in all ages, but God's incomprehensible majesty is damning rather than saving. God cannot be directly known by our climbing the scale of being, but can only be known in and through the Mediator. Calvin explained,

> When faith is discussed in the schools, they call God simply the object of faith, and by fleeting speculations, as we have elsewhere stated, lead miserable souls astray rather than direct them to a definite goal. For since "God dwells in inaccessible light" (1 Tim. 6:16), Christ must become our intermediary . . . Indeed, it is true that faith looks to one God. But this must also be added, "to know Jesus Christ whom he has sent" (Jn. 17:3). (III.2.1)

While a theology of glory presumes to scale the walls of God's heavenly chamber, a theology of the cross will always recognize that although we cannot reach God, he can reach us and has done so in his Word.

The Reformers' insistence upon God's incomprehensible majesty had clear precedent in the ancient church. Preserving the distinction between creaturely knowledge of God, and God in his hidden, transcendent, and incomprehensible majesty, the fourth-century Eastern theologian Gregory of Nyssa, for example, explores a series of divine attributes. "But in each of these terms," he cautions, "we find a peculiar sense, fit to be understood or asserted of the Divine nature, yet not expressing that which that nature is in its essence."[4]

Similarly, John of Damascus (d. 749) counsels, "As knowing all things, therefore, and providing for what is profitable for each, He revealed that which it was to our profit to know; but what we were unable to bear He kept secret. With these things let us be satisfied, and let us abide by them, not removing everlasting boundaries, nor overpassing the divine tradition." With Scripture, we must "express ourselves according to our limited capacity; as, for instance, when we speak of God we use the terms sleep, and wrath, and regardlessness, hands, too, and feet, and such like expressions."[5] We know God by his works, not in his hidden essence.[6]

---

[4] Gregory of Nyssa, "On 'Not Three Gods' to Ablabius," in *A Select Library of Nicene and Post-Nicene Fathers of the Christian Church*, second series, vol. 5, tr. S.D.F. Salmond (Grand Rapids: Eerdmans, 1973), 333.

[5] John of Damascus, "An Exact Exposition of the Orthodox Faith," in *A Select Library of Nicene and Post-Nicene Fathers of the Christian Church*, second series, vol. 9, tr. S.D.F. Salmond (Grand Rapids: Eerdmans, 1973), 1.

[6] John of Damascus, "An Exact Exposition," 2.

Trying to probe the mysterious divine essence or will apart from Christ and his written Word is the essence of idolatry, Calvin argued. We only know God by means of his works, as he is toward us, not as he is in himself.[7] While medieval systems contained lengthy treatments of the divine essence, Calvin moves quickly through a necessary affirmation of God's spirituality and immensity to discuss the Trinity. "They are mad who seek to discover what God is," he says. "The essence of God is rather to be adored than inquired into" (I.2.2). Early Reformed writers such as Musculus repeated this approach, explicitly launching their discussion of God with the question of who God is rather than what God is.[8] Francis Turretin wrote,

> But when God is set forth as the object of theology, he is not to be regarded simply as God in himself (for thus he is incomprehensible (*akataleptos*) to us), but as revealed and as he has been pleased to manifest himself to us in his word, so that divine revelation is the formal relation which comes to be considered in this object.[9]

Although a sympathetic interpreter of Aquinas, Turretin is simply following this Reformation insight when he adds,

> *Nor is he to be considered exclusively under the relation of deity* (according to the opinion of Thomas Aquinas and many Scholastics after him, for in this manner the knowledge of him could not be saving but deadly to sinners), but as he is *our* God (i.e., *covenanted in Christ as he has revealed himself to us in his word not only as the object of knowledge, but also of worship*).[10]

---

[7] Benjamin B. Warfield, *Calvin and Augustine*, ed. Samuel Craig (Phillipsburg, N.J.: Presbyterian & Reformed Publishing Co., 1956), 153. As B.B. Warfield noted, "He is refusing all a priori methods of determining the nature of God and requiring of us to form our knowledge of him a posteriori from the revelation He gives us of Himself in His activities." See further his excellent summary of this reticence in Calvin and the tradition generally to explore the "whatness," 139–40.

[8] Richard A. Muller, *Post-Reformation Reformed Dogmatics: The Rise and Development of Reformed Orthodoxy*, vol. 3, *The Divine Essence and Attributes* (Grand Rapids: Baker Academic, 1993), 228.

[9] Francis Turretin, *Institutes of Elenctic Theology*, vol. 1, ed. James T. Dennison, Jr., tr. George M. Giger (Phillipsburg, N.J.: Presbyterian & Reformed Publishing Co., 1992), 16–17.

[10] Turretin, *Elenctic Theology*, 16–17.

"Deity" is not something that is available to us—and in any case, the God of Israel is not a species of a genus known as "God." We only have access to this particular God as "covenanted in Christ," revealed in his Word, to the practical end that we will know him in a saving rather than deadly way.

2 God's condescension

Calvin shared Luther's concentration upon God's descent to us in contrast with attempts to ascend to God. Like God's redemptive agency, which it serves, God's revelation is always a sovereign act in which God takes the initiative. God does not reveal himself as he is in himself, which would be devastating rather than saving; rather, he graciously condescends to wrap himself in human language, however much it is beneath the dignity of his infinite majesty. Furthermore, Calvin shared Luther's emphasis on Christ—the hypostatic Word—as the mediator of revelation and redemption. Only when we are led to the Father in and through the mediation of the Son incarnate are we assured that we will meet a gracious and welcoming God instead of a terrifying judge.

We are not left in silence on this side of an unbridgeable gulf, but it is because God has stooped to our feeble capacity. Revelation is always, therefore, accommodated discourse, even "baby-talk" in which God "must descend far beneath his loftiness," as Calvin puts it (I.13.1; III.11.20). Not even in revelation, according to Calvin, does the believer "attain to [God's] exalted state," but one does receive truth "accommodated to our capacity so that we may understand it" (I.17.13). "Better to limp along this path," Calvin cautioned, "than to dash with all speed outside it" (I.6.3).

3 God's Word

3.1 The forms of God's Word

In Calvin's thinking, the Word of God has several referents: first, the hypostatic Word, Jesus Christ; second, the lively speech by which God created the heavens and the earth and upholds all things; third, the written Scriptures; and fourth, the public preaching of Christ by ministers. Throughout all of these forms, the Word of God must be distinguished in terms of law and gospel. Both Lutheran and Reformed traditions have insisted on this point. Law and gospel are correlated not with the Old and New Testaments, respectively, but with everything in both Testaments that is either in the form of a command or a saving promise in Christ.[11] "Hence," wrote Luther, "whoever knows well this art of distinguishing between the Law and the Gospel, him place at the head and call him a doctor of Holy Scripture."[12]

Calvin and his Reformed colleagues and theological heirs underscored this point as well.[13] Wilhelm Niesel observes, "Reformed theology recognises the contrast between Law and Gospel, in a way similar to Lutheranism. We read in the Second Helvetic Confession: 'The Gospel is indeed opposed to the Law. For the Law works wrath and pronounces a curse, whereas the Gospel preaches grace and blessing.'"[14] Ursinus, chief author of the Heidelberg Catechism, called this "the chief division of Holy Scripture" and Beza insisted in his catechism that "ignorance of this distinction is one of the causes of the many abuses in the church" throughout history.[15] The great Elizabethan Puritan, William Perkins, taught that this was the first principle for preachers to learn in interpreting and applying passages.[16] More recently, Herman Bavinck and Louis Berkhof have observed the significance of this distinction for the whole Christian system of faith and practice.[17] As covenant canon, these two parts of the Word

[11] See the Apology to the Augsburg Confession (1531), Article 4. Article 5 of the Formula of Concord adds, "We believe, teach, and confess that the distinction between the Law and the Gospel is to be maintained in the Church with great diligence . . ." (F. Bente and W.H.T. Dau (eds. and trs.), *Triglot Concordia: The Symbolical Books of the Evangelical Lutheran Church* (St. Louis: Concordia Publishing House, 1921)).

[12] Martin Luther, *The Proper Distinction Between Law and Gospel: Thirty-Nine Evening Lectures*, ed. F.W. Walther, tr. W.H.T. Dau (St. Louis: Concordia, 1986 (1899)).

[13] See Michael Horton, "Calvin and the Law–Gospel Hermeneutic," *Pro Ecclesia* 6 (1997), 27–42.

[14] Wilhelm Niesel, *Reformed Symbolics: A Comparison of Catholicism, Orthodoxy and Protestantism*, tr. David Lewis (Edinburgh: Oliver & Boyd, 1962), 217.

[15] Zacharias Ursinus, *The Commentary of Dr Zacharias Ursinus on the Heidelberg Catechism* (Phillipsburg, N.J.: Presbyterian & Reformed Publishing Co., 1985 (1852)), 1; Theodore Beza, *The Christian Faith*, tr. James Clark (Lewes: Christian Focus Ministries, 1992), 41–3.

[16] William Perkins, *The Art of Prophesying* (Edinburgh: Banner of Truth Trust, 1996), 54–6.

[17] See Herman Bavinck, *Reformed Dogmatics*, vol. 4, ed. John Bolt, tr. John Vriend (Grand Rapids: Baker Academic, 2003–2008), 450. Louis Berkhof writes, "The

of God consist of stipulations (things to be done) and the historical narra-tive of God's deliverance (things to be believed). As sacramental Word, the law kills and through the work of the Spirit the gospel makes alive (2 Cor. 3:6–11). Of course, the law also guides, as the gospel also instructs. Hence, the Reformers affirmed a three-fold use of the law: to arraign us before God's judgment and prove the world guilty; to remind all people, even non-Christians, of their obligations to the moral law written on their con-science; and to guide believers in the way of gratitude.[18]

3.2 General revelation

As even Karl Barth reluctantly conceded, Calvin clearly taught that God revealed himself in nature and history. This did not mean that he revealed himself apart from Christ since, according to Calvin, the Father was the origin, the Son the medium, and the Spirit the perfecting power of every external act of the Trinity.

Furthermore, Calvin's affirmation of general revelation is distin-guished from the dominant view in Roman Catholic thinking. First, *Calvin's approach is distinguished by its view of the content of such revelation.* If God reveals himself by his works, then in Calvin's view this original revelation demonstrated God's power, glory, wisdom, and goodness. It did not reveal God's grace and mercy, since there was not yet any fault and therefore no promulgation of the gospel. There is no revelation of God's saving purposes in Christ that can be derived from this original revelation. As a form of law, it is the basis for any sense of justice, truth, and love in human society, but it is not a redemptive revelation.

Chapter 3 of Book I begins, "There is within the human mind, and indeed by natural instinct, an awareness of divinity. This we take to be beyond controversy" (I.3.1). "Indeed, even idolatry is ample proof of this conception" (I.3.1). The *sensus* "can never be effaced" entirely (I.3.3). However, this knowledge is suppressed as idolatry. "They do not there-fore apprehend God as he offers himself, but imagine him as they have fashioned him in their own presumption (I.4.1). Zealous superstition is

---

(cont.) churches of the Reformation from the very beginning distinguished between the law and the gospel as the two parts of the Word of God as a means of grace. This distinction was not understood to be identified with that between the Old and New Testament, but was regarded as a distinction that applies to both Testaments. There is law and gospel in the Old Testament, and there is law and gospel in the New" (*Systematic Theology: A New Combined Edition* (Grand Rapids: Eerdmans, 1996), 612).

[18] The Formula of Concord, Article 6; Calvin, *Institutes*, II.7.6, 10, 12.

sufficient evidence of both of these points (I.4.3). Unbelievers remain in their ignorance "because they are confident that they can perform their duty toward [God] by ridiculous acts of expiation" (I.4.4).

Second, *Calvin's view differs from the Roman Catholic view concerning the status of the receiver of general revelation.* If there had been no Fall, there would be no conflict between faith and reason, obedience to God's Word and sense-experience, revelation and science. It is not *reason* that is opposed to faith, but the *reasoner.* Clearly, then, the problem is not with general revelation but with the moral condition of its interpreter.

It is enough for the common people to see the "sparks of his glory" in the "beautiful system of the universe," but how much more are those engaged in "astronomy, medicine, and all natural science" confronted with God's work each day (I.5.2). Calvin's assessment of the natural person surrounded by general revelation is that of one who is "struck blind in such a dazzling theater" (I.5.8). Calvin seems to have been more favorable toward the natural sciences than toward philosophy as the medium of general revelation. The works of God's majesty "can be observed with the eyes and pointed out with the finger." This is "not that knowledge which, content with empty speculation, merely flits in the brain, but that which will be sound and fruitful if we duly perceive it, and if it takes root in the heart" (V.1.9). It is one thing to observe certain divine attributes from the things that God has made and quite another to offer speculations deduced from our own ideas of a perfect being. Calvin writes,

> Consequently, we know the most perfect way of seeking God, and the most suitable order, is not for us to attempt with bold curiosity to penetrate to the investigation of his essence, which we ought more to adore than meticulously to search out, but for us to contemplate him in his works whereby he renders himself near and familiar to us, and in some manner communicates himself. (I.5.9)

Besides his vivid analogy of being struck blind in a beautiful theater, Calvin thinks of the fallen mind as a labyrinth or maze

> For each man's mind is like a labyrinth, so that it is no wonder that individual nations were drawn aside into various falsehoods; and not only this—but individual men, almost, had their own gods. For as rashness and superficiality are joined to ignorance and darkness, scarcely a single person has ever been found who did not fashion for himself an idol or specter in the place of God . . . It is therefore in vain that so many burning lamps shine for

us in the workmanship of the universe to show forth the glory of its Author. Although they bathe us wholly in their radiance, yet they can of themselves in no way lead us into the right path. Surely they strike some sparks, but before their fuller light shines forth these are smothered. (I.5.12, 14)

We need special revelation even "to direct us aright to the very Creator of the universe" (I.6.1). Scripture provides the "spectacles," allowing us rightly to interpret general revelation (I.6.1). Only in this way does God step forward to reveal himself—not the existence of a god, but himself as the only true God, and "to recognize God not only as Creator but also as Redeemer" through his Word (I.6.1).

Just as Rome regards special revelation as differing only in degree, it sees human beings as standing in varying degrees of truth, righteousness, and grace. However, Calvin held that the mind as well as the will was fal-len. Therefore, although God's revelation in creation continues to speak, the hearer's ears are dull and eyes dim; one needs special revelation as the "spectacles" through which to rightly interpret even God's work in creation. In Calvin's view, therefore, grace (and special revelation) does not supplement nature (and general revelation), but redeems and restores it.

Total depravity means that there was not any part of humanity left unsullied by the Fall, not that human beings are as bad (or as ignorant) as they could possibly be. As Calvin recognized, the *sensus divinitatis* (sense of divinity) is common to all human beings as "the law of their creation."[19] It is not that general revelation is denied, but that it becomes the material out of which we, employing all of the gifts of our nature, corrupt, distort, deface, and suppress the truth. As soon as we, in our fallen humanity, see a glimmering ember of divine truth we smother it and this is why there can be no true natural theology (I.4.1–I.45.14). For a true theology (even of nature), humanity needs another word, another revelation other than the *sensus divinitatis* (natural revelation), to announce God's free grace and reconciliation through the mediation of Christ. This revelation "alone quickens souls" (I.6.1–3). Natural theologies will always be some form of our native theology of glory, while the gospel reveals the theology of the cross.

Calvin could therefore speak almost glowingly of the "admirable light of truth shining in secular writers . . ." teaching us that the human mind, "though fallen and perverted from its wholeness, is nevertheless clothed and ornamented with God's excellent gifts." He continues,

---

[19] See especially, *Institutes*, I.3.1–3.

What then? Shall we deny that the truth shone on the ancient jurists who established civic order and discipline with such great equity? Those whom Scripture calls "natural men" were, indeed, sharp and penetrating in their investigation of earthly things. Let us, accordingly, learn by their example how many gifts the Lord left to human nature even after it was despoiled of its true good. (II.2.15)

On this basis, Calvin challenged the view that the state (lower in rank) must take its cues from the church (higher in rank). With Luther, he spoke of two kingdoms or "a two-fold government." Just as the body and soul are distinct without being intrinsically opposed, "Christ's spiritual kingdom and the civil jurisdiction are things completely distinct . . . Yet this distinction does not lead us to consider the whole nature of government a thing polluted, which has nothing to do with Christian men." These two kingdoms are "distinct," yet "they are not at variance" (IV.20.1–2). Grace is not a higher sphere than nature, the soul is not higher than the body, the church is not higher than the state, and special revelation is not higher than general revelation. Rather, grace redeems nature and special revelation not only discloses God's redemptive actions but gives us the "spectacles," to borrow Calvin's metaphor, through which we can properly interpret general revelation as well.

Like Augustine in the *City of God*, Calvin moves dialectically between an affirmation of the natural order and its inability, because of sin, to generate an *ultimate* society. The goal of common grace is not to perfect nature, but to restrain sin and animate civic virtues and arts, so that culture may fulfill its own important, but limited, temporal and secular ends, while God simultaneously pursues the redemptive aims of his everlasting city. Especially with radical Protestants like Thomas Müntzer in mind, Calvin—following Paul's claim that the moral law revealed in Scripture is the natural law revealed in creation—strongly opposed the idea that a valid civil order must be based on the Bible.[20] In addition to these natural remnants of the image of God in every person, Calvin speaks of God's common grace: "not such grace as to cleanse it [nature], but to restrain it inwardly." This common grace is tied to providence, to restraint; "but he does not purge it within" (IV.20.8, 14). Only the gospel can do this. Thus, common grace and natural law are complementary, not contradictory, concepts for Calvin.[21]

---

[20] *Institutes*, IV.20.8, 14. The basic ligaments of Calvin's political theology can be found in IV.20.1–32.

[21] For precisely the same view, see Philip Melanchthon, *Loci Communes* (1543), tr. J.A.O. Preus (St. Louis: Concordia, 1992), 70.

Because one cannot suppress everything at the same time, the ineradicable sense of justice (natural law) engenders secular community while only the gospel can create a church. The internal word (*verbum internum*) will always be in the form of law (which is why religion is naturally associated with morality and eternal rewards), but the external Word (*verbum externum*) announced by a messenger creates saving faith. This distinction in content does not imply a dualism between creation (general revelation) and redemption (special revelation), since these are not separate spheres but distinct acts and covenants—and in both instances they are the effect of the Father's speaking in the Son and by his Spirit. Here dualism is vanquished, notes Herman Bavinck. "The foundations of creation and redemption are the same. The Logos who became flesh is the same by whom all things were made."[22] Calvin therefore disagreed with Rome at a fundamental level of ontology. For the latter, human existence is not divided between higher and lower realms. There is only a whole person who is created in God's image, fallen in the totality of his or her existence, and redeemed in that same totality. The problematic with which Reformation theology works is sin-and-grace, not nature-and-grace.

3.3 Special revelation

3.3.1 Scripture

Special revelation not only communicates the gospel (which is not revealed in creation), but also corrects our distorted lenses through which we view general revelation. Calvin observes in I.6.2 that the patriarchs had received God's revelation in various ways, sometimes directly and other times indirectly. In any case, God "put into their minds what they should then hand down to their posterity." They knew that "what they had learned proceeded from God. For by his Word, God rendered faith unambiguous forever, a faith that should be superior to all opinion" (I.6.2). The law was clearly published on tablets and in the gospel God is truly known in Christ the Mediator, says Calvin. Therefore, we cannot make any progress in true religion apart from Scripture. As we have seen, Calvin thought of the mind of fallen humans as a labyrinth. The only way through the labyrinth is to be "conducted into it by the thread of the Word; so that it is better to limp along this path than to dash with all speed outside it" (I.6.3).

---

[22] On this point, see Herman Bavinck, *The Philosophy of Revelation* (Grand Rapids: Baker Academic, 1979, paperback; originally published by Longmans, Green and Co., 1909), 26–8.

Next, Calvin argues that Scripture's authority derives from God rather than from the church (I.7.1). "Hence the Scriptures obtain full authority among believers only when men regard them as having sprung from heaven, as if there the living words of God were heard" (I.7.1). Paul "testifies that the church is 'built upon the foundation of the prophets and apostles' (Eph. 2:20). If the teaching of the prophets and apostles is the foundation, this must have had authority before the church began to exist" (I.7.2). We learn to distinguish colors, sweet things and bitter things, and so on without recourse to the church or other authorities; similarly, we learn to respect the authority of God's Word simply because of what it is, not because of the church's approval (I.7.2).

Roman Catholic theologians had repeatedly appealed to Augustine's comment in *Contra epistolam Manichaei quam vocant fundamenti* that he would not believe the gospel if he had not been moved by the church's authority. Calvin reminds readers in I.7.3 that this was a dispute with Manicheanism. The context is all important, Calvin observes. While the Manicheans simply declared their convictions, demanding assent without any argument or evidence, the church persuades. "Augustine is not, therefore, teaching that the faith of godly men is founded on the authority of the church; nor does he hold the view that the certainty of the gospel depends upon it. He is simply teaching that there would be no certainty of the gospel for unbelievers to win them to Christ if the consensus of the church did not impel them." It is precisely that consensus that the Manicheans reject. Later in this work, says Calvin, Augustine argues that those who are still infants in the faith should not abandon it for the Manichean heresy, but should accept the church's authority as teacher, to learn the gospel and grow up into Christ.[23] The consensus of the whole church is indeed weighty evidence. This gospel has been "handed down from the time of the apostles through a sure succession," Calvin willingly affirms. "But it never occurs to [Augustine] to teach that the authority which we ascribe to Scripture depends upon the definition or decree of men" (I.7.3). The church's consensus is an argument, not the premise.

At the end of the day, it is the testimony of the Spirit rather than that of the church that is the foundation for our confidence (I.7.4). This is not apart from the "manifest signs of God speaking in Scripture" (I.7.4), but through them. "Yet they who strive to build up firm faith in Scripture through disputation are doing things backward" (I.7.4). It is fine to offer arguments for the Bible's authenticity and authority, as Calvin will do,

23 Bavinck, *The Philosophy of Revelation*, 136.

but these must be supports rather than the foundation of faith. Otherwise, faith will always waver, depending on the strength of arguments rather than the nature of Scripture itself. Calvin writes,

> For my part, although I do not excel either in great dexterity or eloquence, if I were struggling against the most crafty sort of despisers of God, who seek to appear shrewd and witty in disparaging Scripture, I am confident it would not be difficult for me to silence their clamorous voices. And if it were a useful labor to refute their cavils, I would with no great trouble shatter the boasts they mutter in their lurking places. But even if anyone clears God's Sacred Word from man's evil speaking, he will not at once imprint upon their hearts that certainty which piety requires. Since for unbelieving men religion seems to stand by opinion alone, they, in order not to believe anything foolishly or lightly, both wish and demand rational proof that Moses and the prophets spoke divinely. But I reply: the testimony of the Spirit is more excellent than all reason. For as God alone is a fit witness of himself in his Word, so also the Word will not find acceptance in men's hearts before it is sealed by the inward testimony of the Spirit. The same Spirit, therefore, who has spoken through the mouths of the prophets must penetrate into our hearts to persuade us that they faithfully proclaimed what had been divinely commanded. (I.7.4)

Scripture, added Calvin, is "self-authenticated" (*autopiston*) (I.7.5). Once this is accepted, and certainty is founded on God's own testimony, external arguments may be put forward; in fact, they are then "very useful aids" (I.8.1). Scripture is clearly not divine in its eloquence, which is inferior to many of the pagan orators. Yet its content is such that it "could not be humanly conceived" (I.8.2). Calvin offers an argument from the antiquity of Scripture (I.8.3) and defends the church's contention that Moses wrote "under heavenly inspiration" (I.8.4).

Besides offering positive arguments, Calvin also responds to criticisms concerning the miracles and prophecies (I.8.5–8). "For they ask, Who assures us that the books that we read under the names of Moses and the prophets were written by them? They even dare question whether there ever was a Moses." Yet no one asks "whether there ever was a Plato, an Aristotle, or a Cicero . . . Josiah did not put it [the law] forward as something unknown or new, but as something that had always been of common knowledge, the memory of which was then famous. The archetypal roll was committed to the Temple; a copy was made from it and designated for the royal archives" (Deut. 17:18–19) (I.8.9).

Calvin further defends the trustworthiness of Scripture on the basis of its transmission and preservation. "Even though all wicked men, as if conspiring together, have so shamelessly insulted the Jews, no one has ever dared charge them with substituting false books" (I.8.10). The divine origin of the New Testament is evident in the fact that its history and doctrine, though communicated "in humble and lowly style," convey the most profound truths (I.8.11).

> Matthew, previously tied to the gain of his table, Peter and John going about in their boats—all of them rude, uneducated men—had learned nothing in the school of men that they could pass on to others. Paul, not only a sworn but fierce and murderous enemy, was converted into a new man; this sudden and unhoped-for change shows that he was compelled by heavenly authority to affirm a doctrine that he had assailed. (I.8.11)

Finally, despite the repeated attempts of the world to silence this Word and despite the threats of internal heresies and schisms, the church's consensus is a stirring testimony and martyrs willingly gave their lives for its heavenly doctrine (I.8.12–13).

While Calvin's focus has thus far been on the objections of scoffers—those whom we might call (anachronistically) rationalists, Calvin shifts attention in chapter 9 to the radical Anabaptists or "enthusiasts." These are

> not so much gripped by error as carried away with frenzy. For of late, certain giddy men have arisen who, with great haughtiness exalting the teaching office of the Spirit, despise all reading and laugh at the simplicity of those who, as they express it, still follow the dead and killing letter. But I should like to know from them what this spirit is by whose inspiration they are borne up so high that they dare despise the Scriptural doctrine as childish and mean. (I.9.1)

Spirit and Scripture are held together by an inviolable bond. "Therefore the Spirit, promised to us, has not the task of inventing new and unheard-of revelations, or of forging a new kind of doctrine, to lead us away from the received doctrine of the gospel, but of sealing our minds with that very doctrine which is commended by the gospel" (I.9.1). The Spirit illumines the Word; he does not give new words (I.9.1).

While special revelation radically corrects our unfaithful interpretations of creation, nature, and history (the purview of general revelation), the principal focus is the good will of God toward sinners in Jesus Christ. The gospel is the heart of Scripture. Calvin's colleagues and heirs were fully agreed on this point and they treated the characteristics of

Scripture (namely, inspiration, authority, and sufficiency) as inseparable from its scope and content (law and gospel, with the unfolding plan of redemption in Christ through the covenant of grace).[24] "Thus, the *scopus* or center "toward which all the Scriptures tend . . . is Jesus Christ," wrote Jerome Zanchi.[25] "Scripture, argues [Edward] Leigh, is called the Word of God because of 'the matter contained within it.'"[26] Christ as mediator of the covenant of grace is the scope of all Scripture.[27] The Reformed orthodox never veer from the Reformers' emphasis on "the priority of the *material* over the *forma*, the priority of the Word of saving doctrine mediated by the text over the text as such."[28] Calvin's friend and fellow Reformer, Peter Martyr Vermigli, wrote, "'Thus says the Lord' (*Dominus dixit*) ought to be held as a first principle (*primum principium*) into which all true theology is resolved."[29] Perspicuity, sufficiency, scope and analogy of Scripture all converge into one practice: Christ-centered exegesis. Vermigli adds,

> Moreover, every rational faculty and intellectual discipline derives its worthiness from the subject matter with which it deals . . . Wherefore, since our [theological] *scientia* treats of nothing other than Christ, it ought all the more to be acknowledged as the highest knowledge, since Christ is most excellent above all things. I suppose no one doubts that the New Testament speaks chiefly of Christ; but because some doubt that the Old Testament does likewise, let them attend to Paul writing in the tenth

---

[24] Richard A. Muller, *Post-Reformation Reformed Dogmatics*, vol. 2, *Holy Scripture: The Cognitive Foundation of Theology* (Grand Rapids: Baker Academic, 1993), 119.

[25] Quoted in Muller, *Post-Reformation*, 98.

[26] Muller, *Post-Reformation*, 198.

[27] See Martin Luther, Preface to James and Jude, *Luther's Works*, vol. 35, tr. Jaroslav Pelkian (St. Louis: Concordia, 1962), 396; Luther, *The Schmalkald Articles*, II.i; Calvin, *Institutes*, II.6.2; and 1 Cor. 3:11. "Covenant" is "the essence of all revealed truths" for the Reformed scholastics (RD, 43ff.). Yet, "Christ is the scopus of faith, indeed Christ, as he is presented to us in the Word of God" (Beza, *Confession*, IV.6). "Christ himself is the sum of doctrine (*Christus ipse summam doctrinae*)," according to Ursinus (*Loci Theologici*, col. 427). So, too, for Perkins' Exposition of the Creede: "There Perkins writes that 'the foundation and ground worke of the Covenant is Christ Jesus the Mediatour, in whome all the promises of God are yea and amen'" (cited 224, from *Workes*, I, 165).

[28] Muller, *Post-Reformation*, 277.

[29] Quoted in Muller, *Post-Reformation*, 342.

chapter of Romans: "Christ is the end of the law"; and in the fifth chapter of John, when the Lord said . . . "Search the Scriptures," he added . . . "For they bear witness of me"; and in the same chapter it is said of Moses, "He has written of me."[30]

Inspiration extends both to the form and the content, "Law and Gospel, and is wholly perfect in both," Edward Leigh observed.[31]

In Calvin's treatment of Scripture we also discern a greater emphasis on the role of the Spirit than in Luther and other Reformers. The same Spirit who inspired the sacred texts also indwells believers so that they can understand its central message. This is the doctrine usually referred to as the "inner testimony of the Spirit." The Spirit's illumination is of two kinds, *internal* and *external*. The Spirit witnesses to the truth of Scripture within us to win our consent. "The internal mean is the principal organ or instrument of God's Spirit in this work, and it is that very light which shineth in the Scripture." The Spirit brings forth the internal evidences of Scripture: its harmony, the grandeur of its message, the miracles, and the celestial doctrine.[32] God is the *principium essendi* (source of existence) and therefore also the *principium cognoscendi* (source of knowledge). Scripture is the *principium cognoscendi externum* (external source of knowledge), while the operation of the Spirit who inspired the Scriptures is the *principium cognoscendi internum* (internal source of knowledge).[33] The same Spirit who inspired the Scriptures testifies both externally and internally to their divine origin and content.

This excluded the church as the basis for receiving the Scriptures as divinely given. Though hardly alone, Calvin is generally regarded as having formulated the doctrine of the inner testimony of the Spirit. D.F. Strauss called the *testimonium internum* "the Achilles' Heel of the Protestant system," because it shifted objectivity away from external revelation to the human heart.[34] There is no doubt that this happened in Protestantism, especially in pietism. However, it was only possible by radically changing its original meaning, by separating the external and internal witness of the Spirit, which was precisely the move that Calvin attributed to the radical "enthusiasts" above. From Jesus' upper room discourse especially we see that the Spirit's testimony is to the Son and the

---

[30] Quoted in Muller, *Post-Reformation*, 367.

[31] Quoted in Muller, *Post-Reformation*, 335.

[32] Muller, *Post-Reformation*, 335.

[33] Louis Berkhof summarizes these traditional distinctions in his *Systematic Theology* (Grand Rapids: Eerdmans, 1996), 170.

[34] D.F. Strauss, *Die Christliche Glaubenslehre* (1840), I, 136.

Word concerning him. In other words, the Spirit brings about the perlocutionary effect of the Father's speaking in the Son rather than issuing a different utterance or content. Further, the context of Calvin's formulation was the late medieval view that belief in Scripture as God's Word rested on the authority of the church's witness. Calvin's point is that "only God himself is a sufficient witness to himself."[35] In fact, Calvin compared Rome to the radical Protestants ("enthusiasts") in their affirmation of continuing special revelation apart from and in addition to the canonical Word (I.7.5).

All the external witnesses in the world could not convince us of the Bible's divine inspiration and it makes no sense to argue that the divine authority of Scripture rests on human authority. The highest human testimony can authenticate merely a human work; a divine Word requires nothing short of divine testimony for its credibility. This is the principal argument behind Calvin's treatment of the inner testimony of the Spirit. As Berkouwer relates concerning Calvin's view, "No matter how large a role the church may play in the genetic process of ascertaining, ultim- ately no one can accept Scripture because the church testifies that it is God's Word. The moving of the church as *praedicatrix evangelii* is not the ultimate explanation of faith in Scripture."[36] Only the Spirit can give us confidence in Scripture because it is the Spirit who inspired the sacred text and unites us to Christ, who is its content. It is the Spirit who unites us here and now in our hearing to the then and there of the original speaking. Faith in Scripture rises and falls with faith in Christ, as Bavinck pointed out.[37]

Against the repeated claim that the doctrine of inerrancy, unknown to the church, arose first with Protestant orthodoxy, we could cite numerous examples from the ancient and medieval church.[38] Down to the Second Vatican Council, Rome has attributed inerrancy to Scripture as the common view of the church throughout its history.[39] And with equal

---

[35] Cited by G.C. Berkouwer, *Holy Scripture: Studies in Dogmatics* (Grand Rapids: Eerdmans, 1975), 41.

[36] Berkouwer, *Holy Scripture*, 41–2.

[37] In Berkouwer, *Holy Scripture*, 44.

[38] See Robert D. Preus, "The View of the Bible Held by the Church: The Early Church through Luther" and John H. Gerstner, "The View of the Bible Held by the Church: Calvin and the Westminster Divines" in Norman Geisler (ed.), *Inerrancy* (Grand Rapids: Zondervan, 1980).

[39] According to the First Vatican Council (1869–70), the Old and New Testaments, "whole and entire," are "sacred and canonical." The Council added, "And the Church holds them as sacred and canonical not because, having been composed by human industry, they were afterwards approved by her authority; nor only because they contain revelation without errors,

clarity Luther and Calvin can speak of Scripture as free from error.[40] It is true that Luther sometimes speaks as if the authority of Scripture is limited to its content—namely, "that which preaches Christ." Wilhelm Niesel observes,

> Reformed theology, just like Lutheran, knows that it is God's Word which addresses us from the Bible and produces faith and that this Word is Christ Himself. But this address does not become an experience within our control on the basis of which we can read through the Bible and test whether it "sets forth Christ." Calvin read the whole Bible expecting to find Christ there.[41]

There is therefore no "canon-within-a-canon"; all Scripture is God-breathed and therefore useful (i.e., canonical) for norming the church's faith and practice.

Like the theologians of the ancient and medieval church, the Reformers could speak of the Spirit's authorship of Scripture in both mechanical and more organic terms without any sense of contradiction.

(cont.) but because, having been written under the inspiration of the Holy Spirit, they have God for their Author." See Alfred Duran, "Inspiration of the Bible," in the *Catholic Encyclopedia*, vol. 8 (New York: Robert Appleton Company, 1910). In his 1893 encyclical, *Providentissimus Deus*, Pope Leo XIII went so far as to speak of inspiration occurring "at the dictation of the Holy Spirit" and asserted that this view was "the ancient and unchanging faith of the Church," held by all the church fathers. Early in the twentieth century, Benedict XV said that it is "necessary to salvation" to affirm that the historical narratives as well as the doctrine are fully inspired and inerrant, and in 1943 Pope Pius XII condemned "limited inerrancy," supported again by Pope Leo XIII's encyclical, *Spiritus Paraclitus*. Quoting the Second Vatican Council, the most recent Catholic Catechism states that, "Since therefore all that the inspired authors or sacred writers affirm should be regarded as affirmed by the Holy Spirit, we must acknowledge that the books of Scripture firmly, faithfully, and without error teach that truth which God, for the sake of our salvation, wished to see confided to the Sacred Scriptures." *Dei Verbum* (Constitution on Divine Revelation, 18 November 1965), Article 11, cited in *The Catechism of the Catholic Church* (Liguori, Mo.: Liguori Publications, 1994), 31.

40 Klaas Runia, "The Hermeneutics of the Reformers," *Calvin Theological Journal* 19 (1984), 129–32.

41 Wilhelm Niesel, *Reformed Symbolics: A Comparison of Catholicism, Orthodoxy, and Protestantism*, tr. David Lewis (Edinburgh and London: Oliver & Boyd, 1962), 229.

Only with later refinement—responding to modern criticism—did evangelical theology develop a consistent doctrine of Scripture (including inspiration) and this view favored organic over mechanical analogies. The key difference between the Reformers (including Calvin) and Rome was not the nature of Scripture as inspired and inerrant, but the sufficiency of Scripture to determine all matters of faith and practice: specifically, the relationship of Scripture and tradition.[42]

First, according to their understanding of *sola Scriptura*, Calvin and his fellow Reformers did not eliminate the need for secondary authorities in the church. The Latin slogan means *"by* Scripture alone," not "Scripture alone" (*solo scriptura*).[43] For example, both Lutheran and Reformed churches include the ecumenical creeds in their confessional standards and, in fact, regard the latter as an interpretation of the former.

The emergence of parity between Scripture and tradition as two sources of a single revelation was due largely to the canon lawyers in the twelfth century onward. Yet still there were theologians of the stature of Pierre d'Ailly who insisted that Scripture was sovereign over tradition. The Council of Trent established the view that Scripture and tradition are actually two forms of God's Word: "written" and "unwritten." Many unwritten (i.e., oral) traditions were passed around by the apostles and their circle, and passed down by them to successive generations. Crucial to this development was the assumption that the apostolic office was still in effect, with the pope and magisterium (the teaching office with the pope as primate) as the successors to Peter and the other apostles.[44] It was not, however, until the First Vatican Council (1870) that papal infallibility became a binding dogma for Roman Catholics.

Vatican II represents a more nuanced view of the relation of Scripture and tradition, thinking through the many variations that had been held before the arteries were hardened in the Counter-Reformation. As Berkouwer, an official observer at Vatican II, relates, "Many Catholic

---

[42] Heiko Oberman, *The Harvest of Medieval Theology: Gabriel Biel and Late Medieval Nominalism*, rev. ed. (Grand Rapids: Eerdmans, 1967), 365–75.

[43] A fruitful study of the Reformation's use is found in Keith Mathison, *The Shape of Sola Scriptura* (Moscow, Ida.: Canon Press, 2001).

[44] Although episcopal (governed by bishops), the East was always suspicious of the hierarchicalism of the West and the former emphasized that the whole body of Christ is infused with the charism of the apostles—not that they are apostles themselves, but they are filled with the Spirit and led by the Spirit. According to the West, the idea gradually emerged that this charism was reserved for the priesthood, and especially for those who were part of the magisterium (cardinals and popes).

scholars today (including Karl Rahner, Hans Küng, Yves Congar, and George Tavard) speak of only one source of revelation, sacred Scripture . . . Congar goes so far as to declare, 'Scripture has an absolute sovereignty.'"[45]

Whatever individual theologians maintain, Vatican II affirmed that sacred Scripture and sacred Tradition flow from the same source. "In order that the full and living Gospel might always be preserved in the Church the apostles left bishops as their successors. They gave them 'their own position of teaching authority.'"[46] One may discern in this statement a subtle form of the traditional Roman Catholic distinction between a written canon and a living community. The Council continues, "Sacred Tradition and sacred Scripture, then, are bound closely together, *flowing out from the same divine well-spring*, come together in some fashion to form *one thing*, and move towards the same goal." In fact, it is sacred Tradition that faithfully "transmits in its entirety the Word of God" in both its apostolic and post-apostolic forms.

> It *transmits it to the successors of the apostles* so that, enlightened by the Spirit of truth, they may faithfully preserve, expound and spread it abroad by their preaching. Thus it comes about that the Church does not draw her certainty about all revealed truths from the holy Scriptures alone. Hence, both Scripture and Tradition must be accepted and honored with *equal feelings of devotion and reverence*. Sacred Tradition and sacred Scripture make up *a single deposit of the Word of God*, which is entrusted to the Church.[47]

Tradition is therefore the process of transmitting the Word of God. Although the magisterium is the servant of this Word, "whether in its written form or in the form of Tradition," the two "are so connected and associated that one of them cannot stand without the other."[48]

---

[45] Berkouwer, *Holy Scripture*, 126.

[46] Austin Flannery (gen. ed.), *Vatican Council II: The Conciliar and Post Conciliar Documents*, 1981 edition (Northport, N.Y.: Costello Publishing Company, 1975), 754.

[47] Flannery, *Vatican Council II*, 755 (emphasis added).

[48] Flannery, *Vatican Council II*, 755–6. Formally, Rome does not hold that private revelations can add anything to the deposit of faith: "Christian faith cannot accept 'revelations' that claim to surpass or correct the Revelation of which Christ is the fulfillment . . ." (*The Catechism of the Catholic Church*, 23). Nevertheless, we have seen that revelation takes two forms: the written (Scripture) and the unwritten (Tradition).

The magisterium proposes or commands dogmas to be believed, since it is held that the apostolic authority that produced the New Testament continues in an unbroken succession through Rome's bishops and popes: "The Roman Pontiff, head of the college of bishops, enjoys this infallibility in virtue of his office, when, as supreme pastor and teacher of all the faithful—who confirms his brethren in the faith—he proclaims by a definitive act a doctrine pertaining to faith or morals."[49] Scripture is an essential source, but not the sole source, of dogmatic authority. While Scripture and post-canonical tradition differ in degree of authority, they belong to the same genus since they are both equally the offspring of divine revelation in the church. From this principle emerges Rome's dogma of implicit faith (*fides implicita*), which requires acceptance of all dogmas commanded by the church. The basis for this implicit faith is the church's own inherent authority. "Sacred theology relies on the written Word of God, taken together with sacred Tradition, as on a permanent foundation."[50]

We have seen from the *Institutes* (I.7–9) Calvin's argument against this interpretation. Although the church is indeed the mother of the faithful, it is not the mother of Scripture: Paul "testifies that the church is 'built upon the foundation of the prophets and apostles' (Eph. 2:20). If the teaching of the prophets and apostles is the foundation, this must have had author-ity before the church began to exist" (I.7.2). Augustine's famous maxim ("I would not have believed that the Scriptures are God's Word unless I had been taught this by the church") is nothing more than the relation of his own experience of *how he came to faith* rather than the source of the faith's authority (I.7.3). Unless the credibility of doctrine is established by divine rather than human authority, our consciences will always waver. Those who seek to first prove the reliability of Scripture by appeals to an authority external to it (whether church or reason) are "doing things backwards" (I.7.4). Thus, ". . . Scripture indeed is self-authenticated (*autopiston*); hence, it is not right to subject it to proof and reasoning" (I.7.5). Once this divine authority is firmly established, we may certainly appeal to such external arguments as "very useful aids" (I.8.1). Protestants had no trouble agreeing that there was a time when written Scripture and oral tradition were two media of a unified revelation, but they denied that this situation obtains in the post-apostolic era. The critical question is whether the traditions of non-inspired ministers of the church can be equated with the revelation that they seek to interpret.

---

[49] Flannery, *Vatican Council II*, 235, citing *Vatican Council I*: DS 3074.

[50] Flannery, *Vatican Council II: The Conciliar and Post Conciliar Documents*, 763.

Sound tradition is the effect of the Spirit's *illumination* rather than *inspiration*. Lutheran and Reformed churches do not regard creeds, confessions, and the decisions of councils and synods as compromising *sola Scriptura*. Rather they regard church dogmas as authoritative because they are "clearly revealed in the Word of God, formulated by some competent Church body, and regarded as authoritative, because they are derived from the Word of God."[51] In its deliberative assemblies, the church has an ordained power to direct the confession and interpretation of the Word of God, but always in subservience to it. Therefore, the church's role in defining faith and practice is always *ministerial* (i.e., serving); only the Scriptures have *magisterial* (i.e., ruling or normative) authority. Where Rome holds that the faithful must believe everything that the church teaches (*fides implicita*), based on the authority of the church, Protestants maintain that we must believe everything that the Scriptures teach even if an angel or apostle were to bring a different gospel (Gal. 1:6–9).

Against Roman Catholic and radical Protestant claims, the Reformers argued that there is no ongoing revelation; the prophetic and apostolic offices were temporary and now it is the Spirit's illumination that the church seeks rather than new revelation. The Scriptures are sufficient. If the ancient church recognized post-apostolic tradition as an extension of apostolic tradition, why did their criteria for recognizing canonicity limit authorized texts to those of apostolic origin? Surely these ancient bishops did not regard tradition as a form of ongoing revelation; in fact, it was precisely against this view of the Gnostics that fathers like Irenaeus inveighed.

No less than the ancient and medieval church did the Reformers view these creeds as "the rule of faith." In fact, they appealed in painstaking detail to citations from the church fathers in support of their claim that the church has no intrinsic authority to prescribe articles of faith or commands to be followed. However, they held that creeds and councils have a secondary authority, binding believers only because they are summaries of Scripture. Scripture alone is "the rule of faith and life" because it alone is given by inspiration from God.[52] The church has a *ministerial* (serving) authority to determine matters of doctrine and life in its representative assemblies, yet only insofar as these conclusions are expressions of and limited to the *magisterial*

---

[51] Berkhof, *Systematic Theology*, 19.

[52] *The [Westminster] Confession of Faith, the larger and shorter catechisms with the scripture proofs at large together with the sum of saving knowledge*, I.2 (Glasgow: Free Presbyterian Publications, 1973), 122.

(reigning) authority of Scripture.[53] Ecclesiastical authority derives from and is subservient to Christ's royal office, which he exercises by his Spirit through his canonical Word. Therefore, the church is always put into question in its faith and life by the Word that created and preserves it and it must always be ready to be reformed by it.

Finally, the sufficiency of Scripture for Calvin is inseparable from both its scope and its perspicuity (or clarity). Rome's contention has been that Scripture itself is difficult to understand, especially by laypeople; therefore, it requires an infallible interpreter. Although this infallible tradition of interpretation is itself far more complicated and voluminous than Scripture, Rome does not see this as an obstacle because its doctrine of implicit faith requires the faithful to yield assent to *all that the church teaches*, not to understand and believe particular dogmas.

As we conclude this section on sufficiency and clarity, I would like to return to a point made at the beginning, even at the risk of repetition. In defending *sola Scriptura*, Berkouwer reminds us that "the sharp criticism of the Reformers was closely related to their deep central concern for the gospel," which is evident in the other *solae*.[54] The "only Scripture" is to be understood as the correlate of *solo Christo* (Christ alone), *sola gratia* (by grace alone) and *sola fide* (through faith alone). As Bavinck and Berkouwer point out, the Reformation was not a criticism of tradition per se, but the demand for the proper criterion for judging the whole tradition or any part of it.[55] "The phrase *sola Scriptura* expressed a certain way of reading Scripture, implying a continual turning toward the gospel as the saving message of Scripture . . . In this light it may be said that the term *sola Scriptura* represented 'the struggle for the genuine tradition' [Ebeling]."[56]

---

[53] The Westminster Confession summarizes the Protestant rule: "The whole counsel of God concerning all things necessary for His own glory, man's salvation, faith and life, is either expressly set down in Scripture, or by good and necessary consequence may be deduced from Scripture: unto which nothing at any time is to be added, whether by new revelations of the Spirit or traditions of men" (I.6). At the same time, "All things in Scripture are not alike plain in themselves, nor alike clear unto all: yet those things which are necessary to be known, believed, and observed for salvation, are so clearly propounded, and opened in some place of Scripture or other, that not only the learned, but the unlearned, in a due use of the ordinary means, may attain unto a sufficient understanding of them" (I.7), 23.

[54] Berkhof, *Systematic Theology*, 302.

[55] Berkhof, *Systematic Theology*, 303.

[56] Berkhof, *Systematic Theology*, 306.

Finally—and related to this last point—Calvin affirmed the sufficiency of Scripture because it is *clear* in its central teaching. Assuming that Scripture is unclear even in such matters, Rome justified the need for a magisterial interpreter. The Reformers countered that Scripture interprets itself. Where a passage seems less clear, we compare it with others. In any case, the failure of the church to provide any greater clarity than Scripture is evident in the fact that Rome requires implicit faith in all that the church teaches. Such faith must be implicit because it is highly unlikely that any-one—especially a layperson—could ever know everything that the church teaches on a given topic. The Reformers also pointed to explicit contra-dictions between various popes and councils regarding important matters of faith and practice, observing that neither side in the debate doubted the consistency of biblical teaching.

The Bible is "not equally clear or equally plain" in all of its parts, as the Westminster Confession freely acknowledged.[57] We must interpret obscure passages in the light of clearer ones. No one denies the need for interpret-ation and at least for the Reformers and their heirs the church, through its representative synods, is given a ministerial authority to offer such com-munal interpretations. The question is whether ecclesial interpretations are always subject to revision by the light of Scripture or whether they are to be believed simply on the authority of the church itself.

Given the analysis above concerning the nature of God's Word as sacramental as well as canonically regulative, *sola Scriptura* is not sim-ply an affirmation of the unique authority of the Bible over tradition but a confession of the sovereignty of God's grace. Because God alone saves, God alone teaches and rules our faith and practice. Because the church is the creation of the Word (*creatura verbi*), rather than vice versa, "Salvation is of the LORD" (Jon. 2:9, KJV). Before becoming Pope Benedict XVI, Cardinal Ratzinger recognized that according to the Reformation perspective, the Word guarantees the ministry, where Rome holds that the ministry guarantees the Word.[58] He adds, "Perhaps in this reversal of the relations between word and ministry lies the real opposition between the views of the Church held by Catholics and Reformers."[59]

---

[57] See footnote 54.

[58] Karl Rahner and Joseph Ratzinger, *Revelation and Tradition*, tr. W.J. O'Hara (Freiburg: Herder, 1966), 29.

[59] Rahner and Ratzinger, *Revelation*, 29.

3.3.2 Preaching
In the words of the Second Helvetic Confession, "The preached Word is the Word of God."[60] In Scripture, we find the canon of saving speech; in preaching, the ongoing means by which this saving speech generates a new creation, so that even in this present evil age we "tasted" of the "goodness of the word of God and the powers of the age to come" (Heb. 6:5, ESV). This is *how* the kingdom comes.

From this line of thinking it has been rightly claimed that the church is the creation of the Word (*creatura verbi*). The new birth, as part of the new creation, is effected *in* the church (i.e., through its ministry of the Word), but not *by* the church. Neither the individual nor the community gives birth to itself, but is born from above. The origin and source of the church's existence is neither the autonomous self in the act of reasoning, feeling, willing, or doing, nor the autonomous church as it confuses itself with its sovereign head. "So then it depends not on human will or exertion, but on God, who has mercy" (Rom. 9:16, ESV).

Nuclear to Lutheran and Reformed ecclesiologies, the notion of the church as *creation of the word* has received renewed attention in ecumenical discussions, as in the Reformed–Roman Catholic dialogue that nicely summarizes the theme:

> The church existing as a community in history has been understood and described in the Reformed tradition as a *creatura verbi*, as "the creation of the word." . . . The church, like faith itself, is brought into being by the hearing of God's word in the power of the Spirit; it lives *ex auditu*, by hearing. This emphasis upon hearing the word of God has been of central importance in Reformed theology since the sixteenth century. This is why the Reformed have stressed "the true preaching of the word" together with "the right dispensing of the sacraments according to the institution of Jesus Christ" as a decisive "mark of the true church."[61]

The dialogue adds, again from the Reformed side,

---

[60] The Second Helvetic Confession, ch. 1, in the *Book of Confessions* (Presbyterian Church (USA): General Assembly, 1991).

[61] "Lutheran–Roman Catholic Dialogue," *Growth in Agreement II: Reports and Agreed Statements of Ecumenical Conversations on a World Level*, 1982–1998, eds. Jeffrey Gros, Harding Meyer, William G. Rusch (Geneva: World Council of Churches; Grand Rapids: Eerdmans, 2000), 802. For the Lutheran–Roman Catholic Dialogue on this point, see 495–8.

Against the appeal to continuity, custom and institution, the Reformed appealed to the living voice of the living God as the essential and decisive factor by which the church must live, if it will live at all: the church, as *creatura verbi* . . . The church is the creation of the word because the word itself is God's creative word of grace by which we are justified and renewed . . . The community of faith is thus not merely the community in which the gospel is preached; by its hearing and responding to the word of grace, the community itself becomes a medium of confession, its faith a "sign" or "token" to the world; it is itself part of the world transformed by being addressed and renewed by the word of God.[62]

As an external Word, God's speech breaks up the presuppositions, attitudes, longings, felt needs, pious impulses, speculations, and ideals of individuals and even of the church itself. Yet as public communication, it is inherently social and reorganizes the creation that it disrupts into the new creation of which it speaks. Conceived in the event of hearing, the church always remains on the receiving end of its redemption and identity.

This "sacramental" aspect of the Word—that is, its role as a means of grace—underlies Luther's teaching, but is also a crucial conviction of other Reformers. B.A. Gerrish observes, "Calvin felt no antagonism between what we may call the 'pedagogical' [teaching] and the 'sacramental' functions of the word."[63] "God's word, for Calvin, is not simply a dogmatic norm; it has in it a vital efficacy, and it is the appointed instrument by which the Spirit imparts illumination, faith, awakening, regeneration, purification, and so on . . . Calvin himself describes the word as *verbum sacramentale*, the 'sacramental word,'" that gives even to the sacraments themselves their efficacy.[64]

It is crucial to Calvin's interpretation that the gospel is not a mere invitation to fellowship with Christ, but the effective means by which the communion with Christ comes about . . . It therefore makes good sense to us when we discover that in Theodore Beza's (1519–1605) edition of the

---

[62] Gros, Meyer, Rusch, *Growth in Agreement*, 803.

[63] Life is found only in God, located in Christ, mediated by his Word. As described by B.A. Gerrish, *Grace and Gratitude: The Eucharistic Theology of John Calvin* (Minneapolis: Augsburg Fortress Press, 1993), 84–5.

[64] B.A. Gerrish, *Grace and Gratitude*, 85. Gerrish refers here especially to Calvin's *Petit tracté de la sancta Cene* (1541), *Opera Selecta*, I:504–5, and the *Institutes*, IV.14.4; cf. III.2.6–7; III.2.28–30, and many other places.

Geneva Catechism the fourth part, on the sacraments, actually begins with the heading 'On the *Word* of God.'[65]

As with baptism and the Supper, the Spirit creates a bond between the sign (proclamation of the gospel) and the reality signified (Christ and all his benefits). The word is a ladder, to be sure, but, like the incarnation, one that *God* always *descends* to us (Rom. 10:6–17).[66] It is important to recognize that while God's Word is living and active, its "two words" of *law* and *gospel* do different things.[67] The law kills by revealing our guilt, while the Spirit makes alive by the gospel (2 Cor. 3:6–18). God's word of law and God's word of gospel are both the effective workings (energies) of God.

Specifically, the *gospel* is that part of God's Word that gives life. While everything that God says is true, useful and full of impact, not everything that God says is *saving*. 1 Peter 1:23–24 adds, "You have been born anew, not of perishable but of imperishable seed, through the living and enduring word of God." Furthermore, it is not the Word in general but the gospel in particular that is credited with this vivifying effect: "That word is the good news that was announced to you" (v. 25). Similarly, Paul says that "faith comes by hearing and hearing by the word of God," and, more specifically, "the gospel of peace" (Eph. 6:15, ESV), "the word of faith that we proclaim" (Rom. 10:8). Salvation is not something that one has to actively pursue, attain, and ascend to grasp, as if it were far away, but is as near as "the word of faith that we proclaim." We do not have to bring Christ up from the dead or ascend into heaven to bring him down, since he addresses us directly in his word (vv. 6–9). The gospel is "the power of God for salvation" (Rom. 1:16).

Sometimes God's speech brings judgment, disaster, fear, warning, and dread, Calvin reminds us (III.2.7; III.2.29). "For although faith believes every word of God, it rests solely on the word of grace or mercy, the promise of God's fatherly goodwill," which is only realized in and through Christ (III.2.28–30). "For in God faith seeks life," says Calvin,

---

[65] B.A. Gerrish, *Grace and Gratitude*, 84. His references to Calvin are from the *Institutes*, III.5.5.

[66] This view integrates the truth in the models of revelation as doctrine, history, and personal encounter.

[67] The identification of the Word of God as consisting of law and gospel is familiar not only in Lutheran but also in Reformed systems, from Ursinus (co-author of the Heidelberg Catechism) to Louis Berkhof, who in his *Systematic Theology* distinguishes law and gospel as the "two parts of the Word of God as a means of grace."

"which is not to be found in commandments or the pronouncement of penalties, but in the promise of mercy—and only a free promise" (III.2.29). The only safe route, therefore, is to receive the Father through the incarnate Son. Christ is the saving content of Scripture, the substance of its canonical unity (I.13.7). "This is the true knowledge of Christ: if we take him as he is offered by the Father, namely, clothed with his gospel. For as he himself has been designated the goal of our faith, so we shall not run straight to him unless the gospel leads the way" (III.2.6).

This emphasis on the external Word as the medium of God's saving action is the line that separates the Reformers from what they regarded as the "enthusiasm" common to Rome and the radical Protestants.[68] Though highly esteemed as divine revelation, Scripture was a dead letter that had to be supplemented by ongoing revelation: the living voice of the Spirit through the church or the contemporary prophet. However, the Reformers emphasized that proclamation of the Word is not simply the preacher's discourse about Christ (much less the myriad other things that preachers are wont to address). Luther famously declared,

> For if you ask a Christian what the work is by which he becomes worthy of the name "Christian," he will be able to give absolutely no other answer than that it is the hearing of the Word of God, that is, faith. Therefore, the ears alone are the organs of a Christian man, for he is justified and declared to be a Christian, not because of the works of any member but because of faith.[69]

The choice of preaching as a medium is not incidental. Putting us on the *receiving* end of things, not only does justification come through faith alone, but faith itself comes through hearing.[70]

---

[68] See Willem Balke, *Calvin and the Anabaptist Radicals*, tr. William J. Heynen (Grand Rapids: Eerdmans, 1981).

[69] Martin Luther, Luther's *Works*, 29, *Lectures on Titus, Philemon, and Hebrews*, ed. Jaroslav Pelikan (St. Louis: Concordia, 1968), 224.

[70] This comparison between hearing and seeing is not meant to suggest that there is some magical quality to hearing or that God is bound by this medium. Rather, it is to say that God has bound himself to the spoken word as the *ordinary* method of self-communication. Like Augustine, many Christians would refer to their reading of Scripture as a moment of conversion. Furthermore, physical disabilities such as deafness are no obstacle to God's grace. Stephen H. Webb offers a well-informed treatment of this issue in *The Divine Voice: Christian Proclamation and the Theology of Sound* (Grand Rapids: Brazos, 2004), 51–5.

We discover the same emphasis on the preached Word in the Reformed confessions. "For Calvin as for Luther," as John H. Leith observes, "'the ears alone are the organ of the Christian.'"[71] Calvin summarized, "When the Gospel is preached in the name of God, it is as if God himself spoke in person."[72] Leith elaborates, "The justification for preaching is not in its effectiveness for education or reform . . . The preacher, Calvin dared to say, was the mouth of God." It was God's intention and action that made it effective. The minister's words, like the physical elements of the sacraments, were united to the substance: Christ and all of his benefits. Therefore, the word not only describes salvation, but conveys it. "Calvin's sacramental doctrine of preaching enabled him both to understand preaching as a very human work and to understand it as the work of God."[73]

Following the Pauline logic in Romans 10, Calvin emphasizes that we must refuse any contrast between the outer and inner word. "We hear his ministers speaking just as if he himself spoke . . . God breathes faith into us only by the instrument of his gospel, as Paul points out that 'faith comes by hearing'" (IV.1.5–6). In fact, Paul "not only makes himself a co-worker with God, but also assigns himself the function of imparting salvation" (IV.1.6). Without the work of the Spirit, the word would fall on deaf ears, but the Spirit opens deaf ears *through* the external word.[74]

Similarly, the Heidelberg Catechism, after treating justification, asks, "If it is by faith alone that we share in Christ and all his benefits, then where does this faith come from?", and answers, "The Holy Spirit produces it in our hearts by the preaching of the holy gospel (Rom.10:17; 1 Pet. 1:23–25) and confirms it through our use of the holy sacraments (Mt. 28:19–20; 1 Cor. 10:16)."[75] According to the Second Helvetic Confession,

> The preaching of the Word of God is the Word of God. Wherefore when this Word of God is now preached in the church by preachers lawfully called, we believe that the very Word of God is proclaimed, and received

---

[71] John H. Leith, "Doctrine of the Proclamation of the Word" in Timothy George (ed.), *John Calvin and the Church: A Prism of Reform* (Louisville, Ky.: Westminster John Knox , 1990), 212.

[72] Quoted by Leith, "Doctrine of the Proclamation of the Word," 211.

[73] Leith, "Doctrine of the Proclamation of the Word," 210–11.

[74] Calvin, *Commentary on the Gospel of John*, on Jn.15:27.

[75] The Heidelberg Catechism, Q. 61, in *Ecumenical Creeds and Reformed Confessions* (Grand Rapids: CRC Publications, 1988).

by the faithful; and that neither any other Word of God is to be invented nor is to be expected from heaven: and that now the Word itself which is preached is to be regarded, not the minister that preaches; for even if he be evil and a sinner, nevertheless the Word of God remains still true and good.[76]

Regardless of the subjective piety or intention of the minister, the Word of God is effective. This should caution us against identifying effectiveness either with the antiquity and prestige of a particular office or with the charisma and communicative gifts of a particular person. The medium is consistent with the message of the cross. The fact that some of the most significant witnesses in the history of redemption are characterized as inferior speakers—Moses (Ex. 4:10), Isaiah (Is. 6:5–8), and Paul (1 Cor. 2:4) among others—is surely of some consequence. Yet all of this is so that the power would not rest in us but in God (1 Cor. 2:5). The power of the Word lies in the ministry of the Spirit, not in the ministers themselves. This is just as true of the church more generally.

"The supreme judge of all controversies," according to the Westminster Confession, "is the Holy Spirit speaking in the Scripture."[77] Challenging the radical sects for their contrast between the Word that "merely beats the air" and the "inner Word" resident within the individual, the Second Helvetic Confession continues, "Neither do we think that therefore the outward preaching is to be thought as fruitless because the instruction in true religion depends on the inward illumination of the Spirit, or because it is written, 'And no longer shall each one teach his neighbor . . . for they shall all know me' (Jer. 31:34)."[78] That God *can* illumine inwardly apart from the external preaching is not denied, but this work of the Spirit within is in Scripture connected to the outward preaching of mere mortals (the confession cites Mark 16:15; Acts 16:14, and Romans 10:17). The Westminster Larger Catechism adds,

> The Spirit of God maketh the reading, *but especially the preaching* of the Word, an effectual means of enlightening, convincing, and humbling sinners, of *driving them out of themselves*, and drawing them unto Christ, of conforming them to his image, and subduing them to his will; of strengthening them against temptations and corruptions; of building them up in

---

[76] The Second Helvetic Confession, ch. 1, in the *Book of Confessions* (Presbyterian Church (USA): General Assembly, 1991).

[77] Westminster Confession of Faith, 1.10, p. 24.

[78] Westminster Confession of Faith, 1.10, p. 24.

grace, and establishing their hearts in holiness and comfort through faith unto salvation.[79]

It is not only the message but the method that "drives us out of ourselves," which, of course, an "inner word" cannot do. Against the backdrop of God's incomprehensible majesty, which allows no safe passage from us to God, Calvin explores the marvelous condescension of God to our feeble capacity. We could not rise up to God, but he has "descended far beneath his loftiness," assuming our flesh and our language in both the infallible Scriptures and the fallible preaching of his human ambassadors. In this way, he believes, salvation is truly and exclusively "of the LORD" (Jon. 2:9).

---

[79] The Larger Catechism, Q. 155, in *Westminster Confession of Faith*, 247 (emphasis added).

2

Calvin on the Trinity

Kurt Anders Richardson

While there was considerable exegetical and constructive theological work on the core doctrines of Trinity and Christology during the Reformation,[1] ancient problems of the incomprehensibility of homooous-ion and hypostatic union, when not further complicated, simply were not brought closer to solutions or even clarifications. The mysteries of the knowledge of God both internal to the Trinitarian relations and external in the incarnation continued to require fundamental orientation to revelation and its sole implications for the logic of these doctrines. This, however, was a boon for Calvin, and while he would not counte-nance any hint of defection from these doctrines, the real progress that he and the other Reformers made in doctrine was in soteriology, in the Christocentricity of justifying faith and electing grace; the renewal of Christological and thereby Trinitarian doctrines was profound.

It is a commonplace that the Reformers took their cues from the Augustinian traditions in theology and to that extent it will not therefore be a surprise to find the Western tradition of Trinitarian formulations and sensibility in full evidence in Calvin. Quoted so frequently, Augustine's *De Trinitate* looms large in Calvin's account. In explicating the Trinity doctrine in the *Institutes,* Calvin will be shown to have worked with a Christological hermeneutic, one defined according to the soteriological reasoning of the incarnation, extending back to Irenaeus, Athanasius, and Gregory of Nazianzus: "whatever is not assumed is not redeemed," and the Trinitarian work that is the incarnation—although one of the divine Persons, and only one, becomes incarnate, Calvin will deduce that

---

[1] Note the extensive treatments in the magisterial, Carl Andresen, Adolf M. Ritter (eds.), *Handbuch der Dogmen und Theologiegeschichte,* 3 vols. (Stuttgart: UTB, 1998[2]).

nothing short of the fundamental equality of the Three from all eternity is a *sine qua non* of the doctrine. Deity can only be one thing and the Three possess it *autotheos*. Thus, while Calvin will acknowledge "begotten-ness," he regards speculations regarding this term as to be rejected in favor of distinguishing each of the Persons according to a univocal principle of the self-existence of God. But Calvin's fundamental reasoning on several topological connections is in evidence: the Holy Spirit in revelation; the virginal conception; the mediation of the knowledge of God the Father; the prayers of Jesus as demonstrative of the reality of Trinitarian relations; the Holy Spirit as the source of the miraculous and vivifying power in the life, death and resurrection of Christ; the presence of the risen Christ in the church through the Holy Spirit and in vital communion with God the Father until the end of the age; and the participation of believers gathered together sacramentally in the life of the triune God according to the benefits of Christ distributed Trinitarianly to them.

The section in the *Institutes* (I.13) on the Holy Trinity reflects the late medieval, scholastic background. Beginning with the topic of Person, Calvin then focuses upon the deity of the Son and of the Holy Spirit, presupposing that of the Father, and concludes with Trinitarian heresies that continually revive themselves in new forms. Reasoning quite often from biblical citations, Calvin does not merely argue from traditional concepts. Inaugurating, perhaps, the modern problem over the use of the term "Person" for the three identities of the Godhead, Calvin reflects the Western tradition of the doctrine in embracing as normative formulations by Augustine, Hilary, and Jerome. Always in dialogue with ancient philosophical tradition, Calvin's understanding of Scripture is set out repeatedly as correcting the former of its errors, overstatements and confusions. The scriptural depictions of God's self-knowledge in his immensity and spirituality are the foundational tools by which to accomplish this; in terms of the limitations of both human understanding and of that which has been revealed, and through constant references to the intellectual virtues of calmness and moderation, Calvin provides a kind of certitude according to the limits of what can be known about God from revelation.

Calvin's view of revelation is that the knowledge imparted by any means to human beings is always an act of condescension on God's part in which he accommodates his own self-knowledge, or knowledge of creation as he made it and governs it, so that human beings may understand according to the conditions and contingencies of their knowing as human. God is otherwise and on his own terms incomprehensible to the human being and inaccessible according to the natural cognitive and speculative means and apertures of the body and the mind.

From the beginning of his arguments, Calvin is explicit that all Trinitarian knowledge is garnered on the basis of its Christological mediation: that God the Son has appeared in the flesh as the man Jesus Christ, and is the one who incomparably discloses the eternal divine realities of himself (see especially Heb. 1:3; cf. Eph. 4:5; Mt. 28:19) as one, yet differentiated, in the eternal Godhead of Father, Son and Holy Spirit. Calvin seems to focus on the consubstantiality of the three Persons in the one Godhead—the entirety of one is in the entirety of the other and vice versa.[2] The oneness of the Three is best understood as their mutual containment of one another and thus a full embrace of the classic notion of *perichoresis*. In combining this notion with that of the self-existence of each Person of the Trinity, Calvin also eliminated subordinationism from his model. God's essence is primary, such that each member is as fully self-determined as the other, together mutually reinforcing this eternal, immutable being.

The Holy Spirit is co-equal with the Father and the Son and receives emphatic inclusion in this section of the *Institutes*.[3] In addition, because of Calvin's aggressive biblicism, the Western tradition's tendency to occlude the Spirit as the bond of love, the *nexus amoris* or *vinculum*,[4] is bypassed as Calvin makes some of the strongest assertions about the Holy Spirit's identity. Eternal spiration, however, along with eternal begetting as divine, self-determinative acts grounded in the identity of the Father and then the Son together with him, are rejected by Calvin.

But this is getting ahead of ourselves a bit, even for this short chapter. As will be pointed out below, Calvin's penchant for arguing everything Christologically, while fundamentally correct, can have its problems. In his case, because the Christological exegesis of the Reformers tended to get snarled around the formidable problems of expounding the hypostatic union according to the tradition of the *communicatio idiomatum*

---

[2] Not to be confused with the somewhat defective formulation of Rahner, which suggests the reversibility immanent and economic in the Trinitarian life of God; so Karl Rahner, *The Trinity* (New York: Crossroad, 1997).

[3] John Calvin, *Institutes of the Christian Religion*, tr. Henry Beveridge (Grand Rapids: Eerdmans, 1957), I.13.14, 15, 29 (henceforth shown in the text by book, chapter and section).

[4] Aquinas popularizes this term, cf. *In I Sent.*, 31.3.1; *Super ev Joann*, 1.2; cf. Catherine Osborne, *Eros unveiled: Plato and the God of Love* (Clarendon: Oxford University Press, 1996), 201; also, J.J. McEvoy, Thomas Augustine Francis Kelly, Philipp Rosemann (eds.), *Amor Amicitiae: On the Love that is Friendship: Essays in Medieval Thought and Beyond* (Leuven, Belgium and Dudley, Mass.: Peeters, 2004).

("communication of attributes"—incarnational sharing of the divine and the human), the hypostatic reasoning of Trinitarian Persons sometimes fell short in terms of proper distinctions and clarity. Beyond this, the relative confusion of the principles of generation and mediation connected with the Son's incarnate identity, due particularly to Christological apologetics, to some extent muddles the relational aspect of the Spirit's identity and eternal being-ness. Most conspicuously, however, Calvin wishes to assert the co-equal divinity of the Son and the Spirit with the Father by attributing full deity to each "of himself" apart from the others.

The Son is thus *autotheos*,[5] as is the Father and the Spirit. While denying any essential subordination of one Person to the other, Calvin indicates that there is, nevertheless, an order of relations whereby Son and Spirit are derived from the Father according to an internal principle of generation and origination. It is an *ordo trinitatis*, based upon agencies and identities exclusive to the eternal being of God as eternal together (I.13.19). Calvin wishes, however, to distinguish the Son as Person (hypostasis), according to the language of begottenness, not as God (I.13.20, 25). The economic Trinity is without beginning and from all eternity but according to the self-vivifying nature of the Three and in this sense, the interpersonal, so to speak, the Son and the Spirit proceed from the Father according to the grammar of eternal generation and eternal spiration. In this economic sense, the Father has the pre-eminence, but not ontologically, in terms of the divine essence of the Three and therefore as they are one and the same Deity. The distinction of Persons is very evidently perichoretic since each is contained in the personhood of the other. In the grammar of deity, "beginning" is transformed and becomes source or cause, that is, the deity is self-caused, God is the source of God, from all eternity. To speak of the Son apart from the Father is to speak of Deity "beginning" of himself *a se*, but to speak of the Son in relation to the Father is to speak of his beginning in the Father (I.13.19). Such reasoning for Calvin, however, means a necessary reaffirmation of the *filioque* of the Creed and a rejection of the Eastern form.[6]

The problematic of Calvin's formulations is his attempt to distinguish between the un-begottenness of the deity Son and the begottenness of

---

[5] *ex se ipso*, I.13, 29, 25; cf. Benjamin B. Warfield, "Calvin's Doctrine of the Trinity" in *Calvin and Augustine*, ed. Samuel Craig (Phillipsburg, N.J.: Presbyterian & Reformed Publishing Co., 1980), 283, 284.

[6] Calvin, not surprisingly, regards the Greek tradition as erring on this point, cf. *Commentary on the Gospel of John*, on Jn. 15:26.

the person of the Son. As with Christology during the Reformation, in spite of the most assiduous study of Scripture and all the new exegesis it provoked, precious little was done to advance Christological and Trinitarian doctrine beyond the patristic legacy and the historic creeds and councils. Indeed, earlier problems, such as the nature of the hypostatic union and the exchange of attributes, got exacerbated. Here, Calvin is on thin ice as he attempts to resolve Trinitarian conundrums where the immanent attributes both determine and do not determine the econ-omic attributes—or neither may be the case. And of course the econ-omic attributes, since they are fully divine and unconditional, cannot be construed as nevertheless conditional on account of the creaturely contingencies of the incarnation of God the Son. But since the Reformers, particularly Calvin and Zwingli, were wont to make the classical distinction between the awareness of Christ the Son of God and of Christ the Son of Man, the notion of the begotten Person of the Son could mediate these twin poles.

The immanent Trinity indicates for Calvin a unity of Persons in one utterly simple divine essence, where by "Person" is meant "a subsistence in the Divine essence"[7] as distinguished from an attribute or property. The properties or attributes belong to the Person, actually, distinctively and incommunicably to each Person. Therefore the Father is not the Son is not the Spirit and vice versa. This internal conditionality, however, does not result in essential change of God. The deity of the Son is held not only because "God" is ascribed to him by Scripture, but because he participates in creation and is thereby fully God with the Father who creates (I.13.7). It must be recognized that God's being is essentially dynamic, volitional, and therefore living Being, in contrast to analogies and metaphors that would convey a static pattern of attributions.[8] One can hardly underestimate the definitional significance of the *locus classicus* "I am who I am" of Exodus 3:14, not only on ancient and medieval theology but also and especially on the Reformers and the Scotist influences in the air at the time. The "Substantial Word" is always "God and with God . . . together with God the Father, the maker of all things" (I.13.7). But Calvin does not exercise tight Trinitarian reasoning at this point, and can mix the metaphors of Word with those of Sonship, so that given their coeternity, "the Word was eternally begotten by God" (I.13.8). His reasoning that eternity establishes deity is incontestable, but

---

[7] *Personam igitur voco subsistentiam in Dei essentur*, I.13.6.

[8] This problem is evident in the basic reading of Calvin on the subject in the extraordinarily fine treatment: Paul Helm, *John Calvin's Ideas* (Oxford: Oxford University Press, 2004), especially p. 56.

since he will make the new distinction regarding begottenness, the mixture suggests a capacity for infelicitous turns in analogical thought.

Christology is always nearby in Calvin's thinking; appropriately since the Mediator is the most proper orientation of revelatory conveyance, the analogical field of the Word tends to overwhelm that of the Son. Indeed, Calvin gets caught up for a number of paragraphs (8–13) with incarnational rather than strictly Trinitarian concerns. He is of course discoursing about the eternal Word, but in an incarnational context of argumentation and apologetics regarding "the divinity of Christ."[9] This, of course, will have another somewhat disabling effect later, only in reverse, under the Christological *topos* maintaining too radical a distinction between divine and human natures in terms of the formulations used. Calvin emphasizes the revelation of incommunicable attributes reflected in the works of creation and providence in the life of Christ in order to convey the truth of his divinity. But then we are approaching that point of fusion, even in the Pauline epistles, where conceptual frameworks relating to the Trinitarian life and works interpenetrate with the life and works of Christ and are difficult to differentiate precisely from one another. He appeals to the life of Christ as a source of "practical knowledge" (I.13.13), rather than to the speculative abstractions of transcendent simultaneity from notions of oneness and threeness. By this he means, "the best proof to us is our familiar experience" (I.13.14). And yet without appealing to the passages of Scripture, particularly the Gospel of John and especially the prayers of Jesus,[10] which convey something of the inner-Trinitarian relations in which the Son participates with the Father and the Spirit, a stress of hypostases results.

When Calvin moves on to the life of the Spirit within the Trinitarian life of the Godhead he, as always, resorts to a classic set of Scriptures (for example, Ps. 33:6; Mt. 28:19) and sees in them constant reference to creation as the evidence of Trinitarian reality. This move, of course, is typical of the classic, *vestigia trinitatis*, inherited from medieval theology. Interestingly, the subject of the Spirit conveys the aesthetic dimension of creation in terms of the beauty of its ordered existence (I.13.14). In a fascinating passage echoing Genesis, Calvin writes, "The Spirit of God was

---

[9] For example, defending the deity of Christ as God incarnate in the face of Jewish rejection.

[10] The prayers of Jesus in John convey a real relation of God with God, an interpersonal relationality of God, since the prayers are not relational fictions. This is perceived profoundly by Athanasius in *Contra Arianos*, and indeed, the high priestly prayer of John 17, is the most expounded upon passage of Scripture in the entire large thesis.

expanded over the abyss or shapeless matter; for it shows not only that the beauty which the world displays is maintained by the invigorating power of the Spirit, but that even before this beauty existed the Spirit was at work cherishing the confused mass" (I.13.14).

Calvin uses the conceptuality of energies in connection with the Spirit, whose boundless extensity is over and in all things, particularly in vivifying them. By also being the regenerative agent in all redemption, the Spirit completely transcends the creaturely in his nature and action. In a truly profound phrase, whereby we are reminded that Calvin is one of the great pneumatologues of the history of Christian theology, he says that the Spirit, according to Scripture, is "the author of regeneration, not by a borrowed, but by an *intrinsic energy* (*eius modo*) (I.13.14, italics added);[11] and not only so, but that he is also the author of future immortality. Further, the Spirit is always "subsisting in God, will and arbitrary disposal" such that the volitional aspect of the living God is brought to light. The term "will and arbitrary disposal" (*arbitrium et voluntas*) is extremely important in that it conveys, since Scotus, the freedom of God in his eternal self-determination and initiatory action.[12] Indeed, like the Son, the Spirit "dwells hypostatically in God" and cannot be regarded along any other lines than Trinitarian.[13]

The underlying concern on Calvin's part through this section of the *Institutes* is the disputability of its truth, and the text is heavily laden with references to "proof" (*testimoni*) (e.g., I.13.16), and polemical language protective of certitude and correctness. Calvin is not attempting to penetrate the history of exegesis for the doctrine in an exhaustive fashion and to rework the arguments of the fourth to the seventh centuries. He does employ a liturgical analogy as well, based upon the triadic Pauline formula of one God, one faith, one baptism. Because of the truth of each of the three, that the faithful are baptized (as Mt. 28:19) into the threefold name of Father, Son and Holy Spirit, there is an entailment of certain proof of the Trinity (I.13.16). The argument is curious and is not rooted in any kind of metaphysical reasoning.

> . . . since this is the same thing as to be baptized into the name of the one God, who has been fully manifested in the Father, the Son, and the Spirit.

---

[11] Calvin surely has in mind the roots of this term so vital to Aristotle's *Nichomachian Ethics and Metaphysics*. It gains special saliency in the work of Maximus the Confessor in his *Questions to Thalassius* and *Ambigua*.

[12] cf. especially, H. Veldhuis, et al. (eds.), *Duns Scotus on Divine Love: Texts and Commentary on Goodness and Freedom, God and Humans* (Farnham: Ashgate Publishing, 2003).

[13] Veldhuis, *Duns Scotus*.

Hence it plainly appears, that the three persons, in whom alone God is known, subsist in the Divine essence. And since faith certainly ought not to look hither and thither, or run up and down after various objects, but to look, refer, and cleave to God alone . . . Then, as the baptism of faith is a sacrament, its unity assures us of the unity of God . . . is this any thing else than to declare that the Father, Son, and Spirit, are one God? Wherefore, since it must be held certain that there is one God, not more than one, we conclude that the Word and Spirit are of the very essence of God. (I.13.16)

The argument runs like this. Because:

(1) God is truly the object of baptismal faith, and
(2) baptism signifies a unity of the baptizand with God under the threefold name

therefore:

(3) the three-personed God subsists in a unity of being.

Calvin never hesitates to base an argument solely upon revelation and its own inherent rationality, but this may or may not comport with any-thing recognizable in terms of classical metaphysics or logic about the Supreme Being and relations with the world. This must be said since here biblical revelation radically differs from the ancient Greek consensus, particularly at the point of *creatio ex nihilo* and rejection of the eternality of the world. The Creator/creature distinction is the funda-mental biblical metaphysic but as to the nature of God as well, that God is a fundamentally volitional being, even in terms of his own nature, is the best way to understand the classic incommunicable attributes of omnipotence, omnipresence and omniscience. God will be who God will be. What God will be, at most, is always reasoned biblically: "We should speculate soberly and with great moderation" (I.13.21). It is not that the liturgical argument is merely rhetorical and therefore metaphysically inconsequential, but that revelation, which is always address and response, signifies an actuality of being and relations when enacted through liturgical faithfulness.

The distinctions between the three Persons should never be made in such a way that one is considered an abstraction from the other or, indeed, from the unity of God's being. But Calvin does not hasten to defend the *filioque*—that the Spirit proceeds from the Father *and the Son*—and yet he does assume it and believes it to be the testimony of

Scripture: "The Son is said to be of the Father only; the Spirit of both the Father and the Son" (I.13.18). Like Basil, Calvin is happy to defend the distinctions upon prepositions such as "with" and "from" while acknowledging the co-equality of eternity and glory of the Three (I.13.17). By the same token, he is not so emphatic about the Father as eternal source of the Trinity, but instead focuses on economic identities: "That to the Father is attributed the beginning of action, the fountain and source of all things; to the Son, wisdom, counsel, and arrangement in action, while the energy and efficacy of action is assigned to the Spirit" (I.13.18). Because eternity is at the heart of the fundamental distinction between the Creator and the creature in Calvin's understanding, this attribute of the one, equally shared by the others, restores their image of an absolute unity. Nevertheless, to speak of the Son in and of himself, is to speak of God the self-caused.

The embrace of arguments based wholly on Scripture and faithful, liturgical response is for Calvin consistent with sobriety and the "measure of faith" (*fidei mensura*) (I.13.20). This accords with usefulness (*profitemur*) as a principle test for all Christian knowing. Calvin does move beyond the Christological context of the hypostases of divine and human natures. This means that he is always looking for passages and phrases that can be subjected to a stringent Trinitarian hermeneutic. "Personal subsistence" (*personis ordinem*) identifies the Son with the Father in a relation of eternal origin because of the latter's name and its meaning, which has nothing proper to the names "Son" or "Spirit." Unity, however, is always returned to and therefore retained on account of the "simple name God" which "admits not of relation, nor can God, considered in himself, be said to be this or that" (I.13.20). The Christological interpretation of the Tetragrammaton accomplishes this especially well for Calvin in that while differentiated in terms of its identification with the incarnate Lord, it conveys as well the reality of the one God. Calvin, as can be seen here, can even think of the one God apart from immanent relationality—believing this to be one of the proper exercises of Trinitarian contemplation. Again, Calvin's pneumatology comes into play so that the Holy Spirit can be just as robustly foregrounded,

> Thus, too, the Spirit is called God absolutely by Christ himself. For nothing prevents us from holding that he is the entire spiritual essence of God, in which are comprehended Father, Son, and Spirit. This is plain from Scripture. For as God is there called a Spirit, so the Holy Spirit also, in so far as he is a hypostasis of the whole essence, is said to be both of God and from God. (I.13.20)

God as eternal spiritual essence is known hypostatically and reversibly as the Holy Spirit.

Toward the end of the Trinity section of the *Institutes*, Calvin concerns himself with his contemporary context of Trinitarian controversies, particularly that of the Socinian variety. Calvin is never free of theological bellicosity, never fully sheds polemical rhetoric, and with this doctrine least of all. And it is in this vein that the figure of Servetus who, among other "frantic men," is an author of "new devices," "fallacies," and therefore of "confusion," receives mention. Calvin's sense of things is that Trinitarian controversies have been and are those by which Satan has designs "to pluck up our faith by the roots" (I.13.21). Calvin, known to be easily provoked, was provoked by the public rhetoric of Servetus and begins with the latter's table-turning phrase: Trinitarians are atheists.[14] But Calvin is particularly irritated by what he calls Servetus' modalist panentheism. After some polemic with heretical and "impious" speculations, he also takes pains to deny that the distinguishing of the three Persons and their one essence does not at all result in "a quaternion of gods" (I.13.25). But it is here that the odd move appears of reasoning about the Son "regarded as God, and without reference to person" so that he can be said, as is said of God simply, that he is "of himself" (I.13.25). The oddity is the "without reference to person" in theological contemplation in order, clearly, to demonstrate the full deity of the Son. This leads to a most curious phrase: "Thus his essence is without beginning, while his person has its beginning in God" (I.13.25).

"Beginning" is the language of distinction for Calvin, while "essence" indicates fullness of deity. He also wants to avoid any implication that "God" and "Father" could be regarded as synonymous terms, thereby, to his mind, applying creatureliness to the Son and to the Spirit within the Trinitarian union. In order to do this, he distinguishes "beginning"

---

[14] From the everywhere-banned *Christianismi restitutio* of 1553, which had included much of his correspondence with Calvin. It must be remembered that the doctrine of the Trinity and the first edition of the *Institutes'* paucity of reference to it, had, in 1537, earned Calvin a charge of Arianism by the Reformer Pierre Caroli. In 1554, the year following Servetus' execution in Geneva for the religious crime of anti-Trinitarianism, Calvin produced the theological tract *Defensio orthodoxae fidei, contra prodigiosos errores Michaelis Serveti Hispani*, in which he attempted to demonstrate, after the fact, that the doctrine included the necessity of capital punishment for its proper defense. The great irony is that while Michael Servetus was read widely, he had no disciples. Without doubt, his death inspired incalculably more heterodoxy than his life and writings.

from the current heretical term "essentiated" (*essentiando*). But what is crucial to Calvin is to accord to the Son the same deity as to the Father, and thereby to make a complete rejection of subordinationism.[15] In order to defend this, he must also wrest the pre-Nicene theologians, Justin Martyr, Irenaeus and Tertullian, from the appeals of the anti-Trinitarians—no small feat since Trinitarian doctrine only achieves its full definitions by the second half of the fourth century. Stretching a bit, Calvin can lay claim to Tertullian, since it "is easy to collect his meaning from the whole tenor of his discourse" (I.13.28). Calvin, finally appealing to Augustine, asserts that the end of the matter is reached when assigning the beginning of Godhead or the priority of the Father in terms of beginning for the Son and the Spirit, which is only to maintain the essential unity of God.

Finally, most oddly of all, since begottenness has played such a large role in Calvin's argument, he is satisfied that he has left out of the discussion, unlike Peter Lombard who belabored it, the topic of the "continuous generation" or eternal generation of the Son. This entire idea, he declares is "an absurd fiction from the moment it is seen" (I.13.29). Indeed, this final assertion of the entire section is quite amazing since eternal generation appears in Lombard because of its normative status. Calvin is utterly dismissive of the concept. It is enough for Calvin that he has maintained, as much for his own satisfaction as for the sake of his readers, a succinct argument for the three undivided, yet distinct, eternal Persons existing in their own unity of essence, each wholly God and yet not exhausting what it means to be God.

---

[15] *Institutes*, I.13.26, citing John, "declaring that he is the true God, has no idea of placing him beneath the Father in a subordinate rank of divinity."

3

Calvin on Creation and Providence

Oliver D. Crisp

> One does not read Calvin. One does not think of reading him. The prohib-
> ition is more absolute than it ever was against Marx, who always had the
> glamour of the subversive or the forbidden about him. Calvin seems to be
> neglected *on principle*.[1]

For some modern theologians, the doctrines of creation and providence
found in the work of a classical theologian such as John Calvin either
need significant adjustment, or must be done away with altogether in
favor of a very different understanding of God's relation to his creation.[2]
An example of the former, more modest, reassessment can be seen in the

---

[1] Marilynne Robinson, *The Death of Adam: Essays on Modern Thought* (New
York: Picador, 1998), 12.

[2] Back in the 1960s, Langdon B. Gilkey summed up much of the mood of the
(then) modern theology when he said, "Providence, then, is a difficult doctrine for us in our day to ponder, difficult alike to us morally and rationally
and apparently opposed to our fundamental beliefs in creaturely autonomy
and finite causality" ("Providence in Contemporary Theology," *The Journal of
Religion* 43 (1963), 181). But this problem is still in evidence today. Charles
Wood, in commenting on Gilkey's essay, observes, "The situation has not
changed markedly since Gilkey wrote. Put plainly, the doctrine [of divine
providence] has simply been overwhelmed by the challenges it has faced"
("Providence" in John Webster, Kathryn Tanner and Iain Torrance (eds.), *The
Oxford Handbook of Systematic Theology* (Oxford: Oxford University Press,
2007), 93). Things are not quite so bleak for the doctrine of creation, which
has been the subject of considerable theological discussion in recent times (a
good survey can be found in David Fergusson's *The Cosmos and the Creator*
(London: SPCK, 1998)). But the doctrine of a God who creates and *interacts*

work of so-called 'Openness' theologians, who argue that God's knowledge cannot include knowledge of the future actions of (libertarianly) free creatures because presently there are no truths about that segment of the future that is affectable by free will. The future has yet to occur and God, like the created order, is in time. Even if God creates the world out of nothing, he does not know how much of it will transpire, and what choices free creatures will make. He can guess and form beliefs about what we will do, and his ability to approximate to the truth of what will occur is second to none. But because he is a time-bound entity as we are and cannot, as a consequence, know the future, the scope of divine providence is more limited than Calvin conceived it, and is different in nature.[3]

An example of the latter, more radical, readjustment to creation and providence can be seen in the work of the feminist theologian Sallie McFague, who thinks of the theological task as setting forth models describing, among other things, how God and his creatures interact. These models are inherently metaphorical, heuristic constructions that offer imaginative explanations of the God–world relationship, which McFague believes necessary in order "to remythologize Christian faith through metaphors and models appropriate for an ecological, nuclear age."[4] According to McFague, a panentheist understanding of God and creation is a most appropriate model for thinking about creation and providence in the contemporary

---

(cont.) with his world, such as Calvin (in common with other classical divines) envisaged, is a source of discomfort to some theologians.

[3] The *locus classicus* of this movement is Clark Pinnock, Richard Rice, John Sanders, William Hasker and David Basinger, *The Openness of God: A Biblical Challenge to the Traditional Understanding of God* (Downers Grove, Ill.: InterVarsity Press, 1994). The literature in this area is large. But among the recent contributions, Bruce McCormack's essay, "The Actuality of God: Karl Barth in Conversation with Open Theism" in Bruce L. McCormack (ed.), *Engaging the Doctrine of God: Contemporary Protestant Perspectives* (Grand Rapids: Baker Academic, 2008), 185–242, offers an interesting critique of the doctrine of God that Openness theologians assume in the context of wider criticism aimed at the sort of classical theism Calvin (among others) endorsed.

[4] Sallie McFague, *Models of God: Theology for An Ecological, Nuclear Age* (Philadelphia: Fortress Press, 1987), 40. McFague takes a very strong *via negativa* approach to formulating doctrine. She thinks that "we are prohibited from absolutizing any models of God" because "when we try and speak of God there is nothing which resembles what we can conceive when we say

world.[5] That is, the world is somehow contained "in" God, or—to change the metaphor—God's relation to the world is rather like the traditional way in which substance dualists have thought about the connection between the human soul and its body: God is the "soul," the created order is his "body." In which case, God "needs" the creation in order to be fully himself, just as a soul "needs" a body in order to live and move in the corporeal world.[6]

Another influential contemporary school of theology, which offers a different, though not unrelated, sort of criticism of traditional accounts of creation and providence such as Calvin offered while endorsing a variant of panentheism, is Process Theology. For the process theologians, God is not omnipotent, and the creation is formed from some pre-existing chaotic matter, which God shapes, and which he then tries to keep from slipping back into disorder. This is in many ways an attempt to baptize a Platonic account of the creation, where the *Demiurgos*, or Craftsman god Plato conceived of in *Timaeus* as the agent of creation has become assimilated to YHWH of the Old Testament— or, perhaps, where YHWH has been cut down to the size of a demiurge.[7]

These examples illustrate several of the doctrines of creation and/or providence one can find in contemporary theology that are quite different from the classical theological conceptions Calvin would have been familiar with. Much could be said about these various attempts at

(cont.) that word," *Metaphorical Theology: Models of God in Religious Language* (Philadelphia: Fortress Press, 1982), 194.

[5] McFague, *Models of God*, 72. She explains that her panentheistic model of God and the world is a view "in which all things have their origin in God and nothing exists outside God, though this does not mean that God is reduced to these things."

[6] For discussion of this, see, in particular, McFague, *Models of God*, ch. 3. John Cooper offers trenchant criticism in *Panentheism: The Other God of the Philosophers* (Grand Rapids: Baker Academic, 2006), 294–7, as does Randal Rauser in "Theology as a Bull-Session" in Oliver D. Crisp and Michael Rea (eds.), *Analytic Theology: New Essays in the Philosophy of Theology* (Oxford: Oxford University Press, 2009).

[7] See Plato, *Timaeus*, §30. For a serviceable introduction to Process Theology see John Cobb, Jnr. and David Ray Griffin, *Process Theology: An Introductory Exposition* (Louisville, Ky.: Westminster John Knox, 1977). For a careful critical analysis of Charles Harteshorne's version of Process Theology, see Colin E. Gunton, *Becoming and Being* (London: SCM Press, new ed. 2001 (1978)).

revision in contemporary theology.[8] But I shall refrain from doing so here. Instead, this chapter gives a broadly sympathetic account of Calvin's theology of creation and providence. I shall argue that Calvin's view offers a robust description of God's relation to the creation, a description that is both plausible and defensible in the current intellectual climate, despite those who think that both creation and providence need to be rethought for the contemporary world.

The chapter falls into three parts. The first offers some conceptual context for discussion of Calvin's contribution, which, given the constraints of space, can only be an overview of some of the most important dogmatic issues in creation and providence. This is followed by discussion of Calvin's doctrine, where our focus will be upon his understanding of the creation and conservation of the world. A final section sets out some constructive criticism of Calvin's view as a contribution to the continuing discussion of these important dogmatic themes in which Calvin's thought has played, and continues to play, an important role.

1 The dogmatic context

For the most part, Calvin was not a fan of speculative theology, which he often rails against, although, as several recent commentators on Calvin's thought have pointed out, he sometimes indulges himself in theological speculation when it suits his purposes.[9] Yet in order to get a sense of where Calvin's views on creation and providence sit in relation to other accounts of these twin doctrines, including the sorts of revisionist accounts already mentioned, some kind of philosophical and dogmatic

---

[8] Some theologians are deeply concerned by Calvin's doctrine of creation, which they think is perniciously anthropocentric, to the exclusion of important ecological considerations. See, for example, David Kinsley, *Ecology and Religion: Ecological Spirituality in Cross-Cultural Perspective* (Englewood, N.J.: Prentice Hall, 1995), 111. Randal Zachman responds to this sort of concern in "The Universe as the Living Image of God: Calvin's Doctrine of the Universe Reconsidered," *Concordia Theological Quarterly*, 61 (1997), 299–312. He argues, to my mind convincingly, that Calvin's view is precisely the opposite of that which Kinsley imputes to him.

[9] See Paul Helm, *John Calvin's Ideas* (Oxford: Oxford University Press, 2004), 22–9; Richard A. Muller, *The Unaccommodated Calvin: Studies in the Foundation of a Theological Tradition* (New York: Oxford University Press, 2000), passim; and David Steinmetz, *Calvin in Context* (New York: Oxford University Press, 1995).

contextualizing is in order—in which a smattering of theological speculation might be permissible. This falls into two parts, corresponding to
the two doctrines themselves as the two aspects of the *opera naturae*,
although too strict a division between creation and providence is, as we
shall see, artificial.

We begin with creation. Here two, or perhaps three, dogmatic com-
ponents of this doctrine are important, depending on what is made of
the third. The first constituent is the divine motive in creating the world;
the second, the act of creating itself; and the third, the relation between
creation and the sustenance of the created order thereafter.

As to the first, the divine motivation for creating the world is itself connected to at least two further dogmatic issues of importance.[10] The first of
these subsidiary points concerns the doctrine of the divine decrees. The
second and related issue has to do with the divine freedom in creating the
world. The divine decrees touch upon matters that are sublime and difficult. Those classical theologians who think God is atemporal maintain
that God's motivation in creation is logically but not chronologically first
in the order of the external works of God (*opera ad extra*).[11] Some post-
Reformation Reformed divines have further distinguished the external

---

[10] I assume in what follows, as Calvin and all orthodox theologians would, that
all the external works of God are triune works, even if some of these works,
such as the incarnation, terminate on a particular divine person. See John
Calvin, *Institutes of the Christian Religion*, ed. John T. McNeill, tr. Ford Lewis
Battles (Philadelphia: Westminster Press, 1960 (1559)), I.13.20; cf. Heinrich
Heppe, *Reformed Dogmatics*, tr. G.T. Thompson (London: Wakeman Trust, n.d.
(1950)), ch. IX.

[11] For Calvin's endorsement of divine timelessness, see *Institutes*, III.21. There,
in the context of setting forth divine "fore" knowledge, Calvin says, "When
we attribute foreknowledge to God, we mean that all things always were,
and perpetually remain, under his eyes, so that to his knowledge there is
nothing future or past, but all things are present. And they are present in
such a way that he not only conceives them through ideas . . . but he truly
looks upon them and discerns them as things placed before him." See also
similar comments with respect to the Trinity in *Institutes*, I.13.18. Calvin cautions against probing divine election (and, by implication, the divine decrees)
out of intellectual curiosity. This will only result in entry upon a "labyrinth
from which" such persons "can find no exit" (III.21.1). There has been some
recent dispute over whether Calvin did believe God is atemporal. See Henri
Blocher, "Yesterday, Today, Forever: Time, Times, Eternity in Biblical
Perspective," *Tyndale Bulletin*, 52:2 (2001), and the response by Paul Helm,
"Calvin on 'Before All Ages,'" *Tyndale Bulletin*, 53:1 (2002).

divine works into those that are somehow "internal" to God, being works conceived in the divine mind "prior," as it were, to the act of creation, and other works that are "external" to God, being works that are consequent to his "internal" works, and that are directed toward the created order.[12] But in fact such distinctions are, on this way of thinking, merely intellectual devices by which human creatures can make sense of what is not literally distinguishable in the divine nature, because God is essentially metaphysically simple—that is, without any distinct "parts" whatsoever.[13]

However one distinguishes the works of God, the motivation for creation is a matter intimately tied to the eternality of God. If God is atemporal, then his motivation in creation is not something that *happens* at a particular moment in time, but something eternal in the divine nature. On the question of the nature of the divine motivation in creating the world, theological opinions diverge, some opting for the union of the creation or human beings with the divine nature as the crowning glory of the created order, others opting for some weaker account of the reconciliation of fallen humans to God and the restoration of all creation to its former glory prior to the fall of humankind. But these matters are surely subordinate to the overarching divine motivation in all God's works, namely, to bring glory to himself—a matter that received wide agreement in the post-Reformation period immediately after Calvin, from both Lutheran and Reformed dogmaticians.[14]

Divine freedom in creation presents particular theological problems that have been, and continue to be, the source of some difficulty.

---

[12] The external works of God that are (paradoxically) said to be "internal" in some sense, must be distinguished from the internal work of God as such, which has to do with things like the relations of origin, by which the Persons of the Trinity are distinguished (e.g. the eternal generation of the Son; the eternal procession of the Holy Spirit). Traditionally, the doctrine of creation does not include this internal work of God, which is logically prior to any external work he undertakes in the creation.

[13] For an excellent discussion of the development of the doctrine of the divine attributes from the high Middle Ages through to the demise of post-Reformation orthodoxy, see Richard A. Muller, *Post-Reformation Reformed Dogmatics*, vol. 3 (Grand Rapids: Baker Academic, 2003). For Calvin's endorsement of divine simplicity in the context of his discussion of the Trinity, see I.13.2, 19.

[14] See Heinrich Schmidt, *The Doctrinal Theology of the Evangelical Lutheran Church*, tr. Charles A. Hay and Henry E. Jacobs (Philadelphia: Lutheran Publication Society, 1875), chs. 3–4; and Heppe, *Reformed Dogmatics*, chs. 9 and 11.

Although most Christian theologians want to affirm that God is free to create or refrain from creating, precisely what this means is the subject of controversy. For instance, should divine freedom be construed as the freedom to choose to do other than he has in fact chosen? If so, how is this to be squared with an account of the divine nature where God is metaphysically simple, a perfect being without any passivity or unrealized potential? For most contemporary theologians this problem does not arise as it would have done in Calvin's intellectual *milieu*, where a kind of consensus on the divine nature had been handed on from the school theology of the high Middle Ages.

Today, there are other issues to be negotiated for those no longer enamored with this classical picture of the divine nature, issues such as how to make sense of the idea, found in Karl Barth among other modern divines, that God is free to determine who he will be, and (according to some commentators on Barth) in some eternal or primordial divine act decides he will be the God and Father of Jesus Christ, thereby freely choosing to be the sort of God we know him to be in and through Christ.[15] Other theologians and philosophers, objecting to what is sometimes called the "hellenization" of Christian theism, have objected to parts or the whole classical conception of the divine nature, opting instead for the idea that God is in time, is passible, mutable, and so on.[16] And besides these issues, the theological waters have been muddied by those who, as previously mentioned, have adopted some version of panentheism in which the relation between creature and Creator is much closer than in classical theism, to the extent that God must create a world, even if he may have some freedom about the sort of world he creates.

We come to the second dogmatic question concerning the act of creation itself. Here there has been considerable discussion in the modern

---

[15] See Bruce McCormack, "Grace and being: The role of God's gracious election in Karl Barth's theological ontology" in John Webster (ed.), *The Cambridge Companion to Karl Barth* (Cambridge: Cambridge University Press, 2000), 92–110. For a defense of Calvin against McCormack's reading of Barth on this score, see Paul Helm "John Calvin and the Hiddenness of God" in McCormack (ed.), *Engaging the Doctrine of God*, 67–82.

[16] Two recent theological attacks on classical theism can be found in Colin E. Gunton, *Act and Being, Towards A Theology of the Divine Attributes* (Grand Rapids: Eerdmans, 2002); and Robert W. Jenson, *Systematic Theology*, vol. 1. An influential critique from a philosophical perspective comes from Nicholas Wolterstorff, "God Everlasting" in C. Orlebeke and L. Smedes (eds.), *God and the Good: Essays in Honor of Henry Stob* (Grand Rapids: Eerdmans, 1975).

period, with a number of theologians and philosophers claiming that the opening verse of Genesis does not teach the traditional doctrine of creation out of nothing (*creatio ex nihilo*) but something closer to a Platonic doctrine of creation from chaos.[17] Much depends on whether this verse should be translated, "In the beginning, God created the heavens and the earth . . ." as in traditional discussions of creation out of nothing, the default option in the Christian tradition, with which Calvin allied himself. Alternatively, Genesis 1:1 could be translated, "*When God began to create* the heavens and the earth . . ."[18] The dogmatic difference between these views turns on what is entailed by the divine fiat in the act of creation, not on whether God has, in some sense, created the temporal world. But closely related to this is the question of whether the cosmos is created in time, or with time. For those modern theologians who think God is in time, it is natural to suppose that the world is created in time, or at some moment before which God existed. But for those, such as Calvin, who follow the older way of thinking, where God is atemporal, it is impossible to say this.[19]

---

[17] Some theologians, notably St. Thomas Aquinas, have discussed the possibility of creation being metaphysically contingent but having no first moment in time (although St. Thomas dismisses this as contrary to Scripture in *Summa Theologiae*, I.46.1). To my knowledge, Calvin does not discuss this at any length, and given his qualms about speculative theology, would probably have been reticent about doing so.

[18] Typical of those who defend the "revisionist" reading of Genesis 1:1, the Princeton philosopher Harry Frankfurt says: "This is manifestly not an account of creation *ex nihilo*. Whatever basis there may be for supposing that the world was created out of nothing, these opening lines of Genesis seem to be flatly inconsistent with that supposition." Frankfurt, "On God's Creation" in Harry G. Frankfurt, *Necessity, Volition, and Love* (Cambridge: Cambridge University Press, 1998), 119. But compare Robert Jenson's judicious comments in defense of the traditional, *creatio ex nihilo* reading: "The recent preference for translations that make Genesis 1:1 a dependent clause derives from residual prejudices of a now antique form of critical exegesis that tended always to look for the 'real' meaning of texts in some stage of the tradition before and outside the structure of the canonical text and then to interpret the canonical text to fit" (Jenson, *Systematic Theology*, vol. 2, *The Works of God* (New York: Oxford University Press, 1999), 3, n. 2).

[19] Susan Schreiner has recently observed that in his commentary on Genesis 1:5, "Calvin saw no need to insist that the creation of the world was free of temporality," see Schreiner, *The Theater of His Glory, Nature and the Natural Order in the Thought of John Calvin* (Durham, N.C.: The Labyrinth Press, 1991),

There are problems explicating the very notion of a timeless creative act—what does it mean to say there is no time at which God brings about the world, and yet that the world begins to exist at a particular moment in time? One might think that the world is timelessly created "in" time, where time somehow "contains" the created order, as the pan of water "contains" the egg boiling in it. Then, God creates time and creates the world subsequently, so that the world begins to exist in a temporal series that has already been set in motion. But this is not how theologians such as St. Augustine of Hippo understood matters. In *Confessions*, Book XI, he says God timelessly creates the world "with" time: the divine creative fiat begins the whole of creation, time included. So there is no "time" prior to the first moment of creation. And, as such, the questions, "What was God doing before he created the world?" or, "Why did God not bring about the creation sooner than he did?" are idle.[20]

What of the third dogmatic component of the doctrine of creation, concerning the Creator and the sustenance of his creation? For most Christian theists, God is distinct from his creation, exists *a se*, and, as a consequence, is free to refrain from creating this world or any other metaphysically possible world. But is the act of creating the world he does bring about distinct from his act of sustaining that world thereafter? In one sense, it is: if we think of the act of creation as creation from nothing, then the sustaining of a world that has been called into existence by divine fiat must be something different from the act that calls forth that world. So there is a conceptual distinction between these two sorts of divine act.

Yet a number of classical divines have thought that there is no substantive difference between the two acts, because the created order is not merely dependent on God for its preservation in being once created, but is conserved in being by the divine will, without which it would immediately cease to exist. For such theologians the reliance of the creation upon its Creator implies a radical dependence. Consider the act of thinking of the *Mona Lisa*. The first instant at which one calls the thought to mind, it begins to exist. Every moment one thinks of the painting thereafter, provided that one continues to think of this without interruption,

---

(cont.) 15. In other words, Calvin thinks God creates the world in phases, over six days, rather than all at once. But this is consistent with the claim that an atemporal God creates the world with time.

[20] Calvin echoes St. Augustine's language in his *Commentary on Genesis*, tr. John King (Grand Rapids: Baker Book House, 1979 (1554)), 61–2, although, unlike Augustine, Calvin thinks such intellectual curiosity is reprehensible.

and without being distracted by some other thought, one is conserving that initial thought in the mind's eye. But if one were to stop thinking of the *Mona Lisa*, the thought of the painting would cease to exist. So, we might say, the initial thought of the painting perdures provided that I continue to think it. But if, like Professor Albus Dumbledore, one were able to take a thought from one's mind, and deposit it in a magical thought-repository, or Pensieve, then the thought would continue to exist without my continuing to think it. In which case, the relation between my thought and me is much less radical, since, once placed in the Pensieve, the thought can persist without my consciously sustaining it in being.[21]

This thought experiment should not be pressed too hard. It is only intended to show something of the difference between the dependence of the creation upon the Creator where God preserves an existing creation in being, though, in some sense, the creation perdures—that is, continues to exist under its own steam—and the idea of a radical dependence of the creation upon its Creator. The relation of radical dependence (call it, the *radical dependence view*) should be distinguished from what is sometimes called continuous creation, although not all dogmaticians make this clear.[22] If, like Jonathan Edwards, one thinks that God creates the world, which, having no power independent of God to perdure momentarily, ceases to exist, only to be replaced by a numerically distinct replica of the first world, and so on seriatim, then one has dispensed with the idea of divine preservation of the creation. There is no created entity to preserve because no created entity has the power to exist for more than a moment. Continuous creation, then, is a much stronger doctrine than even the robust version of the divine preservation of creation, though both are often referred to as continuous creation doctrines.

This brings us to the doctrine of divine providence, even a cursory consideration of which should be sufficient to demonstrate the intimate connection between it and the doctrine of creation. Common in post-Reformation works of theology is the distinction between divine preservation of the creation (*conservatio*), God's concurrent activity in upholding and sustaining the creation (*concursus*), and his government of it (*gubernatio*). Sometimes the first two of these are conflated, depending

---

[21] The Pensieve makes its first appearance in J.K. Rowling's novel, *Harry Potter and the Goblet of Fire* (London: Bloomsbury, 2000).

[22] It does not help that scholastic theologians sometimes distinguish between *creation continua* (continuous or constant (re)creation) and *creatio continuata* (a creative act that persists from one particular time to another). I am grateful to Ben Myers for directing me to this.

on the theory of divine preservation under consideration. Thus, if God preserves the cosmos via concurrently causing all things to occur alongside mundane causes, then God's concurrent activity is a function of his preservation of the created order. This idea that God orders all things that come to pass, such that no event occurs without his concurrently bringing it about in conjunction with mundane creaturely causes, is usually referred to as *meticulous providence*, in order to distinguish it from those accounts of divine providence where God does not decree or otherwise bring about all that comes to pass.

But there is another distinction to be made, and that is between general and specific divine providence. One might speak of God upholding and sustaining the world in being as a general act of God: he sustains all created things in existence, good and bad, for as long as seems good to him. But God's particular acts, by which he ordains certain things that will take place, things of salvific importance—the election of some to life, and reprobation of others in eternal death—is often thought of as a specific act of providence. The distinction, however, seems somewhat artificial if, with Calvin, we think that God ordains *all* that comes to pass: "For he is deemed omnipotent . . . because, governing heaven and earth by his providence, he so regulates all things that nothing takes place without his deliberation" (I.16.3). If God deliberately decrees all things or events to occur, then all things or events are deliberate acts of God, and it seems that the difference between "general" and "specific" acts of providence evaporates. Still, it does serve to distinguish certain sorts of providential action, whereby God brings about salvation, from other sorts of providential action, whereby God sustains the creation as the "the most beautiful theater" of God's glory (I.14.20), in which the narrative of salvation history is played out. Provided that we understand "general" and "specific" acts of providence in this way, as a means of separating out what, from the human vantage, appears to be different sorts of divine act in creation, rather than as a means of distinguishing different "levels" of divine causal activity in creation, the distinction may be of some theological use.

2 Calvin on creation and providence

With some idea of the major dogmatic structures in the doctrines of creation and providence in place, we can turn to consider what Calvin contributes to these twin *loci*. Here two things are important. First, an understanding of where Calvin's views sit with respect to the spectrum of views just outlined. And, second, several ways in which Calvin introduces important theological nuances that make a considerable difference to how creation and providence are understood.

We begin with Calvin's doctrine of creation. Recalling our three dogmatic questions on creation outlined in the previous section, we can see that under the topic of the divine motive in creating the world, Calvin endorses the traditional view that the ultimate end of all God's works is his own self-glorification, albeit with a Calvinian twist. This is particularly evident in his metaphor of creation as the "theater" and "mirror" of God's glory, tropes that recur in the *Institutes* and elsewhere in his corpus.[23] Thus, for example, in setting out how the knowledge of God shines forth in the created order (though our sin-blind faculties are incapable of apprehending this without the spectacles of Scripture), Calvin says, "This skilful ordering of the universe is for us a sort of mirror in which we can contemplate God, who is otherwise invisible" (I.5.1). And later, in commending the spiritual lessons the doctrine of creation engenders, he says, "Let us not be ashamed to take pious delight in the works of God open and manifest in this beautiful theater." He goes on to encourage his readers to be "mindful that wherever we cast our eyes, all things they meet are works of God," and to "ponder with pious meditation *to what end* God created them" (I.14.20, emphasis added). The "end" in question is, of course, the glory of God.

It is true that Calvin also says things about the purpose of creation that sound at times alarmingly anthropocentric, such as this comment: "God himself has shown by the order of Creation that he created all things for man's sake" (I.14.22). But this must be tempered with what he says elsewhere in the *Institutes*, where he makes clear that human beings are themselves "microcosms" that reflect the divine Artificer (I.5.3; cf. I.5.6). Humanity is as much a work of God as any other created thing, with this important qualification: human beings bear the image and imprint of the Creator upon their souls (I.15.3). It is this that sets human beings apart from the rest of creation, which is why Calvin labors the point about the world being created *for* human beings. But humans are a part of that creation, according to Calvin. Human beings are, in a way, bearers of the glory of God (via the *imago dei*); they show forth God's ultimate end of bringing glory to his name in all his created works—humanity included. As Zachman points out, for Calvin

> the creation of all good things in the world for the benefit and enjoyment of humans is not . . . an end in itself, but is rather the way God initially

---

[23] See, for example, *Institutes*, I.6.2; I.14.20; III.9.2; and Calvin's commentaries on Pss. 104:31; 138:1; and on Heb. 11:3.

reveals to humankind that he is the author and fountain of every good thing. Our use and enjoyment of the good things of creation is not intended by God to be an end in itself, but is rather the way God allures and invites us to seek him as the source of every good thing.[24]

Although Calvin does not use the precise language of later Reformed scholastic theology, it is clear from a careful reading of his comments on the doctrine of election in *Institutes*, III.21–4 that he thinks God has eternally destined human beings to life or death according to the good pleasure of his will alone—a matter that is well known. Was God free to choose to create or refrain from creating the world he did bring about? Calvin does not appear to address this question head-on. But it is clear that he has a high view of divine freedom. God has, he thinks, "in his own hand and will the free disposing of his graces" (II.21.14). What is more, God's will is, he maintains, "the cause of all things that are" (III.23.2). "When, therefore, one asks why God has so done," says Calvin, "we must reply: because he has willed it. But if you proceed further to ask why he so willed, you are asking for something greater and higher than God's will, which cannot be found" (III.23.2). This apparent theological voluntarism is tempered by Calvin's appeal to the divine character: God wills as he does because his nature is perfect (III.23.2). What is important for our purposes is that this suggests that Calvin does think God could have created a world other than the one he did in fact create, although Calvin's aversion to theological speculation means he does not pursue the matter, which, he thinks, is hidden from human scrutiny.[25]

Concerning the second dogmatic issue in creation—the act of creation itself—Calvin sides with the tradition in holding unambiguously to *creatio ex nihilo*. For instance, in commenting on Genesis 1:1, he says that Moses "teaches by the word 'created,' that what before did not exist was now made; for he has not used the term . . . *yatsar* . . . which signifies to frame or form, but . . . *bara* . . . which signifies to create. Therefore his meaning is that the world was made out of nothing." Interestingly, given the attempts of some recent theologians to return to a more Platonic doctrine of creation from existing matter, Calvin goes on to say: "Hence the folly of those is refuted who imagine that unformed matter existed from eternity; and who gather nothing else from the narration of Moses than

[24] Zachman, "The Universe as the Living Image of God," 303–4.

[25] Helm has a helpful discussion of this matter in the context of Calvin's use of the medieval distinction between the absolute and ordained power of God in *John Calvin's Ideas*, ch. 11.

that the world was furnished with new ornaments, and received a form of which it was before destitute." To which he adds, "For Christian men to labor . . . in maintaining this gross error is absurd and intolerable."[26] So Calvin is aware of the sort of thinking that informs some modern revisionist discussions of creation. And it is clear he has little patience with such ideas.[27]

For the modern reader there are curiosities in Calvin's understanding of the act of creation, typical of pre-critical exegesis. For instance, he thinks the created order was brought about through six literal days (I.14.21). And he spends a considerable amount of time dealing with angelic beings and their place in the created order (e.g., I.14.3–19), something that is seldom the subject of serious theological discussion today. But one of the important things Calvin's doctrine implies, in good Augustinian fashion, is that creation, like annihilation, is an act only God can perform. We creatures can make things, just as we can destroy them. But making is no more creating than destroying is annihilating. I make a clay statue; my daughter destroys it. But I cannot *create* a clay statue, because I am incapable of generating the matter of which clay is composed from nothing. Just so, my daughter is incapable of annihilating my statue because she cannot eliminate the energy/matter of which it is made. She can only redistribute it over a different area. This is an important consideration whereby the work of God as Creator is clearly distinguished from the "creative" activity of his creatures—something that defenders of panentheism find much more difficult to do.

It might be thought that Calvin's understanding of creation, when taken together with what he says in *Institutes*, I.1–4 about the *semen religionis* (seed of religion) and the *sensus divinitatis* (sense of the divine) as

---

[26] Calvin, *Commentary on Genesis*, 70.

[27] Calvin, writing before the widespread acceptance of the Copernican understanding of the cosmos, still holds to the geocentric theory: "We indeed are not ignorant, that the circuit of the heavens is finite, and that the earth, like a little globe, is placed in the centre" (*Commentary on Genesis*, argument 61). However, this should not be taken as an indication that Calvin was a scientific Luddite. Unlike contemporary "creationists," Calvin is at pains to align his own theological views with what he understood of the natural sciences. See, for example, his *Commentary on Genesis*, on Gen. 1:16 (praising astronomy), and his remarkable comment on Psalm 136:7, where he says, "The Holy Spirit had no intention to teach astronomy" (*Commentary on Psalms*, vol. 5, tr. James Anderson (Grand Rapids: Eerdmans, 1949), 184). Our understanding of the natural world has overtaken Calvin; but this is no judgment on Calvin himself, or his theological method.

well as his doctrine of the limited role natural theology plays in theology, yields the view that one can know God as Creator without Christian faith. The reasoning here would go something like this: Calvin holds that the natural order reflects the glory of its Creator, though, due to the noetic effects of sin, fallen human beings are no longer in a position to perceive this through the naked contemplation of creation. In this way, we may distinguish between the revelation of God in creation that is *offered* us, and the revelation that is (or is not) *received by* us.[28] Our intellectual equipment, including the sense of the divine with which we are endowed as human beings, is vitiated. At best, fallen humans, through exercising this malfunctioning belief-forming apparatus, can arrive at some notion that there is a Maker of this world, but the revelation of God in nature cannot deliver a saving knowledge of God because of the effects of sin. We are sin-blind. So God has to provide the spectacles of Scripture in order for us to be able to "read" this revelation in creation. But this still means that the heathen can know there is a Creator of some sort without the need for special revelation. And the fact that fallen humans can know this much is a reason for their condemnation in not giving due glory to God.

This is true, as far as it goes. But Calvin does think the role Christian faith plays in human understanding concerning God the Creator is crucial. Take, for instance, what he says in commenting on Hebrews 11:3,

> It is by faith alone that we understand that the world was created by God . . . There has always been a certain supposition that the world was created by God among the heathen, but a vague one. Whenever they imagined some sort of God they quickly became vague in their thinking so that they groped uncertainly at a shadow of deity in the darkness rather than grasping the true God. Furthermore, since it was only a fleeting conjecture that flitted through their minds, it was far from any understanding.[29]

Calvin goes on to say that only those with faith have "a firm conviction deep in their hearts" that enables them to behold the true Creator God.[30]

---

[28] cf. Steinmetz, *Calvin in Context*, 32, who argues that this distinction between "what is given" and "what is received" informs Calvin's theology as a whole, not merely his natural theology. It is certainly present in his sacramental theology.

[29] John Calvin, *The Epistle to the Hebrews*, Calvin's New Testament Commentaries , vol. 12, eds. David W. Torrance and Thomas F. Torrance, tr. W.B. Johnston (Grand Rapids: Eerdmans, 1963), 159. (Hereinafter cited as CNTC.)

[30] Calvin, *Epistle to the Hebrews*, CNTC, vol. 12, 159.

This does seem to be in tension with other things he says in the *Institutes*, where it appears that fallen humans can really *know* that there is a god of some sort via the *sensus divinitatis*, absent special revelation. But perhaps what Calvin means to say is that the epistemic condition in which fallen humans find themselves is such that they have no way of rightly identifying God as Creator without divine assistance in the form of the renewal of the *sensus divinitatis*. This renewal comes about through the internal work of the Holy Spirit in regeneration, and a right reading of Scripture, which, in passages like Psalm 19, helps us through the eyes of faith to comprehend what we could only with faltering steps begin to see, vaguely, inchoately, and lacking understanding without faith. If this is right, then there is an important epistemic role that faith plays in Calvin's doctrine of creation, absent from some later works of Reformed dogmatics.[31]

Concerning the third dogmatic issue, namely, the relation between creation and the sustenance of the created order thereafter, Calvin takes the view that creation and conservation are not properly distinct, but two parts of one whole divine act whereby God creates and thereafter conserves in being what he has brought about. In this way, Calvin's position is a species of the radical dependence view of the relation between the created order and its Creator.

Such a position implies a doctrine of meticulous divine providence. However, Calvin's doctrine is not quite as meticulous as that of his contemporary, Huldrych Zwingli, for whom secondary causes are not real causes. Zwingli thinks God directly causes everything to occur that does occur such that mundane causes are merely the occasions (or something very like the occasions) of God's activity. Calvin, by contrast, wants to uphold some version of concurrence: God causes or otherwise brings about all and every event in the created order, but in a way that is not inconsistent with real creaturely causation.[32] There is a nest of problems

---

[31] But not Barth, for whom the doctrine of creation is properly a piece of dogmatics that can only be understood by faith. See *Church Dogmatics* III/1, §40, eds. G.W. Bromiley and Thomas F. Torrance (Edinburgh: T&T Clark, 1958).

[32] Although he does not call his view occasionalism, Huldrych Zwingli denies the reality of secondary causes in his doctrine of providence—which is tantamount to occasionalism. See his *Sermon on the Providence of God* in *The Latin Works of Huldreich Zwingli*, vol. 2, ed. William John Hinke, tr. Samuel Macauley Jackson (Philadelphia: The Heidelberg Press, 1922), 138. There Zwingli bluntly states, "Secondary causes are not properly called causes. This is of fundamental importance for the understanding of Providence." For comparison between Calvin and Zwingli on this, see Paul Helm, "Calvin (and Zwingli) on Divine Providence" in *Calvin Theological Journal* 29 (1994), 388–405.

in the neighborhood of this assertion, which are well known. For one thing, Calvin, like other theological determinists, wants to affirm significant moral freedom for at least some creaturely actions. He also wants to affirm that human beings are morally responsible for their sins. And, of course, he thinks that the conjunction of these two things is important: there is an intimate connection between moral responsibility and freedom; I am morally responsible for the actions I perform provided that I am free to do them. One way of framing Calvin's response to this sort of problem is by appeal to levels of causal activity. God is the primary cause of every action I perform; but I am the secondary cause. However, there are real problems with this approach if God causes all things. He is not just a *necessary* condition, but a *necessary and sufficient* condition for any creaturely action. In which case, talk of my causing a particular action seems otiose.[33]

What of human freedom and moral responsibility? A theological compatibilist such as Calvin can say human agents are free to the extent that they act voluntarily: I make the moral choices I do, and provided I am not coerced into, or prevented from, making those choices, they are voluntary. Moreover, one might think that I am morally responsible for such acts. Provided that one thinks of human freedom in terms of voluntary actions of the sort just outlined, one can be morally responsible for such actions—even where there is no real alternative open to the human agent concerned (whether she knows that or not).[34]

To illustrate: I chose to stay in the study to work on my book, rather than watch television in the lounge, although (unbeknownst to me) my daughter had locked me into my study, so that I could not have gone to watch television in the lounge even if I had wanted to. Does this diminish my responsibility for choosing to stay in the study and work? This is a hoary philosophical conundrum. But, plausibly, my responsibility for so acting is not diminished, given the compatibilist assumptions about what counts as a voluntary action. After all, I chose to stay. True, I could not have left if I had wanted to. But the point is, I did not *want* to. I

---

[33] A point Paul Helm, among others, raises in *The Providence of God* (Leicester: Inter-Varsity Press, 1993), 178–80.

[34] There is a large contemporary philosophical literature on this matter, which owes its impetus to Harry Frankfurt's paper, "Alternate Possibilities and Moral Responsibility," reprinted in *The importance of what we care about* (Cambridge: Cambridge University Press, 1988), 1–10, and his development of so-called "Frankfurtian counterexamples" to the notion that moral responsibility presumes a choice between alternatives, such as the example given in the text above.

wanted to stay in the study, and chose accordingly. If I had known that the door to my study was locked and I could not leave, then I would not have been able to choose to leave the room. But I would have been able to choose to choose to leave the room. The fact is, whether I knew I could leave the room or not, I still had that choice to make. Perhaps if I could only have chosen to choose to leave the room, I would still have chosen to stay where I was. So, one might think, provided that I have the capacity to choose to choose between options before me, even if I am not in a position to act upon my choice, I am responsible for making the choice I do (even if it is not "formalized" in action, so to speak).[35] And even where I have no obvious alternative, I may still refrain from making a decision (refraining from "choosing to choose," as it were), thus preserving moral responsibility.

Of course, Calvin never takes this sort of line in his work. His thinking is much more "concrete" than this.[36] But what I have just said is consistent with what Calvin does offer. He is set against what he calls "bare permission," that is, the idea that God merely allows certain things to occur. Calvin wants a full-blooded determinism: God ordains all that comes to pass. This poses obvious problems for theodicy. But he is more concerned by the prospect of a world where things happen over which God has no control, than he is about a world where things happen that are evil. There is comfort in knowing that, behind the apparent mare's nest of circumstance, God is in control—even if we cannot always fathom his purposes. So, in essence, Calvin's response is the response of Job: trust in God, sometimes despite circumstances, in the knowledge that he works all things to the good, even though we cannot comprehend that from our limited epistemic vantage.

3 Interrogating Calvin

We are now in a position to scrutinize Calvin's position. In the first place, it is important to ask why contemporary evangelical theologians should prefer Calvin's thinking on creation and providence to alternatives

---

[35] Intentional acts are a good case in point: I may choose to daydream about Gustav Klimt's *Danäe* when I should be concentrating on a committee meeting. My action is determined, but it is my choice; I do so voluntarily.

[36] This is not to say that Calvin does not think about divine providence in a rather philosophical manner, even appropriating the argumentative form of school theology in his treatise *A Defence of the Secret Predestination of God*, as Helm makes clear in *John Calvin's Ideas*, ch. 4.

offered from progressive evangelicals, for example, Openness theology; or theological revisionists, for example, panentheists such as McFague. Much here will depend upon what one makes of the doctrine of God.[37] Calvin's adherence to the main lines of a classical doctrine of God, including divine simplicity, aseity, immutability and atemporality have implications for his account of creation and providence. But these deliverances of a classical doctrine of God are increasingly the subject of dispute within the evangelical theological constituency. Disenchantment with the classical doctrine of God[38] will inevitably mean distance from the sort of notions, culled from this classical picture of God, that inform Calvin's understanding of creation and providence.

That said, a God who is in time, whose nature is strongly unified though not simple, strictly speaking (such that he has distinct properties, say), and who is capable of change, may still be a being able to create the world from nothing and sustain it thereafter. So one could make changes to the classical doctrine of God and retain the core commitments that inform Calvin's understanding of creation and providence, that is, creation *ex nihilo* and a meticulous doctrine of providence. But some changes may be thought a bridge too far. Giving up a strong doctrine of divine aseity in order to endorse panentheism, on the grounds that a God who *must* create may not be said to exist *a se*, is, I imagine, one such. But even with respect to panentheism, there are complications: at least one major theologian beloved of evangelicals embraced a seemingly traditional doctrine of God *and* panentheism.[39] The bottom line seems to have much more to do with whether or not one is convinced by Calvin's attempt to reason from Scripture to certain propositions about the nature of creation and providence, and the God who creates and sustains the world. For it is certainly beyond dispute that Calvin thought of himself as engaged in a theological project

---

[37] Much, but not all. Another important issue Calvin would have taken for granted is metaphysical realism, which is now the subject of dispute —as McFague's work makes clear.

[38] Disenchantment with the classical doctrine of God comes in theological and philosophical varieties, of course, as I have already indicated.

[39] See Jonathan Edwards, *End of Creation in The Works of Jonathan Edwards*, vol. 8, ed. Paul Ramsey (New Haven: Yale University Press, 1989). I suppose most evangelical theologians will not want to follow Edwards in this matter because they think commitment to a robust doctrine of divine aseity precludes it. But Edwards endorses both panentheism and aseity. This does open up an interesting avenue for discussion about whether panentheism is beyond the bounds of evangelical theology.

rooted in Scripture, as his commentaries, treatises and *Institutes* testify. So perhaps the important question is not whether we should adopt Calvin's specific interpretation of Scripture, but whether we should adopt Calvin's commitment to Scripture as a theological criterion, a *norma normans*.

Some contemporary theologians think that the classical picture of God with which Calvin, like so many others, was enamored, is simply hopeless because it is not sufficiently *Christological* in character. Recently Bruce McCormack has taken this line, concluding, "Abstract doctrines of God [namely, classical conceptions of the divine nature such as the one Calvin endorsed] have had their day. It is time for evangelicals to take more seriously their affirmation of the deity of Jesus Christ and begin to think about God on a thoroughly christological basis."[40]

Perhaps there is some truth in this criticism. But consider again Calvin's account of creation and providence in the light of those aspects of his doctrine of God that bear upon these issues. Where does Christology fit in? In reading the *Institutes* one might be forgiven for thinking that Christology enters into the picture only once Calvin has thoroughly prepared the ground in the first book, concerned with the knowledge of God, where creation and providence are discussed. It is in the second book that the knowledge of God the Redeemer is set forth. But here familiarity with Calvin's commentaries is important because what he says in commentating on several New Testament passages throws a rather different light on matters. Thus, in his reflections on the Prologue to the Fourth Gospel, he says,

> So far, he [the Evangelist, in John 1:4] has taught us that all things were created by the Word of God. He now likewise attributes to Him the preservation of what had been created; as if he were saying that in the creation of the world His power did not simply suddenly appear only to pass away, but that it was visible in the permanence of the stable and settled order of nature—just as Heb. 1.3 says that He upholds all things by the Word of command of His power . . . For did not His continued inspiration quicken the world, whatsoever flourishes would without doubt immediately decay or be reduced to nothing . . . It is God, therefore, who gives us life; but He does so by the eternal Word.[41]

And in his *Commentary on Colossians,* on 1:15, he goes as far as to say,

---

[40] McCormack, "The Actuality of God," 242. See also his "Grace and Being" where he deals with Calvin's position directly.

[41] Calvin, *Commentary on the Gospel of John,* CNTC, vol. 4, 10–11.

The sum is, that God in Himself, that is, in His naked majesty, is invisible; and that not only to the physical eyes, but also to the human understanding; and that He is revealed to us in Christ alone, where we may behold Him as in a mirror. For in Christ He shows us His righteousness, goodness, wisdom, power, in short, His entire self. We must, therefore, take care not to seek Him elsewhere for outside Christ, everything that claims to represent God will be an idol.[42]

Finally, with regard to Colossians 1: 20, Calvin says that the Apostle,

declares accordingly, that we are blessed through Christ alone, inasmuch as He is the bond of our union with God (*vinculum nostrae cum Deo coniunctionis*), and, on the other hand, that, apart from Him, we are most miserable, because we are shut out from God.[43]

Seen in the light of these passages, Calvin's doctrines of creation and providence appear much more Christologically focused. Taken together with what we have already seen of Calvin's understanding of these twin *loci*, we see that, for Calvin, only those with faith can apprehend what God is *really* doing in creating and preserving the world: how he glorifies himself in his created order by ensuring human beings can apprehend his perfections, at first in and through the natural order and the in-built divine sense of things, and then, after the fall of humanity, in special revelation, applied to the heart of the believer by the secret working of the Holy Spirit. And only those of faith can see that God creates and sustains the world through Christ, the one who makes the divine nature perceptible to us, through whose work we may be united to God.

Other Calvinian themes could be co-opted here, too. Christ is the supreme *divine accommodation* to human limitations, not merely lisping to us in Scripture, but entering into the creation as a creature.[44] Yet even when "contracted to a span" as a human being, Christ is upholding and

---

[42] Calvin, *Commentary on Colossians*, CNTC, vol. 11, 308.

[43] Calvin, *Commentary on Colossians*, CNTC, vol. 11, 312.

[44] "It is evident from this that we cannot believe in God except through Christ, in whom God in a manner makes himself little (*quodammodo parvum facit*), in order to accommodate Himself to our comprehension (*ut se ad captum nostrum submittat*)," *Commentary on 1 Peter*, on 1:20–21 in CNTC, vol. 12, 250; cf. *Institutes*, II.6.4; and Jon Balserak, *Divinity Compromised: A Study of Divine Accommodation in the Thought of John Calvin* (Dordrecht: Springer, 2006), especially ch. 6.

sustaining the universe he fashioned via the so-called *extra calvinisticum*.[45] It should be tolerably clear from this that Calvin's Christology plays a fundamental role in his doctrines of creation and conservation, and that Calvin sees no tension between such commitment and adherence to a classical conception of the divine nature.[46]

4 Conclusion

In common with several recent commentators on Calvin's work, I have tried to show that Calvin's account of creation and providence only makes complete sense when seen as part of the fabric of his theological project, which is an integrated and organic whole. We are created and conserved in being for the glory of God. But God's delight is to so fashion human beings that they (or at least, the elect) may be united to Christ. I have also highlighted Calvin's Christological development of these doctrines in his commentaries, which do seem to put what Calvin says in his *Institutes* in a rather different light. It turns out that on Calvin's way of thinking, those who believe are not just spectators in this divine theater; they are participants in this glorious work of creation, fashioned by God through the Son to be united via the work of

---

[45] *Institutes*, IV.17.30, "For the very same Christ, who, according to the flesh, dwelt as Son of man on earth, was God in heaven. In this manner, he is said to have descended to that place according to his divinity, not because divinity left heaven to hide itself in the prison house of the body, but because even though it filled all things, still in Christ's very humanity it dwelt bodily (Col. 2:9), that is, by nature, and in a certain ineffable way"; cf. Helm, *John Calvin's Ideas*, ch. 3.

[46] Question: *Why* is it that Calvin's commentaries seem much more Christological on the doctrines of creation and providence than the *Institutes*? Perhaps the answer to this lies in the restructuring of this material in the 1559 *Institutes*, where Calvin separated out the material on providence and the material on election. Paul Helm suggests this move came about because Calvin came to see the need to distinguish human choice as such (part of God's providential rule) from human choice as bound in sin and freed by divine grace, which is properly treated in soteriology. If so, then perhaps structural and systematic considerations in the dogmatic arrangement of material in the final Latin form of the *Institutes* come into play in a way they do not in his commentaries. For discussion of this, see Helm, "Calvin, the 'Two Issues,' and the Structure of the *Institutes*" in *Calvin Theological Journal*, 42 (2007), 341–8.

Christ with the Father by the Holy Spirit, to the praise of his glory. If this is not a recommendation of Calvin's understanding of creation and providence to contemporary evangelicals, I don't know what is.[47]

---

[47] I am grateful to David Gibson, Paul Helm and Benjamin Myers for comments on previous drafts of this paper.

4

Calvin's Theological Anthropology

Henri Blocher

Twofold is our knowledge of ourselves, or it should be, says Calvin. He is not speaking here of its correlation with the knowledge of God, which he so famously posits as the opening thesis of the *Institutes*. He is not marking the correspondence with the twofold character of our knowledge of God, the *duplex cognitio*, which Dowey highlighted, of God as Creator and as Redeemer: Calvin could have set forth our knowledge of ourselves (human beings) as *duplex cognitio* of our creation and redemption, but this is not his point. "Our knowledge of ourselves is twofold: of how we were formed in our first origin, and, then, in what condition we are fallen since Adam's fall."[1] In somewhat parallel fashion, his Response to Pighius on free will insists that, just as Luther did, he affirms a "double nature": "The first as

---

[1] John Calvin, *Institutes of the Christian Religion* (final, 1559–1560), I.15.1 (book, chapter and section henceforth abbreviated in this way in the text). For reasons of availability, and unless otherwise indicated, I will give my own renderings of Calvin's original, either Latin or French (he made or checked the French translations of the works he had first written in Latin). References will be made to the *Calvini Opera (CO)* edited by Baum, Cunitz & Reuss, and a few other editions, especially the *Recueil des Opuscules, c'est à dire, Petits traictez de M. Iean Calvin* (Geneva: Baptiste Pinereul, 1566), abbreviated *Opusc*. Richard A. Muller somewhere recommends using editions of Calvin's epoch; I confess to not having reached such a level of refined scholarship as to be conscious of the difference it makes, but it so happens that I own, and am using, several sixteenth-century editions of Calvinian works (my copy of the *Commentaires de Iean Calvin sur le livre des Pseaumes* unfortunately lacks the title page and preface, but none of the 902 pages in -4°, plus pages of index).

God had created it, which . . . we confess, was pure and whole; and the other, which lost its integrity through the corruption of the human fall."[2]

Apart from a remarkable fondness for binary analysis and presentation,[3] Calvin's emphasis on the duality affecting human nature reflects the decisive significance of *event* for his theology: the event, here, of Adam's disobedience. As Gabriel-Philippe Widmer observes, instead of philosophical prolegomena in the scholastic fashion, Calvin offers a "dramatology" to account for the present state of humankind.[4] His theology could be called "narrative," as it is shaped by the Grand Narrative of the whole Scripture, Creation-Fall-Redemption (his interest lying not in formal features of the telling but in the events as real). Furthermore, discerning between original integrity and subsequent corruption provides the key insight into the character of evil: "It makes a big difference whether our nature was affected from the start or was affected since, and from elsewhere";[5] a *vitium* in human nature from creation would be a valid ground for accusing God (II.1.10). The utter singularity of evil constrains us into paradoxical language, as Calvin expresses forcefully,

> We say that man is *naturally* corrupt and perverse, but that perversity does *not* proceed *from nature*. We deny that it proceeds from nature to show that it is an adventitious quality that came to affect man, rather than a substantial property which was his from the beginning; however, we call it *natural*, that no one should think that we contract it through the influence

---

[2] *Opusc.*, 287.

[3] One is reminded of the "new," anti-Aristotelian, logic of Pierre de la Ramée (Ramus), which was strongly to influence Reformed thinking. However, a Ramist influence looks most unlikely in Calvin's case: Ramus was a few years younger, and dealt first with mathematics; one can only conjecture about the influence of the intellectual climate that prevailed among the "évangéliques." (In ecclesiology, there were some tensions between the two men: together with many among the French Reformed, Ramus championed a more congregationalist polity than was welcome in Geneva.)

[4] Gabriel-Philippe Widmer, "La 'Dramatique' de l'image de Dieu chez Calvin," in *Humain à l'image de Dieu. La théologie et les sciences humaines face au problème de l'anthropologie*, ed. Pierre Bühler, Lieux théologiques, 15 (Geneva: Labor & Fides, 1989), 213.

[5] *Institutes*, II.1.10: "Ce sont choses bien diverses, qu'elle ait esté navrée dès son origine, ou qu'elle l'ait esté depuis et d'ailleurs" (*multum refert accesseritne aliunde, an ab origine insederit*).

of bad custom and example, for it is the case that it affects us all from our first being born.[6]

Calvin's interest in the succession of original events also entails his sharp distinction between creation and redemption.[7] Though the Son of God is the Mediator in both, he became man only to redeem us from our sins, and Calvin tenaciously combats any attempt, such as Osiander's, to relate human creational status or features to Jesus Christ incarnate.[8] Even the fact that we need to look to Christ to find the image of God restored (the texts Calvin often cites being Col. 3:10 and Eph. 4.24), and thus precisely to know what the image implies, does not lead to redemption being included in anthropology proper.

---

[6] *Institutes*, II.1.11: "Nous disons doncques que l'homme est naturellement corrompu en perversité (*naturali vitiositate corruptum*): mais que ceste perversité n'est point en luy de nature (*a natura non fluxerit*). Nous nions qu'elle soit de nature, afin de monstrer que c'est plutost une qualité survenue à l'homme (*adventitiam qualitatem quae homini acciderit*), qu'une propriété de sa substance, laquelle ait esté dès le commencement enracinée en luy (*ab initio indita*); toutesfois, nous l'appelons naturelle, afin qu'aucun ne pense qu'elle s'acquiert d'un chacun par mauvaise coustume et exemple, comme ainsi soit qu'elle nous enveloppe tous dès nostre première naissance" (emphasis added).

[7] Calvin insists on that distinction, and the proper order of treatment—he will not deal with redemption at this stage—in *Institutes*, I.6.1.

[8] *Institutes*, I.15.3, where Calvin grants that a more moderate view than Osiander's, the view that "Adam was created in the image of God because he was conformed to Jesus Christ, who is the [unique, in Latin] image of God" is more attractive, superficially (*Plus coloris habet*), and, yet, he rejects it as unfounded. In *Institutes*, I.6.1, he contrasts the knowledge of God the Creator with that of the Redeemer, whom we know "in the person of our Lord Jesus Christ," and with the covenant of grace "founded on Jesus Christ": this would suggest that the creational relationship was *not* established through Christ. However, many other passages demonstrate that Christ was already the Mediator in creation (cf. *Institutes*, IV.8.5: "None of the saints of ancient times [including Adam] has ever known God apart from beholding him in his Son as in a mirror")—only: not in the flesh, not by virtue of his incarnation. One of the most explicit documents is the Refutation of Stancarus sent to the Polish Brethren (1560), *Response aux Frères de Pologne, comment Christ est médiateur, pour réfuter l'erreur de Stancarus, Opusc.*, 1756 (Latin in *CO* 9, 338): Calvin (with colleagues adding their signatures) affirms that Christ was always Mediator (prince of angels, even

Calvin gave so much weight to the creation/fall duality in his view of the human being that we had to recall some of his strong expressions. Yet, since the present book devotes another chapter to Calvin's doctrine of sin and evil, only the *first* panel will be the object of our inquiry. Within the limits of the space allotted, we propose to explore and to sketch Calvin's teaching on humankind *as created*. It corresponds to the contents of chapter 15 of Book I of the *Institutes*, Calvin's only attempt to deal at some length, *ex professo*, with the question: "What is man?" Since there is a grain of truth in Emile Doumergue's exaggerated statement that "anthropology is nowhere [in Calvin's work] because it is everywhere,"[9] we shall draw from other passages as well—in any case, Calvin never tires of repeating, with slight (though interesting and sometimes fascinating) variations, the same elements of teaching.

Teaching that is *preaching*! This feature is striking: when Calvin theologizes, he is constantly determined by *pastoral* concerns. There is an "existential" edge to every doctrine, as a previous generation would have said. As Wilhelm H. Neuser perceived, "Calvin is not interested in any doctrinal proposition on the Bible which is not, at the same time, relevant to preaching."[10] The frequent warning against speculation

---

(cont.) Head of the church, in the sense of the supreme Authority over the human community called to worship God, at the creation stage) as "the eternal Word (*Parole, sermo*) of God," and then, after humankind's alienation from God, for redemptive purposes, he assumed a mediatorship "of another kind" (d'une autre sorte, *alio modo*); cf. the interpretation of Col. 1:15ff. in *Institutes*, II.12.7: Christ is the "firstborn of all creatures" as the eternal Word (*Logos asarkos*), whereas "inasmuch as he was made man, he is called firstborn of the dead." Such evidence compels one to correct Wilhelm Niesel's misreading in *Die Theologie Calvins (Einführung in die evangelische Theologie*, Band VI (Munich: Chr. Kaiser, 1938)), for example: "Even as we affirm the general human responsibility, we cannot bypass the *incarnandus* and *incarnatus* God," 49. One spots the weakness also in Thomas F. Torrance's synthesis, in many respects a masterpiece (with such a wealth of quotations and references!), *Calvin's Doctrine of Man* (London: Lutterworth, 1949), for example, 42, 69 n. 3, 84f. Pierre Gisel, *Le Christ de Calvin* (Collection, "Jésus et Jésus-Christ, 44), (Paris: Desclée, 1990) emphasizes Christ's mediatorship in creation but acknowledges that it did not imply the incarnation, 38, 66, 125, 147.

[9] Emile Doumergue, *Jean Calvin. Les hommes et les choses de son temps*, IV: *La pensée religieuse de Calvin* (Lausanne: Georges Bridel, 1910), 137, following Dilthey.

[10] "Calvins Vertändnis der Heiligen Schrift," in *Calvinus Sacrae Scripturae Professor* [*Calvin as Confessor of Holy Scripture*] (Grand Rapids: Eerdmans, 1994), 52.

(idle, more often than not) and ideas that "flutter about in the brains" reflects the conviction that "true religion requires a knowledge not speculative, but united with practice."[11] He even makes it a rule of method: "We shall be protected from wandering from the path if we consider the dangers on either side," dangers of unwanted spiritual attitudes.[12] Calvin's developments on human beings as created aim at casting down human pride and presumption on the one hand, and castigating offensive thanklessness on the other—at fostering *humility* and eliciting *gratitude*.[13]

This dual pattern—once more—provides a convenient division of the data, which we adopt. Our overview, inevitably quick and basically descriptive, will first consider what, in the doctrine, should humble us, after Calvin's admonition, and then what should fill us with overflowing thankfulness. Beyond drawing the main features, we will pay attention to a few sensitive spots that have often been disregarded, we feel, in summaries of Calvin's teachings.

1 Humbling: the lowliness of the human condition

Calvin easily adopts the tone of that fellow-preacher of the fear of God, Ecclesiastes: "God is in heaven and you are on earth" (5:2b, ESV). Putting man in his place, smashing to pieces his silly boasting, means first to recall his mere *creatureliness*. There is "a fundamental non-symmetry in the divine–human relationship."[14] The crushing realization of the unthinkable superiority of God *drives* Calvin's theological reflection: no human being can see God and live, as the biblical saints perceived in awe and terror (I.1.3), "the infinity ("infinité," *immensitas*) of his essence must fill us with dread" (I.13.1). Hence Calvin's zeal against all trends or theories that tended to mix Godhood and creaturehood, or to relativize their difference. He opposed "the animistic, vitalistic and hylozoist naturalism that was expanding in his days, and denounced its pantheism and its deism tending to atheism: they ruin ethics and foster a return to paganism."[15] He

---

[11] *Commentaire sur le livre des Pseaumes* (henceforth *Pseaumes*), 881, on Ps. 145:5–6 (Latin, CO 32, 413: *non speculativam, sed practicam notitiam*).

[12] *Institutes*, II.2.1: "Voycy le moyen qui nous gardera d'errer, c'est de considérer les dangers qui sont de part et d'autre," nonchalance, témérité, etc.

[13] Torrance, *Calvin's Doctrine of Man*, 13, 70 ("No theme recurs more constantly throughout Calvin's *Institutes, Commentaries*, and *Sermons* than man's duty of thankfulness, and his sin in ingratitude").

[14] Gisel, *Le Christ de Calvin*, 31.

[15] Widmer, "La 'Dramatique' de l'image," 214.

burned in Elijah-like anger against the pantheistic implications of Michel
Servet's system (chaotic system!), where he saw the same wicked delusion
("resverie mechante," *delirium*) as among the Manicheans of old.[16] He
detected the same poisonous root in the views of the Libertines,[17] and in
the muddled explanations of the non-orthodox Lutheran theologian
Andreas Osiander.[18] Calvin's sense of the *mysterium tremendum* of deity
maintained an infinite distance between Creator and creature;[19] even the
Son's mediatorial role in creation, which could be construed as a glorious
association, Calvin interpreted as a humbling necessity of our condition,
so far down below the Most High![20]

One aspect of creaturely lowliness that is central for Calvin is total
dependence. If there can be no true knowledge of self, among human
beings, apart from the knowledge of God, if "man does not understand
himself in himself, but can only understand himself in and through his
relation with God,"[21] it is because there is not a particle of our being, at

[16] *Institutes*, I.15.5 and II.14.5–8; "Declaration pour maintenir la vraye foy que tiennent tous Chrestiens de la Trinité . . . Contre les erreurs detestables de Michel Servet Espagnol . . ." *Opusc.*, 1315–1469 (with various elements of the case), especially 1435–7 (1445 on deification); also *Commentaires de Jehan Calvin sur le Nouveau Testament*, IV, henceforth abbreviated as *CNT* (Paris: Meyrueis, 1854), on 2 Pet. 1:4 (referring to Manicheans), 748.

[17] "Contre la secte phantastique et furieuse des Libertins, qui se nomment spirituels," *Opusc.* 646–713, especially 666–7.

[18] *Institutes*, III.11.5–6. Though the issue was deeply theological, there may have been a "human" factor in Calvin's distrust of Osiander. P. Tschakert reports: "At Worms [1540] he became acquainted with Calvin, who was offended by his indecorous table-talk," in the art. "Osiander," in Samuel Macauley Jackson (ed.), *The New Schaff-Herzog Encyclopedia of Religious Knowledge*, VIII (New York: Funk & Wagnalls, 1910), 280.

[19] Well characterized by John H. Leith, "Calvin's Awareness of the Holy and the Enigma of his Theology," in *In Honor of John Calvin 1509–1564. Papers from the 1986 International Calvin Symposium, McGill University*, ed. E.J. Furcha, ARC Supplement 3 (Montreal: Faculty of Religious Studies, McGill University, 1987), 204–32.

[20] *Institutes*, II.12.1. The French text only says: too low to reach God, "trop basse pour parvenir à Dieu," but the Latin adds *sine mediatore*.

[21] Jean Boisset, *Jean Calvin et la souveraineté de Dieu, Philosophes de tous les temps* (Paris: Seghers, 1964), 44. This is, according to Boisset, one of the two affirmations one must indispensably have in mind "to understand calvinian anthropology"; the second one is the difference between the original state and the fallen condition—with which we started.

any moment and from any point of view, that could be seen as independent of God. Even the privilege of being created in the image of God, Calvin interprets in a humbling way: the human creature "was not rich with his/her own goods" (II.2.1). A favorite image is that of the mirror, and Torrance, who stresses that choice, comments: "Only while the mirror actually reflects an object does it have the image of that object. There is no such thing in Calvin's thought as an *imago* dissociated from the act of reflecting."[22] The special gifts are "adventitious."[23] Immortality, which is tied to the *imago* privilege, is no inherent property of the soul, of which human beings could boast as something they would own of and by themselves.[24] Susan E. Schreiner ventures the word "precarious": "In Calvin's thought nature was more than merely contingent and dependent; it was also precarious."[25] If one remembers the etymology of "precarious"—bound to *prayer* (*preces*)—the word is not improper; one might say that the ontological truth of humanity *is* prayer, the avowal of dependence in humble gratitude and obedient trust.

At the same time, we must guard against excesses. Claiming that "Calvin ALWAYS think[s] of the *imago* in terms of a *mirror*" goes beyond the evidence; and discounting the numerous statements about the image of God "engraved" ("engravée," *insculptata*) in the soul as negligible metaphors smacks of *petitio principii*.[26] Calvin ascribes an authentic consistency to created being—only, with God governing and sustaining. His point, which he makes with powerful rhetoric, is that every creature, and human creature, remains utterly dependent on God; surrounding statements in the same paragraphs where he speaks of the soul as a mirror irradiated by God's glory, show that he does not wish to deny a true possession of properties, provided that it is acknowledged to be under God, "in God" (Acts 17:28) and in dependence on him. Ownership is not

---

[22] Torrance, *Calvin's Doctrine of Man*, 36.

[23] Torrance, *Calvin's Doctrine of Man*, 53; Torrance quotes from the *Commentary on Genesis*, on Gen. 2:7 (CO 23, 35: "*unde agnoscant adventitium illud fuisse bonum*"; the French uses less technical language: "ce bien leur vient d'ailleurs").

[24] Torrance, *Calvin's Doctrine of Man*, 27, and Niesel, *Die Theologie*, 62, offer many references. Calvin's language is strong and clear, for example, already in his *Psychopannychia, Opusc.*, 48; Thirty-ninth and Fifty-fourth Sermons on Job (Job 10 and 14), CO 33, 491, 674; *CNT* IV, 260, on 1 Tim. 6:16.

[25] Susan E. Schreiner, *Nature and the Natural Order in the Thought of John Calvin* (Durham, N.C.: Labyrinth Press, 1991), 23. I thank Lydia Jaeger for making this text available to me.

[26] Torrance, *Calvin's Doctrine of Man*, 36 (capitals added).

absolute, but not unreal: Calvin can write that "the image of God is the whole excellence of human nature" (I.15.4). To read into his discourse antitheses such as those of "static" and "dynamic"[27] or "substantial" and "functional" can be misleading: anachronistic. Calvin often uses "substance" and "nature" (as an enduring set of properties): Emile Doumergue counted 40 appeals to "nature" in the Sermons on Deuteronomy![28] When Torrance claims: "For Calvin, all secondary causation is highly suspicious, and has no real place in theology,"[29] he sets aside clear statements to the contrary,[30] the basis of Susan Schreiner's conclusion: "Calvin never denied secondary causality. He did believe that God worked immediately and mediately in nature and history . . . he tied God as closely as possible to these secondary means or instruments."[31] The role of secondary causes grounds the distinction between absolute and relative necessity (I.16.9); more important theologically, it enables Calvin to blame the wicked action exclusively on the sinner, though it was foreordained in God's counsel. The very non-symmetry of the Creator–creature relationship entails that one refuses the either/or of independence, *coram Deo*, and the non-reality (nearly so) of the creature's being, which then amounts to the mere phenomenality of a divine act or thought.

---

[27] Torrance, *Calvin's Doctrine of Man*, 106, writes with honesty: "A large part of the difficulty in determining Calvin's views on the depravity of man is due to the fact that he lapses back again and again, at least in language, from a dynamic to a more static conception of man"; this sounds like a confession that the categories do not fit Calvin's discourse.

[28] Doumergue, *Jean Calvin*, IV, 152–3.

[29] Torrance, *Calvin's Doctrine of Man*, 29; cf. 63: "From the point of view of his theology Calvin has nothing to do with second causes." It is true that Torrance hastens to add, "That does not encourage the Christian to overlook inferior causes, but it does mean that we can never think of the world of nature as in any sense independent of the Creator," 63: this addition is perfectly correct (Torrance could not forget what Calvin wrote), but it formally contradicts the main statement.

[30] For example, *Institutes*, I.16.4: all species behave "as their natural make-up requires it, as obeying a perpetual statute to which God has subjected them . . ."

[31] Schreiner, *Nature and the Natural Order*, 36f. She sees a certain ambivalence in Calvin's position, 30, but quotes several passages showing Calvin affirming inferior, secondary, causes, 30–2: he is simply vigilant that they be not considered independent. Lydia Jaeger, *Ce que les cieux racontent. La science à la lumière de la création*, La Foi en dialogue (Cléon-d'Andran/Nogent-sur-Marne: Excelsis/Institut Biblique, 2008), 85f., helpfully touches on the topic.

The humbling truth of creaturely dependence applies in two areas that loom large in Calvin's theological interests, and in Calvinian studies. For that very reason, we are constrained to do little more than mention them: Calvin's unflagging warfare against "free will" as commonly understood[32] and his doctrine of the "sense of divinity" or "seed of religion" in all human beings (I.2–3). Free will, as he rejected it, amounts to independence: in the act of choosing. Total dependence on God, on the contrary, implies that "one chooses good when divine grace assists and one chooses evil when it desists":[33] there is no neutral ground; divine sovereignty requires an infallible determination of all particulars. The *sensus divinitatis/semen religionis*[34] could be considered as an asset to the credit of humankind, but Calvin emphasizes both its ugly distortion in idolatry and its manifestation in horror and terror in those, such as Caligula, who dare insult heaven.[35] Assuredly, the preaching of our human dependence on our Creator is intended to deflate and shatter to the ground all attempts at proud postures.

---

[32] For example, *Institutes*, II.2 (I.16; III.22–3).

[33] *Institutes*, II.2.4 (*"On élit le bien quand la grâce de Dieu assiste: et le mal quand icelle désiste"; bonum eligitur gratia assistente, malum, ea desistente*). This looks equivalent to the distinction in Reformed theology between divine causality as *efficient* for good and *deficient* for evil.

[34] Despite efforts, indeed, I have not found (yet) an answer to the question: Has Calvin coined the phrases, or did someone before him? They are not found in Cicero (whom Calvin closely uses), nor in Tertullian, nor in Lactantius, nor in Thomas Aquinas, nor, it seems (from Migne's indices, only one reference which turns out to be later than Calvin) in any other medieval writer. My doctoral student, Jean D. Decorvet, should complete the search with computer and internet tools, and report on results. Calvin was fond of the "seed" metaphor; I suspect it provided an easy way out of conceptual straits, a way to allow for both presence and absence. In one case, O. Gründler comments that it was "not totally free from ambiguity": "The Problem of the Semen Fidei in the Teaching of Calvin," in *Calvinus servus Christi*, International Congress on Calvin Research, 1986, Debrecen, ed. Wilhelm H. Neuser (Budapest: Presseabteilung des Ráday-Kollegiums, 1988), 207.

[35] I merely refer to two remarkable treatments: Edward A. Dowey, Jr., *The Knowledge of God in Calvin's Theology* (Grand Rapids: Eerdmans, 1994 augmented), 50–5 (on our point, 54); Paul Helm, "John Calvin, the *sensus divinitatis*, and the noetic effects of sin," *International Journal for Philosophy of Religion*, 43 (1998), 87–107, most exact on the contours of Calvin's teaching, and convincing on the gap between Calvin's concerns and those of the advocates of (so-called) "Reformed epistemology," who appeal to the theme.

One dimension of our created being seems even more humbling than the others: our *bodiliness*. On countless occasions, Calvin refers to the body as a "prison,"[36] and he can paint a very grim picture of our physical life.[37] He can reach comical heights (intentionally, I think): he pities Noah and his family, who had to live for ten months in the midst of so much dung and refuse, and draws a comparison with the child's trial during pregnancy: only a divine miracle can explain the child's survival in surroundings that "would be enough to suffocate the most robust within half an hour"![38] Most references do not distinguish between creation and fallenness. A few times, Calvin does marvel at the perfection and beauty of the human body as fashioned by God.[39] But he explicitly interprets our having been drawn from the ground as a humbling trait, a precaution against pride.[40] Of Adam before the Fall, he writes: "He smelt of earth."[41]

Calvin's idiosyncrasies played a part: his experience of bodily life—ill-health, since the harsh treatments of the Collège Montaigu—his personal sensitivity and delicacy, his psychological make-up . . . Undoubtedly Platonism was an influence. It was an attractive option for humanists,[42] helping them to free themselves from Aristotle and Nominalism. Calvin singles out Plato among all philosophers for milder assessment.[43] As a young, but mature scholar, in his *Psychopannychia*, Calvin quotes (approvingly) from the Platonic apocryphal Wisdom of Solomon: "a perishable body weighs down the soul" (9:15).[44] His low estimate of the body was something self-evident to him, and worth preaching in order to humble human beings.

---

[36] Already in the *Psychopannychia, Opusc.*, 23; *Pseaumes*, 641, on Ps. 103:14–16; and in the *Institutes* I quickly collected nine occurrences, I.15.2; II.7.13; III.2.19, 3.9, 9.4; IV.1.1, 15.11–12, 16.19.

[37] *Institutes*, I.17.10; cf. *Pseaumes*, 37, on Ps. 8:5, with comments on the Hebrew word *Enos* ('*enôš*).

[38] *Pseaumes*, 449, on Ps. 71:5.

[39] *Institutes*, I.5.2 (with reference to the Greek physician Galen's book); *Pseaumes*, 855, on Ps. 139:6.

[40] *Commentaire sur la Genèse*, 45, on Gen. 2:7; *Institutes*, I.15.1.

[41] *CNT* III, 503, on 1 Cor. 15:47 ("Il sentoit la terre, de laquelle estoit produit le corps").

[42] Boisset, *Jean Calvin*, 107–20, emphasizes Calvin's participation in that climate; I would insist rather on the mediation of St. Augustine's Platonism.

[43] For example, *Psychopannychia, Opusc.*, 6; *Institutes*, I.15.6 and III.25.2.

[44] *Opusc.*, 23 (see *Opusc.*, 9 for comments on the authority of the Apocrypha). This verse in Wisdom 9 was important for St. Augustine.

It is the more remarkable that Calvin did *not* follow, on one point, the Platonic disparagement of the body: he breaks from the negative view of sexuality that usually went with it. He denounces St. Jerome's asceticism as "wicked" and "perverse," born of Satan's inspiration.[45] Everything in sexual activity that is "unbecoming and dirty" was introduced by human sin.[46] Sex in marriage is not first of all a remedy against fornication—this is only an *accidental* benefit, in a sinful situation;[47] it is essentially a gift of the God who "provides for our pleasure" (III.10.2). Calvin can speak favorably of erotic play.[48] Female beauty comes from grace (despite its dangers) and even the "sons of God," understood as the Sethites, are not blamed for the attraction they felt from the charm of Adam's daughters![49] Reformation was revolution . . .

The fourth "humbling" aspect of Calvin's anthropology has received less attention but deserves some: original human *infirmity*. Calvin uses the word to characterize Adam's condition *before* the Fall: "Man was created *infirmus* and liable to defection,"[50] his goodness was "fragile and liable to fall" and it was by this infirmity that he did fall.[51] Adam did not enjoy "a solid and firm position."[52] Adam was in a "middle condition," being able to sin and not to sin (*posse non peccare*, whereas redemption brings the *non posse peccare*).[53] "He could lean on either side" and possessed "free will."[54] "Had he willed it, he could have gained eternal life," but the gift of perseverance was not given him, and "this is why he

---

[45] *Commentaire sur la Genèse*, 56, on Gen. 2:18; *CNT* I, 491, on Mt. 19:10ff.; *CNT* III, 361, on 1 Cor. 7:1.

[46] *Commentaire sur la Genèse*, 94, on Gen. 4:1.

[47] *Commentaire sur la Genèse*, 57, on Gen 2:18ff.

[48] Commentary on Deut. 24:5, according to André Biéler, *L'Homme et la femme dans la morale calviniste*, Nouvelle série théologique (Geneva: Labor & Fides, 1963), 61.

[49] *Commentaire sur la Genèse*, 536, on Gen. 39:6, and 125, on Gen. 6:2.

[50] "Response aux calomnies . . . touchant la providence secrète de Dieu," *Opusc.*, 1784: "Combien que l'homme aist esté creé & infirme & prompt à revoltement" (". . . de occulta Dei providentia," CO 9, 291: *Quamvis infirmus, et ad defectionem flexibilis*).

[51] CO 9, 291, "bonté, qui estoit fragile et caduque" (*rectitudinem, quae fluxa et caduca erat*); "il est cheu par son infirmité" (*sua infirmitate cecidisse*).

[52] *Commentaire sur la Genèse*, 46, "point de solidité ni de fermeté" (CO 23, 36: *non habebat stabilem fixamque constantiam*).

[53] *CNT* I, 119 on Mt. 4:2.

[54] *Institutes*, II.3.10 and already I.15.8.

fell so quickly"—he was standing on "slippery ground."[55] Calvin avails himself, in the same paragraphs, of the opportunity of belittling *"free will"* whose exercise brought about such sad consequences.[56]

Tensions are hard to deny. Calvin himself, when writing on original infirmity, hastens to claim that "this weakness (*debilitas*) was very good (*valde bona*)": how convincing can he be? His comments on the Fall being so easy on the slippery ground tend to smooth down the disruption between creation and the sinful state—just contrary to his main strategy! And does the "flexible" undecided state of Adam's will in Eden, which Calvin posits after St. Augustine,[57] not look suspiciously like the neutral liberty of indifference against which he waged an unrelenting war through the rest of his theology! If human beings always choose evil when God "desists," and Adam was not given the gift of perseverance, without which he would not persevere, is there any content left to Calvin's *posse non peccare*? Only further reflection on the meaning of "possibility," on the concept of *posse*, would help elucidate the issue, which was bound, in Calvin's reconstruction, on the *probation* understanding of the Eden episode, with the trees and the command: Adam's choice was tested, and, therefore, not yet firm.[58] One discerns also a link with Calvin's tendency so to lower creatures in order to exalt the Lord that he charged the good and faithful angels with uncleanness and

---

[55] *Institutes*, I.15.8, "comme en lieu glissant" (*quasi in lubrico*); a little above: *ideo tam facile prolapsus est.*

[56] One may note that in the *Commentaire sur la Genèse*, 50, the forbidden knowledge of good and evil is said to be the "origin of *free will*," corresponding to Adam's will to be by himself (*CO* 23, 39: *per se esse voluit*). There seems to be a discrepancy here: either *"free will"* is the flexible indetermination of Adam's *arbitrium* or the sinful autonomy he acquired.

[57] *De correptione et gratia* XI, 31ff. In his "Responsio contra Pighium de libero arbitrio," *CO* 6, 403, Calvin adopts the distinction between the *adjutorium* (synonym *auxilium*) *sine quo non* and the *adjutorium quo* (a controversy *de auxiliis* raged between Jesuits and Dominicans and the pope had to forbid any further publication on the topic!).

[58] *Institutes*, II.1.4; *Commentaire sur la Genèse*, 55, on Gen. 2:17 (*CO* 23, 45). Since I find no hint, in the biblical narrative, of such a probationary character, I ask how Calvin could be led to his assumption in this regard. I suggest: (1) that his low estimate of bodiliness and earthly life made it impossible for him to imagine that an earthly paradise could be the ultimate destiny of creatures made in God's image; (2) in the framework of a literal reading of the story, the command looks so arbitrary that the idea of probation is read into the text to "inject" rationality.

guilt:[59] the sense of God's infinite superiority may slide into a non-Calvinistic dualism!

2 Amazing: the excellence of original gifts

To human beings who confess that they are but dust and mud from the ground, prostrate in awe before the Most High and Holy One, the preacher announces good news: already in the doctrine of creation, the good news of "amazing grace." They are God's "masterpiece,"[60] the object of his elective love and *fatherly* care;[61] they have been invested with the highest prerogatives and endowed with the most excellent gifts.

Calvin lavishes the treasures of his eloquence on the praise of human *excellence*, at least among all visible creatures. "They have been adorned with so many excellences that their condition is hardly less than God's heavenly glory."[62] They recapitulate the beauties of the universe, and the word *microcosmos* was well chosen for what they are, by God's original disposition.[63] Bolder still: Calvin can write that the original gifts would have made us (had not Adam lost them) "like half-gods."[64] All the privileges depend on God's sustenance and "virtue," but are truly *given*.[65]

One phrase sums up the gifts that elevate humans above other creatures: they were created *in God's image*. "The problem of the *imago dei*,"

---

[59] *Institutes*, III.17.9; *CNT* IV, 69, on Col. 1:20; Fourth Sermon on Ephesians (*CO* 51, 295), and Sixteenth Sermon on Job (*CO* 33, 207f.), as quoted by Richard Stauffer, *Dieu, la création et la providence dans la prédication de Calvin*, Basler & Berner Studien zur historischen und systematischen Theologie, 33 (Bern: Peter Lang, 1978), 191. Calvin had been impressed by Job 4:18, but the consequences he draws are not obligatory.

[60] Frequently, and already in the early, stylistically brilliant, *"Epître à tous amateurs de Jésus-Christ et de son Evangile, salut,"* as edited by Irena Backus and Claire Chimelli, *"La Vraie Piété"*: *Divers traités de Jean Calvin et Confession de foi de Guillaume Farel*, Histoire et Société, 12 (Geneva: Labor & Fides, 1986), 25.

[61] I owe to my doctoral student Geoffrey M. Ziegler a fine survey of the remarkable prevalence of the sonship/fatherhood language in Calvin.

[62] *Pseaumes*, 37, on Ps. 8:6–7, "Leur condition n'est gueres moindre que la gloire celeste de Dieu."

[63] *Institutes*, I.5.3; *Pseaumes*, 855, on Ps. 139:6; *CNT* II, 805, on Acts 17:27.

[64] *Pseaumes*, 38, on Ps. 8:6–7: "comme demi-dieux" (*CO* 31, 93: *quasi semideos*).

[65] Using scholastic language, Calvin endorses the *donum superadditum* (*praeternaturale*); though "added," it is nonetheless *donum*.

writes Richard Stauffer, "is one of the most difficult in Calvin's theology. The texts that deal with it are as numerous as they contradict each other"; and he criticizes Niesel and Torrance for unilateral systematization.[66] In my estimate, most discrepancies, in formal statements, relate to what is left of the image after the Fall, and lie outside the purview of our inquiry. In creation, what may be disconcerting is the combination of a *moral* interpretation—likeness being identified with righteousness and holiness (Eph. 4:24)—and a *metaphysical* one, with a strong emphasis on the spiritual nature and its faculties (I.15.3–4). That the latter carried weight with Calvin appears when he explains which gifts show that human beings were formed in God's image (with immortal life as their goal),

> In that they were endowed with reason, to be able to discern between good and evil, in that there is a seed of religion engraved within them, that there is among them mutual communication, of which the bonds are holy and sacred: similarly, in that they are concerned for honesty, are ashamed of wrongdoing, that they have laws to govern them, all these things, I say, are obvious signs of a sovereign and heavenly wisdom.[67]

A mediating concept is the soundness, perfect regulation and harmony of the faculties.[68] One may suggest that Calvin's failure to cut through the duality of the "metaphysical" and the "moral" is a sign of his sensitivity to the *truth* of the matter: though the distinction is indispensable, one cannot separate; in Calvin's radical monotheism, if humans live, move and *are* "in God," the quality of their relation with God ("moral") bears upon the character of their being ("metaphysical," if one wishes).[69]

More clearly, probably, than any great doctor of the church before him, Calvin affirmed the full participation of the *woman* in the image of

---

[66] Stauffer, *Dieu, la création et la providence*, 201.

[67] *Pseaumes*, 38, on Ps. 8:6–7.

[68] *Institutes*, I.15.3: "Under this word [image of God] the whole integrity of Adam is subsumed which Adam possessed when he enjoyed rectitude of mind, proper control over his affections, adaptation of the senses, everything well ordered in itself, to represent by such ornaments the glory of his Creator." In his "Consilium. . . contra Osiandrum," *CO* 10,166, Calvin speaks of *symmetria in singulis facultatibus*.

[69] I could have written of a "relational ontology"; I refrained from using a word that has become quasi magical today.

God privilege.[70] "Whatever was said on the man's creation also applies to the female sex";[71] the man (male) could be said to be "half a man" (*dimidium hominem*).[72] "Moses wanted to indicate equality."[73] The subjection of women, which Calvin does teach also, he restrains to an "economic status" (relative to the present economy), an "external honesty and church polity,"[74] belonging to this age. He underscores the "singular honor" that the apostle pays to a woman, Prisca—Paul "does not consider it beneath him to have a woman as fellow-worker in the Lord's work, and is not ashamed to confess it."[75] In his letter to the ladies imprisoned in Paris, several of whom were to die as martyrs of the faith, Calvin points out that God is pleased to work powerfully through female weakness, that he grants the gift of prophecy to sons and daughters and chose a woman to be the messenger of Christ's resurrection.[76]

Though one can glimpse "sparks" of the image of God in the human body, Calvin has no doubt that its seat is the *soul*, or heart, or mind, or spirit.[77] Calvin's first important work in theology, his *De Psychopannychia*, is a powerful demonstration of the soul's distinct existence, and survival after the dissolution of the body: one admires the fullness and thoroughness of the biblical survey (on the presupposition of scriptural consistency), the rigorous philological method,[78] and the use of the

---

[70] This has been highlighted by Jane Dempsey Douglass, *Women, Freedom, and Calvin* (Philadelphia: Westminster Press, 1985); cf. her "Ce qui demeure vivant dans la doctrine calvinienne," in *La Réforme, un ferment dans l'Eglise universelle*, ed. Henry Mottu (Geneva: Labor & Fides, 1987), especially 67–76, to which I responded, 83–5 on the topic. Biéler, *L'Homme et la Femme*, converges; Stauffer, *Dieu, la création et la providence*, 210, charges him with modernizing Calvin a little too much.

[71] *Commentaire sur la Genèse*, 56, on Gen. 2:18, "though at a second stage."

[72] *Commentaire sur la Genèse*, 37, on Gen.1:27 (*CO* 23, 28).

[73] *Commentaire sur la Genèse*, 57, on Gen. 2:17 ("égalité"; *CO* 23, 47: *aliquid aequabile*).

[74] *Commentaire sur la Genèse* for the first phrase; *CNT* III, 427, on 1 Cor. 11:3.

[75] *CNT* III, 262, on Rom. 16:4.

[76] Letter from Geneva, September 1557, *Lettres françaises de Jean Calvin*, II, ed. Jules Bonnet (Paris: Meyrueis, 1854), 145–9.

[77] *Institutes*, I.15.3 and *passim*. On the diversity of names for the soul, *CNT* IV, 454, on Heb. 9:10. The erect posture of the human body is a symbol of human privilege, *Institutes*, I.15.3.

[78] Calvin deals with a sure touch, in perfect accordance with linguistic science, with the polysemy of *nèfeš* (*Opusc.*, 6–7), and easily solves the difficulty of the same phrase *nèfeš hàyâ* being used for animals and for humankind (*Opusc.*, 8).

Christological argument.[79] Calvin is aware of the arguments of what now goes under the name "non-reductive physicalism" and finds them exegetically and theologically wanting; the "virtues" associated with the soul are such that they cannot be reduced to bodily functions.[80] He maintains, non-biblically, the phrase "immortality of the soul," but is aware that the soul also "dies" in a sense—he wants to ward off the idea of extinction.[81] His zeal for dichotomy even leads him to this extreme statement (in a sermon, to be sure!): "Is there anything more different from the soul than the human body?"[82]

Regarding the "virtues" or faculties of the soul, it is well known that Calvin leaves aside St. Augustine's Trinitarian analogy—though sometimes in the mildest fashion[83]—and adopts, again, a binary pattern, with mind (reason, intelligence) and will as the twin powers. He suggests, a bit surprisingly, that when both soul and spirit are found, as in 1 Thessalonians 5:23, the latter "denotes intelligence or reason" and the former "will and all the affections."[84] Since scholars have extensively investigated the relation between the two faculties, we shall be content with receiving their conclusions. Torrance, while urging that the "stress upon the will is of prime importance in Calvin's theology," adds that "Calvin expressly repudiates the idea that the will is primary in man, but he insists that it is not an intellectual fiction."[85] Richard A. Muller's analysis is a model of accuracy and balance: "The soul is understood to be *rational* in both of its faculties"; "Calvin does not oblige any neat 'head/heart,' intellective/affective, rational/experiential dichotomy"; when will follows intelligence, "will may be regarded as the 'affection of the intellect,'" but "choice belongs to the will, including the choice to follow or to disregard the intellect"; "In the order of temporal priority, the intellect must come first, insofar as the will must have a ready object for

---

[79] *Opusc.*, 18f.

[80] *Opusc.*, 6, and especially 28. In *Institutes*, I.5.5 he meets the "reductionistic" argument based on the fact that the faculties are instrumental ("instrumentales," *organicae*).

[81] *Opusc.*, 30.

[82] Twenty-seventh Sermon on 1 Timothy, on 1 Tim. 3:16, *CO* 53, 326.

[83] *Commentaire sur la Genèse*, 36, on Gen. 1:26; Calvin says he does not reject the reference ("je ne veux point rejeter").

[84] *CNT* IV, 148.

[85] *Calvin's Doctrine of Man*, 65f., and Torrance quotes from the commentary on Ephesians 4:17: "The mind holds the highest rank in the human constitution, is the seat of reason, presides over the will, and restrains sinful desires." (There are slight differences in the French version, *CNT* III, 805.)

its act of trust. Nonetheless, temporal priority is not causal priority: the will is free to accept or to reject the knowledge presented by the intellect . . ."[86] The complexity of the account well represents the complexity of Calvin's thought, which may well represent the complexity of human functioning. I would only add two observations lest the points escape notice. Speaking of will, and generally of human gifts, Calvin greatly values choice, discernment, election (*e(x)-legere*), which may be a reflection of his emphasis on election as an exercise of divine willing.[87] On the other hand, Calvin, when writing on Romans 7:7, suggests that there is a concupiscence or desire *deeper* than will.[88] Which makes matters even more complex.

An original feature of Calvin's treatment of the soul's faculties is his emphasis on mobility, nimbleness, agility. He marvels at the ability of the soul or spirit to free itself from the limitations of space and time, and to overcome absence through figuration.[89] The sense of right and wrong and the taste for truth imply reaching out beyond the earthly.[90] This is close to a sense of *transcendence*, and, indeed, Calvin uses the Latin verb *transcendere* for the human soul.[91] Such is the amazing gift of the Creator, for which we give thanks and offer praise!

The excellence of the soul, as compared with the body, must have contributed to Calvin's preference for *creatianism* over against *traducianism*. Creatianism,[92] the official teaching of the Roman Church is the doctrine that teaches that the origin of the soul in each individual is a special act

---

[86] Thomas F. Torrance, *The Unaccommodated Calvin: Studies in the Foundation of a Theological Tradition* (New York: Oxford University Press, 2000), respectively 164, 164, 165, 170.

[87] Jean Boisset, *Jean Calvin*, 51, focuses on the value of the human exercise of election, quoting from a sermon on Deuteronomy (*CO* 26, 438).

[88] *CNT* III, 116 ("encore plus cachée et secrète que la volonté").

[89] *Institutes*, I.5.5 and 15.2.

[90] *Institutes*, I.15.2 and II.2.12.

[91] *Institutes*, I.15.2 (*animas quae mundum transcendunt, esse immortales*), and again in §8 (*usque ad Deum*).

[92] "Creatianism" is not the term generally used today in English; though it is found in Augustus H. Strong's *Systematic Theology*, it is replaced by "creationism" by most writers. Unfortunately so! For then a confusion arises with "creationism" in the proper sense: belief in creation (of the world), and with "creationism" in the very special sense of that interpretation of the days of Genesis 1 which offers a literal chronology of the cosmogonic process! In French, German, Dutch, normally, the distinction is preserved (créatianisme, Kreatianismus).

of creation on God's part. Because of Calvin's caution and sobriety, Otto Weber thought that Calvin had left the question open.[93] E. Doumergue rightly notes that Calvin's language on the transmission of original sin sounds traducianist (with the botanical metaphor of the rotten root), though he is not.[94] But the Reformer's position leaves no ambiguity: it is creatianist, the clearest statement, maybe, being the statement that Job speaks as if, "when God has placed a human creature in the mother's womb, there is no soul: on the contrary, we know that when the creature is conceived in the mother's womb, God inspires a soul in it."[95] Calvin escapes the traducianist argument on original sin by focusing on the negative presentation, the *loss* of original gifts.

A final expression of the high view of humankind that Calvin taught in order to arouse the proper response of gratitude, trust and obedience, is the doctrine of our *ultimate destiny*. To be sure, it will be ours in Christ only, and Calvin realizes (e.g., commenting on 1 Cor. 15) that the promises of the Second Adam exceed those of the first; nevertheless, the logic of Calvin's interpretation of the "probation" in Eden, and of the excellence of the immortal soul, entails that the destiny of humans *as such* was precisely the one Christ has won for us. Incarnation was required because of sin intervening, but had Adam been given the grace of perseverance, he would have reached the enjoyment of God himself in eternal blessedness (III.25.10), the goal of "humanity" as such: this is why Calvin writes that "the state of humanity was not accomplished in the person of Adam."[96] In that perspective, it is relevant for anthropology (creational) that Calvin is able to speak of our being "quasi deified."[97] In one attack on Osiander, whom he charges with mixing God's essence with ours, his reply, "As if we were already such as the Gospel promises we shall be in the last advent of Jesus Christ" (III.11.10), seems to grant the mixing in the final state! This, however, would miss his constant meaning. His fuller explanations emphasize that the sharing in God's nature is a matter of quality, not of substance, and can only occur according to the

---

[93] Otto Weber, *Foundations of Dogmatics*, I, tr. Darrell L. Guder (Grand Rapids: Eerdmans, 1981), 477, n. 37.

[94] Doumergue, *Jean Calvin*, IV, 142.

[95] Twelfth Sermon on Job (Second on Job 3:11–19), CO 33, 162. Other passages include *Institutes*, II.1.7; *CNT* IV, 514; *Pseaumes*, 344, on Ps. 51:7.

[96] *Commentaire sur la Genèse*, 46, on Gen. 2:7, "L'état de l'homme ne fut pas accompli en la personne d'Adam" (CO 23, 36: *non fuisse in persona Adae absolutum Adae statum*).

[97] *CNT* IV, 748, on 2 Pet. 1:4.

"measure" appropriate for us.[98] Suffice it to say that Calvin goes as far as possible on the way to an anthropology of glory!

Contrasting emphases, and yet a deep unity of purpose. The *infirmitas* of Adam's constitution is correlative of the supreme destiny God had in view. The lowliness of our estate is the foil that causes the brightness of the gifts of original grace to radiate with increased splendor. In both movements, the same motto rules: *Soli Deo Gloria*!

---

[98] *CNT* IV, 748, on 2 Pet. 1:4.

5

From Ordered Soul to Corrupted Nature: Calvin's View of Sin

Lanier Burns

This is where his deepest interest lay. What was suffusing his heart and flowing full flood into all the chambers of his soul was a profound sense of his indebtedness as a lost sinner to the free grace of God his Saviour . . . The roots of his zeal are planted, in a word, in his consciousness of absolute dependence as a sinner on the free mercy of a saving God.[1]

"The theologian" of the Reformation, in Philipp Melanchthon's estimation, lived in times of extraordinary change, an early modern world that he addressed theologically in his magisterial *Christianae religionis institutio*. The church was enmeshed in the affairs of the world, experiencing "a hardening of its ecclesiastical arteries."[2] In a prefatory address to Francis I, Calvin expressed his catechetical intent to encourage French believers who were "hungering and thirsting for Christ." He wished to assure the king that the reforming movement was faithful to Christian traditions and not subversive to the monarchy.

Calvin's *Institutes* developed from six chapters in 1536, to seventeen in 1539, to twenty-one in 1543–50, and then to four books in 1559, changing not only in length but also in structure and emphasis. By 1539 the "sum of piety" had become his "sum of wisdom" to defend the French Reformers against charges of heresy. Concurrent with the revisions of the *Institutes* were his New Testament commentaries, which synthesized

---

[1] Benjamin B. Warfield, *Calvin and Augustine,* ed. Samuel Craig (Phillipsburg, N.J.: Presbyterian & Reformed Publishing Co., 1974), 484.
[2] Alister McGrath, *A Life of John Calvin: A Study in the Shaping of Western Culture* (Oxford: Basil Blackwell, 1990), 3.

a historical drama of salvation, combining creedal affirmation with biblical argumentation. Calvin's "stage directions" indicate that by 1559 he was instructing his readers about the true faith of the church. The form and structure of this development govern the interpretation of his finished masterpiece.

Contrary to popular misconceptions, the *Institutes* is a drama about the theater of the world in which God is Author, Producer, and Director. People perform on a stage that has been darkened by sin with dissonant tones. We, his readers, can discern an enhanced lighting of selected players as they are called and illumined by the Spirit and the Word. They are distinguished from other characters by their obedient relationship with God and their understanding of the themes. They brighten the drama and theater as God directs them to their joy in the glory of his Son, which he foreordained. This chapter is about the darkness and dissonance of the drama.[3]

Our approach will be to follow Calvin's form and plot development in his *Institutes* as closely as possible. Thus, the bulk of the chapter will summarize his view of sin as developed in his 1559 revision.[4] Supporting materials from his commentaries and other sources will be introduced as needed. Finally, we will conclude with the abiding importance of his work for perennial issues, such as theodicy and humanity's desperate need for God's grace. I have written the chapter with a conviction that a memorial volume should reflect Calvin's own thoughts and language as much as possible.[5]

1 Depravity as corrupted knowledge of the Creator

Calvin's theology in general and his doctrine of depravity in particular begin with "Knowledge of God the Creator" (Book I), because he was convinced that the interrelationship of our knowledge of God and self should govern our thinking about salvation (I.1).[6] The *Institutes* devel-

---

[3] In my research I have discovered that Calvin's view of sin has been surprisingly neglected.

[4] For this chapter we will use Calvin: *Institutes of the Christian Religion*, 2 vols., ed. John T. McNeill, tr. Ford Lewis Battles et al., The Library of Christian Classics, vol. XX (Philadelphia: Westminster Press, 1960 (1559)). The citations will be by book, chapter, and section. The quotations are so numerous that they have been integrated into the text for the sake of clarity and convenience.

[5] Furthermore, a cardinal rule of "historical integrity" is to represent thinkers on their terms before judging their thought according to the canons of a later era.

ops the thesis that the depravity of humanity drives us "as by rivulets to the springs" of God's grace: "No one can look upon himself without immediately turning to the contemplation of God, in whom he 'lives and moves' (Acts 17:28)" (I.1.1).[7] He concluded, "From the feeling of our own ignorance, vanity, poverty, infirmity, and—what is more—depravity and corruption, we recognize that the true light of wisdom, sound virtue, full abundance of every good, and purity of righteousness rest in the Lord alone" (I.1.1). Thus, he keynoted the polar emphases of his theology: the perfections of God's grace and the depravity of humankind.

Calvin frequently referred to creation metaphorically as a theater (*theatrum mundi*) that exhibits God's glory and gives all people an awareness of the Creator (I.5.8).[8] He used creation as a backdrop of natural law to inform and instruct people rather than as an end in itself.[9] Interestingly, four of his references were added in the final Latin edition of 1559. A fifth reference in I.14.20 replaced "the visible works of God in which we are bidden to recognize the Artificer himself" in earlier editions with "meanwhile let us not be ashamed to take pious delight in the works of God open and manifest in this most beautiful theater."[10] In *Institutes*, I.5.8 Calvin emphasizes the sin-bound blindness of most "spectators" in the "dazzling theater." *Institutes*, I.6.2 relates the contemplation of wisdom in this "glorious theater" to the hearing of God's word in Scripture; II.6.1

---

[6] Calvin's language for knowledge is conceptually unified. The Latin *cognitio, notitia* (knowledge), *agnitio* (comprehension), *intelligentia* (perception), and *scientia* (expert knowledge) can be nuanced, but Calvin rendered them by *cognoissance* (1541), because for him true knowledge is gracious persuasion of the truth of divine revelation more than comprehension by human reason (III.2.14).

[7] The thesis is reversible as "in knowing God, each of us can know himself," which stands at the beginning of every edition of the *Institutes*. McNeill notes, "These decisive words set the limits of Calvin's theology and condition in every subsequent statement" (I.1.1, n. 3).

[8] In *Institutes*, I.14.20, Calvin also refers to heaven and earth as "a spacious and splendid house" that God has adorned with exquisite and abundant furnishings.

[9] He defined natural law as "that apprehension of the conscience which distinguishes between just and unjust, and which deprives men of the excuse of ignorance, while it proves them guilty by their own testimony" (II.2.22).

[10] Earlier references to creation as a mirror (*speculum*) of an otherwise invisible God are synonymous with theater for Calvin (cf. *Institutes*, I.5.1). In usage, Calvin thought of the *imago Dei* as a mirror that was illumined by the Word.

underscores the inexcusability of rebellious unbelief: "Contemplating it [the theater of the world], we ought in wisdom to have known God, a point of focus from Romans 1:19–20" (I.5.1).[11] Consistent with the blindness of unbelief, his commentary on Genesis 1:6 uses the theater image to caution against icons and "artistic idolatry," so that the true "book of the unlearned" is the adornment of that theater that God sets before our eyes.[12] Thus, Calvin uses the metaphor to strengthen his argument that proper self-knowledge praises God the Creator and that all acts of human glorification reflect the depravity of humankind.[13]

1.1 Calvin's description of depravity and evil

Calvin used a colorful vocabulary for sin. The varied terms are coordinated in his view of the fallen world, which is antithetical to divine perfections. Battles has characterized the *Institutes* as a "book of antitheses," a "true/false principle" that Calvin used to sift conflicting teachings and controversies to arrive at his conclusions about truth.[14] Perhaps a better description beneath the antithesis of Creator and sinful creatures would be "dialectical juxtapositions" that revolve around the core of grace and

---

[11] Elsewhere in his commentaries and sermons, Calvin argued that God manifested himself in "visible language" like the "apparel" and "open book" of creation. The use of "visible metaphors" as revelation of God was a common theme in the Middle Ages, as illustrated by Bonaventure. The reader may note Etienne Gilson, *The Philosophy of St. Bonaventure*, trs. Dom Illtyd Trathowan and Frank Sheed (Paterson, N.J.: St. Anthony Guild, 1965), 185–214. For other examples and discussions, see M.-D. Chenu, *Nature, Man, and Society in the Twelfth Century*, trs. Jerome Taylor and Lester Little (Chicago: University of Chicago Press, 1968), 114–19; and Ernst Robert Curtius, *European Literature in the Latin Middle Ages*, tr. Willard Trask (Princeton: Princeton University Press, 1953). The emphasis on humanity's estrangement of mind in spite of creation's evidence is validated in *Calvin's Commentary on the Epistles of Paul the Apostle to the Corinthians*, 2 vols. 1, tr. John Pringle (Grand Rapids: Eerdmans, 1948), 1:84–6, on 1 Cor. 1:21.

[12] John Calvin, *Commentary on Genesis*, tr. and ed. John King (London: Banner of Truth Trust, 1965), 80.

[13] Angels, in turn, observe the mirror of the church, which reflects God's wisdom in the union of Jews and Gentiles. John Calvin, *Commentary on the Epistles of Paul to the Galatians and Ephesians*, tr. William Pringle (Grand Rapids: Eerdmans, 1948), 256, on Eph. 3:10.

[14] Ford Lewis Battles, *Analysis of the Institutes of the Christian Religion of John Calvin* (Grand Rapids: Baker Academic, 1980), 18–19.

depravity.[15] Examples of these contrasts, for our purposes, would be pre-fallen/fallen humanity and true/perverted knowledge. We tend to think more in terms of "sins" than "sin," whereas Calvin used hamartiology, with a general emphasis on the prideful rebellion of Adam that caused the condition of "original sin."

The human condition that leads to "our teeming hordes of infamies" is described with a two-fold emphasis. First, the terms depravity, corruption, perversity, and wickedness are used most emphatically and frequently for humanity's evil condition. They are practically interchangeable within Calvin's view of the fallenness of the world, often occurring together in a single sentence. Depravity (*pravitas*) is a "boundless filthy mire of error wherewith the whole earth was filled and covered" (I.5.12). Corruption is simply described: "The world tries as far as it is able to cast away all knowledge of God, and by every means to corrupt the worship of him" (I.3.3). Again, citing numerous passages, Calvin affirms: "[God] inveighs not against particular men but against the whole race of Adam's children. Nor is he decrying the depraved morals of one age or another, but indicting the unvarying corruption of our nature" (II.3.2).[16] He uses "perversity" to describe "impious" unbelievers, who use their creational knowledge of deity to project their own gods and religions: "They become fools in their perverse haughtiness" (I.4.1; also III.3).[17] Under his description of the hypocrisy of false religions, Calvin speaks of wickedness similarly: "They do not desist from polluting themselves with every sort of vice, from joining wickedness to wickedness, until in every respect they violate the holy law of the Lord and dissipate his righteousness" (I.4.4.)[18] Less frequent terms that are equivalent to depravity are rottenness and accursed.

One should note that Calvin is affirming more than partial depravity or people's inability to save themselves. The whole person is so corrupt that the Holy Spirit must renew every aspect of the individual: "The Spirit is so contrasted with flesh that no intermediate thing is left . . . We have nothing

---

[15] The reader may consult Ford Lewis Battles, *Interpreting John Calvin*, ed. Robert Benedetto (Grand Rapids: Baker Academic, 1996), 155–85.

[16] And in I.14.3, Calvin attributes evil to "depravity of nature" or "the corruption of nature."

[17] cf. Thomas F. Torrance, *Calvin's Doctrine of Man* (London: Lutterworth Press, 1949), 83.

[18] Elsewhere in discussing the inexcusability of human wickedness, Calvin denies that people can plead God's providence "to cloud their own depravity" (I.17.5). Citing Romans 3:10, Calvin emphasized that "all men are both depraved and given over to wickedness" (II.5.3).

of the Spirit, however, except through regeneration" (II.3.1).[19] The "thunderbolts" that he introduced for support include Romans 3 and Psalms 14 and 53. "Let this be argued: that men are as they are here described not merely by the defect of depraved custom, but also by depravity of nature" (II.3.2). Selinger captures Calvin's emphasis as follows,

> Sin was not additive; it was not the sum of individual, separately occurring, and performed sins; it was existence itself, for life was led by one whose total being was sin . . . Calvin maintained that the whole man is overwhelmed—as by a deluge—from head to foot, so that no part is immune from sin and all that proceeds from him is to be imputed to sin.[20]

Calvin's emphasis lies beyond the oft-repeated "sinners in need of a Savior" to a description of the created order after the Fall. Of course, he would affirm the need for salvation, but that can only be met by the foreordaining grace of God.

Second, Calvin uses another set of terms to describe humanity's corruption of the goodness of God's creation. Deformity and ruin are frequently used to complement the aforementioned terms for depravity. He uses deformity in terms of the ruinous consequences of sin on the image of God: "While it would be of little benefit to understand our creation unless we recognized in this sad ruin what our nature in corruption and deformity is like, we shall nevertheless be content for the moment with the description of our originally upright nature" (I.15.1).[21] Thus, "even though we grant that God's image was not totally annihilated or destroyed in him, yet it was so corrupted that whatever remains is

---

[19] Calvin also attributes perseverance of the believer to God's grace and not personal merit (II.3.2). "Any mixture," he later declared, "of the power of free will that men strive to mingle with God's grace is nothing but a corruption of grace" (II.5.15). He forbade any suggestion that fallen humanity could alleviate the consequences of the Fall in any way, because that would blur the distinction between prefallen and fallen human nature.

[20] Suzanne Selinger, *Calvin against Himself: An Inquiry in Intellectual History* (Hamden, Conn.: Archon Books, 1984), 42.

[21] Calvin uses "nature" in two senses as here. It may mean the "nature" of unfallen humanity or the "nature" of man and angels after the Fall (II.1.10–11). Thus, depravity undermined the order of creation, but it is now natural to humanity. McNeill notes, "This distinction is indispensable for understanding the relation of God to creation and sin as well as the precise sense in which a doctrine of 'total' depravity may be attributed to Calvin" (I.2.2, n. 7). The notion of ruin is developed in *Institutes*, II.1.4–7.

frightful deformity" (I.6.4). We might say that the Fall's corrupting effects so warped or distorted God's creation that its goodness was barely recognizable and its restoration was lost apart from his gracious intervention. That is, we can only see glimmers of creation's goodness behind the calamitous consequences of the Fall.

1.2 Calvin's explanation of depravity and evil

Calvin's explanation of how the Fall caused deformity and "original sin" is lengthy and repetitive. From creation all people are aware that God is their Maker. In other words, all people are God-conscious, and a universal knowledge of God is humanly innate rather than arbitrarily "invented" or "imposed" for control of the unlearned masses. His explanation flows from this knowledge, which undergirds the comprehensive antithesis between sinful creatures and divine perfection. In other words, universal human knowledge of the Creator necessarily leads to "total depravity," because all people share this corrupted knowledge. He acknowledged the power of religion from people's soulish drive to know truth, but sin destroyed humanity's prefallen relationship with the righteous God. Everyone, therefore, is pridefully unrighteous. God is the one, true Deity, who is the sole standard of righteousness,

> We always seem to ourselves as righteous and upright and wise and holy—this pride is innate in all of us—unless by clear proofs we stand convinced of our own unrighteousness, foulness, folly, and impurity. Moreover, we are not thus convinced if we look merely to ourselves and not also to the Lord, who is the sole standard by which this judgment must be measured. (I.1.2; also I.2.1)

Calvin's statement places God's sovereign providence in juxtaposition with fallen humanity's attempts to use their religions and "virtues" to disclaim their innate unrighteousness: "They set God aside, the while using 'nature,' which for them is the artificer of all things, as a cloak" (I.5.4).[22] God's providential control of his creation is so complete that all people should worship him alone: "Nothing is more preposterous than to enjoy the remarkable gifts that attest the divine nature within us, yet

---

[22] The noun "sovereignty" is commonly used in connection with Calvin's view of God's absolute control of the world and its history. Some translators, such as Beveridge and Allen, use the term, but it does not occur in Calvin's text. The valid concept is subsumed under his doctrine of providence as an expression of God's omnipotence.

to overlook the Author who gives them to us at our asking" (I.5.6). God "tempers his providence in the best way" with a "fatherly kindness" that offers mercy to his people and judgment for the wicked (I.5.7).

In chapter 16 of Book I, Calvin develops his doctrine of providence to highlight the depravity of the world.[23] False worship is as much a rejection of the Sustainer of the world as of the Creator,

> We see the presence of divine power shining as much in the continuing state of the universe as in its inception . . . For unless we pass on to his providence—however we may seem both to comprehend with the mind and to confess with the tongue—we do not yet properly grasp what it means to say: 'God the Creator.'" (I.14.1)

This means that God's "ever-present hand" is a personal presence to be accepted or rejected rather than fortune or chance, a "watchful, effective, active sort, engaged in ceaseless activity . . . directed toward individual and particular motions" (I.16.3). Calvin explicitly rejected bland terms that restricted God to mere "general providence"; that is, natural terms that reduce God to an idle observer from heaven. Instead, Scripture expresses "more plainly that nothing at all in the world is undertaken without his determination," showing "that things seemingly most fortuitous are subject to him" (I.16.6). Again, "We make God the ruler and governor of all things, who in accordance with his wisdom has from the farthest limit of eternity decreed what he was going to do, and now by his might carries out what he has decreed" (I.16.8).[24]

Divine providence is complete according to the Scriptures, but we cannot know his "secret providence" in mysterious circumstances such as the prosperity or extreme cruelty of wicked people. We can know, on the other hand, that it is "the determinative principle of all things, from which flows nothing but right, although the reasons have been hidden from us" (I.17.2). Humanly speaking, inexplicable events are seemingly fortuitous, and we cannot discern how he will bring his good from the abyss of evil: "For it would not be done if he did not permit it; yet he does not unwillingly permit it, but willingly; nor would he, being good,

---

[23] In the editions of 1539–1554, Calvin treats providence in conjunction with predestination. In our edition they are separated, with providence remaining in the context of the knowledge of God the Creator, while predestination is moved to Book III under the redemptive work of the Holy Spirit.

[24] Similarly, "Not one drop of rain falls without God's sure command" (I.16.5). Calvin sometimes describes his view of providence in terms of Aquinas' First Cause of all motions (see I.16.3).

allow evil to be done, unless being also almighty he could make good even out of evil" (I.18.3). Calvin's answer is simply that we should not presumptuously strive for our own omniscience: "We must cherish moderation that we do not try to make God render account to us, but so reverence his secret judgments as to consider his will the truly just cause of all things" (I.17.1).[25]

Reverential assent to God's supreme authority recognizes that it is not an excuse for our sin and the world's evil or a release from prudential living. Our acceptance of his decree is not a fatalism that covers godless behavior or slovenly living. One cannot claim that evil is God's plan. Instead, it is our deliberate rebellion against his righteous ordinances. On the other hand, believers can be assured of God's providential care (as in the case of Joseph) and will praise God for benefits received with gratitude for his emissaries of kindness. They can know that God's special providence protects them from the effects of evil, even ones that they do not know about, and escape extreme anxieties and fears in this unceasingly perilous world: "You will easily perceive that ignorance of providence is the ultimate of all miseries: the highest blessedness lies in the knowledge of it" (I.17.11).

True and false knowledge of creation and the Creator is traceable to people's humble obedience or prideful rebellion under God's providence with little logical room for middle ground (II.2.11). The narrow way of God's elect is characterized by humble obedience. Calvin explicitly connects humility and proper self-knowledge in Christ,

> In order for Christ to redeem us from sin, it was necessary, Calvin argues, for the primordial human disobedience towards God to be outweighed by an act of human obedience. Through his obedience to God as a *human being*, Christ presented an offering to his father which compensated for sin, discharging any debt and paying any penalty which might be due on its account (II.12.3).[26]

---

[25] The *Institutes* repeatedly cautions against human speculations, "inordinate curiosity" (II.2.10), which can be quite explicit, as in discussions of the Lord's Supper (IV.22) and predestination (III.21–4). Human limitation is implied in the notion of *captus* as the finite capability of the mind, which, for Calvin, was inherent in mankind's creaturely status and was corrupted by the Fall. Speculation about why God allowed Adam to sin, he argues, is pointless: "But the reason he did not sustain man by the virtue of perseverance lies hidden in his plan; sobriety is for us the part of wisdom" (I.16.8). Also, our schemes to gain immortality apart from God are "like applause in the theater . . . they evaporate" (III.9.2).

"Knowledge of God does not rest in cold speculation, but carries with it the honoring of him . . . in lawful worship in order to hold mankind in obedience" (I.12.1).This proper view of oneself under God is "a becoming humility that submits oneself to fear and reverence" (I.17.2; also II.8.1). "The cardinal rule," Parker observed, "is complete humility before God."[27]

The broad way, to the contrary, is populated by prideful rebels: "Since, therefore, men one and all perceive that there is a God, and that he is their Maker, they are condemned by their own testimony because they have failed to honor him and to consecrate their lives to his will" (I.17.1). Similarly, Calvin stated, "For where they ought to have remained consistently obedient throughout life, they boldly rebel against him in almost all of their deeds, and are zealous to placate him with a few paltry sacrifices" (I.5.4).[28] Unbelievers do this because Satan seduces them to worship the Lord's "manifested powers" in nature as mere expressions of their haughtiness and pride (I.14.15–16; also I.4.1 and I.5.4–5). After "superstitions" had bestowed divine honors on idols, "then followed ambition, which, by adorning mortals with the spoils of God, dared profane everything sacred" (I.12.3). The result has been a depraved world that is filled with multitudes of "shadow deities," idols, and impious religions (I.5.9, 15). In his exposition of Romans 3, Calvin related this "arrogance of humanity" to total depravity: "With these thunderbolts he inveighs not against particular men but against the whole race of Adam's children. Nor is he decrying the depraved morals of one age or another, but indicting the unvarying corruption of our nature" (II.3.2).[29]

In summary, the initial section of this chapter has demonstrated that a universal knowledge of God the Creator has been seen in the theater of the world, its drama making human depravity inexcusable. Calvin used vivid terminology for sin, terms that describe the human condi-

---

[26] McGrath, *A Life of John Calvin*, 161–2.

[27] T.H.L. Parker, *Calvin: An Introduction to His Thought* (Louisville, Ky.: Westminster John Knox, 1995), 54.

[28] Later, he would affirm Augustine, "Indeed, Augustine speaks rightly when he declares that pride was the beginning of all evils. For if ambition had not raised man higher than was meet and right, he could have remained in his original state" (II.1.4). Again, "Strange and monstrous indeed is the license of our pride" (II.3.9).

[29] cf. John Calvin, *Commentaries on the Epistle of Paul the Apostle to the Romans*, tr. John Owen (Grand Rapids: Eerdmans, 1947), 140–1, on Rom. 3:23–24.

tion as perverse and corrupt in addition to creation as deformed and ruined. He described the human condition as idolatrous and in rebellion against God as providential Sustainer of the world. God's providence is active, personal, and mysterious as he wills his goodness out of evil. It should not be used as an excuse for our sin or as a release from responsibility. Proper self-knowledge leads to humble submission to God's authority.

2 Depravity as original sin from Adam's fall

We turn now to Calvin's explanation of how the Fall deformed creation and initiated "original sin." Recalling the initial emphasis of Book I, as noted above, he declares that proper knowledge of ourselves, "first is considering what we were given at creation and how generously God continues his favor toward us . . . Secondly, to call to mind our miserable condition after Adam's fall; the awareness of which when all our boasting and self-assurance are laid low, should truly humble us and overwhelm us with shame" (II.1.1).

This section of the chapter will move from the general depravity of the human condition to its source in Adam, focusing on his creation in God's image and his fall. Calvin asked, "What, then, of man: plunged by his mortal ruin into death and hell, defiled with so many spots, befouled with his own corruption, and overwhelmed with every curse?" (II.12.1). The section is about sin, but it leads to "the knowledge of God the Redeemer." Knowledge of God and human sin, emphasizing human depravity, lays the foundation for Calvin's Christology. In order to act as Mediator, the Son of necessity descended to us in full deity and humanity. Who but Life could swallow up death? Who but Righteousness could conquer sin? Who but Omnipotence could "rout the powers of the world and air"? "Therefore our most merciful God, when he willed that we be redeemed, made himself our Redeemer in the person of his only-begotten Son (cf. Rom. 5:8)" (II.12.2).[30]

Calvin's argument is based on humanity's creation in the image of God and on "the faculties of the soul." "This knowledge of ourselves is twofold: namely, to know what we were like when we were first created and what our condition became after the fall of Adam" (I.15.1). His thesis is that depravity stems from Adam's prideful rebellion rather than God's defective plan.[31]

---

[30] cf. Calvin, *Commentary on Romans*, 199–201, on Rom. 5:12.

Calvin's anthropology is dichotomous; the human person is a body and an immortal, essential soul. Though nuanced when used in a single sentence, soul, spirit, mind, heart, and conscience are practically synonymous. The soul is the seat of the image of God, which as mind and heart distinguishes humanity from other creatures (I.15.3). "Now God's image is the perfect excellence of human nature which shone in Adam before his defection, but was subsequently so vitiated and almost blotted out that nothing remains after the ruin except what is confused, mutilated, and disease-ridden" (I.15.4). The prefallen Adam had an ordered image with "full possession of right understanding, when he had his affections kept within the bounds of reason, all his senses tempered in right order, and he truly referred his excellence to exceptional gifts bestowed upon him by his Maker" (I.15.3). This order is Calvin's understanding of the image and the prefallen condition.[32]

The faculties (or powers) of the soul are reason (= understanding or mind) and will (= choice), which account for human aspirations to know God.[33] Understanding is "the leader and governor of the soul; and that the will is always mindful of the bidding of the understanding, and in its own desires awaits the judgment of the understanding" (I.15.7). Adam's mind had the power to distinguish good from evil, "with the light of reason as guide to distinguish what should be followed from what should be avoided" (I.15.8). Since "the will was completely

---

[31] Battles, *Interpreting John Calvin*, 177: "Calvin has chosen to see the line of salvation history, in both its microcosmic and macrocosmic aspects, as the attraction toward, or repulsion from, God, of human souls and the church, by necessity, but not by compulsion. Thus Calvin can claim human responsibility for acts committed by a will bound by the necessity of sin."

[32] Richard Prins, "The Image of God in Adam and the Restoration of Man in Jesus Christ: A Study in Calvin," reproduced in *An Elaboration of the Theology of Calvin*, vol. 8, ed. Richard Gamble (New York, London: Garland Publishing, 1992), 275: "The idea that God is order is a postulate, yet one so basic and almost unconscious that Calvin does not formally list it."

[33] In *Institutes*, I.15.6 Calvin delineated three cognitive faculties of the soul that corresponded to three appetitive faculties. The cognitive faculties are fantasy (*fantasia*) as apprehensions of common sense; reason (*ratio, penes quam universale est iudicium*) as the power of universal judgment; and understanding (*intellectus*) as quiet contemplation with reason. The appetitive faculties are will (*voluntas*) as striving after the content of reason and understanding; anger (*vis irascendi*) as the seizure of reason and fantasy's content; and concupiscence (*vis concupiscendi*) as the apprehension of the content of fantasy and the senses. However, "for the upbuilding of godliness a simple definition will be enough for us."

amenable to the guidance of reason, therefore Adam could have stood if he wished, seeing that he fell solely by his own will" (I.15.8).

The Fall was a consequence of unfaithfulness (or disobedience): "Unfaithfulness, then, was the root of the Fall. But thereafter ambition and pride, together with ungratefulness, arose, because Adam by seeking more than was granted him shamefully spurned God's great bounty, which had been lavished upon him" (II.1.4). The defection was *infidelitas*, a lack of trust in God and his Word. It turned self-knowledge inward, so that people proudly "extol human nature in most favorable terms" to the applause of the masses (II.1.2). Pride, like knowledge of God, is now innate, "so that there is, indeed, nothing that man's nature seeks more eagerly than to be flattered" (II.1.2). Such self-delusion is destructive because the recognition of a lost nobility generated a downward spiral of obstinate disobedience to try to recapture the loss. Sin as concupiscence is "so fertile and fruitful of every evil that it cannot be idle"; it is "a burning furnace giving forth sparks" or "water bubbling up from an opened spring" (II.1.8). Hence, Satan's slanders accused God of falsehood and envy, and Adam's disobedience opened the door to lustful ambition.

The first sin initiated original sin. The subject was so foundational for Calvin that he devoted most of the *Institute's* first chapter of the second book to it. As representative of all humanity, "Adam consigned his race to ruin by his rebellion when he perverted the whole order of nature in heaven and on earth" (II.1.5). The "heavenly image was obliterated in him . . . he also entangled and immersed his offspring in the same miseries." "This is the inherited corruption, which the church fathers termed 'original sin,' meaning by the word 'sin' the depravation of a nature previously good and pure." And he concluded, "Therefore all of us, who have descended from impure seed, are born infected with the contagion of sin. In fact, before we saw the light of this life we were soiled and spotted in God's sight" (II.1.5).

For Calvin, human nature was transmitted (or imputed) through parents to the human race: "When Adam was despoiled, human nature was left naked and destitute, or that when he was infected with sin, contagion crept into human nature" with the consequence that "guilt is of nature, but sanctification, of supernatural grace" (II.1.7).[34] Accordingly, "original sin seems to be a hereditary depravity and corruption of our nature, diffused into all parts of the soul, which first makes us liable to

---

[34] Calvin held to a form of the "mediate imputation" view of the transmission of sin, Adam being both federal and natural head of the human race. All people are judicially guilty, but "inherited corruption and depravity," "infection from birth," and "infection of posterity" indicate the mediate agency of natural generation (II.1.5–8).

God's wrath, then also brings forth in us those works which Scripture calls 'works of the flesh' (Gal. 5:19). And that is properly what Paul often calls sin" (II.1.8). Sin thus became innate in fallen humanity, an "adventitious quality" that has infected every person with a "miserable servitude" to sin. Thus, free will, which Adam and Eve enjoyed before the Fall, became the bondage of their wills to sin after their unfaithfulness. The human condition became hopeless apart from the gracious intervention of God on behalf of his people.

Calvin's argument for total depravity was aimed at Pelagius' "quibble" that sin was transmitted through "imitation" rather than propagation. Calvin used Romans 5:12 to demonstrate "that Adam was not only the progenitor but, as it were, the root of human nature; and that therefore in his corruption mankind deserved to be vitiated" (II.1.6).[35] The Fall was total to the extent that "only Christ's righteousness, and thereby life, are ours by communication, it immediately follows that both were lost in Adam, only to be recovered in Christ" (II.1.6).

The utter depravity of humanity means that "nothing, however slight, can be credited to man without depriving God of his honor, and without man himself falling into ruin through brazen confidence" (II.2.1). Our wisdom and virtue are blessings from God, and all flattery is mere smoke and broken reeds. Calvin acknowledged that many people loathe the notion that "man's power is rooted out from its very foundations that God's power may be built up in man" (II.2.1). Nevertheless, it is "fundamental in religion and most profitable for us," so that we can obey the soul's desire to know God and self in truth.

What about mankind's abiding accomplishments in the arts and sciences? Calvin's answer is that Adam's natural endowments, such as understanding, were not wholly extinguished in the Fall. Natural gifts, such as reason (or soundness of mind and uprightness of heart), were weakened and corrupted, but, in agreement with Augustine, enough remained to distinguish humanity from other creatures. In contrast, "adventitious gifts," such as the light of faith and righteousness, were extinguished, and mankind was "banished from the Kingdom of God" and the blessed life of the soul (II.2.12). In a word, sin perverted all of the image but did not destroy it.

Calvin relates these losses to the soul's division into understanding and will. Human understanding was dulled to the point that its innate

---

[35] In the same section Calvin re-emphasized the point: "Adam, by sinning, not only took upon himself misfortune and ruin but also plunged our nature into like destruction. This was not due to the guilt of himself alone, which would not pertain to us at all, but was because he infected all his posterity with that corruption into which he had fallen."

pursuit of truth was perverted into an "absurd curiosity" that has investigated worthless, religious superstitions. The mind became mired in a "dense ignorance" of "heavenly things," but it retained the ability to foster and preserve public order with equitable laws. In addition to the concept of social fairness, mankind's understanding can still comprehend "truth wherever it appears" in rhetoric, art, math, and related sciences. God alone is the Author of truth, and humanity continues to think well about mundane matters: "We cannot read the writings of the ancients on these subjects without great admiration" (II.2.15). He continued, "These abilities, however, are benefits of the divine Spirit . . . for the common good of mankind . . . if the Lord has willed that we be helped in physics, dialectical mathematics, and other disciplines, by the work and ministry of the ungodly, let us use this assistance" (II.2.16). Without such gracious kindness, our fall would have entailed the destruction of our whole nature (II.2.17).

Consistent with the loss of mental soundness and uprightness of heart is the boundary of what human reason can discern about spiritual insight. By this gift Calvin means knowledge of God, his fatherly favor on our behalf, and knowledge of how his law can frame our lives. Concerning God and his salvific favor, unbelieving philosophers have been "blind as moles." They are like travelers in a lightning storm, who see flashes of truth only to be plunged into night where they defile the insights that they try to recall: "Human reason, therefore, neither approaches, nor strives toward, nor even takes a straight aim at, this truth: to understand who the true God is or what sort of God he wishes to be toward us" (II.2.18, with Jn. 1:4–5, 13; 3:27; 6:44). Without the light of the Spirit, a fallen person is devoid of spiritual discernment. Salvation is not cooperation with grace but rather actuation through the Spirit. Therefore, knowledge of God is totally dependent on the gracious illumination of the Holy Spirit (cf. II.3.6–8).[36]

Concerning knowledge of God's law, Calvin divides the Ten Commandments into two tables, the first part indicating "those duties which particularly concern the worship of his majesty: the second, to the duties of love that have to do with men" (II.8 in general, and section 11 for the quote). Human knowledge is blind regarding the first table, as noted above, but humanity has "some more understanding" about the lawful preservation of society. Even that knowledge of natural law, however, is "miserably subject to vanity," and its function is to deprive

---

[36] Again, in *Institutes*, II.3.9 Calvin states, "The first part of a good work is will; the other, a strong effort to accomplish it; the author of both is God."

people of the excuse of ignorance (II.2.22–5). "We know by experience how often we fall despite our good intention" (II.2.25). Thus, all human insight is a gift of the Spirit.

Disorder from the Fall means that perverted thinking informs the will: "And depravity of the will is all too well known" (II.2.12).The will is subject to discernment of the good by right reason. If reason is fallen, then people will gravitate to sin: "To sum up, much as man desires to follow what is good, still he does not follow it. There is no man to whom eternal blessedness is not pleasing, yet no man aspires to it except by the impulsion of the Holy Spirit" (II.2.26). Even believers constantly feel an internal conflict between flesh and spirit. Steinmetz notes about Calvin's view of the "divided self" in Romans 7, "Human wickedness is made all the more vivid for Calvin when he considers its force and staying power in the lives of the redeemed."[37]

Calvin then acknowledged a "restraining grace" that is not salvific, to account for virtuous people "who conduct themselves most honorably throughout life." They live well by the grace of God, whom he restrains "by throwing a bridle over them only that they may not break loose, inasmuch as he foresees their control to be expedient to preserve all that is" (II.3.3). These restraints are varied and may take the form of social shame or fear and profitability or leadership opportunities. The will, in any case, "remains set in its own perversity," and

> for this reason, we are not afraid, in common parlance, to call this man wellborn, that one depraved in nature. Yet we do not hesitate to include both under the universal condition of human depravity; but we point out what special grace the Lord has bestowed upon the one, while not deigning to bestow it upon the other. (II.3.4)

Virtues, Calvin explained, tend to deceive us with their vain facade. They will have their praise in renown among men, "but before the heavenly judgment seat they shall be of no value to acquire righteousness" (II.3.4).

Because the will is bound by sin, it cannot move toward conversion. Therefore, "simply to will is of man; to will ill, of a corrupt nature; to will well, of grace" (II.3.5). The fallen will, thoroughly guilty, hastens to sin "of necessity, but without compulsion," meaning that Adam lost his freedom.[38] He "sinned willingly, not unwillingly or by compulsion; by the most eager inclination of his heart, not by forced compulsion; by the

---

[37] David Steinmetz, *Calvin in Context* (New York, Oxford: Oxford University Press, 1995), 118.

prompting of his own lust, not by compulsion from without."[39] Accordingly, humanity suffers from a "voluntary servitude" to sin: "We are miserable as to servitude and inexcusable as to will because the will, when it was free, made itself the slave of sin" (II.3.5). Briefly, people sin necessarily and voluntarily. The "spiral of ambition" points to Calvin's emphasis on the inherently active character of the soul. As Adam actively glorified God before the Fall, so mankind seeks truth perversely after his sin. In his words, "The perverse motion of the heart is drawn away to obstinate disobedience" (II.3.9). This declension is most evident in the fallen mind's "workshop of idols," from which "an immense crowd of gods flow forth as waters boil up from a vast, full spring" (I.5.12). Torrance notes that, for Calvin, "The depravity of man's nature must be described as a 'most forward bias of the mind' such that man 'cannot move and act except in the direction of evil.'"[40] However, the ambition of the soul is evident as well in the civic accomplishments of gifted unbelievers for the blessing of their societies.

Calvin, finally, relates humanity's miserable servitude to God's providence. Does willful depravity take place independently of God's providential governance? Calvin answers in the negative. In I.18 and II.4.3 he argues, beyond the permissive will, that God determines whatever comes to pass: "Yet he does not unwillingly permit it [evil], but willingly; nor would he, being good, allow evil to be done, unless being also almighty he could make good even out of evil" (I.18.3).[41] This reprobation takes place with the removal of his guiding Spirit, which hardens human hearts into stones. Thus, God "blinds, hardens, and binds those whom he has deprived of seeing, obeying, and rightly following" (II.4.3). In the end,

---

[38] Susan Schreiner, *The Theater of His Glory: Nature and the Natural Order in the Thought of John Calvin*, Studies in Historical Theology, 3 (Durham: Labyrinth Press, 1991): "According to Calvin, necessity is that inner state of the soul that determines the direction of the will; God necessarily wills the good, sinners necessarily will evil . . . Calvin concluded that people sin out of the inner necessity of their fallen wills, but never because of an external force or compulsion." As always, the problem is Adam's disobedience rather than God's providence.

[39] Schreiner, *Theater of His Glory*. The language is important for Calvin's interpretation of Lombard and Bernard. "Calvin and Bernard agree in affirming an intrinsic bondage of the will to sin and in denying an external constraint" (Anthony Lane, "Calvin's Interpretation of Bernard," *Studies in Reformed Theology and History*, new series, 1 (1996), 43).

[40] Torrance, *Calvin's Doctrine of Man*, 123; cf. Institutes, II.3.5.

[41] cf. Calvin, *Commentary on Genesis*, 283–6, on Gen. 8:21.

our solace is "to know that the heavenly Father so holds all things in his power, so rules by his authority and will, so governs by his wisdom, that nothing can befall except he determine it" (I.17.11).

This section of the chapter transitioned from the general depravity of the human condition to its source in Adam's fall. Calvin's discussion is based on the image of God in man, specifically the ordered soul that characterized Adam's prefallen nature. The soul's understanding guided the will until Adam's rebellious disobedience. Thereafter, the will was bound to lustful ambition under perverted reason, which could comprehend only the natural gifts of God's restraining Spirit for the lawful preservation of society. Thus, sin bound humanity in its corruption but did not destroy the image. This bondage enslaved everyone with "inherited corruption," redeemable only by God's calling through his Son. "Secret providence" assures us that our heavenly Father graciously determines history for the enjoyment of his people in his glorious presence.

3 Depravity as a contribution to knowledge

Calvin is popularly associated with his distinctive emphasis on predestination and his concomitant denial of free will. This chapter has summarized his equally distinctive view of sin and his concomitant emphasis on grace. The importance of Calvinism's "total depravity" in intellectual history will be briefly discussed in three parts: its explanatory value for issues of theodicy and human responses to its evil, its spiritual value for the necessity of grace, and its theological importance in Calvin's systematic and biblical understanding of life.

First, Calvin offered an explanation for theodicy, a dilemma that seeks to reconcile God's attributes (e.g., wisdom, goodness, justice, and omnipotence) and the existence of evil (often catastrophic). If God is sovereign and good, then why does he allow evil in the world? Though Leibnitz coined the term in the 1690s, it has been a perennial problem through history. Theodicy has gained center stage in the modern era, when God has been displaced by social and scientific progress as saviors from suffering and traumatic circumstances.[42]

From the Renaissance, people began to exchange the medieval view of suffering as an indication of eternal opportunity for an ideal of hap-

---

[42] For the urgency of theodicy in the modern era, the reader may consult Odo Marquand, *In Defense of the Accidental: Philosophical Studies*, tr. Robert Wallace (New York: Oxford University Press, 1991), 8–28; also, John Hick, *Evil and the God of Love* (New York, San Francisco: HarperSanFrancisco, 1977).

piness in this life. Now, at the end of a long development of the ideal, we expect the world to make sense on its own terms, so that we can judge God for his failure to prevent evils such as natural catastrophes, pestilences, and acts of war that pillage the planet. Especially painful are instances of inexplicable or unintentional tragedy, where people are harmed even though they "did nothing wrong." We are no longer tolerant of a "secret providence" that stops short of God's full accountability for his failures. We may not know everything yet, but we are "on our own" to gain the omniscience that we need.

From the Enlightenment (c. 1800) the West has experienced intellectual change that has created radical redefinitions of traditional concepts. For example, God as the standard of righteousness is now viewed by consensus "in our image" as a transcendent dimension of the world or self. "Enlightenment," for all its accomplishments, bequeathed its central tenet of human autonomy to modern traditions. This means the independence of people and their societies from all authorities including parents, God, and all in between. We never actually live this way, but we have gained a feeling that we can live as we want—without consequences. Humility under God has been revalued into an open-ended pride to be "god," an unleashing of human potential that incrementally will replace his kingdom with our self-made utopias. Sin and guilt have been camouflaged under "mutual consent" and comedy. The denial of God necessarily means our refusal to admit the existence of sin, individual or corporate.

Consequently, without a Standard we no longer have criteria to evaluate standards in our world. We conduct endless surveys and evaluations to arrive at clues about good and evil that may promote our happiness. We try to avoid large-scale losses, although "collateral damage" is to be expected. Most people agree about the extremes, that the evils of the last century are horrible and that scientific discoveries, artistic achievements, and social innovations are good. A prominent dialectic of the twentieth century is the juxtaposition of the abysses of Stalingrad, Auschwitz, Hiroshima, and genocides with the brilliant gains in transportation, communication, and unparalleled understanding of the universe at micro- and macro-levels. However, the vast majority of the world's populations are mired in a swampy middle ground of petty theft, white lies and constant spins of information, ruptured relationships, and conflicting self-interests that transform successes into survivals. Popular today are theories of "choice-moralities." We simply need to know enough to choose correctly! The problem is that worth is attached to our ability to choose right options rather than the moral status of the option and choice in the first place. In a depraved world, right decisions are "the best of the worst." "Character (virtue)-morality" is an alternative, but its "goodness of humanity" criterion is elusive. It requires "curbing evil," which makes the good life possible, and the pursuit of goods, which gives the ideal its content. The goal and the content are secular. Must the lesser evil be committed for the greater good? What do these words mean, especially when "good" is understood in terms of "evil"!

Calvin's explanation, in the Augustinian tradition of a world ruined by the Fall, is not going to be popular or acceptable for many contemporary audiences on several counts. First, "God" now has no explanatory value in a thoroughly naturalistic and secularized environment. Calvin, of course, defined evil in terms of self-knowledge in the light of God the Creator and Sustainer of the world. His clarity and coherency are a direct result of his rigorously God-centered approach. His God is not anemic but dynamically awesome, requiring a commitment that most people now reserve for entertainment. Second, contemporary thinkers distance themselves from an ancient account of the Fall in a mythological Bible. However, the Bible was Calvin's compass as he traced the confessional faith of the Judeo–Christian tradition. The rejection of the Bible as God's trustworthy revelation has cut the anchor of historical accountability and set us adrift on a sea of "repeating history's tragedies" in spite of our intentions to avoid them. Even good things, in human estimation, such as nuclear experimentation, have turned tragically bad in the exigencies of crises.

Of course, explanations of evil should not be popularity contests. The issue is whether Calvin has given us a plausible explanation of the perpetual pervasiveness of evil. A related issue is whether his explanation stands on his grounds of God, Word, tradition, and the realities of human history. The answer is that Calvin's thought has been an enduring blessing for those in the church who share his foundational assumptions. The issue is not that believers are perfect arbiters of earthly tragedies. It is that, as citizens of this depraved world, they are driven to contemplate God, which was Calvin's intent.

We note as well that Calvin's description of responses to his explanation of evil have been precise. The unbelieving masses will object that a personal God, with watchful, effective providence in and over the world, would not prevent evil, which they have caused. They would refuse to accept the guilt of what they did not do, even though their character replicates Adam's and Eve's desire to be more than human at worst, or more than their proper role in life at best. They would find "the becoming humility of reverential worship" to be strange in a world of rebels where overcoming risks defines personal significance. They would balk at the notion that their prideful ambition is a "workshop of idols." They would flatly reject a "rooting out of man's power so that God's power might increase." "There is nothing," Calvin correctly observed, "that we are more unwilling to do than to bid farewell to our own labors and to give God's works their rightful place" (II.3.9). They would "seem to themselves as righteous and upright and wise and holy" and would not want "clear proofs to convince them of their own unrighteousness." They would be offended that "wellborn and depraved" people are both included under the universal condition of human depravity. Yet this is precisely what the majorities in biblical times, in Augustine's and Calvin's generations, and in our own world have done. And Calvin has not taken an elitist exemption, because "total depravity" includes everyone.

Second, Calvin's doctrine of sin has abiding importance for its uncompromising reminder of humanity's need of grace. People's greatest shortcoming in interpreting Calvin is that they fail to pursue his thinking to its conclusion. This chapter began with his statement that the depravity of humanity drives us as by rivulets to the springs of God's grace. No one is more aware than I am of the apparent negativity of the preceding pages. A biblical view of depravity, however, requires that we relinquish all our attempts to acquire salvation for ourselves or, corporately, to restore paradise on our terms. We are more effective as agents with the gospel than saviors of fellow sinners. In the end, Calvin was more realistic than misanthropic. His aim in his description of the Fall was to open the prison house of sin with the keys of grace, so that lovers of God can live without the shackles of guilt and the burdens of our flawed world. B.A. Gerrish wrote, "For Calvin, too, the divine election was the final proof that everything is of grace, including the division between those who come to faith and those who do not."[43] We would only add "divine election and human depravity." Calvin struck at the heart of merit and deserts, which have perpetually separated depravity and prosperity, and placed all of life under God's providence. In Torrance's words, "Man lives and moves and has his being in the unceasing visitations of the presence of God, and in the constant and continuous repetition of his pure grace."[44] Believers' roles are to be gracious conduits of the Spirit's presence in the midst of needs around us. We do not have to judge or to fix the innumerable imperfections of

[43] B.A. Gerrish, "The Place of Calvin in Christian Theology," in *The Cambridge Companion to John Calvin*, ed. Donald McKim (Cambridge: Cambridge University Press, 2004), 292.
[44] Torrance, *Calvin's Doctrine of Man*, 61.

the fallen world like people who spend their lives with anxiety over every speck of dust in the house. As noted earlier, reverence for God's authority means that we will not blame our sins on God or seek release from God-given responsibilities. And we must not only accept his grace but also live in the example of the Messiah's death and resurrection. In a word, believers must be people of the Word.

Finally, returning to Warfield's introductory quote, what is the place of sin in Calvin's theological system? We can recall that "the roots of his zeal are planted in his consciousness of absolute dependence as a sinner on the free mercy of a saving God." We also described the *Institutes* as an extended development of "dialectical juxtapositions." I am therefore uncomfortable with reducing Calvin to single doctrines such as salvation, providence, or depravity. His drama involves the dynamic tension between God's providential grace and humanity's "spiral of depravity." Our sinful condition is foundationally important as the "polar extreme" of God's foreordaining grace that saves his people, so that "their chief end becomes the glorification of God and the enjoyment of him forever."

6

Calvin on the Cross of Christ

Mark D. Thompson

The cross of Christ lies at the heart of the Christian faith. It is the focus and climax of the Gospel narratives. The apostle Paul told the Corinthians that he was determined to know nothing among them "except Jesus Christ, and him crucified" (1 Cor. 2:2). Later in the same letter he identified as of first importance that which had been delivered to him and which he now proclaimed to others: "that Christ died for our sins in accordance with the Scriptures, that he was buried, that he was raised on the third day in accordance with the Scriptures, and that he appeared to Cephas, then to the twelve" (1 Cor. 15:3–5, ESV). It is hardly surprising, then, that John Calvin, determined as he was to present a genuinely biblical presentation of Christian doctrine, should give careful and sustained attention to the theology of the cross. As he moves towards his treatment of the cross in the *Institutes of the Christian Religion*, he describes the priestly work of Christ as "the principal point (*praecipuum . . . cardinem*) on which . . . our whole salvation turns."[1]

Calvin's understanding of the cross appears repeatedly throughout his literary legacy, in his sermons, his biblical commentaries, and his *Institutes*. Recent research has stressed the need to read widely in Calvin rather than attempting to construct his theology exclusively from one source.[2] However, the *Institutes* do have a special place. Calvin's careful

---

[1] John Calvin, *Institutes of the Christian Religion*, ed. John T. McNeill, tr. Ford Lewis Battles (Philadelphia: Westminster Press, 1960 (1559)), II.15.6.

[2] ". . . investigation of the interrelationship of the various literary forms used by Calvin in the accomplishment of his larger theological task offers no clear sense of the priority of one form over the other . . . To know the whole Calvin one must read the whole Calvin, and then some!" (Richard A. Muller, *The Unaccommodated Calvin: Studies in the Foundation of a Theological Tradition*

revision of the work repeatedly over the course of his lifetime, his concern to present in it a "right order of teaching" and a faithful exposition of the Bible's doctrine, and his own acquaintance with how earlier editions of the *Institutes* had been used as a stand-alone introduction to evangelical doctrine, all suggest that it is not altogether inappropriate to give a certain prominence to the way he expounds the atonement in this key work.[3] In what follows our chief point of reference will be the *Institutes*, without neglecting important comments in the commentaries and sermons.

1 The context of Calvin's exposition of the cross in the *Institutes*

Calvin's treatment of the atonement is found in the final two chapters of Book II of the *Institutes*. It follows his discussion of the Fall (II.1–6), the Law (II.7–8), and the relation of the two Testaments (II.9–11), as part of his exposition of the threefold office of the Mediator (II.12–17). Calvin breathed new life into the ancient formula of the threefold office: the Christ brings together in his person the Old Testament offices of anointed prophet, priest and king while at each point transcending the Old Testament antecedent.[4] The three offices of the Old Testament become

---

(cont.) (New York: Oxford University Press, 2000), 182). Henri Blocher agrees, but insists, "[t]his is not to suggest any substantial difference in doctrine across that diversity: on the contrary, we have been struck by the stability, constancy and consistency—sometimes even the repetitious character—of Calvin's teaching on the atonement" (Henri Blocher, "The Atonement in John Calvin's Theology," in C.E. Hill and F.A. James (eds.), *The Glory of the Atonement* (Downers Grove: InterVarsity Press, 2004), 282).

[3] Though Richard Muller has rightly stressed wide engagement with Calvin's theological work, he nevertheless admits, "His *Institutio* was surely intended as a formal instruction in Christian religion, containing *loci communes* and *disputations*, arranged in a suitable order of teaching—with the result that it was dogmatic, polemical, and pastoral as required by each issue addressed" (Muller, *Unaccommodated Calvin*, 181–2).

[4] This scheme for understanding Christ's work can be found in Eusebius, *Historia Ecclesiastica*, vol. 1, tr. K. Lake (London: William Heinemann, 1926), 29–39 (*H.E.*, I.iii); Aquinas, *Summa Theologia*, vol. 50, *The One Mediator*, ed. and tr. Dominican Order (London: Blackfriars, 1964–81), IIIa.22.1; and in the work of Calvin's mentor in Strasbourg, Martin Bucer, *Enarratio in Evangelion Iohannis*, ed. I. Backus (Leiden: Brill, 1988 (1536, p. 607)), 100.

the threefold office of the New: there is but one "Christ" and "our whole salvation and all its parts are comprehended" in him (II.16.19). Calvin will unfold Christ's work with the aid of this threefold scheme, starting with Christ's "prophetic dignity" (II.15.1–2), then, at greater length, Christ's kingship (II.15.3–5), and finally giving most attention to Christ's priestly office (II.15.6–16.19). Nevertheless, there is an important sense in which these aspects of Christ's work cannot be isolated from one another: his prophetic work centers on his revelation of the way of salvation; his priestly work effects that salvation; and the goal and presupposition of that salvation are Christ's kingly rule. More specifically, the cross is the work of the prophet, priest and king—here the love of God is definitively disclosed; here the necessary propitiation and expiation is provided; here the king rules, extending mercy and accomplishing the most remarkable victory over death and guilt and sin.

Calvin's exposition of the person of Christ forms the most immediate context for his treatment of the cross and atonement. This is the climax of his account of "The Knowledge of God the Redeemer in Christ" (the title of Book II of the *Institutes*). However, there is another facet of this context, which should not be ignored. Calvin's treatment of the person of Christ, so strongly Chalcedonian in its basic contours, refused to locate the saving work of Christ in his divine nature alone but in the one Christ who is both God and man: "Now it was of the greatest import-ance for us that he who was to be our Mediator be both true God and true Man" (II.12.1).

Unlike many before and since, Calvin takes the humanity of Christ with the utmost seriousness: "He is true man (*verus homo*) but without fault and corruption" (II.13.4).[5] This purity, Calvin insists, does not com-promise his genuine humanity, but rather is anchored in the miraculous nature of his conception and the sanctifying work of the Spirit (II.13.4). The divinity of Christ and his human nature grow together (*coalescerent*) "by mutual connection (*mutua coniunctione*)." If this had not been the case, "the nearness would not have been near enough (*nec satis propinqua*

---

[5] However, Colin Gunton would disagree with the suggestion that Calvin gives due attention to the humanity of Christ. He argued that after initial acknow-ledgement of the significance of Christ's humanity, it becomes clouded in his theology as a whole, a defect that was compounded in the treatment of the atonement given by some of his more illustrious successors (Colin E. Gunton, *The Actuality of Atonement: A Study of Metaphor, Rationality and the Christian Tradition* (Grand Rapids: Eerdmans, 1989), 136). As will be obvious in these paragraphs, I do not believe that the evidence sustains Gunton's complaint, at least as far as Calvin is concerned.

vicinitas), nor the affinity sufficiently firm (*nec affinitas satis firma*), for us to hope that God might dwell with us" (II.12.1). With clear allusion to Athanasius and the Nicene fathers, Calvin asks who could have restored us to God's grace "had not the self-same Son of God become the Son of man, and had [he] not so taken what was ours as to impart what was his to us, and to make what was his by nature ours by grace?" (II.12.2). Calvin's summary statement makes clear why the humanity of Christ is so important to him,

> In short, since neither as God alone could he feel death (*mortem nec solus Deus sentire*), nor as man alone could he overcome it, he coupled human nature with divine that to atone for sin he might submit the weakness of the one to death; and that, wrestling with death by the power of the other nature, he might win victory for us. Those who despoil Christ of either his divinity or his humanity diminish his majesty and glory, or obscure his goodness. (II.12.3)

Commenting on 1 Timothy 2, Calvin suggests that gross distortion of the Christian faith has occurred as a result of a false and impenetrable transcendence, predicated of God without due consideration of the incarnation. He then asks, "If it were deeply impressed on the hearts of all men that the Son of God holds out to us the hand of a brother and is joined to us by sharing our nature (*naturae societate nobis coniunctum*), who would not choose to walk in this straight highway rather than wander in uncertain and rough byways?"[6] Similarly, Calvin's comments on the classic atonement passages in Hebrews stress the importance of Christ's humanity as the proper location of the divine work of reconciliation. His mediatorial role necessitates a genuine humanity: "It is necessary (*oportet*) for the one who is the mediator between God and men to be a man."[7] Calvin expands on this simple statement when commenting on Hebrews 8:2: "a minister in the holy places, in the true tent that the Lord set up, not man."

> Certainly He suffered on earth, and atoned for our sins with earthly blood (because he had derived his origin from the seed of Abraham); the sacrifice

---

[6] John Calvin, *The Second Epistle of Paul to the Corinthians, and the Epistles to Timothy, Titus and Philemon*, CNTC, 10, eds. David W. Torrance and Thomas F. Torrance, tr. T.A. Smail (Grand Rapids: Eerdmans, 1964), on 1 Tim. 2:5.

[7] John Calvin, *Commentaries on the Epistle to the Hebrews and 1 and 2 Peter*, CNTC, 12, eds. David W. Torrance and Thomas F. Torrance, tr. W.B. Johnson (Grand Rapids: Eerdmans, 1963), on Heb. 7:26.

of this death was a visible one; indeed to offer Himself to the Father, He had to descend from heaven to earth and be subject as a man to the troubles of mortal life and at the end to death . . . Thus His flesh, which came from the seed of Abraham, was the temple of God and therefore life-giving.[8]

Calvin never abandons this strong sense of Christ's genuine humanity and its critical place in atonement theology. However, he consistently moves beyond this to insist on the unique empowerment of the Spirit, which means that Christ's humanity is an insufficient explanation of his effective redeeming work. So, commenting on Hebrews 9:14, Calvin declares, "Christ suffered as man (*ut homo*), but in order that His death might effect our salvation it came forth from the power of the Spirit (*ex efficacia spiritus*). The sacrifice of eternal atonement was a more than human work (*opus fuit plus quam humanum*)."[9]

The ultimate theological underpinning of this understanding lies not so much in the supernatural endowment of the Spirit as in the hypostatic union of Christ's divine and human natures.[10] That union does not admit of either separation or confusion, as the Chalcedonian Definition made quite clear.[11] Christ's human nature retains its integrity as a genuinely human nature while his divine nature, one in being with the Father, is not in any sense diminished. Calvin is admittedly willing to grant a communication of properties across the natures: "Because the selfsame one was both God and man, for the sake of the union of both natures he gave to one what belonged to the other" (II.14.2). Nevertheless, a critical distinction remains and most importantly, "Those things which apply to the office of the Mediator are not spoken simply either of the divine nature or of the human" (II.14.3). This is why Calvin can speak of "the earthly blood" of the Christ, which is at one and the same time the "blood of the Son of God" and "the whole world and all things deemed precious by men are nothing compared with the excellency of this price."[12]

Interwoven with this literary and theological context of Calvin's exposition is a historical and apologetic one. At various points in this

---

[8] Calvin, *Epistle to the Hebrews*, on Heb. 8:2.

[9] Calvin, *Epistle to the Hebrews*, on Heb. 9:14.

[10] R.C. Doyle, "Penal Atonement: The Orthodox Teaching of the Fathers and Three Conversations with John Calvin, Part 2," *Reformed Theological Review*, 65:2 (2006), 95, 100–1.

[11] The Chalcedonian Definition, in both the original Latin and in English translation, can be found in J. Pelikan and V. Hotchkiss, *Creeds and Confessions of Faith in the Christian Tradition*, vol. I (Yale University Press, 2003), 180–1.

[12] Calvin, *Commentary on 1 and 2 Peter*, on 1 Pet. 1:18.

section of Calvin's *Institutes*, readers are invited into a theological conversation that Calvin is having with his predecessors and contemporaries.[13] Two particularly important conversation partners as Calvin discusses the atonement are Augustine and Lelio Sozzini (Laelius Socinus). Augustine provides a way of clarifying the priority of love without evacuating the biblical language of wrath and judgment of any meaning.[14] Socinus, on the other hand, argued that mercy and merit are irreconcilable, as indeed are the concepts of atonement and forgiveness or love and wrath. Calvin, who was not adverse to describing Christ's obedience as meritorious and who was committed to affirming both the love of God and the wrath of God, was forced to defend this language in the light of Socinus' objections.[15]

2 The heart of Calvin's exposition of the cross

Calvin was well aware of the variety of images used in Scripture to describe the saving work of Christ.[16] In his own exposition, one image gives way to another in quick succession. Of course, the prior decision

---

[13] Twenty-first-century readers have tended to extend the conversation to include some of Calvin's successors, including Theodore Beza, Johannes Piscator, Jacobus Arminius, François Turretin, and Moise Amyraut.

[14] Augustine, *In Iohannis Evangelium Tractatus* in *A Select Library of the Nicene and Post-Nicene Fathers of the Christian Church*, VII: *St. Augustine*, ed. P. Schaff, trs. J. Gibb and J. Innes (Grand Rapids: Eerdmans, 1888, repr. 1978), *CX*, 5–6 (*CCSL XXXVI*, 625–7).

[15] In 1554/5 Socinus addressed four questions to Calvin, two of them dealing directly with the doctrine of the atonement. The document has been lost and our only source is Calvin's reply: *Responsio ad aliquot Laelii Socini quaestiones* (*Corpus Reformatorum*, X.i, 160–5). For some of the background see W. de Greef, *The Writings of John Calvin: An Introductory Guide*, tr. L.D. Bierma (Grand Rapids: Baker Academic, 1993), 211–12.

[16] In his invaluable 1983 study, Robert A. Peterson highlighted six such images in Calvin's presentation: the obedient second Adam, the victor, our legal substitute, our sacrifice, our merit, our example (Robert A. Peterson, *Calvin's Doctrine of the Atonement* (Phillipsburg, N.J.: Presbyterian & Reformed Publishing Co., 1983)). Peterson has since admitted a lack in that work, namely, "a failure to give pride of place to penal substitution" (Robert A. Peterson, "Calvin on Christ's Saving Work" in D.W. Hall and P.A. Lillback (eds.), *Theological Guide to Calvin's Institutes: Essays and Analysis* (Phillipsburg, N.J.: Presbyterian & Reformed Publishing Co., 2008), 245).

to deal with the atonement as the heart of Christ's priestly work gave that exposition a particular character. The various images will be integrated around Calvin's understanding of the one true priest as our Mediator. Yet right from the start Calvin draws from the rich variety of biblical language, concepts and images to ensure that this is not understood too narrowly.

> Now we must speak briefly concerning the purpose and use of Christ's priestly office: as a pure and stainless Mediator he is by his holiness to reconcile (*conciliet*) us to God. But God's righteous curse bars our access to him, and God in his capacity as judge is angry towards us. Hence, an expiation (*piaculum*) must intervene in order that Christ as priest may obtain God's favor for us and appease (*placandam*) his wrath. Thus Christ to perform this office had to come forward with a sacrifice (*sacrificio*). For under the law, also, the priest was forbidden to enter the sanctuary without blood, that believers might know, even though the priest as their advocate stood between them and God, that they could not propitiate God (*non posse tamen Deum propitiari*) unless their sins were expiated (*nisi expiates peccatis*) . . . The priestly office belongs to Christ alone because by the sacrifice of his death he blotted out our own guilt and made satisfaction for our sins (*quia sacrificio mortis suae reatum nostrum delevit, et satisfecit pro peccatis*). (II.15.6)

We might identify in just these opening lines the themes of mediation, reconciliation, expiation (washing away our sin), propitiation (appeasing God's wrath at sin), sacrifice, and satisfaction. Later in this same paragraph Calvin will speak of sanctification (Christ as our High Priest "sanctifies (*sanctificet*) us") and intercession ("he is an everlasting intercessor (*aeternum . . . deprecatorem*)"). Farther on still, he uses the language of redemption and deliverance, insisting that Christ did not fall under a curse that overwhelmed him, "rather—in taking the curse upon himself—he crushed, broke, and scattered (*depressit, infregit, dissipavit*) its whole force" (II.16.6). As one might expect, this theme is developed in his comments on Colossians 2:14–15,

> For although in the cross there is nothing but curse, this was nevertheless so swallowed up (*absorpta fuit*) by the power of the Son of God, that it has put on, as it were, a new nature. For there is no tribunal so magnificent, no kingly throne so stately, no show of triumph so distinguished, no chariot so lofty, as the gibbet on which Christ subdued (*subegit*) death and the devil, the prince of death; more, has utterly trodden them under His feet (*penitus contrivit sub pedibus suis*).[17]

---

[17] Calvin, *Commentary on Colossians*, on Col. 2:15.

In the light of this evidence, attempts to dismiss Calvin's exposition of the cross as indefensibly narrow are almost inexplicable. Calvin's treatment of the biblical data is deeply integrative. Blocher has productively observed the interlacing of two main language-sets in Calvin's presentation: the religious, cultic language of *sacrifice* and the forensic or judicial language of *condemnation*.[18] Rather than being isolated from one another, or proposed as alternatives, the various images belong together. However, they belong together in a particular way. There is an interpretative center and at that center we find the notion of a penal substitutionary sacrifice. So, listing the wonderful facts that should move a person to gratitude and joy, Calvin writes,

> . . . suppose he learns, as Scripture teaches, that he was estranged from God through sin, is an heir of wrath, subject to the curse of eternal death, excluded from all hope of salvation, beyond every blessing of God, the slave of Satan, captive under the yoke of sin, destined finally for a dreadful destruction and already involved in it; and that at this point Christ interceded as his advocate, took upon himself and suffered the punishment (*poenam in se recepisse ac luisse*) that, from God's righteous judgement, threatened all sinners; that he purged with his blood (*sanguine suo expiasse*) those evils which had rendered sinners hateful to God; that by this expiation he made satisfaction and sacrifice duly (*piaculo satisfactum ac rite litatum*) to God the Father; that as intercessor he has appeased God's wrath (*iram eius fuisse placatum*); that on this foundation rests the peace of God with men; that by this bond his benevolence is maintained toward them. (II.16.2)

Throughout chapter 16 of Book II, this central theme keeps resurfacing.

> We could not escape God's dreadful judgement. To deliver us from it, Christ allowed himself to be condemned before a mortal man—even a wicked and profane man . . . Christ was offered to the Father in death as an expiatory sacrifice that when he discharged all satisfaction through his sacrifice (*ut peracta per eius sacrificium litatione*), we might cease to be afraid of God's wrath . . . he in every respect took our place to pay the price of our redemption (*in vicem nostram ubique se supposuerit ad solvendum nostrae redemptionis pretium*). Death held us captive under its yoke; Christ, in our stead (*in loco nostro*), gave himself over to its power to deliver us from it. (II.16.5, 6. 7)[19]

---

[18] Blocher, *Atonement*, 283.

[19] ". . . the legal language of penal satisfaction and substitution predominates in Calvin's discussion of atonement" (Timothy George, *Theology of the Reformers* (Leicester: Apollos, 1988), 222).

"The centrality of this cluster of ideas could just as easily be demonstrated from Calvin's commentaries or from his sermons."[20] From this center the other images gain a deep and rich meaning. The demonstration of love arises not from some sentimental gesture but from the serious engagement with, and exhaustion of, the penalty we deserve. His death is for us (*pro nobis*) because it is a death in our place (*in loco nostro*). The example of self-sacrifice and humble service is inextricably linked to Christ's willingness to bear a burden that was not his—bearing it in all its intensity and with all its terrible consequences—in order that we might not need to bear it. Even the powerful theme of victory over death and the demonic powers "depends on the more central understanding of the atonement in a lucid and consistent way."[21] Views of the atonement that do not trace the connection between the images of loving self-sacrifice, moral example and victory, on the one hand, and the

---

[20] For example, "His death procured satisfaction (*perfunctus est satisfaction*) for us, so that we should not always remain guilty (*iam sub reatu*), not be subject to the condemnation (*iudicio*) of eternal death" (Calvin, "*Praelectionum in Danielem*," tr. T. Myers (1852), repr. in vol. 2 of *Commentaries on the Book of the Prophet Daniel* (Grand Rapids: Eerdmans, 1948), on Dan. 9:25). "This is the material cause—the fact that Christ by His obedience satisfied the judgment of the Father (*patris iudicio satisfecit*), and by undertaking our cause freed us from the tyranny of death by which we were held captive. Our guilt is taken away by the expiatory sacrifice which He offered" (Calvin, *Commentary on the Epistle of Paul to the Romans*, in Calvin's New Testament Commentaries, 8, tr. R. Mackenzie, on Rom. 3:24). "Yet they [the Apostles] insisted principally on showing that by the pouring out of the blood of our Redeemer we are washed and cleansed of all our spots, that He made payment to God His Father for all our debts by which we were obliged, that He acquired for us perfect righteousness" (Calvin, "Second Sermon on the Passion of our Lord Jesus Christ," in *Sermons on the Saving Work of Christ*, tr. L. Dixon (Grand Rapids, Baker Academic, 1980), 80). "If our Lord saved others, it is certain that He could have saved Himself, unless He preferred others to Himself. What can be perceived there except an admirable goodness, that He wished to be cast into the abyss according to men in order to draw us out of the depth of the abysses, that He was willing to suffer everything we deserved in order to acquit us from it (*qu'il a voulu souffrir tout ce que nous meritons, afin de nous en acquitter*) . . ." (Calvin, "Sixth Sermon on the Passion of our Lord Jesus Christ," in *Sermons*, 140–1).

[21] Blocher, *Atonement*, 291. A page earlier Blocher suggests, "Satan and death, as they draw their power from the administration of divine justice, were disarmed by the satisfaction of that justice," 290.

central image of a penal substitution by the one who is both God and man, on the other, lack the richness and depth of Calvin's account.

A number of the contemporary objections to an understanding of the cross of Christ as a penal substitution are effectively answered by Calvin's presentation.[22] We can limit ourselves to three of these. In the first place, his careful consideration of the work of Christ in the context of the person of Christ ensures that the atonement is seen not as God's punishment of an innocent third party instead of us—child abuse on a cosmic scale—but as God himself bearing the penalty we deserve. In Christ, God bears his own judgment and exhausts its demands so that, in Paul's words, "he might be just and the justifier of the one who has faith in Jesus' (Rom. 3:26, ESV). Second, as we shall see, Calvin directly confronts the suggestion that talk of God's wrath and the need of propitiation is incompatible with the foundational biblical description of God as loving and compassionate (for example, Ex. 34:6–7; Jn. 3:16; 1 Jn. 4:7–8). Echoing the Bible's own presentation (where, for example, 1 Jn. 4:9–10 follows immediately 1 Jn. 4:7–8), he will argue that love and judgment are both divine realities that need to be taken seriously. Third, it is evident that Calvin is not committed to a notion of absolute necessity, as if the cross of Christ is demanded by legal realties to which even God is bound. Though at one point Calvin can say that Christ's priestly work was "to render the father favorable and propitious toward us *by an eternal law of reconciliation (ut aeterna reconciliationis lege)*" (II.15.6, emphasis added), he is elsewhere concerned to stress God's freedom and so his loving decision to save us in this manner.

> If someone asks why this is necessary, there has been no simple (to use the common expression) or absolute necessity. Rather, it has stemmed from a heavenly decree (*ex coelesti decreto*), on which men's salvation depended. Our most merciful Father decreed what was best for us. (II.12.1)

In a sermon on Matthew 26:36–39 he is more explicit,

> In fact, [God] was well able to rescue us from the unfathomable depths of death in another fashion, but He willed to display the treasures of His infinite goodness when He spared not His only Son. And our Lord Jesus in this matter willed to give us a sure pledge of the care which He had for us when He offered Himself voluntarily to death.[23]

---

[22] This is the burden of Robert Doyle's helpful article (Doyle, "Penal Atonement").

[23] Calvin, "First Sermon on the Passion of our Lord Jesus Christ," in *Sermons*, 51–65.

Timothy George's conclusion is well grounded in the evidence of Calvin's writing: the atonement "has no necessity outside of God's gracious will toward us."[24]

At the heart of Calvin's understanding of the atonement is the notion of penal substitution. This ought not to be confused with Anselm's account of the atonement, which privileges a particular understanding of "satisfaction." The glib association of the two accounts in some popular critiques fails to notice the very significant differences between them.[25] As we have seen, Calvin, unlike Anselm, pulls back from affirming an absolute or ontological necessity for the incarnation. In addition, Anselm's preoccupation with "satisfaction," understood as recompense for God's offended honor, is not echoed in Calvin, who prefers to speak of the love and wrath of God as well as the satisfaction of God's justice. Further, in his account of Christ's saving work, Calvin gave greater prominence to the life of Christ than Anselm did. As we have seen, in his integrated account of the atonement, he also took account of the variety of biblical language and imagery, including the descriptions of the cross as a victory over death and the devil, in a way that Anselm did not. Finally, Calvin's discussion of the atonement embraces both the objective and subjective dimensions of God's work in Christ whereas the link between our sinful state and the achievement of the cross is not always clear in Anselm's boldly objective account. For Calvin, the cross of Christ makes a difference in the world at large and also calls for a response on the part of all those who hear of it.

3 The distinctives of Calvin's approach to the cross of Christ

Calvin did not think he was saying anything new or novel when he described the saving work of Christ in these terms. His concern was not to create a distinctive and easily recognizable theological system but rather to assist others "to find the sum of what God meant to teach us in his Word."[26] Yet in doing so, Calvin highlighted in a fresh way critical issues arising from the Bible's teaching, resulting in an account that was indeed recognizably

---

[24] George, *Theology*, 221.

[25] The following five points of differentiation were identified by Timothy George (George, *Theology*, 220–3) and have since been endorsed with some minor corrections by Robert Peterson (Peterson, *Christ's Saving Work*, 244–5).

[26] Calvin, Preface to the 1560 French edition of the *Institutes*, 6. It remains true, as Richard Muller has reminded us, that the *Institutes* do indeed constitute a theological system in sixteenth-century terms (which must be distinguished from nineteenth- and twentieth-century terms), (Muller, *Unaccommodated Calvin*, 180).

different from that of many of his contemporaries and those who preceded him, as well. Four important distinctives have often been identified.

3.1 The cross arises from a genuine love and deals with a genuine wrath

In a much studied section of the *Institutes*, Calvin addressed directly an issue that continues to trouble many today. Does the Bible's teaching about God's wrath, about human guilt and the judgment that awaits us all, render meaningless all talk about God as loving and gracious? Put the other way round, if God really does love the world (Jn. 3:16) and really does desire all to be saved (1 Tim. 2:4), is there any reality to the idea of God's wrath? Calvin was not oblivious to this tension,

> . . . before we go any farther, we must see in passing how fitting it was that God, who anticipates us by his mercy (*qui nos misericordia sua praevenit*), should have been our enemy until he was reconciled to us through Christ. For how could he have given in his only-begotten Son a singular pledge of his love to us if he had not already embraced us with his free favor? Since, therefore, some sort of contradiction (*aliqua repugnantiae species*) arises here, I shall dispose of this difficulty (*nodum*). (II.16.2)

Calvin also addresses this issue in his commentaries,

> We were enemies [Paul] says, when Christ presented Himself to the Father as a means of propitiation . . . The apostle, however, seems here to be contradicting himself (*secum pugnare*). If the death of Christ was a pledge of the divine love towards us, it follows that we were even then acceptable to Him. But now he says that we were *enemies*.[27]

> Notice how men return to God's favor—by being regarded as righteous, by obtaining remission of their sins. As long as God imputes our sins to us, He cannot but regard us with abhorrence, for he cannot look with friendship or favor upon sinners. But this may appear to contradict what is said elsewhere (*Sed videtur cum hac sententia pugnare quod alibi*), that "we were loved by Him before the foundation of the world" (Eph. 1:4), and to contradict still more John 3:16 where He says that His love for us was the reason why He expiated our sins by Christ, for the cause must always precede the effect. My answer is that we were loved from before the foundation of the world, but not apart from Christ.[28]

---

[27] Calvin, *Commentary on Romans*, on Rom. 5:10 (emphasis original).
[28] Calvin, *Commentary on 2 Corinthians*, on 2 Cor. 5:19.

There was, of course, a long tradition of wrestling with this seeming contradiction, going back at least to the writings of Augustine of Hippo. Indeed, as Calvin carefully works his way through this problem he cites Augustine and his remarkable conclusion, "Accordingly, in a wonderful and divine manner, even when He hated us, He loved us (*Proinde miro et diuino modo et quando nos oderat, diligebat*) . . ."[29] Calvin's own treatment of the question made use of a concept he had employed elsewhere in the *Institutes*, the concept of divine accommodation.[30] The language of enmity between God and human beings requiring reconciliation, of a curse that is only lifted when iniquity is atoned for, and of an estrangement from God that must be overcome, is used with a purpose: "Expressions of this sort have been accommodated to our capacity (*ad sensum nostrum sunt accommodatae*) that we may better understand how miserable and ruinous our condition is apart from Christ" (II.16.2).

It is significant for Calvin that such an accommodation does not involve distortion to the extent of falsehood. "Though this statement is tempered to our feeble comprehension," he insists, "it is not said falsely." And in support of this he continues, "For God, who is the highest righteousness, cannot love the unrighteousness that he sees in us all. All of us, therefore, have in ourselves something deserving of God's hatred" (II.16.3). As one recent and important study of the concept in this context puts it, the accommodated expression to which Calvin refers tells "the truth but not the whole truth about the atonement and its relation to the Christian."[31] Elsewhere, Calvin acknowledges that a similar tension exists in our descriptions of Christ himself.

> How does it happen, some may object, that a beloved Son is cursed by His Father? I reply, there are two things to be considered, not only in the person of Christ, but even in His human nature. The one is that He was the

---

[29] Augustine, *Iohannis Evangelium Tractatus*, CX.6, 411 (*CCSL* XXXVI, 626).

[30] For a treatment of this issue in these other contexts, strangely without reference to Calvin's use of it here, see F.L. Battles, "God was Accommodating Himself to Human Capacity," *Interpretation*, 31 (1977), 19–38; cf. D.F. Wright, "Calvin's 'Accommodation' Revisited" in Peter de Klerk (ed.), *Calvin as Exegete: Papers and Responses Presented at the Ninth Colloquium on Calvin and Calvin Studies 1993* (Grand Rapids: CRC, 1995), 19–38.

[31] Paul Helm, *John Calvin's Ideas* (Oxford: Oxford University Press, 2004), 395. Helm's study critically engages with comments on the topic by Gerrit Berkouwer and Robert Peterson (Gerrit C. Berkouwer, *The Work of Christ*, tr. C. Lambregste (Grand Rapids: Eerdmans, 1953), 269; Peterson, *Calvin's Doctrine*, 7–10).

unspotted Lamb of God, full of blessing and grace. The other is that He took our place and thus became a sinner and subject to the curse, not in Himself indeed, but in us: yet in such a way that it was necessary for Him to act in our name. He could not be outside God's grace, and yet He endured His wrath (*Itaque neque extra Dei gratiam esse potuit et tamen sustinuit iram eius*).[32]

The language of judgment, wrath and enmity is both true and necessary in order to teach us to take seriously our predicament outside Christ. Calvin nowhere attempts to back away from the reality of God's wrath, nor its appropriateness given the reality of our sin. Yet he refuses any suggestion that a wrathful God has to be made loving: "By his love God the Father goes before and anticipates our reconciliation in Christ (*Proinde sua dilectione praevenit ac antevertit Deus Pater nostram in Christo reconciliationem*). Indeed, 'because he first loved us,' he afterward reconciles us to himself" (II.16.3). As we have already noted, Calvin cites Augustine at length on this point,

> For it was not after we were reconciled to him through the blood of his Son that he began to love us. Rather, he has loved us before the world was created, that we also might be his sons along with his only-begotten Son—before we became anything at all. The fact that we were reconciled through Christ's death must not be understood as if his Son reconciled us to him that he might now begin to love those whom he had hated. Rather, we have already been reconciled to him who loves us, with whom we were enemies on account of sin.[33]

It is all too easy to give a one-sided explanation of the atonement that proclaims one of these aspects but excludes or minimizes the other. The atonement is in fact the evidence that both are true: atonement is necessary because God's wrath is real; atonement is provided because God's love is real. Nevertheless, God's love has a priority because it is eternally characteristic of his being.[34] In Calvin's words, "I do agree that the

---

[32] Calvin, *Commentary on Galatians*, on Gal. 3:13. On this basis, Robert Doyle urges that Calvin controlled the significance he drew from the logic of judicial descriptions of the death of Christ "by appeal to the ontological context" (Doyle, "Penal Atonement," 99).

[33] *Institutes*, II.16.4, citing (with the omission of two clauses) Augustine, *In Iohannis Evangelium Tractatus*, CX.6, 411 (*CCSL* XXXVI, 626).

[34] The ultimate priority of the eternal intratrinitarian love is not developed by Calvin at this point in the way it has been by some of his successors. See

love of God was first in time and in order also as regards God (*quantum ad Deum*); but, as regards us (*respectu nostri*), His love has its foundation in the sacrifice of Christ."[35]

3.2 The cross is the critical element of "the whole course of Christ's obedience"

Calvin gives the incarnation and the sinless life of Jesus greater prominence than many other treatments of the atonement. Here he is confident that he is following the example of the apostle Paul: "Paul extends the oasis of the pardon that frees us from the curse of the law to the whole life of Christ," he observes, after quoting from Romans 5:19. The life of Christ is not just a precondition of the saving work of Christ but part of that saving work. A line or two later Calvin summarizes the point: "From the time when he took on the form of a servant, he began to pay the price of liberation in order to redeem us" (II.16.5).

Calvin does not intend his emphasis on "the whole course of Christ's obedience" to take away from the significance of the cross and resurrection. Indeed, the very next paragraph in the *Institutes* begins, "Yet to define the way of salvation more exactly, Scripture ascribes this as peculiar and proper (*quasi peculiare ac proprium*) to Christ's death" (II.16.5). However, explicitly following the lead suggested by Philippians 2:7–8, Calvin wishes to stress that Christ's sacrificial death was an act of obedience, in fact the act of obedience par excellence,

> Even in death itself his willing obedience is the important thing because a sacrifice not offered voluntarily would not have furthered righteousness . . . no proper sacrifice to God could have been offered unless Christ, disregarding his own feelings, subjected and yielded himself wholly to his Father's will. (II.16.5)

There are three immediate effects of giving Jesus' life-long obedience a distinctive prominence in this way. The first is an underscoring of the

---

(cont.) Doyle, "Penal Atonement," 104. Paul Helm goes further, insisting ". . . in fact there is no change in God; he loves us from eternity. There is, however, a change in us . . . from regarding God as a judge to regarding him as Saviour" (Helm, *Calvin's Ideas*, 395, 398).

[35] Calvin, *Commentary on 2 Corinthians*, on 2 Cor. 5:19. Henri Blocher's comments are entirely in the same vein: "Substitution under the curse we had deserved, so that divine justice is satisfied and we go free, marks the culmination of God's love for us, the ultimate point on the road of self-denial and self-giving, farther than which none can be conceived" (Blocher, *Atonement*, 286).

genuine humanity of Christ. In this very context Calvin speaks of Christ's "struggle" (*certamine*), "weakness" (*infirmitates*), "terrible fear" (*horribili formidine*) and "cruel torments" (*diros cruciatus*). The atonement is not made at some distance from us or from the dreadful consequences of sin that plague us in the world. The eternal Son genuinely entered into our condition, not superficially but profoundly. Just as the deep reality of the incarnation remains critical for understanding what was happening in Jesus' life, it is critical for understanding what took place in his death and resurrection.[36]

The second effect is to return to the love that suffuses the saving work of Christ. Not only is this the Father's love, which caused him to send the Son, it is the Son's love, which motivates every step toward the cross and his voluntary self-giving in it. "And here was no common evidence of his incomparable love toward us," Calvin insists, "to wrestle with terrible fear, and amid those cruel torments to cast off all concern for himself that he might provide for us" (II.16.5). The Gospels reveal a loving determination on the part of Jesus Christ to bear the penalty due to all on account of their sin and this can too easily be obscured when his death is treated in isolation from his lifelong pattern of obedience to his Father.

Third, Calvin's understanding of "the whole course of Christ's obedience" provides him with the foundation for his discussion of Christ's merit in response to the objections of Socinus. It is telling that Calvin reserves his discussion of merit until chapter 17 of Book II. The language of merit does not in fact feature in the main exposition. Nevertheless, Calvin is prepared to affirm that "By his obedience . . . Christ truly acquired and merited (*acquisierit ac promeritus sit*) grace for us with his Father" (II.17.3). He will insist that "it is absurd to set Christ's merit

---

[36] Thomas F. Torrance has often reflected upon the profound implications this has for the Christian life, a life lived in response to God's action in Christ: "It is curious that evangelicals often link the substitutionary act of Christ only with his death, and not with his incarnate Person and life—that is dynamite for them! They thereby undermine the radical nature of the substitution, what the New Testament calls *katallage*, or Christ in our place and Christ for us in every respect. Substitution understood in this radical way means that Christ takes our place in all our human life and activity before God, even in our believing, praying and worshipping of God, for he has yoked himself to us in such a profound way that he stands in for us, and upholds us at every point in our human relations before God" (Thomas F. Torrance, James B. Torrance and David W. Torrance, *A Passion for Christ: The Vision that Ignites Ministry* (Edinburgh: Handsel Press, 1999), 24).

against God's mercy" and yet "Christ's merit" remains "subordinate to God's mercy" (II.17.1). Merit and mercy are held together in the person and work of Jesus Christ as in grace the Son empties himself, embraces genuine human existence and consistently submits his will to that of his Father. The cross is not just another instance of that obedience, for in dying in the place of sinners he bears all the burdens of the Law of Moses and pays what we could not pay (II.17.5).

3.3 The cross deals with the fullness of the penalty we all deserve—the descent into hell

The central section in Calvin's account of the saving work of Christ follows, in large part, the order of the Apostles' Creed. It is in this context that Calvin presents his own distinctive explanation of the clause "he descended into hell (*descendit ad inferna*)." He introduces it as "a matter of no small moment in bringing about redemption" (II.16.8). He acknowledges that there has been a variety of explanations of this clause. Some have even considered it otiose, being just another way of saying he was buried or counted among the dead, which is the subject of the immediately preceding clause. Is this just an example of useless repetition (*superfluam battologiam*)? Calvin concludes that this is unlikely (II.16.8).

Calvin also considers the traditional explanation associated with the Roman Church and some Anabaptists. Aquinas had suggested that "immediately after his death Christ's soul descended into hell (*ad infernum descendit*), manifesting to the saints detained there the fruit of his passion."[37] Once again Calvin is unconvinced, this time because the biblical expectation is that believers who have died share the same grace with us and so are not languishing in any prison awaiting release of some kind. They are safe in the Lord's hands not in any "limbo." Calvin recognizes that he has to deal with 1 Peter 3:19, which speaks of "the spirits in prison" (*tois en phulaka pneumasin*). However, he considers that a better translation, "watchtower" (*specula*) rather than "prison" (*carcer*), and a better appreciation of the context, both lead away from the interpretation of Aquinas and others (II.16.9).[38]

Calvin's preferred explanation of this article of the Creed was not entirely original.[39] According to him, the Creed at this point was reflecting

---

[37] Aquinas, *Summa Theologiae*, vol. 54, *The Passion of Christ*, IIIa.52.6.

[38] cf. Calvin, *Commentary on 1 Peter*, on 1 Pet. 3:19.

[39] See the editor's footnote (no. 23) at this point in the *Institutes*. He mentions the prior work of Nicholas of Cusa and Pico della Mirandola (*Institutes*, II.16.10).

the awful reality expressed in the cry of dereliction: "My God, my God, why have you forsaken me?" (Mt. 27:46, ESV). Jesus underwent, not only the physical trauma of death by crucifixion, but also the fullness of what was owing to us, "the severity of God's vengeance" and "the terrible torments of a condemned and forsaken man" (II.16.10). On this view, the order of the Creed takes on a new importance. That order is not simply or strictly chronological. What is affirmed at this point is not merely the next in a sequence of events from Jesus' history following his suffering, death and burial. In Calvin's words,

> The point is that the Creed sets forth what Christ suffered in the sight of men, and then appositely speaks of that invisible and incomprehensible judgement which he underwent in the sight of God in order that we might know not only that Christ's body was given as the price of our redemption, but that he paid a greater and more excellent price in suffering in his soul the terrible torments of a condemned and forsaken man. (II.16.10)

The horror of crucifixion with all that it entails was certainly not minimized by Calvin. His sermons are eloquent testimony to this. However, more was going on at that point than simply the extinguishing of a life. On the cross Jesus was suffering "*everything* we deserved in order to acquit us from it."[40] He was bearing "the weight of divine severity" (II.16.11). This is what leads Calvin to suggest right at the outset that should this affirmation be omitted from the Creed "much of the benefit of Christ's death will be lost" (II.16.8). The Creed and the testimony of Scripture that supports it call for a sober view of the judgment we deserve and confidence that it has been borne in its entirety by Christ on the cross. "This is our wisdom," Calvin concludes, "duly to feel how much our salvation cost the Son of God" (II.16.12).

3.4 The cross has both a universal and a particular scope

Over the centuries since Calvin penned the *Institutes*, no aspect of his treatment of the atonement has attracted more controversy than the question of its extent.[41] The debate surrounding Jacobus Arminius' objection to the teaching of Calvin's successor Théodore de Bèze—resolved, at least

---

[40] Calvin, "Sixth Sermon on the Passion of our Lord," in *Sermons*, 141 (emphasis added).

[41] Some representative works on either side of the twentieth-century debate include B. Hall, "Calvin against the Calvinists," in G. Duffield (ed.), *John Calvin* (Grand Rapids: Eerdmans,1966), 23–7; R.T. Kendall, *Calvin and*

officially, by the Synod of Dort in 1618—and the heated discussions surrounding the teaching of Moïse Amyraut and the Reformed seminary in
Saumur later that century, have tended to dominate most treatments on
Calvin's teaching on the cross. Did Calvin believe that Christ died for all or
only for the elect? Could he actually affirm both in some sense? Further, if
the extent of the atonement is limited, is it limited by intention or at the
point of application?

There is a sense in which these questions are anachronistic. They
import a debate from a later period, expecting to resolve it by appeal
to theological work done when the issue was not a focus of controversy.[42] The difficulty is compounded, as Richard Muller has made
clear, when the expressions "limited atonement" and "universal
atonement" are employed. These are categories from a much later
period and they would not have been recognized by many in the sixteenth century. It is worth quoting Muller's important critical study at
this point.

> The terms "universal" and "limited atonement" do not represent the six-
> teenth and seventeenth century Reformed view—or for that matter, the
> view of its opponents. The issue was not over "atonement," broadly
> understood, but over the "satisfaction" made by Christ for sin—and the
> debate was never over whether or not Christ's satisfaction was limited: all
> held it to be utterly sufficient to pay the price for all sin and all held it to

---

(cont.) *English Calvinism to 1649* (Oxford: Oxford University Press, 1979),
13–28; J.B. Torrance, "The Incarnation and Limited Atonement," *Evangelical
Quarterly*, 55 (1983), 82–94; M.C. Bell, *Calvin and Scottish Theology: The
Doctrine of Assurance* (Edinburgh: Handsel Press, 1985), 13–40; and W.R.
Godfrey, "Reformed Thought on the Extent of the Atonement to 1618,"
Westminster Theological Journal, 37 (1975), 137–8; Paul Helm, *Calvin and the
Calvinists* (Edinburgh: Banner of Truth Trust, 1982); R. Nicole, "John Calvin's
View of the Extent of the Atonement," *Westminster Theological Journal*, 47
(1985), 197–225; Richard A. Muller, "Calvin and the 'Calvinists': Assessing
Continuities and Discontinuities between the Reformation and Orthodoxy,
Part I," *Calvin Theological Journal*, 30 (1995), 345–75; Richard A. Muller,
"Calvin and the 'Calvinists': Assessing Continuities and Discontinuities
between the Reformation and Orthodoxy, Part II," *Calvin Theological Journal*,
31 (1996), 128–9, 151–7.

[42] Though Roger Nicole is right to note that the question had been debated cen-
turies before, in connection with the teaching of Godescalc of Orbais
(Gottschalk), particularly as this was later defended by Remigius of Lyons
(Nicole, "Extent of the Atonement," 197).

be effective or efficient only for those who were saved. The question concerned the identity of those saved and, therefore, the ground of the limitation—God's will or human choice.[43]

Muller's basic observation that "Calvin, Bullinger, and others of their
generation did not make a major issue of the limitation of Christ's aton-
ing work to the elect alone" is amply supported by the evidence. Both
sides in the modern debate have been able to appeal to passages in
Calvin's commentaries, though, significantly, the *Institutes* appear to be
silent on the issue. Some acknowledge the paucity of explicit statements
from Calvin on the subject and appeal instead to "the logic of his position," or a correspondence between the extent of Christ's intercession
and the extent of the atonement on one side or between the scope of the
general resurrection and that of the atonement on the other, or even
inferences drawn from the fact that those closest to Calvin and trusted
by him unambiguously taught on the subject.[44]

There are, in fact, a number of passages in which Calvin seems to
affirm two dimensions of impact when it comes to the atonement of
Christ. On the one hand, he is the Redeemer of the human race; on the
other, his redeeming work takes effect only in those drawn to Christ by
the Spirit in faith. In his "Fourth Sermon on the Passion of our Lord,"
Calvin contrasts Peter and Judas. Both men fail to persevere in faith, but
Peter is restored while Judas is ultimately lost. This leads Calvin to
reflect on the fact that "the death and passion of our Lord Jesus does not
bear fruit in all men." He then goes on to say,

> For as [God] declared His love toward mankind (*le genre humain*) when He
> spared not His Only Son but delivered Him to death for sinners, also He
> declares a love which He bears especially toward us (*qu'il nous porte spe-
> cialement*) when by His Holy Spirit He touches us by the knowledge of our
> sins and He makes us wail and draws us to Himself with repentance.[45]

In the *Institutes* themselves, within a few pages of the section we have
been examining, Calvin will begin Book III with the bold declaration
that "as long as Christ remains outside of us, and we are separated from
him, all that he has suffered and done for the salvation of the human

---

[43] Richard A. Muller, *After Calvin: Studies in the Development of a Theological Tradition* (New York: Oxford University Press, 2003), 14.

[44] See, for example, Blocher, *Atonement*, 280–1; Peterson, "Christ's Saving Work," 247.

[45] Calvin, "Fourth Sermon on the Passion of our Lord," in *Sermons*, 108.

race remains useless and of no value to us." At the end of that first paragraph he will sum up with the words, "The Holy Spirit is the bond by
which Christ effectually unites us to himself" (III.1.1).

Christ is the only hope for the world. There is no other Savior and his
saving work is undoubtedly sufficient for the entire world. Yet clearly
not all are saved. Not all are given the Spirit and united to the Son so that
they might share all that is his. This Calvin was prepared to leave in the
hands of a loving and merciful God as he addressed his own call to
repent and believe to everyone with ears to hear.

4 Calvin on his own terms

John Calvin was passionate about the cross of Christ. That is evident in
his sermons, in his commentaries, and supremely in his *Institutes*. He
knew that this priestly work of Christ is the principal point on which our
whole salvation turns. He knew that a proper understanding of the cross
shapes Christian theology and the Christian life. It frees us from doubt,
from superstition, and from a false and dangerous reliance upon our
own religious accomplishments.

It has become fashionable in some circles to caricature the
Reformation doctrine of the cross of Christ. It is offensive in all the
wrong ways, so its critics say. It assumes the worst about us, is ultimately inconsistent with the open-handed generosity of God, and it
relies on primitive and discredited notions of divine wrath, propitiation,
and substitutionary sacrifice. However, a return to a careful study of
Calvin's exposition of the cross exposes the caricature drawn by so
many of the critics. Calvin's understanding of the cross is neither narrow
nor superficial and yet it could be explained in simple language and
with profound pastoral impact.

> Now the power arises solely from the fact that the Son of God was cruci-
> fied as the price of our righteousness (*iustitiae nostrae pretium*). (II.17.5)

> This is our acquittal: the guilt that held us liable for punishment has been
> transferred to the head of the Son of God. We must, above all, remember
> this substitution, lest we tremble and remain anxious throughout life . . .
> (II.16.5)

7

Calvin, the Theologian of the Holy Spirit

Elias Dantas

My goal in writing this chapter is to talk about Calvin, the theologian of the Holy Spirit. I must say upfront that he did not receive this title from one of his friends or fellow theologians. It was given to him almost 350 years after his death by one of the most famous Reformed theologians of the twentieth century, Dr. B.B. Warfield. His are the following words,

> The fundamental interest of Calvin as a theologian lay, it is clear, in the region broadly designated soteriological. Perhaps we may go further and add that, within this broad field, his interest was most intense in the application to the sinful soul of the salvation wrought out by Christ, – in a word in what is technically known as the *ordo salutis*. This has even been made his reproach in some quarters, and we have been told that the main fault of the *Institutes* as a treatise in theological science, lies in its too subjective character. Its effect, at all events, has been to constitute Calvin pre-eminently the theologian of the Holy Spirit.[1]

In the introductory note for the outstanding book written by Abraham Kuyper, Warfield adds, "It is to John Calvin that we own the first formulation of the doctrine of the work of the Holy Ghost; he himself gave it a very rich statement developing it especially in the broad departments of 'Common Grace', 'Regeneration', and the 'Witness of the Spirit.'"[2]

---

[1] Benjamin B. Warfield. This essay appeared in a booklet published by the Presbyterian Board of Education in 1909. The electronic edition of this article was scanned and edited by Shane Rosenthal for *Reformation Ink*.

[2] Abraham Kuyper, *The Work of the Holy Spirit*, Introductory Note by Benjamin B. Warfield (Grand Rapids: Eerdmans, 1959), 34.

Applied to Calvin, the title can generate some confusion in some people's minds. It can give the impression that the Holy Spirit was the chief theme of Calvin's writings. That was not the case. Although he wrote extensively about the subject, especially in his *Institutes* III, it was always in the context of some other major theme. In the volume mentioned above, he addresses the benefits believers draw from the redeeming work of God in Jesus Christ. The title for the whole book reveals Calvin's soteriological focus in writing it: "The Way in which We Receive the Grace of Christ: What Benefits Come to Us from It, and What Effects Follow." As he addresses each one of the sections of the book, Calvin makes it clear that the applications and imputation of those benefits in the lives of individual believers are direct results of the sovereign action of the Holy Spirit.[3]

As we study Calvin's literary legacy, we recognize that he never wrote a theological document dealing specifically with the person and work of the Holy Spirit. During the last hundred years especially, this fact has generated many criticisms from several high-profile Christian theologians and leaders. The criticism, though, seems to be unfair in the light of what Calvin wrote in the above-mentioned book, in some of his commentaries, and in many of his sermons.

What some of Calvin's critics seem not to understand is that the Reformer spoke to his context. He wrote to the church of his day. For that church the major theological themes were not necessarily the same as ours. In Calvin's day, the doctrine of the Holy Spirit was neither the central focus of his debate with the Roman Catholic Church, nor the content of his discussions and sometimes heated disagreements with other leaders of the broad Reformation movement. Calvin only dealt with the work of the Holy Spirit as that particular topic was essential to the logic of his theological argument, especially in relation to the doctrine of salvation, the Scriptures, the sacraments, and the Christian life.

Perhaps we could properly say that most of the criticism against Calvin and his teachings on the Holy Spirit is due not so much to his theological works, as to the general portrayal of him established by his

---

[3] Book III of the *Institutes* is basically a theological treaty on the topic of salvation. In considering the Holy Spirit, Calvin examined the doctrine of regeneration—that is, how we are saved. He claimed that salvation is only possible through the grace of God. Even before creation, God chose some people to be saved. This is the bone most people choke on: predestination. Curiously, it isn't particularly a Calvinist idea. Augustine taught it centuries earlier, and Luther believed it, as did most of the other Reformers. Yet Calvin stated it so forcefully that the teaching is forever identified with him.

spiritual heirs. Perhaps because churches in the Reformed tradition tend to attract middle-class people, typically more formally educated individuals, and because congregations are generally led by a well-trained ministry with an overwhelming focus on doctrinal preaching, Reformed Christians are inclined to be more reserved about their faith. It is probably not unfair to describe them as cool and philosophical in contrast to the warm enthusiasm and spontaneity of other charismatic and Pentecostal traditions.

Lewis Mudge says that part of the problem may be theological. Our creeds and confessions do not do justice to Calvin's emphasis on the work of the Holy Spirit: "The result is that in reading what the Bible says about the Spirit we are blind and deaf."[4] The reality, though, is that Calvin was not the loveless, spiritless dogmatician that he has so often been portrayed in popular caricature. In fact, "A strong case can be made for the thesis that Calvin was more a theologian of the heart than of the head, with 'heart' for him meaning not so much the seat of the emotions or affections, as in contemporary usage, but rather the existential core of the personality."[5]

Taking issue with those who stress only the objective side of Calvin's teaching, and with others who hold that the Calvinistic Reformation was chiefly a political or scientific movement, Professor S. Vander Linde declares that the movement was pre-eminently religious in nature. Books III and IV of the *Institutes*, with their focus on soteriology, Christian piety, and the external means of grace, are clear evidences of that fact. In developing this thesis he writes,

> The most sensitive, most vulnerable, and at the same time the most distinguishing traits of Reformed folk do not lie in the more objective sphere of dogmatics or ethics, but in what follows from the practice of faith. Consequently the work of the Holy Spirit has a great and wholesome emphasis in Calvin and the Reformed pietists.[6]

---

[4] Lewis S. Mudge, *One Church: Catholic and Reformed* (Philadelphia: Westminster Press, 1963), 63. Mudge is presently Professor Emeritus of Theology at San Francisco Theological Seminary and in the Graduate Theological Union. He is also the author of *The Crumbling Walls* (Philadelphia: Westminster Press, 1970). He is editor of *Essays on Biblical Interpretation*, by Paul Ricoeur (Philadelphia: Fortress Press, 1980).

[5] I. John Hesselink, *On Being Reformed: Distinctive Characteristics and Common Misunderstandings* (New York: Reformed Church Press, 1988), 70.

[6] See M. Eugene Osterhaven, *The Spirit of the Reformed Tradition* (Grand Rapids: Eerdmans, 1971), 140.

1 The Holy Spirit and faith

Calvin's writings on the topic of faith are very revealing of his heart. For him, faith from beginning to end is a work of the Holy Spirit. And not only one of the many works of the Spirit but, "Faith is the principal work of the Holy Spirit."[7]

In his first catechism Calvin begins his discussion of true faith in this way: "Now we are to conceive the Christian faith as no bare knowledge of God or understanding of Scripture which rattles around the brain and affects the heart not all."[8] Later in the same work, he adds, "Therefore it is perfectly clear that faith is the enlightenment of the Holy Spirit by which our minds are illumined and our hearts confirmed in a sure persuasion within, which establishes that God's truth is so sure that He cannot but supply what He has promised to us He will do by His Holy Word."[9]

This is an emphasis from which Calvin never deviates. In the last edition of the *Institutes*, written over twenty years after the first, he constantly reiterates this theme: "Faith requires knowledge and understanding, but it is above all a matter of the heart."[10] James W. Jones puts his finger on the motivation for this emphasis, namely, Calvin's constant quest for assurance and certainty in matters of faith.

> For Calvin, authority lies in something being confirmed as authoritative in the heart of the individual . . . The mind cannot give certainty, Calvin says, because its knowledge always comes through the senses and is therefore subject to doubt. The will can give no certainty either for it is dependent upon the mind. But the heart is the seat of certainty and assurance for Calvin.[11]

2 Assurance of faith

The above affirmation brings us to another important understanding of Calvin's doctrine of faith as it relates to the saving work of the Holy

---

[7] John Calvin, *Institutes of the Christian Religion*, ed. John T. McNeill, tr. Ford Lewis Battles, (Philadelphia: Westminster Press, 1960 (1559)), Book III, ch. 1, sect. 4 (III.1.4, henceforth abbreviated and shown in the text).

[8] John Calvin, *Instruction in Faith*, tr. and with comments by Paul T. Fuhrman, (Philadelphia: Westminster Press, 1949), 17.

[9] Fuhrman, *Instruction*, 19.

[10] Hesselink, *On Being Reformed*, 70.

[11] James W. Jones, *The Spirit and the World* (New York: Hawthorn Books, 1975), 131.

Spirit. Calvin says that faith is never merely assent (*assensus*), but involves both knowledge (*cognitio*) and trust (*fiducia*). He affirms that knowledge and trust are saving dimensions of the life of faith rather than notional matters. For him, faith is not historical knowledge plus saving assent, as his successor, Theodore Beza, was to teach, but faith is a saving and certain knowledge joined with a saving and assured trust.

Calvin held that knowledge is foundational to faith. Knowledge rests upon the Word of God, which is essentially the Holy Scriptures as well as the gospel and its proclamation. Faith originates in the Word of God. Faith rests firmly upon God's Word; it always says amen to the Scriptures. Hence assurance must be sought in the Word and flows out of the Word. Assurance is as inseparable from the Word as sunbeams are from the sun.

It is true, according to Calvin, that although the external proof of the Word of God should have been amply sufficient to engender faith, "Our mind has such an inclination to vanity that it can never cleave fast to the truth of God; and it has such a dullness that it is always blind to the light of God's truth" (III.1.33). For that reason, without the illumination of the Spirit, the Word can do nothing: "And it will not be enough for the mind to be illumined by the Spirit of God unless the heart is also strengthened and supported by his power" (III.1.33).

In one of his most famous statements, Calvin says, "Indeed, the Word of God is like the sun, shining upon all those to whom it is proclaimed, but with no effect among the blind. Now, all of us are blind by nature in this respect. Accordingly, it cannot penetrate into our minds unless the Spirit, as the inner teacher, through his illumination makes entry for us" (III.1.33). In this respect, as the Word relates itself to the matter of faith and trust, Calvin says,

> Faith, thus, is a singular gift of God, both in that the mind of man is purged so as to be able to taste the truth of God and in that his heart is established therein. For the Spirit is not only the initiator of faith, but increases it by degrees, until by it he leads us to the Kingdom of Heaven. "Let each one," says Paul, "guard the precious truth . . . entrusted by the Holy Spirit who dwells in us (2 Tim. 1:14)." (III.1.33)

Faith is also inseparable from Christ and the promise of Christ, for the totality of the written Word is the living Word, Jesus Christ, in whom all God's promises are "yea and amen." Faith rests on scriptural knowledge, and on promises that are Christ-directed and Christ-centered. True faith receives Christ as he is clothed in the gospel and graciously offered by the Father.

Thus, illuminated by the Spirit, true faith focuses upon the Scriptures in general, and particularly the promise of the grace of God in Christ. Calvin makes much of the promises of God as the ground of assurance, for these promises are based on the very nature of God, who cannot lie. Since God promises mercy to sinners in their misery, faith relies upon such promises. The promises are fulfilled by Christ; therefore Calvin directs sinners to Christ and to the promises as if they are synonyms. Rightly understood, faith rests on and appropriates the promises of God in Christ made known in Scripture.

Since faith takes its character from the promise on which it rests, it takes on the infallible stamp of God's very Word. Consequently, faith possesses assurance in its very nature. Assurance, certainty, trust—such is the essence of faith. This assured and assuring faith is the Holy Spirit's gift to the elect. The Spirit persuades the elect sinner of the reliability of God's promise in Christ and grants faith to embrace that Word. In short, for Calvin, assuring faith necessarily involves saving knowledge, the Scriptures, Jesus Christ, God's promises, the work of the Holy Spirit, and election. God himself is the assurance of the elect. Assurance is gratuitously founded upon God.

We take up again the point made at the beginning of this section on faith: for Calvin, faith is above all a matter of the heart. He clearly affirms,

> For the Word of God is not received by faith if it flits about in the top of the brain, but when it takes root in the depth of the heart that it may be an invincible defense to withstand and drive off all the stratagems of temptation . . . It is harder for the heart to be furnished with assurance than for the mind to be endowed with thought. The Spirit accordingly serves as a seal, to seal up in our hearts those very promises the certainty of which it has previously impressed upon our minds; and takes the place of a guarantee to confirm and establish them. (II.1.3, 6)

Consequently, Calvin's formal definition of faith reads like this: "Now we shall possess a right definition of faith if we call it a firm and certain knowledge of God's benevolence toward us, founded upon the truth of the freely given promise in Christ, both revealed to our minds and sealed upon our hearts through the Holy Spirit" (III.2.7). In essence, Calvin stresses that faith is assurance of God's promise in Christ and involves the whole person in the use of the mind, the application to the heart, and the surrendering of the will. Assurance is of the essence of faith.

3 Life in faith and a faithful life in the Holy Spirit

One of the central pillars of Christianity and of all human existence is that humanity is in the presence of God. One need only read the chapters on living the Christian life in the third book of the *Institutes* to observe how large a place this theme of living in the presence of God occupied in Calvin's thinking. His discussion of the life of the Christian, self-denial, cross-bearing, the right use of the present life, and meditation on the future life, his broad treatments of faith, justification, prayer, and Christian freedom, is that section of the *Institutes* that is closest to Calvin's heart.

As we tried to demonstrate in the initial section of this chapter, John Calvin was no armchair theological strategist, no mere theoretician who had little practical interest in the day-to-day life of human beings. "Empty speculations which idle men have taught apart from God's Word" (I.14.4) held little interest for him. Calvin's conviction was that Christianity is a life to be lived before the face of God.

3.1 Life in faith in the Holy Spirit

Human beings can live before the face of God only on the condition that they receive grace. Because they are sinners, they need the salvation worked out by God in history and its application to them through the work of the Holy Spirit. As Calvin says, "No one is a son of God until he has been renewed by . . . the Spirit who cleanses us anew . . . The newness of life comes from the Spirit alone."[12]

Birth and rebirth. Both are the result of the operation of the Holy Spirit. Just as nothing can live biologically apart from the power of the Holy Spirit, so no human being can come alive to God apart from the Spirit's work. In his discourse with Nicodemus, Jesus said this about the Holy Spirit: "Most assuredly, I say to you, unless one is born again, he cannot see the kingdom of God" (Jn. 3:3, NKJV).

Nicodemus, and all of us, need to be reminded that we are not capable of receiving the gospel until we begin to be new creatures.[13] As Calvin goes on to say, "It is a simple statement, that we must be born again, in order that we may be the children of God, and that the Holy

[12] John Calvin, *Commentary on the Gospel of John*, tr. William Pringle (Grand Rapids: Baker Academic, 2003), 111–12.

[13] For a complete view of Calvin's understanding of this topic, I recommend the reader to study Calvin's commentary on this whole passage—*Commentary on the Gospel of John*, chapter 3, 101–18.

Spirit is the Author of this second birth . . . we are born a second time when we are renewed in mind and heart by the grace of the Spirit."[14] Regeneration is the sovereign work of God the Holy Spirit. The initiative is with him, not with us.

The Genevan Confession of Faith of 1536, attributed to Calvin by Beza, says the following in its affirmation number VIII,

> We acknowledge that the Spirit regenerates us into a new spiritual nature. That is to say that the evil desires of our flesh are mortified by grace, so that they rule us no longer. On the contrary, our will is rendered conformable to God's will, to follow in his way and to seek what is pleasing to him. Therefore we are by the Spirit delivered from the servitude of sin, under whose power we were of ourselves held captive, and by this deliverance we are made capable and able to do good works and not otherwise.[15]

For the purpose of this chapter, it is necessary to affirm once again that ". . . newness of life and free reconciliation are conferred on us by Christ, and both are attained by us through faith" (III.3.1).

In which part of the order of salvation does faith play its vital role? The answer to this question is a matter of great and intense debate in Christian circles. Nonetheless, the vast majority of Calvin's heirs are prompt to affirm that the new life must precede faith, and is logically the cause of faith. Faith does not cause the new birth, the new birth causes faith.[16]

It is the Holy Spirit who produces the new birth and confers on us the grace and ability to believe with a true and saving faith. This true faith, ignited by the Holy Spirit, will manifest itself in all the other steps of the order of salvation, namely, the regenerated person will then repent in

---

[14] Calvin, *Commentary on the Gospel of John*, 111.

[15] The Genevan Confession was credited to John Calvin in 1536 by Beza, who said Calvin wrote it as a formula of Christian doctrine suited to the church at Geneva. More recent scholarship attributes it to William Farel but in all likelihood Calvin did have considerable influence on the document. Indeed, the records of the Senate at Geneva indicate that the Confession was presented by both Farel and Calvin to the magistrates, who received it and set it aside for more detailed examination.

[16] The reader can study more about this subject by consulting several good works written by Calvinists. Louis Berkhof, *Systematic Theology*, Part 4 (Grand Rapids: Eerdmans, 1996); Abraham Kuyper, *The Work of the Holy Spirit*, ch. 4 (Grand Rapids: Eerdmans, 1979); or the contemporary writer R.C. Sproul, *The Mystery of the Holy Trinity* (Wheaton, Ill.: Tyndale House, 1979).

faith, will be justified in Christ by faith, will walk faithfully in obedience to God, will persevere in faith on the basis of the merits of Christ and the continuous work of the Spirit, and will receive the fulfillment of his or her belief in God's faithful promises in the glorification of the saints.

Perhaps we should conclude this section by quoting a few more of Calvin's affirmations on this topic.

> Hence it follows, first, that faith does not proceed from ourselves, but is the fruit of spiritual regeneration; for the Evangelist affirms that no man can believe, unless he be begotten of God; and therefore faith is a heavenly gift. It follows, secondly, that faith is not bare or cold knowledge, since no man can believe who has not been renewed by the Spirit of God.[17]

> The illumination of our minds by the Holy Spirit belongs to our renewal, and thus faith flows from regeneration as from its source; but since it is by the same faith that we receive Christ, who sanctifies us by his Spirit, on that account it is said to be the beginning of our adoption.[18]

3.2 A faithful life in the Holy Spirit

I want to move our study now to what Calvin called the "double grace of justification and sanctification," and the ministry of the Holy Spirit in applying this double grace to the life of the elect.

3.2.1 The double grace of justification and sanctification
The call to holiness in the biblical sense cannot be adequately understood apart from an examination of the relation between justification and sanctification. Justification in the New Testament has primarily the forensic meaning of being accounted righteous before the divine tribunal. Sanctification means to be engrafted into the righteousness of God. Justification is imputed righteousness, whereas sanctification is imparted righteousness. In justification the guilt of sin is removed, and in sanctification the stain of sin. Justification makes human beings acceptable to God; sanctification makes God desirable to human beings. As Bloesch says, "Justification confers a new status whereas sanctification instills in the human being a new character. As justification is related to faith, so sanctification is related to love."[19]

---

[17] Calvin, *Commentary on the Gospel of John*, 44.

[18] Calvin, *Commentary on the Gospel of John*, 44.

[19] Donald G. Bloesch. *Essentials of Evangelical Theology*, vol. 2, *Life, Ministry and Hope* (Peabody, Mass.: Prince Press, 1988), 42.

Calvin sees this whole notion of justification and sanctification as the two complementary sides of a single coin. Here is a powerful summary,

> Christ was given to us by God's generosity, to be grasped and possessed by us in faith. By partaking of him, we principally receive a double grace: namely, that being reconciled to God through Christ's blamelessness, we may have in heaven instead of a Judge a gracious Father; and secondly, that sanctified by Christ's spirit we may cultivate blamelessness and purity of life. (III.11.1)

So grasping Christ by faith, we receive a "double grace"—justification and sanctification.

3.2.2 Justification: reconciled through Christ's blamelessness

When we grasp Jesus with the hand of faith, we are "reconciled to God through Christ's blamelessness." This is clearly Calvin's meaning, for he goes on to say, "Justified by faith is he who, excluded from the righteousness of works, grasps the righteousness of Christ through faith, and clothed in it, appears in God's sight not as a sinner but as a righteous man" (III.11.2). " . . . Therefore, we explain justification simply as the acceptance with which God receives us into his favor as righteous men. And we say that it consists in the remission of sins and the imputation of Christ's righteousness" (III.11.2).

Calvin's emphasis on faithful acceptance of Christ and his benefits as the basis of justification points toward the profound connection in his theology between justification and the substitutionary atonement effected by Christ. Believers are counted righteous because of the righteousness of Christ who stands in their place and fulfills the righteousness and obedience required by God of human beings. Since no sinner can find favor in God's eyes, he or she must be clothed in Christ in order to be justified in God's sight. The one justified has no part in works righteousness, for such a person "grasps the righteousness of Christ through faith, is clothed in it, appears in God's sight not as a sinner but as a righteous man" (III.11.2.).

The only means of reconciliation with God is in the doing and dying of Jesus on our behalf. He not only lived the life we should have lived, but also died the death we should have died. God treated Jesus like a sinner so he could treat us like Jesus.

The Father accepts us as righteous before him, not because of anything we do, and not even because of anything he has done in us, but solely because of what Jesus Christ has done for us. Distinct from the role that Christ plays as the mediating bond, the Spirit is the unitive

bond of our union with Christ. Appropriating the Augustinian notion of
the Spirit as the bond of love between the Father and the Son, Calvin
claims that the Holy Spirit is the bond by which Christ effectually unites
us to himself.

3.2.3 Sanctification: the cultivation of a blameless life through the sanctifying ministry of the Holy Spirit

But there's more. We are not only reconciled through Christ's blamelessness, we are also sanctified by Christ's Spirit so that we may
cultivate blamelessness and purity of life. Justification is joined with
sanctification.

Sanctification is a major part of God's redemptive plan and the primary work he does to develop a godly character in his people. The word
has been used in a variety of ways, but Calvin understood it as primarily pertaining to Christian conversion, and secondarily to growth in the
Christian life. Sanctification is thus very Christological, for it is through
identification with Jesus that one becomes sanctified and grows in sanctification. But as much as sanctification is Christological, it is also pneumatological, for it is the Spirit who, at every level, makes identification
with Christ both a possibility and a reality for the believer.

For Calvin, the sanctification process following the imputation of
righteousness is a direct result of being "in Christ." By giving the previously independent elements of justification and sanctification a common
ground, that is, union with Christ, Calvin was able to reconcile the free
gift of justification with the subsequent demand for sanctification.
Calvin makes justification and sanctification distinct but nonetheless
integrated; their unity is found in Christ. Here are some of his words on
this idea.

> We see that our whole salvation and all its parts are comprehended in
> Christ (Acts 4:12). We should therefore take care not to derive the least
> portion of it from anywhere else. If we seek salvation, we are taught by the
> very name of Jesus that it is "of him" (1 Cor. 1:30). If we seek any other
> gifts of the Spirit, they will be found in his anointing. If we seek strength,
> it lies in his dominion; if purity, in his conception; if gentleness, it appears
> in his birth. For by his birth he was made like us in all respects (Heb. 2:17)
> that he might learn to feel our pain (cf. Heb. 5:2). If we seek redemption,
> it lies in his passion; if acquittal, in his condemnation; if remission of the
> curse, in his cross (Gal. 3:13); if satisfaction, in his sacrifice; if purification,
> in his blood; if reconciliation, in his descent into hell; if mortification of the
> flesh, in his tomb; if newness of life, in his resurrection; if immortality, in
> the same; if inheritance of the Heavenly Kingdom, in his entrance into

heaven; if protection, if security, if abundant supply of all blessings, in his Kingdom; if untroubled expectation of judgment; in the power given to him to judge. In short, since rich store of every kind of good abounds in him, let us drink our fill from the fountain, and from no other. (II.16.19)

As Sinclair Ferguson, an outstanding theologian, pastor, writer and teacher, so clearly and profoundly summarizes,

> If we are united to Christ, then we are united to him at all points of his activity on our behalf. We share in his death (we were baptized into his death), in his resurrection (we are resurrected with Christ), in his ascension (we have been raised with him), in his heavenly session (we sit with him in heavenly places, so that our life is hidden with Christ in God), and we will share in his promised return (when Christ, who is our life, appears, we also will appear with him in glory) (Rom. 6:14; Col. 2:11–12; 3:1–3). This, then, is the foundation of sanctification in Reformed theology. It is rooted, not in humanity and their achievement of holiness or sanctification, but in what God has done in Christ, and for us in union with him. Rather than view Christians first and foremost in the microcosmic context of their own progress, the Reformed doctrine first of all sets them in the macrocosm of God's activity in redemptive history. It is seeing oneself in this context that enables the individual Christian to grow in true holiness.[20]

Calvin's preferred term for sanctification was repentance. Repentance can thus well be defined: it is the true turning of our life to God, a turning that arises from a pure and earnest fear of him; and it consists in the mortification of our flesh and of the old man, and in the vivification of the Spirit (III.3.5).

Such a definition, as applied to the life of the regenerated by the Spirit and justified by the imputation of the merits of Christ, suggests that those who are enjoying this new creation and new status will invariably find that a new life follows, and, conversely, that a new life necessarily presupposes a new birth and a new status, so that regeneration, faith, conversion, justification, and sanctification, although they may be distinct steps as individual sections of the order of salvation, and although they are individual chapters of the outlines of systematic theology, are inseparably conjoined in the life of every individual elect. In other words, a renewed heart will be followed by practical reformation, and a

---

[20] Sinclair B. Ferguson, *The Christian Life: A Doctrinal Introduction* (Edinburgh: Banner of Truth Trust, 1990), 113.

holy life can only spring from an inward change of heart. Regeneration is where everything starts. It is the spring, sanctification is the stream; if we live in the Spirit, we shall also walk in the Spirit; but we cannot walk spiritually unless we are spiritually alive.

It is equally clear that every sinner who has been quickened by the Spirit and justified by the merits of Christ will also walk in the Spirit. If he or she is alive, he or she will walk. And the inseparable connection that subsists between a new birth, faith, conversion, justification, and the progressive course of sanctification is well worth a deeper and serious consideration. Unhappily, the limits of space and time for this chapter will require leaving these other necessary themes for another opportunity.

4 Conclusion

Perhaps the best way to conclude this chapter is by bringing to the reader's attention two important statements from two very distinguished Calvinists. The first one comes from the introductory notes from Professor Warfield as he relates the participation of John Calvin to the systematizing of the doctrine of the Holy Spirit for the purpose of the edification of the church. He says,

> It is to John Calvin that we owe the first formulation of the doctrine of the work of the Holy Ghost; he himself gave it a very rich statement, developing it especially in the broad departments of "Common Grace" "Regeneration" and "the Witness of the Spirit" . . . It is simply true that these great topics received their formulation at the hand of John Calvin; and it is from him that the Church has derived them, and to him that it owes its thanks for them.[21]

The second statement is found in the concluding words of Kuyper in his monumental work about the work of the Holy Spirit. In these words he reminds us of the focus of Calvin's teaching and life. It is only God who shall receive all the final and complete glory for everything we are, and from everything we produce. Kuyper says,

> It is He that is the divine Bearer of every higher conception and holier consciousness in the children of men; He, the Spirit of the Father and of the

---

[21] Benjamin B. Warfield. "Introductory Note" in Abraham Kuyper, *The Work of the Holy Spirit* (Grand Rapids: Eerdmans, 1979), xxxiv.

Son, that exhibits all the riches of the Mediator to the Bride, making her eager to possess them; He that quickens the treasures of the Word by the spark of His holy fire, bringing them to the consciousness of the inward man. Blessed is the man to whom has been given a taste of the work of the Holy Spirit in his own experience. Blessed is the Church which in its service has proved the in-working of the Spirit of grace and of supplication. Blessed is he who, constrained to love by the love of the Holy Spirit, has opened his heart in thanks, praise and adoration, not only to the Father who from eternity has chosen and called him, and to the Son who has brought and redeemed him, but also to the Third Person in the Holy Trinity, who has kindled in him the light and keeps it burning in the inward darkness; to whom, therefore, with the Father and the Son, belongs forever the sacrifice of love and devotion of all the Church of God.[22]

Sola Deo Gloria.

---

[22] Kuyper, *The Work of the Holy Spirit*, 649.

8

Calvin on Justification in Evangelical and Ecumenical Perspective

Gabriel Fackre

Evangelical thought in the twenty-first century turns increasingly ecumenical.[1] Indeed, the focus may even be on the doctrine at hand.[2] How would Calvin on justification appear if read with an evangelical eye looking through an ecumenical lens? Inviting such scrutiny is a significant ecumenical statement set forth on the eve of our century, the 1999 Lutheran–Roman Catholic *Joint Declaration on the Doctrine of Justification*.[3] A dialogue with this declaration would be a fruitful case study of how Calvin's thought, evangelically understood, can play a vital role in ecumenical exchange. Further, it can bring out aspects of Calvin's own views on justification that deserve more attention than they receive.

---

1 For example, "Evangelicals and Catholics Together: The Christian Mission in the Third Millennium," *First Things*, 43 (May 1994), 15–22. So, too, many evangelical blogs on the internet. See also the commentary of Phyllis Tickle reported by Terry Mattingly, the religion editor of the Scripps Howard Foundation News Service (Cincinnati, Ohio), 28 November 2007. The "post-conservative" evangelical movement has its own ecumenical tendencies, as in Roger Olson, *Reformed and Always Reforming: The Postconservative Approach to Evangelical Theology* (Grand Rapids: Baker Academic, 2007). The writer of this chapter is part of that stream, as in the writer's *Evangelical Faith in Ecumenical Perspective* (Grand Rapids: Eerdmans, 1993).

[2] See Thomas C. Oden, *The Justification Reader* (Grand Rapids: Eerdmans, 2002).

[3] The Lutheran World Federation and the Roman Catholic Church, *Joint Declaration on the Doctrine of Justification*, English language edition (Grand Rapids: Eerdmans, 2000). Interestingly, it was a Reformed publishing house that printed this declaration.

"Might other ecclesial bodies sign the Lutheran–Catholic *Joint Declaration*?" The question was put to Roman Catholic ecumenist (then Bishop, now Cardinal) Walter Kasper, in 2000, at a Yale consultation on this document, which declared that whatever the continuing differences in interpretation, there is sufficient consensus on the main points of justification to render the doctrine no longer "church-dividing."[4] Probably not a simple sign-on, he replied, because of some specific Catholic–Lutheran issues, ones worked on over a long period of preliminary studies and statements.[5] However, he saw no reason why parallel agreements with Rome could not be developed, with the *Joint Declaration* as a model. Cardinal Kasper's comment suggests that whatever formal actions of this sort might be taken—and they are long shots at this time, especially for evangelicals—the "Augsburg accord" provides a fruitful occasion for wider ecumenical and evangelical inquiry.[6]

"Ecumenical" here refers to the world-wide movement, with notable twentieth-century lineage, that explores and seeks to advance intra-Christian relationships. Some stretch the meaning of the term to include, or even to signify, interfaith connections. However, the word is

---

[4] Cardinal Kasper, secretary of the Pontifical Council for the Promotion of Christian Unity, represented the Vatican at the consultation on the *Joint Declaration*. This consultation was sponsored by Yale Divinity School and Berkeley Divinity School and was held at Yale, 4–6 February 2000. Responses included papers from representatives of the Anglican and Reformed traditions as well as Catholic and Lutheran, setting the stage for the question posed. The papers, along with several others, were published in William Rusch (ed.), *Justification and the Future of the Ecumenical Movement: The Joint Declaration and the Doctrine* (Collegeville, Minn.: Liturgical Press, 2003). This chapter draws heavily on material from the writer's Reformed paper given at that conference, which appears in the latter work. It is used with the permission of Liturgical Press.

[5] An assessment of the document was made by a group of Reformed theologians, including the writer, in *The Reformed World*, 52:1 (March 2002), but no action has been taken by the World Alliance of Reformed Churches or comparable Reformed entities.

[6] In spite of Kasper's reserve, a world Methodist body has "signed on." For a more reserved response to the *Joint Declaration* with criticisms entailed, see Avery Cardinal Dulles, "Saving Ecumenism from Itself," *First Things*, 178 (December 2007), 23–7, and also Avery Cardinal Dulles, "Justification: The Growing Consensus," in Skye Fackre Gibson (ed.), *Story Lines: Chapters in Thought, Word and Deed, For Gabriel Fackre* (Grand Rapids: Eerdmans, 2002), 16–21.

employed in its intra-Christian sense in the *Joint Declaration*[7] with recognition that interfaith dialogue has an integrity of its own.[8] The meaning of "evangelical" presupposed here is that of the writer's entry in *The Westminster Dictionary of Theology*: it relates the current word to its roots in the material and formal principles of the Reformation. Thus, evangelicals, as comprising a movement subsequent to the Reformation, are "those who espoused and experienced justification [the material principle] and scriptural authority [the formal principle] in an intensified way: personal conversion and a rigorous moral life, on the one hand, and concentrated attention on the Bible as guide to conviction and behavior [as in inerrantist, infallibilist and related forms of hermeneutics], on the other, with a special zeal for the dissemination of Christian faith so conceived (evangelism)."[9]

1 Calvin on justification in its fullness

First, a review of the highlights of Calvin's doctrine of justification, with the *Joint Declaration* not far from the writer's mind. Often Calvin's understanding of justification is interpreted with its relation to the believer to the fore. Thus, the accent is on salvation of persons by grace received by faith alone, with its sequential partner, sanctification. This is fundamental to Calvin's view, and of particular importance to evangelicals. In a key section of the *Institutes*, however, Calvin develops the doctrine of justification in a more encompassing fashion. And he does it in conjunction with John 3:16, a favorite evangelical text: "For God so loved the world that he gave his only Son, so that everyone who believes in him may not perish but may have eternal life." Calvin's use and

---

[7] "2.The Doctrine of Justification as Ecumenical Problem" in *Joint Declaration on the Doctrine of Justification*, 14–15. This is hereafter referenced in the footnotes as *JD*, with section and paragraph.

[8] Better the plural, "dialogues"? The Jewish–Christian dialogue is unique, given the commonalities, and, for an increasing number of Christians, its anti-supersessionist entailments.

[9] See "Evangelical, Evangelicalism" in Alan Richardson and John Bowden (eds.), *The Dictionary of Christian Theology* (Philadelphia: Westminster, 1983), 191–2, and also similar pages in Alan Richardson and John Bowden (eds.), *A New Dictionary of Christian Theology* (London: SCM Press, 1983). For an analysis of the variety of evangelical hermeneutics, see Gabriel Fackre, *The Christian Story*, vol. 2, *Authority: Scripture in the Church for the World* (Grand Rapids: Eerdmans, 1987), 62–73.

exposition of this verse are significant because they press justification back to its origins in the being and actions of the triune God. As such, this move reflects the characteristic Reformed accent on *divine sovereignty*. Justification is therefore conceived in macrocosmic as well as microcosmic terms.

Driving justification back to its source in the sovereign will and way of God explains why "election" has been a constant in the Reformed tradition, and especially so in its evangelical stream. Indeed, the discussion of justification in the *Institutes*, in the Reformed confessions, and by classic Reformed theologians, is set in the context of predestination, an expression of the Reformed accent on the divine sovereignty. Given both the contributions and the pitfalls of this latter preoccupation, I shall return to it as an occasion for some "mutual admonition" between the Reformed and other Christian traditions. But my point is that Calvin's perspective on justification as here articulated, shaped by its stress on the divine sovereignty, puts to the fore the will and way of the triune God manifest in Christ. This theocentric, rather than anthropocentric, reading is illustrated by Calvin's frequent counsel on matters of election regarding the assurance of salvation, in which he urges attention not to the state of our faith, weak and ambiguous as it always is, but to the trustworthiness of the divine deed and promise.[10] For him, Jesus Christ is the "mirror" in which we look for that assurance, an assertion, not unlike that of Luther's allusion to Christ as the "Book of Life," which makes for the same confidence, a theme, echoed, in fact, in the *Joint Declaration* itself.[11]

In a chapter entitled "The Beginning of Justification," Calvin takes the doctrine on a "writ large" to "writ small" journey, following the grand narrative of John 3:16, albeit stated in the causal categories of his time.

> The efficient cause of our eternal salvation the Scripture uniformly proclaims to be the mercy and free love of the Heavenly Father toward us; the material cause to be Christ, with the obedience by which he purchased righteousness for us; and what can be the formal or instrumental cause

---

[10] John Hesselink traces this in Calvin's catechism, and throughout the *Institutes*. See I. John Hesselink, *Calvin's First Catechism: A Commentary* (Louisville, Ky.: Westminster John Knox, 1997), 96–8.

[11] John Calvin, *Institutes of the Christian Religion*, vol. II, tr. Henry Beveridge (Grand Rapids: Eerdmans, 1957), Book III, chapter 24, section 5 (henceforth referred to in the text by book chapter and section). See the reference to the Book of Life in *The Formula of Concord*, art. 11, sect. 2. And in *JD*, all the paragraphs on assurance, in 4.6, 34–6.

but faith? John includes the three in one sentence when he says, "God so loved the world, that he gave his only begotten Son, that whosoever believeth in him should not perish but have everlasting life" (John iii. 16). (III.14.17)[12]

Calvin adds that Paul gathers up the three in his own formulas in both Romans and Ephesians (III.14.17). And he describes justification elsewhere in explicitly Trinitarian terms: "The efficient cause of our salvation is placed in the love of the Father; the material cause in the obedience of the Son; the instrumental cause in the illumination of the Spirit, that is in faith . . ." (III.14.21).[13]

Calvin's wide-ranging view was carried forward in traditional Reformed teaching where the objective and subjective are brought together, as in the 1559 French Confession of Faith, which declares that "on the cross we are reconciled to God and justified before him" and then "made partakers of this justification by faith alone."[14] However, this is increasingly done in a decretal manner, as in the distinction between "the decree of justification" and "justification . . . made in this life," yet always entailing the narrative of the electing Father, the accomplishing Son, and the *applicatio salutis* by the work of the Holy Spirit.[15]

For all the Reformed scholasticism that pressed justification in a supralapsarian direction, with its elect "us" and reprobate "them," another Reformed theologian was to come along who gave the same priority to election, and even double predestination, but took these things in a quite different direction. Thus Karl Barth speaks of a divine decision and action into which the whole of the human race is gathered up in the judgment rendered on the cross,

> the verdict in Jesus Christ by which man is justified. This justifying sentence of God is His decision in which man's being as the subject of that act [of human pride] is repudiated, his responsibility for that act, his guilt is pardoned, canceled and removed . . . Justification definitely means the sentence executed and revealed in Jesus Christ and His death and resurrection,

---

[12] Calvin includes a fourth, citing Paul, a "final cause" being the demonstration of the divine righteousness.

[13] See also II.17.17, where John 3:16 is exegeted and causal language deployed.

[14] "The French Confession of Faith, 1559," XVII, XX, in Arthur C. Cochrane (ed.), *Reformed Confessions of the 16th Century* (Philadelphia: Westminster Press, 1966), 150, 151.

[15] See Heinrich Heppe, *Reformed Dogmatics*, tr. G.T. Thompson (Grand Rapids: Baker Book House, 1978), 557 and *passim*.

the No and Yes with which God vindicates Himself in relation to covenant-breaking man.[16]

True to the Reformed stress on the divine sovereignty, this verdict is rendered, "certainly on behalf of man, but primarily for His [God's] own sake, to assert His honor and to maintain His glory against him."[17]

The worthy stress on the *objective* dimension of justification found in both traditional Calvinist and contemporary Barthian views does have its downside. It can become so dominant that it threatens the importance of the *subjective*, issuing, in the former, in a hyper-Calvinist double pre-destination in which the significance of the decision of faith, so important for evangelicals, erodes, or, in the latter, in justifying faith becoming the knowledge given to some of the justification of all, rather than the graced medium through which the baptized believer is justified before God. I shall return to this later when considering the admonitions that the Reformed, including evangelicals in that tradition, need to hear from others. For now, let it be noted that the defining characteristic of Reformed teaching on justification as expounded by Calvin and others who follow him here is that the microcosmic "for me" is placed against the background of the macrocosmic "for the world." Justification in Calvin and, thereafter, in much of the Reformed tradition, begins in the sovereign purposes of the Father, is accomplished in the saving person and work of the Son, and is brought through the church to persons by the Holy Spirit's gift of faith and its sanctifying consequences. Interestingly, the Leuenberg Agreement (between Lutheran and Reformed churches) on justification sets forth this wide-ranging view.

> The true understanding of the gospel was expressed by the fathers of the Reformation in the doctrine of justification. In this message, Jesus Christ is

---

[16] Karl Barth, *Church Dogmatics*, IV/1, tr. Geoffrey Bromiley (Edinburgh: T&T Clark, 1956), 145, 96. See also how Eberhard Jungel has incorporated this aspect into his reading of justification, a factor that may have contributed to his initial questioning and later endorsement of the *Joint Declaration*. Eberhard Jungel, "On the Doctrine of Justification," *International Journal of Systematic Theology*, 1:1., 25: "The centre of Christian proclamation is that the history of Jesus Christ is not a private affair, but that, in that history, God's history with the whole of humanity takes place, and that in this one, unique history there occurs a liberating change of direction in the deadly fate of sin-dominated humanity . . ." See also his *"Kardinale Probleme," Stimmen Der Zeit, Heft* 11 (November 1999), 727–35.

[17] Barth, *Church Dogmatics*, IV/1, 9.

acknowledged as the one in whom God became [human] and bound himself to [humanity]; as the crucified and risen one who took God's judgment upon himself and in so doing demonstrated God's love to sinners . . . Through his word, God by His Holy Spirit calls all . . . to repent and believe, and assures the believing sinner of his righteousness in Jesus Christ. Whoever puts his trust in the gospel is justified in God's sight for the sake of Jesus Christ and is set free from the accusation of the law. In daily repentance and renewal he lives within the fellowship in praise of God and in the service of others.[18]

2 Mutual affirmation and mutual admonition

Ecumenist Harding Meyer commended the linkage of the concept "mutual admonition" to that of "mutual affirmation" in the formula put forward by yet another Lutheran–Reformed exchange, the recent four-year segment of a long-term North American Lutheran–Reformed dialogue.[19] Mutual affirmation applies where there is a unity discernible in core beliefs. But what of the undeniable disunities? He found, approvingly, that "a clearly *positive function* is being attributed to the differences, the function of mutual admonition, or mutual correction, of being 'no trespassing signs.'"[20] The *Joint Declaration* and its predecessor texts, while not using the same language, strike just these notes, speaking of the "concerns" and "emphases" of each partner and the "salutary warnings" rightfully given one to another.[21] This mutuality of concern and recognition of difference as

[18] "The Message of Justification as the Message of the Free Grace of God," *Leuenberg Agreement*, II/6/1, in *Invitation to Action: The Lutheran-Reformed Dialogue, Series III, 1981–1983*, eds. James E. Andrews and Joseph A. Burgess (Philadelphia: Fortress Press, 1984), 67.

[19] Keith F. Nickle and Timothy Lull, *A Common Calling: The Witness of Our Reformation Churches in North America Today* (Minneapolis: Augsburg Fortress, 1993), 65–7.

[20] Harding Meyer, "A Common Calling in Relation to International Agreements," *Ecumenical Trends*, 23:8 (September 1994), 4/116–5/117.

[21] As in Karl Lehmann, *The Condemnations of the Reformation Era: Do They Still Divide?* ed. Wolfhart Pannenberg, tr. Margaret Kohl (Minneapolis: Augsburg Fortress, 1990), 38, 40, 52, 68–9. The *JD* cites approvingly the phrase from the foregoing—"salutary warnings"—as the continuing function of the sixteenth-century condemnations (5/43). For an attack on the idea of differences as "emphases" and "concerns," see Gerhard Forde, "What Finally To Do About the (Counter-) Reformation Condemnations," *The Lutheran Quarterly*, XI (1997), 3–16.

occasions for admonition about emphases is an ecumenical "method" that has four aspects: (1) each partner admonishes the other not to caricature its position, attributing to it views it does not espouse; (2) each partner admonishes the other that what it accents does not, as such, exclude what the other emphasizes; (3) each partner admonishes the other to avoid reducing the meaning of the doctrine to its particular emphasis; (4) each partner admonishes the other to receive its own accent as a charism necessary for a fuller understanding of the doctrine. The affirmation/admonition formula is an ecumenical contribution to relating an evangelically-oriented appropriation of Calvin on justification to the Lutheran–Roman Catholic document at hand, as well as to intra-Reformation issues.

3 The *Joint Declaration* on justification

And what of that newly stated Lutheran–Roman Catholic convergence on the doctrine of justification? Are there any grounds for "mutual affirmation"—Reformation and Roman—including evangelical Calvinist and contemporary Catholic? Interestingly, it is John 3:16 that heads the biblical section of the *Joint Declaration*: "For God so loved the world that he gave his only Son, so that everyone who believes in him may not perish but may have eternal life." Out of it grows a key paragraph of the *Joint Declaration*, which describes "justification" in this way,

> In faith we together hold the conviction that justification is the work of the triune God. The Father sent his Son into the world to save sinners. The foundation and presupposition of justification is the incarnation, death and resurrection of Christ. Justification thus means that Christ himself is our righteousness, in which we share through the Holy Spirit in accord with the will of the Father. Together we confess: by grace alone, in faith in Christ's saving work and not because of any merit on our part, we are accepted by God and receive the Holy Spirit, who renews our hearts while equipping and calling us to good works.[22]

Intrinsic to its meaning, therefore, is its Christological "foundation and presupposition," the justifying work of the incarnate Son. Indeed, such is the very "heart" of the gospel,

> We also share the conviction that the message of justification directs us in a special way toward the heart of the New Testament witness to God's

---

[22] *JD*, 3/15.

saving action in Christ: it tells us that because we are sinners our new life is solely due to the forgiving and renewing mercy that God imparts as a gift and we receive in faith, and never can merit in any way.[23]

The description of justification that grounds it in the deed of God done in Jesus Christ reflects a key theme in the documents on which the *Joint Declaration* draws. Such is the case in the U.S. dialogue, italicized there for emphasis,

> Our hope of justification and salvation rests in Christ Jesus and on the gospel whereby the good news of God's merciful action in Christ is made known; we do not place our ultimate trust in anything other than God's promise and saving work in Christ."[24]

The European dialogue takes note approvingly of this accent in its U.S. counterpart,

> . . . the barricades can be torn down only if we remain unswervingly on the Christological foundation expressed—with particular reference to the doctrine of justification—in the Lutheran–Catholic dialogue that took place in the United States: "Christ and his gospel are the source, center and norm of Christian life, individual and corporate, in church and world. Christians have no other basis for eternal life and hope of final salvation than God's free gift in Jesus Christ, extended to them in the Holy Spirit."[25]

George Tavard echoes the importance of this Christocentricity in his "ecumenical study" of the doctrine of justification, declaring it the determinative "focus" of Roman Catholic–Reformation convergences.[26] The *Joint Declaration* puts it in just those terms as the basis for the agreement,

> Lutherans and Catholics share the goal of confessing Christ in all things, who alone is to be trusted as the one Mediator (1 Tim 2:5f) through

---

[23] *JD*, 3/17.

[24] "Common Statement, Introduction," *Justification by Faith: Lutherans and Catholics in Dialogue VII*, eds. H.G. Anderson, T. Austin Murphy, Joseph A. Burgess (Minneapolis: Augsburg, 1985), 16.

[25] "Justification," in Lehmann, *Condemnations of the Reformation Era*, 36. The quotation is from "Common Statement," *Justification by Faith: Lutherans and Catholics in Dialogue* VII, 71.

[26] George Tavard, *Justification: An Ecumenical Study* (New York: Paulist Press, 1983), 62.

whom God in the Holy Spirit gives himself and pours out his renewing gifts.[27]

What is identified as a "Christological foundation" is, as can be seen in the last citation as well as in the earlier ones, a *Trinitarian–Christological* one. The person and work to which allusion is made are about "the Father" who "sent his Son into the world to save sinners," and thus "justification is the work of the triune God" (3/15). Markus Barth in his biblical study of justification refers to this Trinitarian reading as a narrative view of justification, a "drama" found in "the liturgies of the Eastern Church and the passion plays of the Western Church, and the works of a writer like Dorothy Sayers," which traces justification from the electing decision of the Father through the being and doing of the Son to a receiving faith busy in love, and on to its eschatological finale, "five days in the process of justification."[28]

An encompassing view, of course, includes "justification writ small," the *pro me* dimension. In addition to the above reference, the *Joint Declaration* asserts that it comes to us

> through Christ alone when we receive this salvation in faith . . . God's gift through the Holy Spirit who works through Word and Sacrament . . . and who leads believers into the renewal of life . . . (3/16); When persons come by faith to share in Christ, God no longer imputes to them their sin and through the Holy Spirit effects in them an active love (4.2/22); We confess together that sinners are justified by faith in the saving act of God in Christ . . .They place their trust in God's gracious promise by justifying faith, which includes hope in God and love for him (4.3/25).

In carefully worded sentences, the *Joint Declaration* moves narratively from "God's gracious promise" and "Christ's saving work" to the Holy Spirit's gift of faith and the renewal of life by sharing in Christ. What is said here *together* is: (1) "justifying faith" is "trust" in the "promise" that they may share in Christ and his righteousness; (2) this faith that justifies cannot be what it is without "hope" and "love," or, otherwise stated, without genuine "renewal" and thus "the equipping and calling to good works"; (3) throughout, all is by grace alone, excluding any human merit. Whatever other questions are involved—the naming of sin ruled by grace, the language and location of merit, the assurance of

---

[27] *JD*, 3/18.

[28] Markus Barth, *Justification: Pauline Texts Interpreted in the Light of the Old and New Testaments*, tr. A.M. Woodruff III (Grand Rapids: Eerdmans, 1971), 21.

salvation—a consensus is asserted on these three points of subjective soteriology.

The "foundation" has as its superstructure justification *pro nobis* and *pro me*. To change the figure, justification "writ large" runs down toward justification "writ small." Or again, the drama moves to the next act when what is wrought by the Father through the Son in the Spirit in "the incarnation, death and resurrection of Christ" comes to us in the church by faith. At this ecclesial cum personal end of justification, "Christ himself is our righteousness, in which we share through the Holy Spirit in accord with the will of the Father" (3/15). Justification "achieved" in Christ as "applied" to us by a grace received in faith is a veritable participation in the person and his Trinitarian relations. To "share in Christ" (4.2/22) is by the "will of the Father" through the power of the Holy Spirit. Thus, whatever the metaphor—up from the foundation, down from large to small, or along the path of the drama—it is Trinitarian–Christological all the way.

By locating the standard discussion of justification—"subjective soteriology" entailing questions about the relation of faith to works, faith to love and hope, forensic to infused grace—in the larger Trinitarian– Christological framework, the *Joint Declaration* and its predecessor documents have set forth an encompassing understanding of the doctrine. This *focus* had its effect, I believe, on the way long-standing disputed questions were treated. Indeed, it made for a new *method* of discussing them. The agreement on the Trinitarian–Christological focus constituted a "mutual affirmation" on commonalities that enabled the partners to judge the continuing differences as no longer church-dividing. In a time when Jesus Christ, the Mediator, this "one Word we have to trust and obey," must be boldly declared, divided Christians find one another so they might speak it with one voice and live it out together.[29]

Contributing to the possibilities of mutual affirmation for Calvinists is the use of John 3:16 in the *Joint Declaration* in a way comparable to its use by Calvin. So understood, justification is viewed as "the work of the triune God." The Father sent the Son to "save sinners" in "the incarnation, death and resurrection of Christ." The Holy Spirit applies the benefits of Christ's righteousness, without "any merit on our part," by grace through faith "while equipping and calling us to good works."

---

[29] A conclusion to which Avery Dulles seems to come, after raising questions about how much reconciliation of views was in fact achieved by the *Joint Declaration*, see "Two Languages of Salvation: The Lutheran-Catholic Joint Declaration," *First Things*, 98 (December 1999), 29–30.

If a Calvin-drenched "Amen" can be said to an encompassing view of justification, why not with it an evangelical echo? Here is an "inclusive" understanding of justification *received*. Justifying personal faith is union with Christ and his righteousness. "Union with Christ" is a long-standing Reformed accent with its roots in Calvin.[30] This union means that faith shares in Christ's righteousness, the obedience of Christ fulfilling what we could not and cannot. It also means the pouring into us of "the life flowing forth from the Godhead" (IV.17.9), a theme stressed by the self-described "evangelical catholic" Mercersburg theology of the Reformed tradition.[31] This faith that shares in Christ cannot be what it is without its consequences in a grateful obedience. Justification is distinct from, but also inseparable from, sanctification (4.2/22), language identical to Calvin's and that of the Westminster Larger Catechism.[32] Conjoined are the "declaration of forgiveness" and "the renewal of life," or in Reformed

---

[30] So Calvin: "So long as we are without Christ and separated from him, nothing which he suffered and did for the salvation of the human race is of the least benefit to us. To communicate the blessings which he received from the Father, he must become ours and dwell in us . . . Christ is not external to us, but dwells in us: and not only unites us to himself by an undivided bond of fellowship, but by a wondrous communion brings us daily into closer connection, until he becomes altogether one with us (III.1.1, and III.2.24). For a searching inquiry into the Reformed view(s) on union with Christ, see Lewis B. Smedes, *All Things Made New: A Theology of Man's Union with Christ* (Grand Rapids: Eerdmans, 1970). For an incarnational cum sacramental reading of Calvin, see John Williamson Nevin, *The Mystical Presence and Other Writings on the Eucharist*, eds. Bard Thompson and George H. Bricker, Lancaster Series on the Mercersburg Theology, vol. 4 (Philadelphia: United Church Press, 1966).

[31] See Nevin, *Mystical Presence, passim*. The parallels here with the new Finnish school of Luther studies is interesting, speaking as it does of faith as both "favor" and "gift." See Tuomo Mannermaa on the "Doctrine of Justification and Trinitarian Ontology," in Colin Gunton (ed.) *Trinity, Time and Church: A Response to the Theology of Robert Jenson* (Grand Rapids: Eerdmans, 2000), 139–45, and his extended inquiry into the same, *Hat Luther eine trinitarische Ontologie? Luther und die trinitarische Tradition: Okumenische und philosophische Perspectiven* (Erlangen: Luther-Verlag, 1994).

[32] "Although sanctification be inseparably joined with justification, yet they differ, in that God in justification imputeth the righteousness of Christ; in sanctification, his Spirit infuseth grace, and enableth to the exercise thereof; in the former sin is pardoned; in the other, it is subdued" (Westminster Larger Catechism, Q. 77).

language, "regeneration." And like Calvin's accent on the divine sovereignty, grace is all the way down from justification's "beginning" to its ending, as "all persons depend completely on the saving grace of God for their salvation"(4.1/19).

So far so good. But, as with the Lutheran–Catholic exchange, there is "evidently a clear difference."[33] Following the "method" of mutuality of admonition, here is a conceivable give-and-take, Reformed cum evangelical admonitions given and received.

4 Admonitions

4.1 To Roman Catholic and Lutheran together

4.1.1 The theocentric and anthropocentric
If the achievement of the *Joint Declaration* is related to its grounding in a Trinitarian–Christological focus of the doctrine, then this "theocentric" reading should not be obscured by an anthropocentric reductionism. That is, a sole focus on the *pro me* of justification—whether justification is received by faith alone, or by faith, hope and love, whether by imputation or impartation—will miss the big picture of justification. Whatever criticisms we might have of Karl Barth's theology, his reinterpretation of justification did bring again to the fore its Trinitarian–Christological grounding, and may well have played some background role in the new consensus.[34] Here is an admonition to keep our ecumenically oriented evangelical eyes on the ultimate source and center of justification in the sovereign freedom and mercy of God manifest in the person and work of Jesus Christ. In the light of its own periodic drifts into anthropocentricity, this is both an evangelical and a Reformed self-admonition as well as one to its partners.

---

[33] Lehmann, *The Condemnations of the Reformation Era*, 47.

[34] The possibility of this is suggested by Barth's commendation of Hans Kung's study, *Justification: The Doctrine of Karl Barth and a Catholic Reflection*, tr. Thomas Collins, Edmund E. Tolk and David Granskou, with a letter by Karl Barth (New York: Thomas Nelson, 1964), xix–xxii. However, there is a misreading of Barth by Kung traced in detail by Alister McGrath in "Justification: Barth, Trent and Kung, *The Scottish Journal of Theology*, 34 (1981), 517–29. Nevertheless, Kung's discernment of the "objective" dimension in Barth as "the primary and decisive aspect of the theology of justification" (72) is correct and the point at hand. This point is made in Eberhard Busch's essay written against the background of the current discussion of the *JD*, "Karl Barth's Doctrine of Justification," typescript, 1,999.

4.1.2 Baptism

A refrain in the *Joint Declaration* is the linkage of justification and baptism.[35] The biblical witness and ecumenical consensus expressed in the Lima document of the World Council of Churches, *Baptism, Eucharist and Ministry*,"[36] is reinforced and interpreted in accord with a common Catholic and Lutheran stress on the *solidarity* of Christ with ecclesial givens, in this case in the firm linkage of baptism and justification. A Calvinist admonition based on its *sovereignty* accent points to the dangers of allowing this "haveability" of Christ (Bonhoeffer) to slide into a domestication of grace that precludes both the freedom of God and the response of faith. Yes, given Calvin's "high" view of the Lord's Supper, contra Zwinglian distancing of Deity from the meal, the promise of the divine Presence in the sacramental means of grace is trustworthy, but its efficacy is inextricable from the response of personal faith so fundamental to evangelical piety. Interestingly, this accent is found in the ecumenical document, BEM: "The necessity of faith for the reception of the salvation embodied and set forth in baptism is acknowledged by all churches."[37] Surely this is a further area of inquiry, one where mutual admonition is in order, for a sovereignty that separates baptism from justifying grace by an abstract doctrine of predestination or universalism, on the one hand, or by an anti-sacramental memorialism, on the other, is as reductionist as a haveability emphasis that takes grace captive in our means or excludes the place of personal faith by a too narrowed *ex opere operato* interpretation.

4.1.3 The public import of justification

The twin Calvin-grounded Reformed accents on "sovereignty" and "sanctification"[38] press the question of the implications of any agreement on justification for public issues. Calvin's Geneva set the precedent for asserting the Lordship of Christ over the social-economic and political realms. Why not more about this in the *Joint Declaration*? Surely this undeveloped theme must be taken up in subsequent exploration of the agreement. Here Moltmann has a point in his judgment that "we need a

---

[35] *JD*, 4.4, 28–30.

[36] As in "The Meaning of Baptism," *Baptism, Eucharist and Ministry* (Geneva: World Council of Churches, 1982), 2–4.

[37] *Baptism, Eucharist and Ministry*, 3.

[38] For the argument that these are defining characteristics of the Reformed tradition, see the writer's section in Gabriel Fackre and Michael Root, *Affirmations and Admonitions* (Grand Rapids: Eerdmans, 1997), 21–43.

common doctrine of righteousness-justice-justification for the 21st century."[39]

The warrants for this are found in the view of justification writ both large and small in the document itself. As seen through Calvinist eyes, the redemption of the world through the will of the Father and obedience of the Son—the Trinitarian–Christological justification writ large—is inseparable from *sanctification* writ large. As well as being declared forgiven by the act of God in Christ, the world has been given both the gift and the call to holiness.[40] Divine sovereignty over the public sector has been worked out in the Reformed tradition, following Calvin's initial formulations, in terms of the royal office of Christ within the *munus triplex*.[41] The victory of Christ over the powers and principalities extends his rule over the counting house and voting booth as well as the soul and the church, calling the public world to accountability and rendering possible its transformation.[42]

The grounds for public witness lie in sanctification writ small as well as large. As the objective sanctification of the world provides the range of concern and hope, the impulse and mandate in the Christian life come from the inseparability of justification and sanctification *pro me*. The personal justification of the sinner is inseparable from a personal sanctification that issues in public witness to the rule of Christ over the political, social and economic principalities and powers, one implemented by the church as well as persons in the struggles for social change. Thus a Calvinist/Reformed reading of justification will press for its "world-formative" outworking.[43]

---

[39] Mimeographed remarks of Moltmann, *"Bermerkungen zur 'Gemeinsamen Erklarung zur Rechfertigungslehre' (GER) und zur 'Gemeinsamen offiziellen Feststellung' (GOF),"* 2.

[40] Developed by Barth in IV/2 as the exaltation of the Son, and the transformation of the world *de iure*.

[41] For an illuminating treatment of the three-fold office, see Geoffrey Wainwright, *For Our Salvation: Two Approaches to the Work of Christ* (Grand Rapids: Eerdmans, 1997), 97–186.

[42] A theme explored by W.A. Visser t'Hooft in *The Kingship of Christ* (New York: Harper & Brothers, 1948) and expressed with power during World War II by Karl Barth in his *Letter to Great Britain from Switzerland* (London: Sheldon Press, 1941), 9–11ff.

[43] On the Reformed tradition as "world-formative," see Nicholas Wolterstorff, *When Justice and Peace Embrace* (Grand Rapids: Eerdmans, 1983), 3–22.

4.1.4 Evangelism

Some have made the charge that Calvin's view of election cuts the nerve of evangelism and that the *Institutes* provides little warrant for missionary activity.[44] However, recent research on the range of Calvin's writings, including the *Institutes*, has shown otherwise.[45] Not only is the mandate for evangelism integral to Calvin's theology, but the actual practice of it by Calvin and those associated with the early Reformed movement was much in evidence.[46] Evangelism, as the natural accompaniment of a belief in the cruciality of a personal appropriation by saving faith of justification writ large is, therefore, integral to Calvin's belief system.

The question must be asked of the signatories of the *Joint Declaration*: Where is this evangelistic passion to be found in this document? At best, it is by implication, given the "justification writ small" end of the narrative. However, nowhere does it appear with the prominence to which it is due. Calvin, read with an evangelical eye, must enter an admonition at this point. No doctrine of justification can reach its proper end without the evangelistic imperative.

4.2 To the Lutheran tradition

Lutheran–Reformed differences emerged early in Reformation history, and especially so in Christological and eucharistic controversies, rooted in the respective *capax* and *non capax* accents, Lutheran "solidarity" and Reformed "sovereignty."[47] In the specifics of justification, the Reformed stress on the divine sovereignty moves naturally, via its focus on election, to "justification writ large," and in so doing challenges any Lutheran preoccupation with the *pro me*, as noted by Barth.[48] From Luther's anxiety and quest for assurance, through Lutheran pietism to modern existentialisms from Kierkegaard to Bultmann, the subjective

---

[44] For example, A. Mitchell Hunter, *The Teaching of Calvin, a Modern Interpretation* (Glasgow: Maclehose, Jackson & Co., 1920), 154.

[45] See the well-documented essay by Ray Van Neste, "John Calvin on Evangelism and Missions" in *The Founders Journal*, published on the internet by *Founders Ministries*.

[46] Calvin personally trained clergy with a view to evangelizing Europe and the British Isles. The "Venerable Company of Pastors" was one vehicle for such missionary work. See James Galyon data in blog, "Europe," 24 March 2007.

[47] See Fackre and Root, *Affirmations and Admonitions*, 1–43, and Gabriel Fackre, "What the Lutherans and Reformed Can Learn From One Another," *The Christian Century*, 114:18 (4–11 June 1997), 558–61.

[48] Barth, *Church Dogmatics*, IV/1, 150.

dimension of justification has bulked large, threatening to obscure its objective Trinitarian–Christological foundations, ones basic to the agreement reached in the *Joint Declaration*.

Sanctification, another key Calvinist accent, is acknowledged as well in the Lutheran tradition. However, fears of works–righteousness and ambivalence toward, or rejection of, the third use of the law, have so surrounded it with qualifications that the stress on believer's persistence in sin (the Lutheran *simul*) can obscure the possibilities of growth in grace, and counsel retreat into an apolitical "interiorization of piety." Here Calvin and the Reformed tradition joins the Roman Catholic in a history of insistence on the inextricability of sanctification and justification, as well as a stress on the political mandates and possibilities of sanctification.[49] Yet for all the kinship between Reformed stress on the regenerate life and the Catholic accent on the renewed life, serious differences continue. Thus, some Calvinist admonitions to the other partner.

4.3 To the Catholic tradition

Calvin joins Luther in the emphasis on the radical character of the Fall. Nothing in us warrants or contributes to the sinner's salvation. Hence the shared Reformation commitment to the *sola fide*. And with it the common suspicion that a Roman Catholic theology of infused righteousness invites human capacities into an equation that has room only for the divine pardon received by faith. The stress on the empowering grace of sanctification, which the Reformed tradition shares with the Roman Catholic, is located, therefore, as sequential to justification, not coterminous with it as in the latter.

The same determination to give the sovereign God, rather than ourselves, all that is due is at work in Calvinist wariness about inordinate claims for human institutions, as well as persons. The church is such an institution. While different from all others, being the Body of Christ, divine as well as human, and steward of the means of saving grace, it is not the unqualified extension of the incarnation. Further, no organ constitutes the whole Body, each being a part awaiting final wholeness and

---

[49] Indeed, Calvin uses the language of "reward" alluded to in the *JD*'s "Catholic understanding" of good works, declaring that "the works of the faithful are rewarded with the promises which God gave in his law to the cultivators of righteousness and holiness," surrounding it, however with the "threefold" qualification that works have nothing to do with justification, which comes by faith alone, that they are God's own gift being so honored, and that their manifest pollutions are pardoned (III.17.3).

healing. Hence Reformed cautions about delimiting the promises of God to any part of the household of faith. Given its finitude and flaws, the church on earth is always *ecclesia reformata et semper reformanda*.

And, a final admonition, one earlier noted. Calvin's right stress on the divine sovereignty reminds Catholics as well as Lutherans of the limitations of a too exclusively anthropological reading of justification, with the *pro me* preoccupation neglecting its *soli Deo gloria* source and center.

4.4 To the Reformed—from Lutherans and Roman Catholics

What happens when Reformed "sovereignty" takes charge of the doctrine of justification, rather than being a perspective on it? The answer is in the history of Reformed thought on predestination. From Calvin forward, the sound impulse to ground justification in the eternal purposes of God has been accompanied by a speculative leap into the workings of the divine mind as to who is elect and who is reprobate. Thus sovereignty cum justification eventuates in theories of double predestination, and controversies as to whether such is supralapsarian, infralapsarian or sublapsarian and the like.[50] All this with a painful history of internal disputes in which one reductionism matches another, from the Dutch Arminians forward. In the same Reformed stream appears the twentieth-century Karl Barth with his new reading of the sovereign purposes of God, Christ being both elect and reprobate, with all of humanity in the Son's humiliation and exaltation. But then comes the lingering suspicion of a structural universalism, however disavowed.[51] In all cases a single-minded stress on the divine sovereignty seems to be at work.

The admonitory corrective from other traditions comes in various ways. Lutherans have treated election as the existential testimony of the believer to the surety of election rather than a speculative theory on the source of belief and unbelief.[52] And Catholics have been concerned to assert the call for personal responsibility. These are legitimate admonitions. They counsel us to read "predestination" as the confidence that God shall be "all and in all" without the speculative details. And to be

---

[50] For a comparison of the three, see Paul K. Jewett, *Election and Predestination* (Grand Rapids: Eerdmans, 1985), 83–105.

[51] On the disavowal, see Karl Barth, *Church Dogmatics*, IV/3/1, tr. G.W. Bromiley (Edinburgh: T&T Clark, 1961), 477–8.

[52] See this observation in the North American Lutheran–Reformed dialogue, Keith F. Nickle and Timothy F. Lull (eds.), *A Common Calling: The Witness of Our Reformation Churches in North American Today* (Minneapolis: Augsburg Fortress, 1993), 54–5.

wary of "the tendency to 'explain' the doctrine by pressing the logical implications of the divine sovereignty,"[53] thereby erasing personal responsibility. Wiser, argues the evangelical Reformed theologian Paul Jewett, to assert *both* a pure electing grace *and* human responsibility, and understand that as a "paradox" that may be explored but can never be explained.[54]

And admonitions are in order as well concerning aspects of Reformed thinking on sanctification. Certainly, the Lutheran stress on the *simul* must be clearly heard, reminding the Reformed tradition of its own professed realism about continuing sin, one too often overwhelmed by its stress on growth in the sanctified life. Reinhold Niebuhr made the point tellingly vis-à-vis the Reformed tradition's exuberant historical expectations and theocratic pretensions when it too quickly transferred the confidence in personal growth to the public arena. Sin persists at every stage of historical advance and therefore sobriety demands awareness of the hubris that plagues the most "righteous" social, economic and political causes. While the Roman Catholic tradition also finds a large place for sanctification and growth, personal and public, its ecclesial lens discerns another dimension of holiness not limited to personal or social performance. Thus the "holy" church of the creeds has to do with a conferred status, not an achieved one: a warning to Reformed tendencies, with their legitimate emphasis on discipline, not to reduce the church to the morally and spiritually "pure." This is a temptation not only of Reformed, but of all evangelicals—the temptation to make too simple a division between the converted and the unconverted, the former no longer subject to the Lutheran *simul*. It is a tendency that can be carried over into the political arena, with a too simple, even Manichean, distinction between the righteous "us" and the unrighteous "them," producing a self-righteous fury and lack of self-criticism in the "righteous," with disastrous results.[55] The Reformed tradition, in its evangelical form and otherwise, needs to remember that sin persists in the righteous. Further, it needs an enlargement of its concept of the church when it limits it to the "visible saints," for holiness finally roots, as the Reformed

[53] Jewett, *Election and Predestination*, 78.

[54] Jewett, *Election and Predestination*, 92, 106–9, 113–14, 136–9. See also Donald Baillie on "the paradox of grace," in *God Was in Christ: An Essay on Incarnation and Atonement* (New York: Charles Scribner's Sons, 1948), 114–18. So, too, Jonathan Edwards on "efficacious grace" in "Miscellaneous Remarks," Works, vol. VII, iv, 48.

[55] See the writer's *The Religious Right and the Christian Faith* (Grand Rapids: Eerdmans, 1982, 1983), *passim*.

tradition should know from its own accent on sovereignty, not in our performances but in God's purposes.[56] Indeed, it has not been without this emphasis on the objectivity of Christ's ecclesial grace, as in the evangelical catholic Mercersburg theology.[57]

Jürgen Moltmann's "remarks" on the *Joint Declaration* bring together both the strengths and weaknesses of the Reformed focus on sovereignty and sanctification.[58] While rightly urging the development of a new dimension of the doctrine for a new age (thus the characteristic Reformed stress on a contextualizing *semper reformanda* under the divine sovereignty), and pressing the justice import of justification (thus the characteristic Reformed stress on society's sanctification), his comments can be read as diminishing the personal problematic of sin as the concern of another era, reflected in the medieval practice of penance, to be superseded now by the twenty-first century problematic of justice.[59] Yet the sin in the heart of every human being is a perennial problem entailing the perennial word of judgment and justification, a truth to which evangelicals must constantly bear witness.

5 Conclusion

The vision of a genuine ecumenism will be diminished if the evangelical voice is not heard. For evangelicals, Calvin's full-orbed understanding of justification as he expounds it in his interpretation of John 3:16 is an important entry point into the ecumenical discussion.[60] Remarkably, the

---

[56] Ironically, here the Reformed tradition's own teaching of the divine sovereignty, muted in this case by its zealous partner, sanctification.

[57] See the earlier references to Nevin and Schaff.

[58] Moltmann, *Bermerkungen zur "Gemeinsamen Erklärung zur Rechtfertigungslehre."*

[59] The industrial missioner Horst Symanowski anticipated Moltmann's point in the heyday of the secular theologies of the 1960s in oft-repeated words: In the sixteenth century, Luther lay awake at night asking, "How can I find a gracious God?" Today we lie awake asking, "How can we find a gracious neighbor?" Thus yesterday the problem was the alienation between the soul and God, today it is the estrangement between black and white, rich and poor, East and West, men and women, young and old. This is not an either/or today, either in a descriptive or normative sense.

[60] Interestingly, Charles Taylor in his widely acclaimed, and rightfully so, enlargement of his Gifford lectures, argues that Calvin fatefully narrows the Christian understanding of faith, thus preparing the way for secularization

most important recent exchange in those fora, *The Joint Declaration on the Doctrine of Justification*, makes use of that text as the point of orientation for Lutheran–Roman Catholic convergences, in spite of inherited controversies, and continuing differences on this doctrine. Yet one must ask if the personal appropriation of "justification writ large" integral to Calvin's understanding can be given its full due without that evangelical voice. Surely this is an invitation to evangelicals to find their place at this table and make their witness.

(cont.) *A Secular Age* (Cambridge: The Belknap Press of Harvard University Press, 2007), 77–80, 82, 86, 104–5, 107, 119, 230–1, 278, 624, 652, 772). In this chapter, we find another Calvin, one whose understanding of justification enlarges rather than narrows that understanding.

9

Taking up Our Cross: Calvin's Cross Theology of Sanctification

Sung Wook Chung

Ever since the sixteenth century European Reformation, Martin Luther has been regarded as a theologian of the cross.[1] This is because Luther stressed the cross as the event of God's self-revelation of who he is, what he does, and what he requires of human beings. In particular, in the *Heidelberg Disputation* of 1518, Luther delineated the essence of genuine theology as the theology of the cross of Jesus Christ, contrasting the theology of the cross with the theology of glory. As Paul Althaus has argued, "The theology of glory knows God from his works; the theology of the cross knows him from his sufferings."[2] This means that the theology of the cross focuses on God's sufferings, pain, disgrace, and death rather than his power, glory, and majesty in order that we may know who God is.

Then, what about John Calvin? Calvin has been regarded as one of the representative theologians for the second generation of the Reformation. He has been praised for his astute mind, systematic and critical thinking, clear and concise style of writing, and great passion for the truth and the glory of Jesus Christ. Calvin, however, has never been viewed as a theologian of the cross! Rather, he has been well known for his emphasis upon God's absolute sovereignty over the entire universe and the whole course of human history and his infinite glory manifested in the natural

---

[1] See Alister E. McGrath, *Luther's Theology of the Cross* (Oxford: Basil Blackwell, 1985) and W. von Loewenich, *Luther's Theologia Crucis* (Erlangen: Luther-Verlag, 19544).

[2] Paul Althaus, *The Theology of Martin Luther*, tr. Robert C. Schultz (Philadelphia: Fortress Press, 1966), 26.

order.[3] For this reason, Calvin has been misunderstood as a theologian of glory in contrast to Luther, a theologian of the cross.

It is indeed true that Calvin did not stress the cross as the event of God's self-revelation. He seldom discussed the cross in the context of the doctrine of God or the theology proper. Rather, he put a greater emphasis on the cross as the event of Christ's atonement for sinners. According to Calvin, Christ paid all penalties for sinners (penal sub-stitutionary atonement) through his suffering and death on the cross. Therefore, the cross is the place where God's redemptive purpose was accomplished. It is undeniable that Calvin's soteriological under-standing of the cross permeates the entire scope of his theological thinking.[4]

It is important to appreciate, however, that Calvin can be viewed as a theologian of the cross, especially in relation to his doctrine of sanctifi-cation. Unlike Luther, Calvin put a greater stress on the significance of taking up the cross in the context of the progressive sanctification of the Christian.[5] For Calvin, without taking up our cross, we cannot be con-formed to the image of Jesus Christ. Calvin affirmed repeatedly that when God called us to be the disciples of Jesus Christ, he called us to take up our cross. In this sense, we can think of Calvin as a theologian of the cross in the context of the doctrine of sanctification. In the following sections of this article, I will explore and peruse Calvin's cross theology of sanctification, meticulously following his own arguments in the *Institutes of the Christian Religion*.[6] And then I will suggest that Calvin's cross theology of sanctification should be recaptured and revived in the context of modern evangelical theology. First of all, then, let us move to Calvin's theology of self-denial before exploring his cross theology of sanctification.

[3] See Susan E. Schreiner, *Theater of His Glory: Nature and the Natural Order in the Thought of John Calvin* (Grand Rapids: Baker Academic, 2001).

[4] See John F. Jansen, *Calvin's Doctrine of the Work of Christ* (London: James Clarke, 1956).

[5] Ronald S. Wallace and John H. Leith treated this theme in their works on Calvin's doctrine of the Christian life. See Ronald S. Wallace, *Calvin's Doctrine of the Christian Life* (Grand Rapids: Eerdmans, 1961), 68–77, and John H. Leith, *John Calvin's Doctrine of the Christian Life* (Louisville, Ky.: Westminster John Knox, 1989), 74–82.

[6] John Calvin, *Institutes of the Christian Religion*, ed. John T. McNeill, tr. Ford Lewis Battles, The Library of Christian Classics XXI (Philadelphia: Westminster Press, 1960 (1559)). (Hereafter, referred to in the text by book, chapter and section.)

1 Self-denial: the context of Calvin's cross theology of sanctification

1.1 Self-denial in relation to God

In the seventh chapter of the third book of his *Institutes*, Calvin explores and discusses the character and nature of the Christian life, which is closely connected with the process of sanctification. For Calvin, the sum of the Christian life is the denial of ourselves. This truth is grounded upon the fact that we are not our own masters, but belong to God. Calvin continues to contend,

> We are not our own: let not our reason nor our will, therefore, sway our plans and deeds. We are not our own: let us therefore not set it as our goal to seek what is expedient for us according to the flesh. We are not our own: in so far as we can, let us therefore forget ourselves and all that is ours. Conversely, we are God's: let us live for him and die for him. We are God's: let his wisdom and will therefore rule all our actions. We are God's: let all the parts of our life accordingly strive toward him as our only lawful goal. (III.7.1)

For Calvin, the Christian life should be characterized by self-denial. The pursuit of self-interest and self-aggrandizement is the characteristic of the life without God. Since the Christian is born again through the grace of God, his or her life should be a life of following the leading of the Lord alone. In this sense, self-denial is the core of the character of the Christian life and the process of being conformed to the image of Jesus Christ.

Calvin describes the life of self-denial as the life lived in the service of God. He exhorts, "Let this therefore be the first step, that a man depart from himself in order that he may apply the whole force of his ability in the service of the Lord" (III.7.1). Calvin believed firmly that God called the Christian out of the power of sin, death, and the devil so that he or she may concentrate all of his or her energy on serving the Lord in an appropriate manner. Then what does Calvin mean by "service" here? Calvin continues,

> I call "service" not only what lies in obedience to God's Word but what turns the mind of man, empty of its own carnal sense, wholly to the bidding of God's Spirit . . . The Christian philosophy bids reason give way to, submit and subject itself to, the Holy Spirit so that the man himself may no longer live but hear Christ living and reigning within him. (III.7.1)

Calvin construed the Christian's life in the service of the Lord not as a life of self-isolation or world-negation but as a life in submission to the leading of the Holy Spirit. The Christian should subject himself or herself to the sovereign reign of the Lord Jesus Christ who lives within the Christian in and through the Holy Spirit. In this context, one can find an aspect of Calvin's pneumatological doctrine of sanctification. Calvin believed firmly that apart from the person and work of the Holy Spirit, the Christian's sanctification can never be achieved. Benjamin B. Warfield's comment on Calvin's being a theologian of the Holy Spirit seems to be appropriate.[7]

According to Calvin, another characteristic of the Christian life of self-denial is devotion to God. In other words, the Christian should focus on God and his commandments throughout his or her entire life. Devotion to God is an essential factor in the process of sanctification. Calvin contends,

> For when Scripture bids us leave off self-concern, it not only erases from our minds the yearning to possess the desire for power, and the favor of men, but it also uproots ambition and all craving for human glory and other more secret plagues. Accordingly, the Christian must surely be so disposed and minded that he feels within himself it is with God he has to deal throughout his life. (III.7.2)

For Calvin, the Christian life should demonstrate the characteristic of a life centered and focused on God alone. The Christian should remember that he or she is accountable to God alone. God is the only one with whom the Christian should have things to do. The Christian should learn how to glorify God alone throughout his or her life. Calvin continues, "In this way, as he will refer all he has to God's decision and judgment, so will he refer his whole intention of mind scrupulously to Him" (III.7.2). Calvin argues that without self-denial no one is able to succeed in pursuing a life not tainted by pride, arrogance, ostentation, avarice, lasciviousness or effeminacy. It is because all evils come from self-love.[8]

Calvin is convinced that Christians who lead the life of self-denial trust in God's blessings alone. They do not greedily strive after riches and honors. Calvin exhorts the Christian to believe "that every means

---

[7] Benjamin B. Warfield, "Calvin the Theologian," in *Calvin and Augustine*, ed. Samuel G. Craig (Phillipsburg, N.J.: Presbyterian & Reformed Publishing Co., 1956), 484–5.

[8] This demonstrates Augustine's considerable impact upon Calvin's theological thought.

toward a prosperous and desirable outcome rests upon the blessing of God alone. When this is absent, all sorts of misery and calamity dog us" (III.7.9). Furthermore, self-denial helps the Christian to bear all kinds of adversities. This is one of the most valuable spiritual blessings that come from the life of self-denial. Heavenly and spiritual blessings have nothing to do with self-confidence or self-glorification. Calvin states, "Therefore, he alone has duly denied himself who has so totally resigned himself to the Lord that he permits every part of his life to be governed by God's will. He who will be thus composed in mind, whatever happens, will not consider himself miserable nor complain of his lot with ill will toward God" (III.7.10).

1.2 Self-denial in relation to other people

For Calvin, self-denial gives benefits to the Christian not only in his or her relationship with God but also in his or her relations with other people. The first benefit is that self-denial gives the Christian the right attitude toward other people. When the Christian is immature, he or she is prone to self-pride and self-love. The Christian's self-pride leads him or her to belittle and revile the gifts and endowments that other people manifest. The Christian's self-love causes him or her to exaggerate hatefully the faults in others. Although the Christian is commanded by the Lord to forgive and cover the faults and transgressions of others, the immature Christian is inclined to accuse others of their weaknesses, flattering himself or herself. In this sense, Calvin believed that self-denial is one of the most dramatic signs of the Christian's maturity. He argues,

> For thus we are instructed to remember that those talents which God has bestowed upon us are not our own goods but the free gifts of God; and any persons who become proud of them show their ungratefulness. "Who causes you to excel?" Paul asks. "If you have received all things, why do you boast as if they were not given to you? (III.7.4)

According to Calvin, the second benefit of self-denial is that it leads the Christian to proper helpfulness toward his or her neighbors. For Calvin, the Christian is commanded by the Lord to love her neighbors as herself. In order to accomplish what the Lord requires of us, our self-denial is absolutely essential. Calvin raises a valid question: "For how can you perform those works which Paul teaches to be the works of love, unless you renounce yourself, and give yourself wholly to others?" (III.7.5). In addition, Calvin connects the idea of self-denial with the important theological notion of stewardship. For Calvin, only those Christians who have learned how to deny themselves are able to lead their lives as genuine stewards of God's blessings. "We are stewards of everything God has conferred on us by which we are able to help our neighbor, and are required to render account of our stewardship" (III.7.5). By sharing their possessions generously with others, Christians demonstrate that they are true Christians who have learned how to renounce themselves. For Calvin, self-renunciation is closely connected with the practice of Christian stewardship and generous giving.

2 Taking up our cross: a part of self-denial

2.1 Christ's cross and our cross

In the eighth chapter of the third book of his *Institutes*, Calvin discusses the notion of bearing the cross as a part of self-denial (III.8.1). First of all, he compares Christ's cross and our cross. According to Calvin, God "puts his own children to a definite test," namely, "a hard, toilsome, and unquiet life, crammed with very many and various kinds of evil" (III.8.1). This means that the life of the Christian is characterized by suffering, hardships, and tribulations. God allows his children to suffer in order that they may become mature and complete in terms of their obedience to God. Even Christ was not exempt from this test. Calvin continues,

> For even though that Son was beloved above the rest, and in him the Father's mind was well pleased, yet we see that far from being treated indulgently or softly, to speak the truth, while he dwelt on earth he was not only tried by a perpetual cross but his whole life was nothing but a sort of perpetual cross. (III.8.1)

This means that Christ our Lord not only died on the cross for our sins but also lived a life of the cross. This means that Christ himself took up his own cross in order to set up a great example for the Christian.

It is important to note here that Calvin believed that Christians called as Christ's disciples are not exempt from the life of the cross, that is, "from the condition to which Christ our Head had to submit, especially since he submitted to it for our sake to show us an example of patience in himself" (III.8.1). Then, what is the purpose of the life of the cross? Why does God allow us to suffer? It is because God's vision toward the Christians is for them to be conformed to the image of the Son of God. Christians are destined to imitate the character of Jesus Christ through participating in the life of the cross and suffering. Calvin also believed that sufferings are necessary and essential for our becoming conformed to the image of Jesus Christ. We as Christians do not fall into despair in conditions of hardship and tribulation. Rather, we are full of comfort and hope for the glories that we will enjoy in the future with the Lord Jesus Christ. Calvin continues,

> Hence also in harsh and difficult conditions, regarded as adverse and evil, a great comfort comes to us: we share Christ's sufferings in order that as he has passed from a labyrinth of all evils into heavenly glory, we may in like manner be led through various tribulations to the same glory. (III.8.1)

On the basis of this conviction, Calvin urges Christians to have a positive attitude toward sufferings and afflictions. It is because "the more we are afflicted with adversities, the more surely our fellowship with Christ is confirmed. By communion with him the very sufferings themselves not only become blessed to us but also help much in promoting our salvation" (III.8.1). For Calvin, Christians can welcome the sufferings and adversities as divine instruments and blessings in and through which God makes them Christlike children of his own. Just as Jesus Christ learned obedience through what he suffered, so the Christian learns how to obey God's holy and perfect will. Taking up our own cross is the only way for us to be conformed to the image of our Lord Jesus Christ.

In this context, it is important to appreciate that Calvin's understanding of the significance of sufferings in the Christian life is squarely contrasted to the Buddhist understanding of suffering. According to the Buddhist doctrines, suffering is the ultimate evil from which human beings must be liberated through the practice of eight paths of moral righteousness. Suffering does never promote human morality but rather human morality emancipates human beings from the vicious cycle of suffering, namely, the cycle of life, death, and rebirth. Although we can find many significant points of contact between Christianity and Buddhism, it is undeniable that there is a profound difference in terms of the significance and place of suffering in the life of the Christian and of the Buddhist.[9]

---

[9] See my article, "Christianity and Buddhism: Significant Points of Contact and their Missional Implications," in *Christ the One and Only: A Global Affirmation of the Uniqueness of Jesus Christ*, ed. Sung Wook Chung (Grand Rapids: Baker Academic, 2005), 223–40.

2.2 The benefits of taking up our cross

Calvin discusses the concrete benefits of our taking up our own cross. First of all, Calvin says that the cross leads us to perfect trust in God's power (III.8.2). Human beings are naturally prone to pride and self-confidence. Christians are no exception. We Christians are also easily inclined to self-praise and self-aggrandizement unless our weakness and defilement are shown vividly to us. Thus, God allows us to suffer physically, mentally, and spiritually in order that we may realize our need to trust in and depend on God alone. Calvin argues,

> As we are by nature too inclined to attribute everything to our flesh— unless feebleness be shown, as it were, to our eyes—we readily esteem our virtue above its due measure. And we do not doubt, whatever happens, that against all difficulties it will remain unbroken and unconquered. Hence we are lifted up into stupid and empty confidence in the flesh; and relying on it, we are then insolently proud against God himself, as if our own powers were sufficient without his grace. (III.8.2)

Therefore, the cross makes a great contribution to the self-knowledge of Christians. By allowing his children to be afflicted by all kinds of suffering and adversities, God humbles them and leads them to a deeper knowledge of themselves. Considering Calvin's emphasis upon the importance of the knowledge of God and of ourselves in relation to the true Christian piety[10] it is very important to appreciate that for Calvin there is a close connection between suffering and our advancement in self-knowledge.[11]

Second, the cross helps the Christian experience God's faithfulness and gives him hope for the future, Calvin says (III.8.3). When the Christian is afflicted by tribulations and hardships, she is reminded that God has promised to be with her in suffering. Therefore, because God keeps his word faithfully by helping the Christian endure tribulations, she experiences God's faithfulness. God's unchanging faithfulness is demonstrated conspicuously especially when Christians are in sufferings

---

[10] Calvin said in the very beginning of the first chapter of the first book of the *Institutes*, "Nearly all the wisdom we possess, that is to say, true and sound wisdom, consists of two parts: the knowledge of God and of ourselves."

[11] On Calvin's doctrine of the knowledge of God and ourselves, see the following two classical works: Edward A. Dowey, Jr., *The Knowledge of God in Calvin's Theology* (Grand Rapids: Eerdmans, 1994) and T.H.L. Parker, *Calvin's Doctrine of the Knowledge of God* (Edinburgh: Oliver & Boyd, 1969).

and tribulations. For Calvin, "The saints, therefore, through forbearance experience the fact that God, when there is need, provides the assistance that he has promised" (III.8.3). In addition, the cross gives the Christian an opportunity to gain invincible hope for the future. His hope is grounded upon God's promise and faithfulness. Calvin continues,

> And it is of no slight importance for you to be cleansed of your blind love of self that you may be made more nearly aware of your incapacity . . . to distrust yourself that you may transfer your trust to God; to rest with a trustful heart in God that, relying upon his help, you may persevere unconquered to the end; to take your stand in his grace that you may comprehend the truth of his promises; to have unquestioned certainty of his promises that your hope may thereby be strengthened. (III.8.3)

By saying this, Calvin affirms that many good things spring from the cross. Sufferings, tribulations, and hardships are not the signs of God's curse or abandonment but rather testimonies of God's promises and faithfulness as well as our hope for a better future in terms of our progressive sanctification and being conformed to the image of our Lord Jesus Christ.

Third, the cross trains the Christian to patience and obedience, Calvin states (III.8.4). According to Calvin, God makes the best use of sufferings and adversities in order to test the patience of Christians and to teach them to obey. Through the afflictions of the saints, Calvin argues, God teaches them what forbearance is: "They are also instructed by the cross to obey, because thus they are taught to live not according to their own whim but according to God's will" (III.8.4).

Fourth, the cross is medicine for the Christian's wantonness, Calvin says (III.8.5). Calvin reminds the Christians that the wanton impulse of their flesh is powerful. Thus, according to Calvin, "If we even for a moment softly and indulgently treat that impulse," it leads us to shake off God's yoke and to rebel against his law (III.8.5). In this context, Calvin compares God to a great physician. The cross is medicine that God employs to cure the wantonness of the Christians. Calvin argues,

> Thus, lest in the unmeasured abundance of our riches we go wild; lest, puffed up with honors, we become proud; lest, swollen with other good things—either of the soul or of the body, or of fortune—we grow haughty, the Lord himself, according as he sees it expedient, confronts us and subjects and restrains our unrestrained flesh with the remedy of the cross. (III.8.5)

This means that as the heavenly physician, God makes use of the cross as remedy and medicine for the spiritual diseases of pride, haughtiness, and wantonness. Assuredly, Calvin acknowledges that God does not treat all Christians equally. He "treats some more gently but cleanses others by harsher remedies" (III.8.5). It is important to understand, however, that God leaves no Christian free and untouched by the cross because he knows that all Christians are diseased in some way and he wants them to be healthy and mature spiritually.

Fifth, the cross comes to Christians as God's fatherly chastisement (III.8.6). When Christians committed grave sins against God in the past, and become obstinate and stubborn in disobedience in the present, God brings the cross of suffering and adversities to them in order that the cross may correct their past transgressions and present stubbornness. However, it is important to appreciate that God's chastisement is not a sign of his condemnation of us but rather a sign of his "fatherly" love and care. Calvin continues,

> Therefore, also, in the very harshness of tribulations we must recognize the kindness and generosity of our Father toward us, since he does not even then cease to promote our salvation. For he afflicts us not to ruin or destroy us but, rather, to free us from the condemnation of the world. (III.8.6)

This means that as God's legitimate children Christians maintain a very different attitude toward God's chastisement from unbelievers. For Calvin, unbelievers, "like slaves of inveterate and double-dyed wickedness, with chastisement become only worse and more obstinate" (III.8.6).[12] However, the Christians attain repentance and correction because they are freeborn and legitimate sons and daughters.

2.3 The cross in persecution and its comfort

So far we have examined Calvin's discussion of Christians taking up their cross in the process of progressive sanctification. This section will deal with a different kind of cross that the Christian should take up, namely, the cross of persecution (III.8.7). In the process of sanctification, Christians encounter not only physical sufferings and natural disasters but also deliberate persecution from the evil world. In other words, they are called to experience persecution for righteousness' sake and for the

---

[12] In *Institutes* III.4.33, Calvin calls God's chastisement for unbelievers "judgment of vengeance" in contrast to "judgment of chastisement" for believers.

sake of the name of Jesus Christ. According to Calvin, "Not only they who labor for the defense of the gospel but they who in any way maintain the cause of righteousness suffer persecution for righteousness" (III.8.7). Because the world hates the Christians, they can undergo exile, poverty, contempt, prison, disgrace, and even death for the sake of the gospel and for Christ's name.

Calvin encourages Christians not to lose heart in the face of these persecutions. Rather, they should remember that persecutions are disguised blessings from God the Father. He argues,

> But when the favor of our God breathes upon us, every one of these things turns into happiness for us. We ought accordingly to be content with the testimony of Christ rather than with the false estimation of the flesh. So it will come about that we shall rejoice after the apostle's example, "whenever he will count us worthy to suffer dishonor for his name". (III.8.7)

This means that if we lose our possessions for the sake of the gospel, "in God's presence in heaven our true riches are thus increased" (III.8.7). If we are expelled from our own family, "then we will be the more intimately received into God's family" (III.8.7).

For Calvin, when the Christian suffers from persecution, he can find comfort and consolation in the Lord (III.8.8). Calvin continues,

> Scripture, then, by these and like warnings gives us abundant comfort in either the disgrace or the calamity we bear for the sake of defending righteousness. Consequently, we are too ungrateful if we do not willingly and cheerfully undergo these things at the Lord's hand; especially since this sort of cross most properly belongs to believers, and by it Christ wills to be glorified in us, just as Peter teaches. (III.8.8)

It is important to note here that Calvin encourages the Christian to have a cheerful heart when she undergoes persecutions for the sake of the gospel and Jesus Christ. One may raise a valid question, however, on how the Christian can maintain cheerfulness in the context of the extreme pain and agony that her persecutors bring to her. In response to this legitimate question, Calvin answers, "Yet such a cheerfulness is not required of us as to remove all feeling of bitterness and pain. Otherwise, in the cross there would be no forbearance of the saints unless they were tormented by pain and anguished by trouble" (III.8.8). This means that in spite of all kinds of pain, agony, bitterness, and torment the Christian can keep a cheerful heart internally with the help of the Holy Spirit.[13] "Here his cheerfulness shines if, wounded by sorrow and grief, he rests in the spiritual consolation of God."[14]

2.4 The difference between Christianity and Stoicism

For Calvin, the cheerfulness that the Christian can maintain internally with the help of the Holy Spirit's spiritual consolation is the very thing that distinguishes Christianity from Stoicism. Calvin believed that Stoicism as a philosophical system emphasizes insensibility and indifference in the face of pain and agony because of its fatalistic tendencies. Calvin also said that among his contemporary Christians "there are new Stoics, who count it depraved not only to groan and weep but also to be sad and care ridden" (III.8.9). It is important to appreciate in this context that Calvin rejected Stoic indifference and fatalism.[15] He states,

> You see that patiently to bear the cross is not to be utterly stupefied and to be deprived of all feeling of pain. It is not as the Stoics of old foolishly described "the great-souled man": one who, having cast off all human qualities, was affected equally by adversity and prosperity, by sad times and happy ones—nay, who like a stone was not affected at all . . . Yet we have nothing to do with this iron philosophy which our Lord and Master has condemned not only by his word, but also by his example. (III.8.9)

This means that the Christian has every right to give expression to his pain and sorrow. In order to explicate this idea more vividly, Calvin appeals to the example of our Lord Jesus Christ. "For he groaned and wept both over his own and others' misfortunes . . . He openly proclaimed, 'Blessed are those who mourn'" (III.8.9).

In this context, Calvin acknowledges frankly that Christians may experience a contradictory state of mind when they are afflicted. This is because they are in the process of sanctification toward the goal of spiritual maturity and completion. They are not yet perfect. Although they have already been liberated from the rule of sin, sin still remains within

---

[13] Besides the word "cheerfulness," Calvin uses the phrase "sweet obedience." See I. John Hesselink, "Calvin, Theologian of Sweetness" (unpublished paper delivered as The Henry Meeter Center for Calvin Studies Spring Lecture, 9 March 2000), 10–16.

[14] Hesselink, "Calvin," 10–16.

[15] On Calvin's evaluation of Stoicism, see Charles B. Partee, *Calvin and Classical Philosophy* (Leiden: E.J. Brill, 1977), 105–25.

them. In the meantime, their hearts still harbor a contradiction between their natural sense, which flees and dreads what it feels to be adverse to itself, and their disposition to godliness, which even through these difficulties presses toward obedience to the divine will (III.8.10).

This means that Christians may have a double will in the face of extreme hardships such as martyrdom. However, Calvin encourages them to keep their patience firm in adverse situations by saying the following,

> This, therefore, we must try to do if we would be disciples of Christ, in order that our minds may be steeped in such reverence and obedience toward God as to be able to tame and subjugate to his command all contrary affections. Thus it will come to pass that, by whatever kind of cross we may be troubled, even in the greatest tribulations of mind, we shall firmly keep our patience . . . But the conclusion will always be: the Lord so willed, therefore let us follow his will. Indeed, amid the very pricks of pain, amid groaning and tears, this thought must intervene: to incline our heart to bear cheerfully those things which have so moved it. (III.8.10)

Calvin urges his fellow Christians to demonstrate cheerfulness in bearing the cross of persecution. This cheerfulness is the very thing that distinguishes Christians from other people, including Stoics. The Christians are free to express their feelings of sadness, grief, and even despair in the face of tribulations. However, as disciples of Jesus Christ, they should remember that they are required to follow the steps of their Lord with cheerful hearts with the help of the Lord's comfort and the Holy Spirit's empowerment. Calvin wants his fellow Christians not to forget that by testing us through afflictions, God wants us to be equipped with righteousness and equity. Furthermore, through patiently bearing the afflictions, God wants us to grow in salvation, which means that he wants us to be mature and conformed to the image of the Lord Jesus Christ. Therefore, Calvin concludes,

> In patiently suffering these tribulations we do not yield to necessity but we consent for our own good. These thoughts, I say, bring it to pass that, however much in bearing the cross our minds are constrained by the natural feeling of bitterness, they are as much diffused with spiritual joy. From this, thanksgiving also follows, which cannot exist without joy; but if a cheerful and happy heart—and there is nothing that ought to interrupt this is us—it thus is clear how necessary it is that the bitterness of the cross be tempered with spiritual joy. (III.8.11)

2.5 Bearing the cross and meditation on the future life

In the ninth chapter of the third book of the *Institutes*, Calvin explores another important dimension of the cross theology of sanctification. He examines the relationship between the cross of tribulations and meditation on the future life in heaven. For Calvin, when the Christian takes up his cross of sufferings and tribulations, he is given an opportunity to reflect on his future life with the Lord in heaven. This means that the Christian's bearing the cross has a close connection with her eschatological faith and spirituality. By bearing the cross, the Christian grows in renouncing worldly desires as well as in meditating upon his death and life beyond it, heavenly immortality. Calvin contends,

> Whatever kind of tribulation presses upon us, we must ever look to this end: to accustom ourselves to contempt for the present life and to be aroused thereby to meditate upon the future life. For since God knows best how much we are inclined by nature to a brutish love of this world, he uses the fittest means to draw us back and to shake off our sluggishness, lest we cleave too tenaciously to that love. (III.9.1)

For Calvin, the cross of tribulations and sufferings helps the Christian maintain her hope of eternity after death as vividly as possible. Although the Christian has already been born again, she is inclined to the desires of the flesh and of the world unless she is awakened from time to time by the cross of hardships. God knows this fact so well that he makes the best use of the cross of tribulations to awaken Christians from their spiritual slumber and sluggishness. By allowing the Christian to experience the miseries and vanities of this life, God draws her attention to the eternal life of bliss and true happiness. For Calvin, this is another aspect of God's fatherly and gracious care and love toward his children. Calvin states,

> To counter this evil the Lord instructs his followers in the vanity of the present life by continual proof of its miseries. Therefore, that they may not promise themselves a deep and secure peace in it, he permits them often to be troubled and plagued either with wars or tumults, or robberies, or other injuries. (III.9.1)

For Calvin, God is well aware that the cross is one of the best instruments through which he can teach the Christian what this life is truly like. God wants his children to realize that the good things of this present life are "uncertain, fleeting, vain, and vitiated by many intermingled evils" (III.9.1). For this reason, God frequently employs the cross of tribulations for the purpose of educating his children. "Then only do we rightly advance by the discipline of the cross, when we learn that this life, judged in itself, is troubled, turbulent, unhappy in countless ways," Calvin remarks (III.9.1). From God's perspective, the cross is essential, especially because "the present life has very many allurements with which to entice us, and much show of pleasantness, grace, and sweetness wherewith to wheedle us" (III.9.1). Therefore, only when the Christian is afflicted by the cross of the miseries of this present life, can he hold the world in contempt and strive with all his heart to meditate upon the eternal life of the future. In his wise and fatherly providence, God allows his children sufficient afflictions to keep them holding fast to the hope for immortality. In this sense, the true Christian can maintain a positive attitude toward the cross of sufferings. With the help of the cross, the Christian advances in patience with all kinds of hardships and in obedience to the will of God. This means that bearing the cross is an essential aspect of the Christian's sanctification, that is, the process of becoming conformed to the image of the Son of God.

3 The need for recapturing Calvin's cross theology of sanctification

3.1 In the Western and North American context

I believe that Calvin's cross theology of sanctification must be recaptured and revived in the context of the global evangelical movement and theology. In particular, the need to recapture Calvin's valuable insights in the context of the Western and North American evangelical movement is far more urgent than it has ever been. As many evangelical historians and theologians have pointed out,[16] contemporary evangelicalism in the West has been suffering from all kinds of spiritual diseases.

---

[16] See David Wells, *God in the Wasteland: The Reality of Truth in a World of Fading Dreams* (Grand Rapids: Eerdmans, 1994); David Wells, *Losing Our Virtue: Why the Church Must Recover Its Moral Vision* (Grand Rapids: Eerdmans, 1999); David Wells, *No Place for Truth or Whatever Happened to Evangelical Theology* (Grand Rapids: Eerdmans, 1993); Michael S. Horton, *Made in America: The Shaping of Modern American Evangelicalism* (Eugene, Ore.: Wipf & Stock Publishers, 1998); Mark Noll, *The Scandal of the Evangelical Mind* (Grand Rapids: Eerdmans, 1995); Alister E. McGrath, *Evangelicalism and the Future of Christianity* (London: Hodder & Stoughton, 1996).

Among them are the pursuit of instant gratification, impatience with hardships, indifference to discipleship, and shallowness of spirituality. One conspicuous example is the fact that the divorce rate among evangelical Christians is higher than that among non-evangelicals and non-Christians.[17] This is a truly shameful situation.

For maintaining a Christian marriage, one of the most essential things is mutual patience. If husbands are not patient with their wives and vice versa, marriage cannot stand. The married life itself and the hardships arising from it is the cross that Christians should take up. Since as evangelical Christians we are not well trained and disciplined in bearing our own cross in the life of marriage, we have been treacherously unsuccessful in setting a good example for the world. We have miserably failed to shine our light to the world.

In this context, we need to recapture the biblical insights of Calvin's theology of the cross. We should remember that our present life is supposed to be filled with all kinds of sufferings, hardships, and tribulations. We should not forget that God allows us to suffer them in order that we may grow spiritually as we imitate our Lord's patience. By permitting us to be afflicted, God wants us to grow in the knowledge of, and obedience to, the will of God. Therefore, we should not seek to escape from any difficulties and hardships that our married life brings to us. Rather, we should bear the cross of marriage and in doing so progress in the process of our sanctification.

In this postmodern and relativistic society, people tend to pursue instant gratification of their desires and needs. Thus, if husbands do not satisfy instantly the desires of wives, wives get upset easily. This results in dispute, fighting, violence, and extramarital affairs. Although evangelical Christians should be different from unbelievers, sadly, it is not the case. This means that the evangelical movement has been failing in its task of producing spiritually mature Christians. Unfortunately, it is undeniable that most evangelical Christians have been demonstrating their spiritual immaturity and childishness. In order to overcome this problem, we need to learn from Calvin's cross theology of sanctification.

---

[17] In addition to the divorce rate among evangelical Christians, we have other examples, such as indifference to the poor and to the need for social justice, lack of stewardship and generous giving, lack of passion for evangelism and mission, and lack of an intellectual defense of the evangelical truth.

3.2 In the Chinese context

I believe that Calvin's profound insights should be revived in the Asian context as well. It is important to appreciate that evangelical Christians are the objects of severe persecution in many Asian countries. In particular, Chinese Christians have been suffering serious persecution from Chinese society in general and the Chinese government in particular. I admire those Chinese brothers and sisters who have been bearing their cross of persecution for the sake of the gospel and the name of the Lord Jesus Christ. Many of them have demonstrated their impregnable faithfulness to the Lord. Many have been imprisoned, tortured, and even martyred. We have numerous wonderful stories and testimonies about those persecuted Christians and martyrs.

Although our Chinese brothers and sisters have been doing a great job in taking up their cross of persecution, I believe that Calvin's cross theology of sanctification can make a significant contribution toward equipping and reinforcing Chinese evangelical Christians who are struggling with sufferings and persecutions. Calvin's insights can instruct Chinese Christians, showing them that they can suffer persecutions with cheerful hearts with the help and empowerment of the Holy Spirit. Probably, many Chinese evangelical Christians resonate with Calvin's thought that God allows them to suffer persecution in order that they may grow in patience and obedience, taste the glories of heaven, and experience God's comfort and consolation.

3.3 In the Korean context

I also believe that Calvin's cross theology of sanctification should be retrieved in the Korean context. Korean Christianity has been enjoying an exponential growth for the last 30 years. As a result, Korea now has the largest churches in the whole globe and Korea is sending a great number of missionaries all over the world, second only to America.[18] In spite of these praiseworthy facts, Korean evangelical Christianity has recently been suffering from spiritual sluggishness and numerical stagnation. In particular, prosperity theology grounded upon the secular philosophy of positive thinking, has been so prevalent in Korean evangelicalism that many Korean evangelicals do not want to take up their own cross and are not ready for persecution for the sake of the gospel

---

[18] See my unpublished article, "Korean/Korean-American Evangelical Theology and Spirituality: Its Contribution to the Diversity and Unity of Evangelical Tradition," delivered in the AAR Annual Meeting of 2007.

and righteousness. Simply speaking, it is undeniable that many Korean Christians believe in Jesus Christ for the sake of wealth, health, and peace of mind.

One of the most unfortunate consequences of this trend is that Korean evangelicalism has been losing its attractiveness to unbelievers, who think of evangelical Christianity as not differentiated from other religious traditions. For them, evangelical Christianity is merely an option among other mediocre religions. In particular, Korean youth and young adults are leaving the church, and evangelical Christianity is no longer a meaningful and attractive option.

In this context, Calvin's cross theology of sanctification may be able to remind Korean evangelical Christians that they are not sent to the world to be healthy and wealthy but rather to suffer for righteousness' sake and for the glorious name of Jesus Christ. In addition, Calvin's theology of the cross can help Korean evangelical Christians remember that they are called to be disciples of Jesus Christ, and can deny and renounce themselves and take up their own cross of tribulations and persecutions.

4 Conclusion

I have argued so far that John Calvin was a theologian of the cross: a different kind from Martin Luther. Calvin was a theologian who emphasized bearing the cross in the process of the Christian's sanctification. If Calvin's cross theology of sanctification is recaptured and revived in the global evangelical context, global evangelicalism will be able to get another chance for renewal and maturity. In this sense, we can conclude that Calvin bequeathed an invaluable legacy for global evangelicalism. And the future of global evangelicalism depends on how creatively it will be able to reappropriate the profound theological insights of its forbear.

10

Election, Predestination and the Mission of God

Antonio Carlos Barro

1 Introduction

Election and predestination are largely interchangeable and are used as synonyms in much Reformed literature. However, there are some who will point out that the terms differ. The difference lies in the fact that election is the power God exercises to choose who will be saved, while predestination is the actual work of salvation. God chooses and has all the power to carry on that election until it is accomplished. In *The Gospel Standard, or Feeble Christian's Support*, published in 1867 by Oxford University, we read the following distinction: "election is the first act in the mind of God, whereby he chose the persons of the elect to be holy and without blame, and that predestination was the second act, which ratified by fixed decree the state of those to whom election had given birth."[1] We conclude, therefore, that predestination always follows election. One does not occur without the other. For the sake of simplification, I will use the word doctrine in this chapter to refer to these two biblical terms.

As we approach our theme we need to bear in mind the difficulties that it presents to the Christian community of believers, regardless of theological background. But it has been particularly hard for those who adhere to the Reformed faith to live with the misunderstanding of the doctrine. I agree with Stickelberger when he pointed out years ago that: "the doctrine of predestination . . . is the most disputed teaching of the

---

[1] Oxford University, *The Gospel Standard or Feeble Christian's Support* (London: 1867), 153–4. Digitalized 12 October 2006 by Google Library.

Reformer,"[2] and he went on to add: "With a certain discomfort one begins to read the expositions on this question . . . Predestination! The word is repugnant to the modern frame of mind."[3] If this was true in 1954 when these statements were issued, one can only imagine what the postmodern world, where religious relativism and pluralism are widespread, would say about this doctrine!

Besides the discomfort that this doctrine brings, another hindrance to the understanding of it is the idea that this is the major and most important theme of Calvin's theology. The tendency is to equate Calvin with predestination. The problem is that most of the Christian population inside and outside Reformed circles knows neither Calvin's theology nor the meaning of predestination, and they speak of what they hear about without making the effort really to understand the importance of this theological teaching and how Calvin dealt with it.

> If it is concluded, however—as a host of the ignorant has done—that Calvin, proceeding from the thought of eternal election, had developed, so to speak, as a consequence the doctrine to which he gave such impetus so that there is no chance, and every good and evil act—as a matter of fact, every event, even the smallest one—has been predestined by God, then this is a gross distortion. When Calvin speaks of the doctrine of predestination, he does not refer in any way to his doctrine of providence, which has determined all events of the world for all times. And as much as we are tempted in little penetrating studies of Calvin's writings to understand the doctrine of predestination only as a particular part of his doctrine of the providence (*providentia*) of all things, just as carefully does the Reformer separate the two dogmas in their description. He is almost afraid to draw relations between them.[4]

We may then take into consideration that ". . . we should not surrender too easily to the notion that predestination is simply a stigma that we must bear."[5] The wealth that this doctrine brings is much greater than the trouble to explicate it. We need to bear in mind that in the Reformed tradition the most important and distinctive doctrine is not election or predestination but the doctrine of the sovereignty of God and from this

[2] Emanuel Stickelberger, *Calvin: A Life*, tr. David Georg Gelzer (Richmond: John Knox Press, 1954), 31.
[3] Stickelberger, *Calvin*, 31.
[4] Rudolf Grob in Stickelberger, *Calvin*, 157.
[5] Walter L. Lingle and John W. Kuykendall, *Presbyterians: their history and beliefs* (Atlanta: John Knox Press, 1977), 102.

all the others are derived. Our purpose here is not to deal with our theme from a theological standpoint. That has been done extensively by those who are in favor or against this doctrine. Our goal is to look at this teaching from a missiological perspective and draw practical implications for the mission of the church today.

2 Election and predestination in the Old Testament

John Calvin was not the original architect of this doctrine—though he is regarded, together with Augustine, as the leading theologian on this topic. The doctrine is above all else rooted in the Bible, both the Old and the New Testaments. The call of Abram in Genesis 12:1–3 marks the start of Israel's election as the chosen people, a people chosen to carry out a mandate from God,

> The Lord had said to Abram, "Leave your country, and your people and
> your father's household and go to the land I will show you.
> I will make you into a great nation
> and I will bless you;
> I will make your name great,
> and you will be a blessing.
> I will bless those who bless you,
> and whoever curses you I will curse;
> and all peoples on earth
> will be blessed through you." (NIV)

This is a sovereign calling whereby God exercises his power and autonomy to call the one who is to become the father of a great nation for the purpose of carrying his blessings to all peoples of the earth. Walter Brueggemann is correct to point out that "God does not depend on any potentiality in the one addressed . . . The speech of God presumes nothing from the one addressed but carries in itself all that is necessary to begin a new people in history."[6] This interdependency is shown in the format of the calling. There is no dialogue between God and Abram. Here God speaks; Abram listens and follows the direction given to him. To make this calling more meaningful Abram ("exalted father") has his name changed to Abraham ("father of many multitudes"). As the saga continues, God promises Abraham a son and it is through Isaac that his

---

[6] Walter Brueggemann, *Genesis: Interpretation: A Bible Commentary for Teaching and Preaching* (Louiseville, Ky.: Westminster John Knox, 1984), 117.

offspring, or we should say the *missio Dei*, will continue. The election of Isaac as opposed to Ishmael is also God's prerogative (Gen. 21:12).

From Isaac two sons, Esau and Jacob, are born and they become an illustration of God's election and predestination; later on they will influence the way the apostle Paul deals with this doctrine. According to the tradition of those days, the oldest son had the rights to his father's inheritance. There was no question about this, and to change this tradition was to change the *status quo* of that society. God, however, making use of his power, subverts the cultural order and appoints Jacob to be the bearer of his father's blessings. God's words to Rebekah were,

> "Two nations are in your womb,
> and two peoples from within you will be separated;
> one people will be stronger than the other,
> and the older will serve the younger" (Gen. 25:23, NIV)

This was exactly what happened years later when Isaac on his deathbed decided to overlook God's plan and bless Esau. Rebekah intervened and prepared the way for Jacob to receive his blessings according to God's wishes. This is an illustration of the teaching that we pointed out in the first paragraph of the Introduction. Election is God choosing and predestination is the action of making it happen.

God's calling of Abraham, Isaac and Jacob narrows down to what we know as God's calling of Israel to become the apple of his eye. The Scriptures will make many references to Israel as the people chosen from among many nations, the choice not being motivated by their goodness or by how extraordinary they were. The calling of Israel can be understood only from the servanthood perspective—election to serve God in the world. This becomes very clear when the Lord meets Moses at Mount Sinai, according to the narrative in Exodus 19:3–6. The language that God uses to inform Moses about his will for the people is very clear and points to the *missio Dei*,

> "Here is what I want you to say to my people, who came from Jacob's family. Tell the Israelites, 'You have seen for yourselves what I did to Egypt. You saw how I carried you on the wings of eagles and brought you to myself. Now obey me completely. Keep my covenant. If you do, then out of all of the nations you will be my special treasure. The whole earth is mine. But you will be a kingdom of priests to serve me. You will be my holy nation.' That is what you must tell the Israelites." (Ex. 19:3–6, NIrV)

One should note here the difference between the covenant with Abraham and the covenant with Moses. With Abraham, God points toward the future and Abraham accepts the commandments based on divine promises. With Moses, God makes promises based on his past action. He has the power to deliver Israel from bondage and to use the nation as a testimony of his power. Israel is chosen to become the people of God among all the nations. This is a repetitive idea throughout the Old Testament (Deut. 7:6; 14:2; 26:18; Ps. 135:4). The whole nation is called "kingdom of priests" and the purpose for this call is left in no doubt: it is to serve God. This service, however, is not confined to the realm of Israel. The scope of God's mission is the whole earth, which is declared as his possession. The Mosaic covenant is a renewal of the covenant made with Abraham, according to Genesis 17:4: "As for me, this is my covenant with you: You will be the father of many nations" (NIV). Here at Mount Sinai God is reminding Moses and Israel that all the nations will receive the benefit of that particular election. This commandment was well received by the people and later on, just before entering the promised land, Moses urged them to remember the covenant,

> I will die in this land; I will not cross the Jordan; but you are about to cross over and take possession of that good land. Be careful not to forget the covenant of the LORD your God that he made with you; do not make for yourselves an idol in the form of anything the LORD your God has forbidden. For the LORD your God is a consuming fire, a jealous God. (Deut. 4:22–24, NIV)

In order to maintain its integrity and give validity to its election, Israel was absolutely forbidden to divide its loyalty. God alone was to be adored and revered as the only God. This was essential for the carrying out of the mission. If Israel became like any other nation, the peculiarity of being a special people vanished. The main aspect of the *missio Dei*, which was to convert the nations to worship a holy God, would be totally lost. If Israel, which was the chosen people, was not capable of maintaining the commandments, how would other peoples, with pagan behavior, be encouraged to do so? Consequently, it was of supreme importance that Israel should understand who God was and what he required from all peoples of the earth. It is quite possible, however, that despite Israel's verbal commitment to obey the commandments, the nation never understood clearly what God expected from it. The result was the loss of its missionary presence in the earth.

Joshua was another leader who understood the call of Israel as a call to serve God. He invites the people for his farewell and he takes this occasion to remind them of the covenant. The fundamental aspect of his speech is the theme of servanthood. In Joshua 24:14 he says: "serve him" and "serve the Lord." Joshua goes on to summarize the whole problem with Israel as he charges them with these strong words,

> "But suppose you don't want to serve him. Then choose for yourselves right now whom you will serve. You can choose the gods your people served east of the Euphrates River. Or you can choose the gods the Amorites serve. After all, you are living in their land. But as for me and my family, we will serve the Lord". (Josh. 24:15, NIrV)

This is a heartbreaking perception for this important leader in the history of that people. When Joshua concludes that even if the people want to serve the gods, he and his house have decided to serve the true God, it seems that he is almost coming to the point where he would give up on them.

It is interesting to note that the people were totally involved in adoring the gods of the land. Thus the dialogue that follows these words of Joshua sounds strange,

> Then the people answered Joshua. They said, "We would never desert the Lord! We would never serve other gods! The Lord our God himself brought us and our parents up out of Egypt. He brought us out of that land where we were slaves. With our own eyes, we saw those great and miraculous signs he did. He kept us safe on our entire journey. He kept us safe as we traveled through all of the nations. He drove them out to make room for us. That included the Amorites. They also lived in the land. We too will serve the Lord. That's because he is our God."
>
> Joshua spoke to the people. He said, "You aren't able to serve the Lord. He is a holy God. He is a jealous God. He won't forgive you when you disobey him. He won't forgive you when you sin against him. Suppose you desert the Lord. Suppose you serve the gods that people in other lands serve. If you do, he will turn against you. He will bring trouble on you. He will destroy you, even though he has been good to you."
>
> But the people spoke to Joshua. They said, "No! We will serve the Lord."
>
> Then Joshua said, "You are witnesses against yourselves. You have said that you have chosen to serve the Lord."
>
> "Yes. We are witnesses," they replied.

"Now then," said Joshua, "throw away the gods that are among you. People from other lands serve those gods. Give yourselves completely to the Lord, the God of Israel."

Then the people spoke to Joshua. They said, "We will serve the Lord our God. We will obey him." (Josh. 24:16–24, NIrV)

There is no other place in the Old Testament where the election for servanthood is clearer than this dialogue between the leaders of the people and Joshua. If this was the understanding of Israel, the question that remains to be answered is why did they not fulfill the mission entrusted to them? That willingness to obey did not last long. In Judges 6:10 we see this direct word from God: "I am the Lord your God. Do not fear the gods of the Amorites whose land you live in. But you did not obey me" (HCSB).

There are two other instances of God talking about the covenant. When King David wished to build the Temple, feeling, perhaps, that he could do as his heart desired, God used the prophet Nathan to tell David that he was a servant of God and as such he had to ask for direction before going ahead with any project. The message that the prophet brought had a double meaning. David wanted to build a house for God; however, God would build a dynasty for him (2 Sam. 7:11). Another passage that gives us details about the covenant is found in Jeremiah 31:31–34. The message here is not for repentance or about giving up the selfish way in which the nation has been walking. God speaks of a new era, of a time when the people will have the laws not on a piece of stone but in their hearts.

3 Election and predestination in the New Testament

The doctrine of election and predestination will find its substantial rationale in the pages of the New Testament, especially among some sayings of Jesus Christ and the writings of the apostle Paul. It is clear from the pages of the New Testament that Jesus is the divisive waters regarding eternal salvation. Either one accepts God's offering of a new life that is only found in Jesus, or one rejects it as pure fic- tion.

The question then is: "Am I saved because Christ found me or am I saved because I found him?" We may start answering this question with Paul's declaration in Romans 3:11: "There is no-one who understands, no-one who seeks God" (NIV). Calvin points out that "empty is the man in whom there is not the knowledge of God, whatever other learning he may possess . . ."[7] We can only affirm the truthfulness of this statement because this was the reality Christ faced when he declared to the Jews that he was the Messiah sent from God. Even though they were anxiously waiting for him, the religious leaders were inflexible in their refusal to believe that he was in fact the Redeemer sent from heaven. If those who were waiting for him did not accept him, despite the concrete evidence shown during his ministry, we can only imagine how difficult it must be for someone to come to Christ if there is no desire to do it! After seeing his disciples complaining that his teaching was very hard to accept, Jesus Christ turned to them with some questions that he himself answered,

> "Does this upset you? What if you see the Son of Man go up to where he was before? The Holy Spirit gives life. The body means nothing at all. The words I have spoken to you are from the Spirit. They give life. But there are some of you who do not believe." Jesus had known from the beginning which of them did not believe. And he had known who was going to hand him over to his enemies. So he continued speaking. He said, "This is why I told you that no one can come to me unless the Father helps him." (Jn. 6.61–65, NIrV)

Here Jesus makes a very interesting connection, pointing out that it is the Holy Spirit who gives life and that his words are the words of the Spirit. Consequently, if people do not believe his words, they will not have life. It means that there is a need for an outside power to operate in people's hearts and move them toward Christ. There are many passages in Jesus' preaching that underline that only those who are elected by the Father will accept his salvation.

> "Many are invited, but few are chosen." (Mt. 22:14, NIV)

> "If the Lord had not cut the time short, no one would live. But because of God's chosen people, he has shortened it." (Mk. 13:20, NIrV)

> "God's chosen people cry out to him day and night. Won't he make things right for them? Will he keep putting them off? I tell you, God will see that things are made right for them. He will make sure it happens quickly." (Lk. 18:7–8, NIrV)

---

[7] John Calvin, *Commentary on the Epistle of Paul to the Romans*, tr. and ed. John Owen (Grand Rapids: Baker Academic, rpt. 1979), 127.

"And this is the will of him who sent me, that I shall lose none of all that he has given me, but raise them up at the last day. For my Father's will is that everyone who looks to the Son and believes in him shall have eternal life, and I will raise him up at the last day." (Jn. 6:39–40, NIV)

Christ issues the invitation with a promise: "Come to me, all you who are weary and burdened, and I will give you rest. Take my yoke upon you and learn from me, for I am gentle and humble in heart, and you will find rest for your souls. For my yoke is easy and my burden is light" (Mt. 11:28–30, NIV). When they experience salvation they will realize, due to the internal work of the Holy Spirit, that they did not come by their own will or strength but because God had led them to come to his beloved Son.

The apostle Paul is undoubtedly the theologian who systematizes this doctrine. In Romans 8:29–30, we have one of his strongest statements about election and predestination: "For those God foreknew he also predestined to be conformed to the likeness of his Son, that he might be the firstborn among many brothers. And those he predestined, he also called; those he called, he also justified; those he justified, he also glorified" (NIV). From this short summary of how God works toward the salvation of humankind many conclusions can be drawn, but the main one is that predestination begins and finishes with God. He is the one who elects and the elected are glorified by him. Apart from God no one will be saved.[8] For Paul, election and predestination is an act of a God who is sovereign. This sovereignty was exercised when he elected Jacob and rejected Esau (Rom. 9:11). Calvin, commenting here, makes the following remark,

> We have then the whole stability of our election enclosed in the purpose of God alone; here merits avail nothing, as they issue in nothing but death; no worthiness is regarded, for there is none; but the goodness of God reigns alone. False then is the dogma, and contrary to God's word, —that God elects or rejects, as he foresees each to be worthy or unworthy of his favor.[9]

God also gives people to Jesus Christ and according to his will these people are predestined to be adopted into his family (Eph. 1:5). The whole text of Ephesians 1:3–14 is foundational for the understanding of

---

[8] For the way Calvin deals with the term "foreknowledge," see *Commentary on Romans*, 317, and chapter 11 of the *Institutes of the Christian Religion*, ed. John T. McNeill, tr. Ford Lewis Battles (Philadelphia: Westminster Press, 1960 (1559)).

[9] Calvin, *Commentary on Romans*, 351.

the doctrine. Calvin comments on this passage at great length and from here he draws proof that election is free from any merit on the part of human beings. The first proof is that God has chosen us before the foundation of the world and the second is that we are chosen in Christ.[10]

God's choice reverses the natural order of this fallen world. It is common sense to elevate the good and strong among human beings. The chosen ones, however, were the foolish, the weak, the despised and those who are not (1 Cor. 1:27–29). This means that election and predestination have nothing to do with merit and performance on the part of the elected (Eph. 2:9–10; 2 Tim. 1:9). Salvation is a free gift bestowed by God, excluding any self-accreditation on our part. Salvation has nothing to do with the sinners but it rests solely on God's will and grace.

This is precisely the point Paul makes in Ephesians 1:3–14: God chose us in Christ. If election is not based on any merit on our part, it is also not done in a vacuum. Christ is the Lamb promised before the foundation of the world. He is elected first of anybody else. He is the holy and blameless one. He is the pure and meek. Therefore, we understand that if it were not for Christ, no one could be chosen for salvation. We did not have any beauty to move God's will to accept us before his holy throne.

When Paul began his ministry among the Gentiles, many of them rejoiced and glorified the word of the Lord, and those who were appointed for eternal life believed in Jesus Christ (Acts 13:48). In the same book of Acts there is another occasion when we can infer that God is talking about the elected. Facing hardship in the city of Corinth, Paul received these words from God: "For I am with you, and no-one is going to attack and harm you, because I have many people in this city" (Acts 18:10, NIV).

The apostle Peter also refers to this doctrine. He begins his first letter saluting the believers "chosen according to the foreknowledge of God the Father, by the sanctifying work of the Spirit, to obey Jesus Christ and be sprinkled with his blood" (1 Pet. 1:1–2, NASB). Later on in this same letter he admonishes the believers not to return evil for evil or insult with insult, "but giving a blessing instead; for you were called for the very purpose that you might inherit a blessing" (3:9–10, ISV).

4 The purpose of election and predestination

Speaking of God choosing Jacob instead of following the tradition of the culture of the patriarchs, Paul says that this choice took place "before the

---

[10] John Calvin, *Commentary of the Epistle of Paul to the Ephesians*, tr. and ed. John Owen (Grand Rapids: Baker Academic, rpt. 1979), 200–1.

twins were born or had done anything good or bad—*in order that God's purpose in election might stand*" (Rom. 9:11, NIV). The question is very simple: What is the purpose of election? The final section of this work is a tentative attempt to bring an answer to this question.

Election and predestination has, according to Calvin, one chief design: "for the glory of God is the highest end . . ."[11] Every other Christian virtue, such as sanctification, holiness and purity, is the fruit of election. However, we can also state two other purposes, which, of course, are subordinated to God's glory: to separate a holy people and to confer a singular mission to this people. Within the Reformed tradition and theology, greater stress is placed on sanctification and it is natural that emphasizing only this aspect of the doctrine should generate confusion and misunderstanding. The elected may be led to think that election is an end in itself. Because of this feeble comprehension of the teaching of the Reformers, adherents of the Reformed theology are accused of not having a missionary mind. It is possible that some Calvinists may hold this view, which is a gross mistake. One reads, for instance, in the Second Helvetic Confession, chapter X, *Of the Predestination of God and the Election of the Saints*, that "the saints are chosen in Christ by God for a definite purpose, which the apostle himself explains when he says, 'He chose us in him for adoption that we should be holy and blameless before him in love. He destined us for adoption to be his sons through Jesus Christ that they should be to the praise of the glory of his grace'" (Eph. 1:4ff.). The mistake the Helvetic Confession makes is failing to include the other purpose of election, that is, that the elected ones must render service to God by being the bearers of the good news to all peoples of the earth.

The Westminster Confession of Faith also lacks the proclamation purpose of election. However, it goes beyond the Helvetic Confession, devoting chapter XVI, *Of Good Works*, to teaching about the results of salvation as a free gift from God. Article II states very clearly,

> These good works, done in obedience to God's commandments, are the fruits and evidences of a true and lively faith: and by them believers manifest their thankfulness, strengthen their assurance, edify their brethren, adorn the profession of the Gospel, stop the mouths of the adversaries, and glorify God, whose workmanship they are, created in Christ Jesus

---

[11] Calvin, *Commentary on Ephesians*, 198, on Eph. 1:4. God's glory has been a strong theological argument for mission within the Reformed circle. For more on this, see David J. Bosch, *Transforming Mission: Paradigm Shifts in Theology of Mission* (Maryknoll: Orbis Books, 1991), 255–61.

thereunto, that, having their fruit unto holiness, they may have the end, eternal life.

We need to highlight the words *good works, done in obedience to God's commandments, are the fruits and evidences of a true and lively faith.* For me, this is the crux of the matter. Paul, on two occasions, made this point very clear. Writing to the Ephesians he says, "for by grace have ye been saved through faith; and that not of yourselves, it is the gift of God; not of works, that no man should glory. For we are his workmanship, created in Christ Jesus for good works, which God afore prepared that we should walk in them" (Eph. 2:8–10, ASV). Before we go on, we need to mention another statement from Paul, in which he continues this line of thought: "[Jesus] who gave himself for us, that he might redeem us from all iniquity, and purify unto himself a people for his own possession, zealous of good works" (Tit. 2:14, ASV). The apostle Peter applies an Old Testament concept to this new people of God, which is the church: "But you are a chosen generation, a royal priesthood, a holy nation, His own special people, that you may proclaim the praises of Him who called you out of darkness into His marvelous light; who once were not a people but are now the people of God, who had not obtained mercy but now have obtained mercy" (1 Pet. 2:9–10, NKJV). Accordingly, one cannot understand salvation apart from good works and proclamation.

Election and predestination are for service. Shirley C. Guthrie, Jr. is right when he affirms in a logical manner that the people of God "are chosen not to be God's pets or privileged elite but to be God's *servants*, chosen not to receive and enjoy for themselves all the benefits of God's saving grace others do not have but to be instruments of God's grace so that others may receive and enjoy these benefits also."[12] We need to emphasize and make this point clear. "Election," says Richard de Ridder, "is always for a purpose. The uniqueness of God's choice of Israel was the uniqueness of the work which God planned to accomplish through Israel."[13] The mistake Israel made was to believe that election was for its own pleasure and as such it regarded God not as a God for all nations but only for itself. Consequently, Israel forgot its role as God's servant among the nations.

There can be no excuse for this failure. The vocation was made plain. Abraham was called to bless all the nations (Gen. 12:2–3). The people were blessed with a bountiful harvest so that they could lead other nations to

---

[12] Shirley C. Guthrie, *Christian Doctrine* (Louisville, Ky.: Westminster John Knox, rev. ed., 1994), 139.

[13] Richard de Ridder, *Discipling the Nations* (Grand Rapids: Baker Book House, 1971), 31–2.

the path of salvation (Ps. 67), and the Temple was called "a house of prayer for all nations" (Isa 56:7). de Ridder adds, "The Christian church constantly faces the same temptation to which Judaism succumbed when it rejected its fulfillment: the purpose of God's covenant is greater than our personal salvation; it is a taking of us up to the service of God in his plan for mankind."[14] When the church fails to respond to God's call and mission, this failure cannot be laid on the shoulders of Calvin or any other biblical doctrine, for that matter. Calvin says: "If the temptation be to contempt or dislike of the gospel, let us remember that its power and efficacy have been manifested in bringing to us salvation."[15]

5 Calvin and the *missio Dei*

What was John Calvin's relationship between this doctrine and the proclamation of the gospel? To think that his theology about election and predestination would lead him to downplay the role of Christian testimony to the unbelievers, is to be far from the truth. According to Samuel M. Zwemer, "It was the Roman Catholic Church historian and missionary professor, Joseph Schmidlin of Münster, who asserted that all the Reformers . . . were not conscious of the missionary idea and displayed no missionary activity."[16] This was not the case, however, with Calvin. He was conscious of the biblical mandate to proclaim the Word of God. Commenting on the Great Commission he says, "The Lord commands the ministers of the Gospel to go a distance, in order to spread the doctrine of salvation in every part of the world."[17] By this we can understand that he saw the missionary dimension of the church as being important: after all, the proclamation of the gospel is one of the marks of the true church. The gospel was to be preached everywhere in order to bring all nations to the obedience of faith.[18] On 1 Timothy 2:4, Calvin states: "There is no people and no rank in the world that is excluded from salvation; because God wishes that the gospel should be proclaimed to all without exception."[19]

---

[14] de Ridder, *Discipling*, 36.

[15] Calvin, *Commentary on Ephesians*, 206, on Eph. 1:13.

[16] Samuel M. Zwemer, "Calvinism and the Missionary Enterprise," *Theology Today*, 7:2 (July 1950), 206.

[17] John Calvin, *Commentary on a Harmony of the Evangelists, Matthew, Mark, and Luke*, vol. III (Grand Rapids: Baker Book House, 1979), 384.

[18] Calvin, *Harmony*, 383.

[19] John Calvin, *Commentary on the Epistles to Timothy, Titus, and Philemon* (Grand Rapids: Baker Book House, rpt. 1979), 54.

We believe that there is very strong evidence that election and pre-destination do not prevent anyone from sharing the news found in the gospel of Jesus Christ. Calvin's theology, as we have seen, unmistakably points out that Christ is the only hope for humankind. Commenting on many scriptural passages, he made that point very clear: the gospel is offered to the wise and unwise (Rom. 1:14–16); it is to be preached in every place through God's special providence (Rom. 10:14); it is to be preached among all nations consistently with the prophetic writings (Rom. 15:21); and Christ is Lord and Savior of all (1 Tim. 2:4–6).

6 Reformed mission to Brazil

In Calvin's life, one can find many practical instances of gospel proclamation. We just want to point out one missionary endeavor that happened right after the first steps of the Reformation. In 1555, under the leadership of Nicolas Durand de Villegagnon, a group of 600 Frenchmen reached the Bay of Guanabara, Rio de Janeiro, to establish a French colony in Brazil. Having trouble controlling his men, Villegagnon wrote a letter to John Calvin requesting that some ministers be sent to help to establish order and religion among the colonists.[20] Jean de Lery, who was one of the missionaries, wrote, "The church of Geneva at once gave thanks to God for the extension of the reign of Jesus Christ in a country so distant and likewise so foreign and among a nation entirely without the knowledge of the true God."[21] This testimony of Lery shows that the leadership in Geneva was willing to participate in the missionary work when the opportunity was presented.

The church sent a group of ministers in 1556. In the new land many problems arose between the ministers and the colonists, and Villegagnon expelled the missionaries from Fort Coligny, killing several. Those who managed to save their lives went to live with the Tupinambás Indians while waiting for a ship to take them back to Europe. When a small ship arrived, passage for 15 was arranged. While still in coastal waters, the ship submerged and five men returned to Fort Coligny. Eventually three of them, Jean du Bordel, Mathieu Vermuil and Pierre Bourdon, were killed by Villegagnon. This became known as "The Martyrdom of Guanabara."

---

[20] Amy Glassner Gordon, "The First Protestant Missionary Effort: Why Did it Fail?" *International Bulletin of Missionary Research* (January 1984), 12.

[21] R. Pierce Beaver, "The Genevan Mission to Brazil," *The Reformed Journal* (July–August 1967), 16.

"The short-lived mission," says Beaver, "had no statistical fruits in conversions. Yet it has historical importance. The Church of Geneva, when confronted with the challenge to undertake mission had responded immediately."[22] Amy Gordon states,

> If the mission to Brazil accomplished nothing else, at least it raised for Calvinists, and indeed for Calvin himself, some of the fundamental issues that needed to be dealt with before the Protestant churches could become seriously involved in and conscious of their missionary vocation. The episode in Brazil, seen from this perspective, takes on an importance in Protestant missionary history that extends beyond the brief history of the colony itself.[23]

The importance of this enterprise is valuable not only for the history of Christian development from the Reformation perspective, but because it offers a valuable testimony that Calvin and the Reformers were not passively waiting for election and predestination to take place. They were not fatalistic, as people suppose to be the case if one holds this doctrine.

7 Implications of election and predestination for the *missio Dei*

In our Latin American context the formulation of this doctrine is not very attractive and may sound unsympathetic and difficult to appreciate. Despite the growth of the Protestant churches in our lands, we are very much influenced by Roman Catholic theology, tradition and culture, in which there is a very strong emphasis on the place of good works to merit salvation. Accordingly, the teaching that one will be saved without working hard to achieve salvation sounds very strange. It would be much easier to work under the concept of salvation by works and merit.

On the other hand, people, in general, live in such miserable economic and social conditions and experience so many hardships in their lives that they quite often think that they deserve to gain access into heaven. This view is also inherited from the missionary work of the Roman Catholic priests who helped the Portuguese and Spaniards to conquer the New World. Suffering on earth is an exchange for a reward in heaven. If people are already suffering, it makes no sense to talk about eternal condemnation in hell. It also makes less sense to talk about a God

---

[22] Beaver, "The Genevan Mission," 20.
[23] Gordon, "The First Protestant Missionary Effort," 17.

who elects some to be saved. What kind of God is this, who puts people on earth to suffer and on top of everything else will allow them to be lost forever? This is the question that one should answer in a plausible and concrete way. Henri Rondet helps us to start a formulation of an answer that might be helpful,

> The theology of predestination must bear two elements in mind. All the good which we do comes from God. In a supernatural order, nothing good can be done without grace . . . Further it must be maintained that final perseverance is a greater gift than all the others taken together . . . Our life as a whole is in fact in the merciful hands of God. Our spiritual life is a dialogue with a personal God, not a mere relationship to an absolute being.[24]

In a continent of poverty and misery, we as people of God cannot neglect the fact that God is good and is actively blessing our people.[25] It is here that producing good works will make an enormous difference. If we are not saved by works, we are saved *for* good works. The second important aspect mentioned above is that people are not the subject of religiosity. Human beings are the object of God's love and care. In a place where human dignity is very low, it is marvelous to point to a God who sees people as the object of his love and compassion.

From a praxiological perspective, those who hold the doctrine of election and predestination cannot step back and wait for God to save the elected. Election and predestination do not remove the necessity of proclamation. One is saved by hearing and accepting the offer of salvation in Jesus Christ, as Paul rightly teaches,

> How, then, can they call on the one they have not believed in? And how can they believe in the one of whom they have not heard? And how can they hear without someone preaching to them? And how can they preach unless they are sent? As it is written, "How beautiful are the feet of those who bring good news!" (Romans 10:14–15, NIV)

Calvin has a very humorous comment here: "It is enough for us to bear this only in mind, that the gospel does not fall like rain from the clouds, but is

---

[24] Henri Rondet, "Predestination" in Karl Rahner (ed.), *Encyclopedia of Theology* (New York: Crossroad, 1991), 1279.

[25] For a discussion of common grace see chapter XVI, "Calvinistic culture and common grace" in Henry R. Van Til, *The Calvinistic Concept of Culture* (Grand Rapids: Baker Academic, 1959 (1972)), 229–45.

brought by the hands of men wherever it is sent from above."[26] If in the past the misconception about this doctrine prevented the work of evangelism and mission, today this is a mistake that should be avoided by all means.

This doctrine is an incentive to preach the gospel and to perform the good works that will bring glory to God. Every true believer should thank the Lord for his or her election for salvation, even more when we learn that this was a choice based only on his mercy and love and has nothing to do with merit or recompense. The apostle Paul teaches us how to do it: ". . . I was shown mercy so that in me, the worst of sinners, Christ Jesus might display his unlimited patience as an example for those who would believe on him and receive eternal life. Now to the King eternal, immortal, invisible, the only God, be honor and glory for ever and ever. Amen" (1 Tim. 1:16–17, NIV). Election is not for self-pleasure. It is for the pleasure of God and he delights in us when we fulfill his commandments—the *missio Dei*.

Every believer is an ambassador for Christ (2 Cor. 5:20), and "[our] labor in the Lord is not in vain" (1 Cor. 15:58). Therefore, we spread the message of salvation knowing that conversion does not depend on our work or the free will of the listener. This is very comforting news. It releases the messenger of the burden concerning who is going to accept the message, as if the messenger were responsible for the salvation of the human race. One must only imagine the impact that fully grasping this theology would make on the development of the missionary movement!

I recall a lesson I learned from my evangelism professor, who was from a Baptist background. He was the most successful church planter among the missionaries of his denomination in Brazil. Responding to the question why he was planting more churches than the others, he said: "When I go to a new neighborhood I stop at the entrance of it and pray to God: 'Dear Lord, you have many people here that are elected for salvation. I do not know them but you do. Please, as I knock their doors, show me those whom you are going to save.'" This is was the simple but profound explanation of his evangelistic methodology. I wonder how many who hold the Reformed tradition have this theological and missiological understanding of election and predestination!

8 Conclusion

Personally, I do not see election and predestination as a setback for the *missio Dei* and it is useless to get into an argument with those who hold

---

[26] Calvin, *Commentary on Romans*, 399.

the theological position in which the focus is human free will in relation to conversion. From a pragmatic point of view, it does not matter what position one embraces. The gospel of hope and goodness should be preached to all peoples of the earth. If someone is accepting Christ because he or she is predestined, the preacher has no previous knowledge of it and as such needs to preach to every person he or she encounters. On the other hand, if someone is accepting because he or she is exercising free will, again, there is no previous knowledge of that decision. Consequently, the carrier of the good news has to preach the message and wait upon an answer. In the end, only one thing remains certain—people will be saved by grace through faith in Jesus Christ.

11

Calvin's Ministry in Geneva: Theology and Practice

Jung-Sook Lee

John Calvin ministered in Geneva from 1536 to 1564 without halt except for the years between 1538 and 1541 when he was exiled to Strasbourg. His life as a minister began with an unexpected and sudden call from Guillaume Farel, a call that turned his life completely around when he only wished to live peacefully as a scholar. Calvin, an immigrant pastor and teacher in Geneva, had to deal with all the opposition and xenophobic prejudices from the authorities of Geneva to the commoners on the street. Over and against such an unfavorable and sometimes hostile situation, Calvin was an extremely efficient and influential pastor, not only for his own time, but also for many generations of pastors across the world.

Recent Calvin studies have paid more attention to Calvin as a pastor. Without any doubt this interest and concern has a lot to do with the transcription and English translation of the Registers of the Consistory of Geneva by Robert M. Kingdon and his team.[1] The

---

[1] The transcriptions of the Registers of the Consistory of Geneva during the time of Calvin have been completed by Robert M. Kingdon and his team. Most are awaiting publication, but the years between 1541 and 1542 have been published in an annotated critical edition and translated into English. *Registres du Consistoire de Genève: au temps de Calvin*, Thomas A. Lambert et Isabella M. Watt; sous la direction de Robert M. Kingdon; avec l'assistance de Jeffrey R. Wattè (Genève: Libr. Droz, 1996); *Registers of the Consistory of Geneva in the Time of Calvin*, eds. Robert M. Kingdon, Thomas A. Lambert and Isabella M. Watt, with the assistance of Jeffrey R. Watt, tr. M. Wallace McDonald (Grand Rapids: Eerdmans, 2000).

Registers of the Consistory of Geneva reveal two things about which there can be no doubt. First of all, it shows how strenuously Calvin as a pastor made efforts to root his theological ideals and convictions into the depth of people's minds so as to reshape their daily lives in accordance with the Word. Second, it demonstrates the extent to which Calvin's teaching and advice for the Christian life was understood and actually lived out by the people of Geneva. In particular, this second point provides many Calvin scholars with a novel and edifying insight. When reading the Genevan Reformer's writings, it is easy to overlook what it took to foster reform not only in church and society, but also in people's lives. The study of the Registers of the Consistory of Geneva, however, provides plenty of mundane cases that help us to understand the kinds of ministries that Calvin and other pastors had to undertake, as well as the collegial nature of the pastors and elders within the "plural ministry."[2]

Calvin's theology and his own practice of ministry showed several characteristics. First of all, it is clear that he was thoroughly convinced of the necessity of the church and its ministry, although he denied the Roman Catholic concept of the church as a means of grace. Second, he believed that the primary form of church ministry is education through the Word of God in order for believers to live by the Word. Third, he believed that church ministry must be a cooperative work between pastors and lay leaders through the fourfold office system, which is represented by pastor, teacher, elder and deacon. Fourth, this fourfold office worked with four different organizations—some already existing and some newly established—seeking mutual cooperation and quality control in order better to minister to the people of Geneva. Fifth, Calvin worked closely with the City Council as long as it did not encroach upon the fundamental principles of the church. These characteristics worked together for good to help Calvin's ministry and its influence become influential and widely accepted within a short period of time in Geneva. Eventually these characteristics became an exemplary model for other reforming groups in surrounding regions. Now let us explore each factor in more detail.

---

[2] Elsie A. McKee calls this Genevan ministry the "plural ministry" based upon Calvin's fourfold office. She expounds it most thoroughly in her books, *Elders and Plural Ministry: the Role of Exegetical History in Illuminating John Calvin's Theology* (Geneva: Droz, 1988), and *Diakonia in the Classical Reformed Tradition and Today* (Grand Rapids: Eerdmans, 1989).

1 Calvin's understanding of the church and its ministry

In a recent study, Selderhuis critically appraised previous studies of Calvin's ecclesiology, which had laid an undue emphasis on the organizational aspect of the church and as a result created an image of the church as a "building with rigid laws and rigid liturgy, with discipline and doctrine."[3] He emphasized that for Calvin, the church was "not just an organization but a demonstration; it is not something passive, just standing there. It is dynamic, it is a show on the road, it is a show in progress—yes, even a 'traveling salvation show.'"[4] Drawing on *Calvin's Commentary on Psalms*, Selderhuis demonstrated that Calvin understood the church as a "source of revelation and its place amidst the daily turmoil of world history."[5] Selderhuis pointed out many references in the Commentary in which Calvin speaks about the indispensable value of the church for the Christian life in all circumstances, but especially in France, where the church was undergoing much persecution.

Selderhuis' observation on Calvin's view of the church as a moving entity incorporating many aspects of the Christian life and empowering the churches under persecution certainly provides refreshing insights. Having the same sympathy and concern over what Selderhuis described as a "static and rigid" image of the church in Calvin, I am convinced that such a negative view of the church came from previous Calvin studies, which for many years, as Selderhuis maintains, focused on the theoretical or theological understanding of the church found primarily in the *Institutes*. Nonetheless, it is not clear how understanding the church via its "organizational aspects" can necessarily bring forth this "static and rigid" view of the church. A breakthrough in understanding the dynamic nature of Calvin's church can be found from more historical and practical sources, such as the Registers of the Consistory of Geneva and the Company of Pastors, as well as the ordinances and laws stipulated by the City Councils. When an organization is understood with people who operate and utilize that organization, it becomes dynamic and exciting because people tend never to be the same, especially when working together within a community.

---

[3] Herman J. Selderhuis, "Church on Stage: Calvin's Dynamic Ecclesiology," in *Calvin and the Church: Papers Presented at the 31th Colloquium of the Calvin Studies Society, May 24–26, 2001*, ed. David Foxgrover (Grand Rapids: CRC Product Services, 2002), 63.

[4] Selderhuis, "Church on Stage," 46.

[5] Selderhuis, "Church on Stage," 46.

Although the *Institutes*, by its nature, is somewhat limited in its expression of the full scale of the church Calvin tried to establish, we still need to start with Book IV in order to understand on what basis Calvin says we need the church. Calvin believed that the church was a public and organized gathering of believers. The reason for the necessity of the church in a public and organized form was derived from his theological and existential observation of human nature and its condition. He said that due to "our ignorance, sloth, and fickleness of mind" we cannot maintain our fellowship with God without outside help. Already having experienced the case of the Libertines, Calvin, as a champion theologian of the total depravity of human nature, foresaw a possible danger lying in front of people when they are not properly guided and taught by the church. Calvin therefore believed that we need the church as "external means or aids" to tactically control our weaknesses and to effectively materialize salvation in our earthly life.[6]

Further, Calvin had no scruples about adopting the ancient title "mother" for the church. The church is the mother from whom we are born and grow into maturity of Christian life (IV.1.8). In his *Commentary on Psalms* Calvin also said about the church, "[W]e are being reborn to the heavenly life in no other way than through the ministry of the church."[7] In another place he said, "He who wants to be considered a child of God has to search for a place in the church in order to practice brotherly unity with the other believers in this way."[8] Calvin understood church ministry as essential for the beginning, progress, and goal of our faith. In other words, apart from the church there is no forgiveness or hope for salvation (IV.1.4).

Throughout their lives on earth believers, having weak natures, constantly need the help of the church to make their confession of faith more accurate and their lifestyles more adequate to the gospel as reflected in the mirror of the church. The best method the church can employ to assist her believers is education through the preaching and teaching of the Word. Calvin knew well, however, that there would be some who would say that they could read and meditate on the Word by themselves without attending the church or listening to the preaching of the pastors

[6] John Calvin, *Institutes of Christian Religion*, 2 vols., ed. John T. McNeill, tr. Ford Lewis Battles (Philadelphia: Westminster Press, 1960 (1559)), IV.1.1. (Hereafter, references to the *Institutes* are indicated by book, chapter, and section.)

[7] *Calvini Opera* (CO), 31:803, on Ps. 87:5, in Selderhuis, "Church on Stage," 54.

[8] CO, 31:471, on Ps. 47:10, in Selderhuis, "Church on Stage," 54.

or to the teaching of the teachers. Calvin, in response, said that such an attitude comes from mere "pride, dislike, or rivalry" and causes a break in the holy unity of the church (IV.1.5).

Calvin also speaks of the sacraments rightly administered. Preaching is the Word you can hear, while the sacraments are the Word you can see. For Calvin, preaching and sacraments together present the best of what God wants us to know and experience. These are unmistakably related to the marks of the church (*notae ecclesia*) by which believers can identify the true church and be properly led to the necessary knowledge Christians should acquire and enjoy (IV.1.9–10).

While education can be used by the church to help believers be equipped with knowledge to understand the character of Christ, discipline can be exercised by the church to transform the daily lives of believers in accordance with the Word heard and seen at the church. As to discipline, Calvin pointed out the threefold profit to be gained from its proper usage. From the *Institutes* of 1536 and the *Articles* of 1537 through to the last edition of the *Institutes*, Calvin laid out the same three purposes. The first purpose, which is unique to Calvin, affirms that his foremost interest was no more and no less than the preservation of the honor of God. To safeguard the honor of the name of God, the church has to maintain the integrity of its community, otherwise great injury would be brought to the glory of God. Calvin said,

> For since the church itself is the body of Christ (Col. 1:24), it cannot be corrupted by such foul and decaying members without some disgrace falling upon its Head. Therefore, that there may be no such thing in the church to brand its most sacred name with disgrace, they from whose wickedness infamy redounds to the Christian name must be banished from its family. (IV.12.5)

The second and third purposes together focus on the spiritual welfare of human beings at both the individual and communal levels. The second purpose (or third in the *Articles* of 1537) is to protect the church community from being contaminated by fellowship with bad members. As François Wendel correctly points out, this second purpose should not be used primarily to refer to the safeguard of public order.[9] Similarly, it should not be understood simply as an "effective tool for social and political control" as Robert Kingdon described in his discussion of

---

[9] François Wendel, *Calvin: Origins and Development of His Religious Thought*, tr. Philip Mairet (Durham, N.C.: Labyrinth Press, 1987), 300.

excommunication in Geneva.[10] Doubtless such social effects are the natural outcome of an intelligent and proper execution of discipline by the church. The result, however, should not be replaced by the purpose. Instead, we again have to pay proper attention to the fact that this communal aspect of discipline deals with the very nature of the human condition, which is so susceptible to temptation and sins. Our sinful nature as human beings requires some sort of mechanism to prevent us falling into the same disgraceful status that sinners in the church community have already experienced. In this sense, church discipline is by intention conducive to the protection and preservation of the purity of the Christian community as a whole.

Lastly, church discipline purports to save sinners themselves from their sinful and reprehensible situation by granting them a chance to repent and correct their behavior (IV.12.5). Here the biggest stumbling block for sinners is the shame involved in the punishment. Since the last step of discipline, that is, excommunication,[11] inevitably includes punishment in a public manner, it is important that the person overcomes the shame for the purpose of sanctification. For modern minds, shame may be considered an inappropriate or even repressive approach when seeking to encourage better behavior. It was also not easily accepted in Geneva, but for a different reason during the early period of Calvin's ministry. As was explicitly seen in the Berthelier brothers' case, many who were excommunicated objected to discipline being decided by the church (as opposed to the City Council). As such, it was thought to be not an appropriate act and many showed great resistance instead of compliance, especially in the beginning of the Consistory's work among people in Geneva.[12]

---

[10] Robert M. Kingdon, "Social Control and Political Control in Calvin's Geneva," *Archiv für Reformationsgeschichte* (special volume, 1993), 523.

[11] In Geneva excommunication meant temporary exclusion from the sacraments. During excommunication one must abstain from the sacraments, mainly the Lord's Supper, but was still required to come to the worship, in fact, more often so that correction could be received through the Word that was heard.

[12] The Berthelier brothers' case can be followed in the records related in *The Register of the Company of Pastors of Geneva in the Time of Calvin*, ed. and tr. Philip Edgcumbe Hughes (Grand Rapids: Eerdmans, 1966), 283–95. This case is introduced in many different places. It is found within the larger political context in chapter 5 of Ronald Wallace, *Calvin, Geneva and the Reformation: A Study of Calvin as a Social Worker, Churchman, Pastor, and Theologian* (Grand Rapids: Baker Book House, 1988). The Berthelier brothers' case indirectly

Once again, for Calvin, the church was the external means by which believers were helped to maintain and advance in their faith and truly experience the benefits of salvation in Christ through the Holy Spirit. The church as the external means to aid weak human beings ironically requires weak "human ministry" whereby weak human beings become the agents of God's ministry. Human ministry, like a "chief sinew" in a body, makes the church's rule orderly so that believers are held fast together as one body, able to enjoy the benefits made available for them (IV.3.2). Here "human ministry" refers primarily to the education and discipline of the church by which believers are edified and trained into the depth of faith and the well-ordered life guided by the Holy Spirit. In other words, education and discipline together become the chief methods used by the church to enable it truly to function as an external means. These methods work in line with both *notae ecclesiae* (marks of the church) and also *notae fidelium* (marks of the Christian).[13] The marks of the church correspond to the marks of the Christian: as long as the church faithfully bears the marks of the church, believers have a better chance of representing the marks of the Christian, namely, "confession of faith, example of life, and partaking of the sacraments." Therefore, Calvin's understanding of church ministry, characterized mainly by education and discipline, corresponds adequately to the marks of the church and the marks of the Christian.

2 Calvin's ministry through the fourfold office

Calvin's theology and practice of church ministry is called "diversity of ministries"[14] or "plural ministry." It is characterized as cooperative (and

(cont.) deals with shame when both brothers, first Philibert and then François, strongly resisted the excommunication imposed on them on account of disobedience and affront against the authorities. Although it seems true that they could not accept what excommunication entailed in both their spiritual and social lives, their undue reaction arose mainly from political and xenophobic motives. It is possible that they preferred the Zwinglian understanding of discipline, which conceded its power to the hands of the civil authority.

[13] The marks of the Christian are a "certain charitable judgment" which God made available for us to distinguish the true church from the visible church. They include "confession of faith, example of life, and partaking of the sacraments" (IV.1.8), see Wilhelm Neuser, "Teaching on the *notae fidelium*," in Elsie McKee and Brian Armstrong (eds.), *Probing the Reformed Tradition* (Louisville, Ky.: Westminster John Knox, 1989).

[14] Wendel, *Calvin*, 303.

collegial) ministry between clergy and laity, namely, pastor, doctor (teacher), elder, and deacon. This fourfold ministry was based upon the Scriptures and the theology and practice of Calvin's colleagues, such as Johannes Œcolampadius in Basel and Martin Bucer in Strasbourg. This type of ministry was differentiated from the Catholic ministry, which was operated mainly by priests, and was also differentiated from the Anabaptists, who obliterated boundaries between priest and laity. Calvin believed that the fourfold ministry was firmly biblical and permanent so that its operation and usage are not bound to time and place.

How did Calvin come up with the four offices from the Scriptures when they speak of more than four offices in relation to ministry? To this question, Elsie A. McKee's work, *Elders and Plural Ministry*, provides a rather exhaustive answer through a study of the exegetical history of the verses that delineate these multiple offices. According to McKee, in Calvin's exegesis of those verses, like that of other Reformers, there is a strong continuity with tradition. However, Calvin also moved beyond tradition to add something of his own in order adequately to understand and utilize the ministries in his own particular context. For example, while he expounded various offices mentioned in the Scriptures, he differentiated the permanent ones from the temporary ones. From Ephesians 4:11, he considered apostles, prophets, and evangelists as temporary, and the offices of pastor and teacher as permanent (IV.3.4–5). After defining pastor and teacher as permanent offices, he then speaks of two other offices necessary for the ministry. He says,

> Here it must now be noted that to this point we have considered only those offices which are engaged in the ministry of the Word; nor does Paul mention the others in the fourth chapter of the letter to the Ephesians, which we have cited (Eph. 4:11). But in the letter to the Romans (Rom. 12:7–8) and in the first letter to the Corinthians (I Cor. 12:28), he lists others, as powers, the gift of healing, interpretation, government, and caring for the poor. Two of these I omit as being temporary, for it is not worthwhile to tarry over them. But *two of them are permanent: government and caring for the poor*. (IV.3.8, emphasis added)

Thus Calvin again differentiated permanent from temporary offices: permanent offices are elders for government and deacons for caring for the poor. Therefore, from verses such as 1 Corinthians 12:28, Romans 12:8, and some from 1 Timothy and Titus, which mention offices either in a partial or fuller form, Calvin came to list four offices, namely, pastor, teacher, elder and deacon. For Calvin, these four offices are meant to be permanent, for the ministry of the church in every time and place.

Having said this, it is important to mention that it is the offices per se that are permanent. It does not necessarily mean that people holding each office cannot have a limited term of service. While some of the passages speak about gifts instead of offices, Calvin believed that gifts and offices are not separate entities; in fact, all offices originate from God, and are coupled with the necessary gifts without which they cannot be properly performed.[15]

It was Calvin's view that the offices of pastor and teacher were directly related to the Word of God and the sacraments, while those of elder and deacon were related to lay ministries since they were primarily concerned with the daily lives of people in the church. McKee explains this plural ministry in the light of the *pietas* and *caritas* tradition: the first two offices work mainly within the parameter of worship, which engenders *pietas*, the love of the Lord, while the latter two in supervision and charity, represented by *caritas*, the love of neighbor.[16]

Of the four offices, the first and primary office was that of the pastor since the preaching of the Word of God was essential to the marks of the church and of the Christian. Calvin believed that there were two types of pastor for believers: one was the external pastor in the church, and the other the internal pastor of the Holy Spirit. The external pastor in Geneva was chosen by the City Council based upon the recommendation of the Company of Pastors. In order to recommend someone, the Company examined candidates by two standards: the first was related to their preaching and teaching, and the second to their life and character. Concerning preaching and teaching, the Company of Pastors checked on two things: first, whether the candidate had an adequate knowledge of Scripture and sound doctrine; second, whether the person had effective communication skills so that the people in the church could understand the Word of God without hindrance.[17] It is noteworthy that one of the important qualifications for pastors in Geneva was the ability to communicate. Having a sound and thorough knowledge of the Word and doctrine was one thing, delivering that knowledge to commoners in the church was quite another. With no microphones or aids for amplification, Calvin and other pastors in Geneva were asked to be

---

[15] Calvin, *Commentary on Ephesians,* on Eph. 4:11. Summary of the scriptural background regarding different offices can be found in Elsie McKee, *Diakonia in the Classical Reformed Tradition and Today* (Grand Rapids: Eerdmans, 1989), 39–44.

[16] McKee, *Diakonia,* 28–31.

[17] "Ecclesiastical Ordinances of 1541," in Hughes, *The Register of the Company of Pastors of Geneva,* 35–49.

practical enough to consider how loud the voice of the pastor should be in order to communicate the preached Word effectively to the people gathered in a Gothic church building.[18] Once examined in both preaching and life, the candidate was presented to the City Council for approval. The Council usually approved the Company's recommendation without much deliberation. Then the candidate preached to the whole church so that the congregation too had an opportunity to give their consent to this important decision. If he was not accepted by the congregation, then the whole process of election had to be gone through again until the right person for the church was found.

Although Calvin believed that ordination by the laying on of hands was biblically and traditionally sound, he himself did not undergo such a ceremony to become a pastor in that city. It is not clear whether Geneva had a laying on of hands ceremony for the pastors.[19] Whether or not they were ordained with the laying on of hands ceremony, pastors in Geneva were appointed through a civil ceremony. According to the *Ecclesiastical Ordinances*, pastors took some form of oath in front of the Council. By becoming a "salaried civil servant of the state" pastors were the direct responsibility of the city, which provided for and protected pastors as well as discharging them from their duties when they were proven to be incompetent or ethically scandalous according to the list of vices provided in the *Ecclesiastical Ordinances* of 1541.[20]

---

[18] Kingdon shares the case of Claude Baduel, an outstanding scholar who could have been assigned to a city church, but due to his "small voice" was appointed to a small village church (Robert M. Kingdon, "Calvin and 'Presbytery': The Geneva Company of Pastors," *Pacific Theological Review*, xviii (winter 1985), 48).

[19] Both Alexandre Ganoczy and Kingdon agree that Calvin did not believe in the laying on of hands ceremony, so that the Protestant ministry might be distinct from the Catholic one. But McKee says that the pastor had the laying on of hands ordination ceremony in Geneva. See Alexander Ganoczy, "Calvin's Life," in Donald McKim (ed.), *The Cambridge Companion to John Calvin* (Cambridge: Cambridge University Press, 2004), 6–7; McKee, *Elders and Plural Ministry*, 29.

[20] The Council provided pastors with a parsonage, an allowance of grain and of wine (two liters a day—obviously a generous amount!). In addition, they were paid a modest cash salary quarterly (Kingdon, "Calvin and 'Presbytery,'" 50). Regarding the discipline of pastors, the *Ecclesiastical Ordinances* lists the kinds of vices that were intolerable and tolerable. I believe this list became the grounds for the dismissal of pastors in Geneva. From my reading of the Registers of the Company and of the Consistory

In Geneva, the office of teacher was closely connected to that of pastor: teachers, who were members of the Company, actively sought what and how to teach children in order to help them acquire a more responsive faith. This they did in consultation with the pastors in the Company. According to Calvin, pastors could become teachers, but not vice versa. After the Geneva Academy was established, the teacher's role became more distinct. In the *Ecclesiastical Ordinances* teachers were responsible for teaching not only sound doctrine and the Bible, but also language and humanities so that the city would not experience any shortage of ministers and civil officers. Teachers were to be approved first of all by ministers and then presented to the Council. Once approved by the Council, they also became civil officers for whom the Council provided the necessary means for life.

The offices of elder and deacon were what made Calvin's understanding and practice of the plural ministry special and unique. In the medieval period, these offices were part and parcel of the ministry of the clergy. With Calvin it became clear that these were lay ministries set up separately from the office of the Word and sacrament. In reality, however, despite Calvin's wish, the office of elder in Geneva seemed to operate more or less like that of Christian magistrates in Zurich, who attempted to take control of both civil and ecclesiastical jurisdictions. It was only in 1561 that a syndic, the president of the Consistory, was enjoined not to bring his baton, the symbol of his political position, to the Consistory but to perform his job purely as an elder.[21] Prior to that a syndic, who should be performing his duty as an elder in the Consistory, would nevertheless act as a civil officer. This confusion over the role of the elder is nonetheless understandable. It is not too strange if we consider that the church and society were often coterminous during this century. It should be noted, however, that from the beginning Calvin endeavored to select elders from among the civil rulers according to the standards set in the Scriptures, which outline the duties of overseer and censor of morals.

In the *Ecclesiastical Ordinances* elders are identified as "delegates" when they are in the state of "good living and honorable men, without

---

(cont.) I found one case of the dismissal of a pastor from his duty during Calvin's time, though the dismissal was not a permanent one, see Kingdon, Lambert and Watt, *Registers of the Consistory of Geneva*, XI:1, 7.7v; Hughes, *The Register of the Company of Pastors*, 315. See also Jung-Sook Lee, *Excommunication and Restoration in Calvin's Geneva, 1555–1556*, Ph.D. Dissertation (Princeton Theological Seminary, 1997), 198f.

[21] Lee, *Excommunication*, 81–4.

reproach and beyond all suspicion, above all who fear God and possess the gift of spiritual prudence."[22] Such people were elected to "watch over the life of each person, to admonish in a friendly manner those whom they see to be at fault and leading a disorderly life, and when necessary to report them to the Company, who will be authorized to administer fraternal discipline and to do so in association with the elders." Once they were elected as elders, they were subject to annual evaluation, being examined at the end of the year to see if they had fulfilled their duties with diligence and care. Based upon the examination, either their jobs were renewed or they were replaced by another person. As in other matters, Geneva believed that frequent changes in the list of elders may cause inefficiency in ministry.[23] From this we see that an appointment to the office of elder was not a permanent appointment in Geneva but was renewable depending upon the quality of the elder's performance for the sake of the ministry.

From the beginning of the Christian church as described in Acts 6, the office of deacon was established mainly for helping the poor. It was in the late medieval period that becoming a deacon was a prior transitional step to becoming a priest. When Calvin separated the lay office of deacon exclusively for *diakonia*, charity work, it was to revive the scriptural tradition. Regarding the distinctive understanding of deacon in Calvin, McKee clarified,

> For most Protestants, though, the office of the deacon of poor relief was not necessarily ecclesiastical in a Christian society. Calvinist Reformed, however, understood deacons to be a permanent office of the church, and interpreted 1 Cor. 12:28 and Rom. 12: 8 in this light.[24]

In Geneva, there were two kinds of deacons, which, it was believed, was the pattern of the early church. One was the procurator (*procureur*) to help with the administration of charity work in the General Hospital, including receiving, keeping and dispensing goods for the poor. The other was the hospitaler (*hospitallier*), who did the actual care work for the poor and the sick. The hospitaler's work involved administering the allowance for the poor. The *Ecclesiastical Ordinances* specified that there should be four procurators in the Hospital, of whom one should take chief responsibility for receiving and dispensing the goods. They were

---

[22] *Ecclesiastical Ordinances* of 1541, in Hughes, *The Register of the Company of Pastors*, 41–2; cf. *Institutes*, IV.3.9.

[23] Hughes, *The Register of the Company of Pastors*, 41–2.

[24] McKee, *Elders and Plural Ministry*, 217.

elected according to the qualifications laid down in 1 Timothy 3 and Titus 1.

In sum, the fourfold ministry of John Calvin, faithfully delineated from the Scriptures and in the writings of the early church fathers and other Reformers, was a unique example from the sixteenth century of clergy and lay ministers working together to enhance the quality of church ministry by interpreting the Word, administering the sacraments and encouraging a disciplined life befitting the gospel. Calvin's genius in ministry was not only in the fourfold ministry, but also with its linkage with organizations, to which we will now turn our attention.

2.1 Cooperative ministry: the fourfold office and organizations

Calvin linked the fourfold office closely with four specific organizations either that already existed or that he established after he came back to Geneva: the Company of Pastors (pastor), schools and the Geneva Academy (teacher), the Consistory of Geneva (elder), and the General Hospital (deacon). Close cooperation between each office and organization was possible because of the politico-religious context of the sixteenth century. Since all citizens of the city were Christians, leaders of the city were easily identified with church leaders, and this is why the Council members elected every February could be selected to function as church elders as well. As an inevitable consequence of such a political arrangement, linkage between the fourfold office and these organizations did not take place randomly, but with mutual understanding and collaboration. Moreover, when one takes a closer look at this cooperative system, one sees its indispensability for mutual efficiency and effectiveness, especially in the light of the rapid growth and change in the city of Geneva. Let us look at these cases one by one.

First of all, the pastors: Calvin organized the Company of Venerable Pastors in 1541 as a way of providing continuing education, to seek administrative cooperation, and to facilitate self- and mutual evaluation and criticism for discipline. The company met once a week and hired a secretary to keep the records of the meetings. Although fragmentary and incomplete, the records from 1546 are still available in French,[25] and of these, the records taken during Calvin's lifetime have been translated into English.[26] The Company started with nine pastors and grew to twenty-two

---

[25] Jean-François Bergier and Robert M. Kingdon (eds.), *Régistres de la Compagnie des Pasteurs de Genève*, vols. 1–2, 1964.

[26] *The Register of the Company of Pastors of Geneva in the Time of Calvin*, ed. and tr. Philip Edgcumbe Hughes (Grand Rapids: Eerdmans, 1966).

during the time of Calvin. It included pastors not only from the city but also from outside the city walls. Since the population of Geneva and outer areas was about 25,000, one pastor had to minister to more than 1,000 people, even when the number of pastors had reached the maximum.[27]

Attendance at regular meetings was mandatory for the pastors within the city, but the pastors who ministered outside the city walls only had to come once a month. Calvin was the moderator of the Company until he died. As moderator, he led meetings by setting up the agenda, and if necessary he facilitated the decision-making process. In his capacity as moderator, he represented the pastors at the meetings of the Small Council, taking not only the role of spokesperson for the church's interests but also of mediator between the church and the state. Another function of the moderator was to lead pastors in the Consistory, where elders had the main role in terms of presiding over the meetings and reporting what they had observed from the people's lives. Although it is not specified anywhere, it is a natural conclusion that pastors contributed to the theological review of each case, providing edifying admonitions, rebukes, exhortation, and even deciding on excommunication.

Kingdon summarized the company's main functions in terms of four areas: election of pastors, continuing education for members, self- and mutual evaluation and criticism, and mission work.[28] One could add almsgiving or social welfare work because Calvin and other French pastors started the *Bourse des pauvres étrangers français* to help French refugees settle and live in Geneva.

Second, teachers, who in Geneva seemed to teach the whole age range. Moreover, all teachers were directly involved in teaching at educational institutions. As the *Ecclesiastical Ordinances* reveal, Geneva had a plan to establish a "college" early in the Reformation. It took, however, a long time to see its actual opening. To ensure the teaching of sound doctrine and Scripture, Calvin wrote the first catechism, *Instruction in Faith*, in 1537, revising it in 1545. All children and adults who needed it were required to attend a catechism class.[29] Obviously

---

[27] Kingdon suggested that the small numbers of pastors in relation to the population was a possible reason for Calvin's heavy use of lay leadership in his ministry in Geneva, see Kingdon, "Calvin and 'Presbytery,'" 45. It sounds plausible; nonetheless, one should not forget that Calvin strongly affirmed the use of lay leaders who would represent the whole congregation.

[28] Kingdon, "Calvin and 'Presbytery'," 47–53.

[29] For Calvin's catechism, see ch. 6 of Randall C. Zachman, *John Calvin as Teacher, Pastor and Theologian: The Shape of His Writings and Thought* (Grand Rapids: Baker Academic, 2006).

pastors could have served as teachers as well, but when the Geneva Academy was established, the role of teachers was more vividly and distinctively acknowledged. The Geneva Academy was able to recruit first-class teachers when, in 1558, the Lausanne Academy experienced conflict with the city authorities. One of these teachers was Theodore Beza, who became the first rector of the school.[30] The Academy was a success from the beginning: it attracted students from all over Europe because it was known as a place where one could find academic excellence, teaching of the pure gospel, and good discipline. All students were required to attend worship, catechism class, and sing Psalter hymns. They were also asked to reflect on their life on a daily basis.[31] Soon the Academy became the place where local pastors were raised to work with French pastors.

The third organization in relation to the fourfold office was the Consistory of Geneva. As already mentioned, the elder was the main office in this organization. However, pastors, *ex officio*, participated in its operation. Upon his second arrival in the city, Calvin wanted to have the Consistory established to deal with "bad Christians"[32] who did not live according to the Word of God. Unlike Zwingli and Bulinger in Zurich, Calvin believed that church discipline was the prerogative of the church and that the Consistory should be the appropriate organization to deal with this issue. The *Ecclesiastical Ordinances* of 1541 makes it clear that elders had to meet every Thursday, together with the ministers, to see if there was "any disorder within the Church and to consult together concerning remedies when necessary."[33]

Elders were paid for their attendance, though pastors were not as they attended *ex officio*. As stated previously, elders were the primary members within the Consistory and one of the syndics of the year took the moderator's position. The Consistory hired a secretary for the purpose

---

[30] Ronald Wallace, *Calvin, Geneva and the Reformation*, 98f. Regarding the Geneva Academy, outstanding research is found in Karin Maag's study, *University or Seminary: The Genevan Academy and Reformed Higher Education 1560–1620* (Aldershot, England: Scholar Press, 1995).

[31] See Karin Maag's study, *University or Seminary*, 186. Specifically on the worship at the school, Maag's article, "Change and Continuity in Medieval and Early Modern Worship: The Practice of Worship in the Schools," in *Worship in Medieval and Early Modern Europe* (Notre Dame, Ind.: University of Notre Dame Press, 2004), 134–49 is very informative.

[32] Theodore Beza, *The Life of John Calvin*, tr. Francis Gibson (Philadelphia, 1836), n. 1, 25–6, quoted in Steven Ozment, *The Age of Reform 1250–1550* (New Haven and London: Yale University Press, 1980), 366.

[33] *Ecclesiastical Ordinances* in Hughes, *The Register of the Company of Pastors*, 47.

of taking the minutes and keeping the records. They also hired a civil officer to summon anyone whom they needed to admonish, since the Consistory by itself did not have jurisdiction over the people. The Consistory made a conscientious effort to deal with each case with fairness and pastoral care. Many times the Consistory took several weeks to investigate a case, summoning whoever was involved to verify the testimonies given by the people. Extra meetings were sometimes necessary and were arranged to meet with such needs. In addition, the Consistory provided education and counseling services to those for whom it was necessary. Therefore, when Kingdon defined the Consistory of Geneva as "a hearing court, a compulsory counseling service, and an educational institution," he was making a succinct observation.[34]

In my research on excommunication and restoration cases in Geneva, I have found it noticeable that Consistorial discipline served to maintain and promote the marks of the church and of the Christian. There were numerous reasons for excommunication in Geneva; nonetheless, these reasons generally corresponded to the *notae fidelium* with which we can identify the true church. The marks of the Christian were used as the guiding criteria for worthy reception of the Lord's Supper; their absence as the criteria for excommunication. The Consistory expressed deep concern over a lack of religious knowledge and ignorance of the faith and recommended some feasible solutions, such as more sermons or catechism classes, in addition to individual help through visitations. Through this process, the Consistory helped to keep the marks of the church intact and to promote the marks of the Christian.

Two types of deacons worked in the General Hospital in Geneva, which was established in 1535, before Calvin arrived. Since Jeanne Olson's and Elsie McKee's excellent studies on this hospital and the deacon's ministry within the hospital have given a full picture of the charity work in Geneva,[35] it will suffice to speak briefly on this matter. The hospital was not a modern hospital in which the primary concern and

---

[34] Robert M. Kingdon, *Adultery and Divorce in Calvin's Geneva* (Cambridge: Harvard University Press, 1995), 4. Kingdon's articles on the Consistory are numerous; see, for example, "Calvin and the Establishment of Consistory Discipline in Geneva: The Institution and the Men Who Directed It," *Netherlands Archief voor Kerkgeschiedenis* (Dutch Review of Church History) 70 (1990), 158–72.

[35] Jeannine E. Olson, *Calvin and Social Welfare: Deacons and the Bourse francaise* (Selingsgrove, Penn.: Susquehanna University Press, 1989). Elsie A. McKee, *John Calvin on the Diaconate and Liturgical Almsgiving* (Genève: Libr. Droz, 1984).

responsibility was to cure the sick; it would be more appropriate to call it a general welfare center. It functioned to provide aid to the poor, to accommodate travelers, to cure the sick, and then, later, to assist the poor among foreign refugees. Procurators and hospitalers worked together to take care of these duties.

2.2 Co-partnership: church and state

Scholars have emphasized that Calvin had struggles and disagreements with the City Councils in Geneva and experienced more conflict than cooperation. It is certainly true that Calvin had a long-lasting struggle with the City Councils in the area of ecclesiastical discipline. It was for this reason that he and other Reformers had to leave the city in 1538. It was also because of church discipline issues that Calvin and other pastors had to plunge into the court of the Council several times. Calvin was not afraid to make public statements or take action until the Council gave up their misunderstanding of disciplinary power along with any usurpation of authority: often attempted in this respect.[36] Unlike Zwingli, Calvin did not consider the magistrate to be "the church" of Matthew 18:17, which was the last resort of fraternal discipline. Calvin neither followed the Catholic Church's practice of clergy monopoly over discipline, nor endorsed the Anabaptist insistence on congregational discipline. Instead, Calvin believed that "the church" was, like the Sanhedrin in the Bible, an institution composed of both clergy and lay representatives with authority to deal with any disorder—ignorant faith, wrong religious practices, or immoral behavior (IV.11.1).[37] Out of this conviction, Calvin could not relinquish to the Council the power of excommunication and restoration. If he had to do this, it would have contradicted what he had originally asked for when he returned to the city in 1541.

In principle, Calvin believed that the state existed for the maintenance, order, and peace of society, and the magistrates were God's agents to do that work. Since believers were to live under this temporal power, it was important to have a good government. As a French immigrant living in Geneva, Calvin existentially understood the importance of good government. He was grief-stricken by the news that his Protestant brothers and sisters in France were being tormented under an ignorant king who usurped his temporal power in matters of religion. Calvin acknowledged that the positive role of the state was to protect

---

[36] Hughes, *The Register of the Company of Pastors*, 305.
[37] Cf. *Commentaries on the Harmony of the Gospels*, CO 45, 514–15, on Mt. 18:18.

and preserve good order for believers on earth. In this sense, he was faithfully Augustinian; yet he also leaves room for the possibility that one can properly resist civil authority. As a non-citizen immigrant for most of his life in Geneva, Calvin had to deal constantly with the political authorities.[38] It is noticeable that he did not necessarily fight with them over every detail, even when decisions from the Council did not reflect his convictions. The frequency of the Lord's Supper in Geneva could be a good example: he accepted the decision of the Council, which had decided upon administrating it four times a year. Though he did not agree with this, Calvin went along without a fight. However, on disciplinary issues, he did not retreat but insisted on an ecclesiastical court.

2.3 Insights and limitations for today's church

Calvin's ministry in Geneva was special in many ways, but here the fourfold office and its close connection with the four organizations has been highlighted. The strategic partnership between the church and the state to explain Calvin's success as a pastor in Geneva has also been elaborated. It is well known that his ministry has been so influential upon churches both inside and outside the Reformed tradition that his theology and practice of ministry are still a frame of reference for many. What insights does his ministry provide for us today around the world? I can speak about a few findings from my own experience as a Calvinist affiliated to a Korean Presbyterian church.

First of all, warning us against any tendency to annul the corporate nature of the church, Calvin puts stress on the benefit of the corporate church for the faith of believers. Calvin's emphasis on the necessity of the church brings a strong sense of community, much needed when people become more individualized and compartmentalized in this high-tech century. The church encourages people to come out from their shells and comfort zones to find themselves in a community in order to live in service for others. While churches in Korea often have a strong emphasis on church services and programs, they also provide public space where people can experience not only spiritual renewal but also communal support. For example, when a member goes through various kinds of family occasions, happy or sad, the church often plays the role of a support group, whether it be spiritual or physical. Surely this is not

---

[38] Regarding this matter, William Naphy's works, such as "Baptisms, Church, and Social Unrest in Calvin's Geneva," in the *Sixteenth Century Journal* 26 (1995), 85–97, and *Calvin and the Consolidation of the Genevan Reformation* (Manchester and New York: Manchester University Press, 1994), are useful.

just a Korean phenomenon; nevertheless, members within a Korean church tirelessly work to build community in various ways. When a church functions as a community, people experience a strong sense of God's presence and grow into active and vital members.

Second, Calvin believed that the church could fulfill its mission as a community through education and discipline. By education he meant the preaching and teaching of the Word of God by pastors and teachers who are well trained in the Bible and in doctrine. In Calvin's Geneva the church initiated plenty of educational opportunities, such as daily worship services, special services on Mondays, Wednesdays, and Fridays, catechism classes, and, of course, Sunday worship. Consistorial discipline was another factor that made churches in Geneva more functional and responsive to the needs of the people. By means of its visitation to members, which began in 1556, the Consistory helped people to understand and actualize the Protestant faith and practice on a more personal level.[39] As a result of these visitations, future discipline became more efficient. Thus, education and discipline characterized Calvin's ministry as special and successful.

Many churches today, including my own church in Korea, are heeding the need for good education, but are not paying the same attention to discipline. Discipline is a sensitive and often unspeakable topic for most of today's churches. Words of warning and excommunication are scarcely heard before the Lord's Supper even in the churches affiliated to the Reformed tradition. Discipline is often shunned for fear of losing members, and is obviously powerless because people can easily float around from one church to another without being held accountable. Undoubtedly, we cannot and do not have to revive the degree of discipline practiced in Geneva. Nonetheless, it is useful and salutary to teach the meaning and history of its use in order for believers today to ponder on what Calvin meant when he taught "the example of life" as a mark of the Christian.

Third, Calvin's use of the fourfold office in cooperation with its respective organizations is another area where today's church can gain some insights. With such a plural system Calvin was able to make good use of lay leaders and let them participate in different kinds of ministry, in particular, discipline and social welfare. While the ministry of pastors and teachers was the preaching and teaching of the Word of God, lay ministry was the application of the Word in the daily lives of people. These two are independent from, and at the same time complementary to, each other. The way in which Calvin used the fourfold office to

---

[39] Prior to this year, visitations were only made to the sick and the imprisoned.

strengthen the mission of various organizations illustrates well how the churches ought to give each office a proper place within the grand picture of church ministry, and possibly create and use organizations within which each office can take a leadership role. In the Korean context, this collegial and cooperative culture, which Calvin promoted and in which he participated, appears to be lacking. Perhaps we in the Korean church, whether we are deacons, elders or pastors, need to re-examine what it means to be in mutually honoring relationships rather than a disparity-laden hierarchy.

Fourth, Calvin's active cooperation with the City Council is also a powerful example for churches today wherever the church and the state are completely separate. Of course, there are countries where the Christian church is under severe persecution and hence any sort of cooperation is unimaginable. However, if churches are allowed to have religious freedom, active cooperation can become an important principle. More recently, Korean churches have been taking the initiative in providing social welfare programs for neighbors while establishing a conscientious and strategic partnership with local governing bodies. When welfare programs were not properly funded or executed by governmental authority, churches used to fill the gap by providing funds and volunteers in the name of Christian service in an independent and non-systematic way. Now we see the church's approach to its *diakonia* ministry as being a more organized and intentional cooperation with government agencies. Thus, the Korean church's ministry of mercy becomes a better witness to a world that is often antagonistic to the Protestant church.

The Christian church in this century faces numerous challenges to its ministry. This is true no matter where the church is, but where Christianity is a relatively new religion, or where churches coexist with indigenous religions, those challenges can be particularly complex and difficult to respond to. Calvin's ministry in Geneva, despite its distance in time from today, still offers relevant insights in our own struggle to perform effectively the "human ministry" of assisting people to bear their proper marks as God's children.

12

Exploring the Usefulness of Calvin's Socio-Political Ethics for the Majority World

Dieumeme Noelliste

John Calvin had a very modest estimate of his accomplishment. In the farewell address delivered to his ministry colleagues just a few months before his death, Calvin states, "All I have done is of little value."[1] And although he knew that such an admission would be used by his critics to justify their devaluation of his work, Calvin went on to repeat the self-deprecating comment.[2]

But as it turned out, Calvin's self-assessment was wide of the mark. History has shown that his work has not only been highly valued, but its impact has been far more lasting and far-reaching than he imagined. Few would contest the judgment that the jurist turned theologian remains a thinker of multiple achievements. Through hard work in the face of daunting challenges, Calvin has bequeathed to humanity an intellectual legacy that is massive in content, expansive in scope, and innovative in originality.

Having said that, however, I must stress that there is something that cannot escape the heat of legitimate debate. I refer to the interpretation of the French Reformer's mountainous corpus and the impact of that debate on the question of the pertinence of his thought for today. And this should not be surprising given the breadth, the complexity, and the subtlety of his voluminous literary output.

Perhaps in no other aspect of Calvin's thought is the diversity of interpretative viewpoints more apparent and the debate more acute than in his ethics. In his book entitled *Calvin and the Foundation of Politics*, Ralph Hancock has shown that in the past two centuries scholarly opinions on

---

[1] Cited in Georgia Harkness, *Calvin: The Man and His Ethics* (Nashville, Tenn.: Parthenon Press, 1961), 57.

[2] Harkness, *Calvin*, 57.

the contribution of Calvin's ideas to the rise of modern political thought have swung from enthusiastic acclaim to categorical denial.[3] Whereas earlier thinkers found reasons to hail Calvin as "the founder of the modern world,"[4] some later interpreters are adamant that "there is no spiritual kinship between the Reformation and modern democracy."[5] In his *History of Political Thought in the Sixteenth Century*, J.W. Allen states the denial even more bluntly, "If the essence of Protestantism is a claim to liberty for the individual," he asserts, "certainly Calvin was not a Protestant."[6]

In the economic field, the controversy is no less ardent. Here, the debate sparked a century ago by Max Weber's provocative thesis that links Calvinism and modern capitalism continues to rage. It continues to pit those who side with the German sociologist in crediting Calvinism with the emergence of the capitalistic spirit against those who vehemently deny the Reformer such an accomplishment. But even when the connection is granted, the conversation seldom ends with a round of applause and a standing ovation. Rather, the debate often turns on the question of the role played by Calvin's theological and ethical teaching in the development and entrenchment of certain features of the capitalistic system considered less than socially sensitive and progressive.

The question of relevance is further compounded when one takes into account the features of Calvin's ethics that have clearly fallen into obsoleteness by virtue of their affinity with the mindset and the mores of an age that was far more stern and less tolerant than the present one. The result of the joining of these two factors is a nonchalance regarding the usefulness of Calvin's ethical teaching for today. The nonchalance seems apparent even among Calvin's sympathetic critics. Some have taken pains to admonish against parroting and dogmatizing his views, advising that our focus be placed instead on the spirit that he has bequeathed and/or the model of obedience he has set.[7]

---

[3] Ralph Hancock, *Calvin and the Foundations of Politics* (Ithaca, N.Y.: Cornell University Press, 1989), 1–8.

[4] Hancock, *Calvin*, 1–8.

[5] Hancock, *Calvin*, 1–8.

[6] Cited in Hancock, *Calvin*, 3.

[7] The former advice is given by Professor L.M. du Plessis, "Calvin and Calvinism in the State and the Law: A Few Perspectives for South Africa Today" in T, van der Welt (ed.), *Our Reformational Tradition: A Rich Heritage and Lasting Vocation* (Potchefstroom Institute for Reformational Studies, 1984), 531. The latter assessment is by Karl Barth and cited by André Biéler in *The Social Humanism of Calvin* (Richmond, Va.: John Knox Press, 1964), 65.

That such a note of caution deserves to be heeded is beyond question. Many an ethical issue tends to be time sensitive and context bound. There is, therefore, the need to avoid any tendency to engage in indiscriminate totality transfer. But such an admission need *not* mean that the pertinence of Calvin's ethical teaching is to be reduced solely to its overall inspirational value and paradigmatic usefulness. In addition to these, I maintain that there are elements in his system that can be salvaged for our time. In this regard, I argue with André Biéler that what is called for is a careful sifting that allows us to "discern in the action and teaching of Calvin what is perishable and what remains valid for today."[8] Our claim is that despite the outdatedness of many of its prescriptions and the deficiencies of several of its features, Calvin's socio-political ethics still contains elements that can help fashion an ethical stance capable of engendering a social ethos conducive to the enhancement of our common life.

To varying degrees, the usefulness that I am arguing for here would obtain in any context. But I believe that it has the potential to be more keenly felt in Majority World contexts[9] where issues of political liberty, economic justice, and overall social well-being have taken on greater urgency than in the Western world. But beside this question of expediency, there is an element of timeliness to this exploration. Missiologically, we have entered an era in history where Christianity in its Protestant expression has made such inroads into the Majority World that numerically its center of gravity has shifted there.[10] Furthermore, this occurrence has coincided with a keen interest in the search for a Christian praxis that would facilitate the creation of a *modus vivendi* amenable to the well-being of the inhabitants of our planet—particularly the poor and the less fortunate. Moreover, in the pursuit of this project, appeal has been made to resources and insights both within and outside the Christian tradition. In the light of this, to explore the usefulness of Calvin for this project is certainly appropriate.

---

[8] Biéler, *Social Humanism*, 65.

[9] The expression "Majority World" has been adopted since the early 2000s as the preferred designation for the non-Western part of the world, replacing earlier expressions such as "Third World," "Two-Thirds World," the "South," etc.

[10] Scholars of global Christianity have estimated that presently some 70 per cent of all Christians now live in the non-Western part of the world.

1 Calvin, the social ethicist

1.1 His praxis

Earlier, I stated that Calvin's accomplishment is multifaceted. But as is well recognized, he is best known by far for his work as a theologian. Yet if due weight is given to the totality of his life and work, it is not far-fetched to say that Calvin can equally be known as an ethicist—with a social bent. Indeed, in his book *Faithful Ethics According to John Calvin*, James Sauer puts forth the claim that for Calvin, ethics took precedence over theology. According to Sauer, "Calvin's doctrine [was] an extension of his ethical intention, rather than his ethics being an extension of his doctrine."[11] Admittedly, Sauer's thesis is debatable. But even if one contests it, a serious look at the evidence must at least lead to the conclusion that ethics was not tangential or peripheral to Calvin's thoughts and actions; it was an integral part of it.

Several things corroborate this judgment. To begin with, ethical reflection permeates the whole gamut of Calvin's literary corpus. It is found in considerable abundance in every category of his works, be it commentaries, sermons, letters, or Calvin's magnum opus, the *Institutes of the Christian Religion*. According to H.G. Stoker, "More or less all the works of Calvin provide us with pronouncements on morality."[12] Nor is volume the only point worth noting; the breadth of scope is also striking. After studying Calvin's work in this field, Harkness states: "It is possible to learn Calvin's view on almost every problem of practical morality."[13] And the reason why Calvin deemed it necessary to pronounce himself on so many issues of ethics was not speculative. Rather, it was to provide answers to the "practical questions of how to live in obedience to the will of God."[14]

Nor should the predominance of that concrete and practical feature be deemed surprising. Calvin knew full well that by answering the Genevan call he had pretty much given up the desire to embark on a career of pure scholarship. A large part of the job description handed to him by his recruiters was the cleansing of what was considered a

---

[11] James Sauer, *Faithful Ethics According to John Calvin* (Lewiston, N.Y.: The Edwin Mellon Press, 1997), 7.

[12] H.G. Stoker, "Calvin and Ethics" in Jacob T. Hoogstra (ed.), *John Calvin: Contemporary Prophet: A Symposium* (Grand Rapids: Baker Book House, 1959), 127, n. 1.

[13] Harkness, *Calvin*, 65.

[14] Harkness, *Calvin*, 63.

morally decadent city. And honest man that he was, he could do nothing less than attend to the execution of that task with great diligence.

Indeed, in the discharge of that responsibility Calvin went beyond concrete ethical reflection to a vigorous ethical praxis, which exhibits at least three discernable aspects. The first aspect of Calvin's threefold ethical action can be termed *moral* and *theological purgation*. He endeavored to accomplish this by imposing on Geneva a stringent disciplinary regime designed to regulate personal conduct and stamp out "heretical" beliefs. To enforce regulations intended to promote moral uprightness, spiritual purity, and doctrinal correctness, Calvin did not hesitate to make use of the power of the state. He condoned the inflicting of physical punishments ranging from the benign to the most severe—including capital punishment. Under Calvin, Geneva was definitely not a pluralistic city. If it could not be classified as a theocracy or a bibliocracy, it was certainly a Christian city-state governed by biblical precepts.

The second feature of Calvin's praxis can be described as *compassionate social action*. Calvin was not solely concerned with matters of public and private morality, ecclesiastical purity and doctrinal orthodoxy. He was deeply interested in the social well-being of the Genevans—particularly the needy and the destitute. He carried out a vigorous ministry of what we would today call pastoral care, counseling parishioners and friends in person or via correspondence on a vast array of issues. Additionally, Calvin put in place an extensive social outreach program that he placed in the hands of the diaconate and that involved them in the provision of a vast array of services to the poor: health care, housing, food, employment, education, skills training, refugee resettlement, etc.[15] Calvin did not hesitate to appeal to the church, the private sector, and the state to fund this program.[16] His main concern was to ensure that Geneva did not become a city of mendicants and indigents.

Most would be satisfied with these achievements, but not Calvin. To the aforementioned, he added another crucial element: *advocacy for structural change*. The socially progressive measures that Calvin endeavored

---

[15] L. Schummer, "Un Aspect Méconnu, Oublié, Caché . . . de le synthèse de Calvin: La Répartition des Richesses" in Wilhelm M. Neuser, Herman J. Selderhuis, Willem van't Spijker (eds.), *Calvin's Books: Festschrift dedicated to Peter De Klerk on the occasion of his seventieth birthday* (Heerenveen: J.J. Groen, 1997), 144.

[16] Ronald Stone, "The Reformed Economics of John Calvin" in Robert C. Stivers (ed.), *Reformed Faith and Economics* (New York and London: University Press of America), 42–3; J.H. Van Wyk, "Calvin on the Christian Life" in Van der Welt, *Our Reformational Tradition*, 248.

to implement, he sought to entrench in the city's legal system in order to ensure their continuity and permanence. And this task was greatly facilitated by the fact that Calvin himself, as a jurist, had a strong hand in the conceptualization and formulation of the laws. James Sauer puts it correctly when he says that, "Calvin the theologian was concretely involved in ethics as a pastor, community leader and at times a quasi civic functionary of Geneva."[17]

1.2 Calvin's teaching

1.2.1 The foundation
Calvin's basis for the vigorous praxis that we have just reviewed, as well as the rigorous reflection we will analyze below, is unashamedly theological. But for him "theological" is not just the application of doctrine to everyday life. Rather, it is the grounding of the entire ethical enterprise in *theos*—God—in accordance with the principle that "of him, and through him, and to him, are all things" (Rom. 11:36, KJV). What we have here is a thoroughgoing theocentrism, which sees God as the pivot around which the ethical life turns.

This theocentrism is clearly seen in Calvin's treatment of the Ten Commandments, which he sees as God's moral law—the expression of his will for all humankind. According to Calvin, the Decalogue, which together with Christ's twofold command, constitutes the essence of ethics, enjoins upon us a twofold obligation, clearly expressed in its two tables. The first and primary obligation is articulated in the first table and directs us Godward. It enjoins the love and worship of God "upon the contemplation of whom the whole of love depends."[18] That obligation, therefore, is foundational. It is a necessary ground for the fulfillment of the duty of love toward the neighbor laid out in the second table. "Apart from the fear of God, men do not preserve love and equity among themselves" (I.8.11) Indeed, efforts to enforce compliance to the injunction of neighbor-love are bound to fail "unless your teaching has fear and reverence toward God as its foundation" (I.8.50). It is, therefore, imperative that "our soul should [first] be filled with the love of God. From this will flow directly the love of neighbor" (I.8.50). We must always bear in mind, Calvin reminds us, that our debt to humankind is "for the sake of God" (I.8.50).

---

[17] Sauer, *Faithful Ethics*, 5.

[18] John Calvin, *Institutes of the Christian Religion*, ed. John T. McNeill, tr. Ford Lewis Battles (Philadelphia: Westminster Press, 1960 (1559)), I.8.50.

But it would be a mistake to view this insistence on the priority of the vertical over the horizontal as a devaluation of the social, or an affirmation of the adequacy of piety. Calvin is clear that to focus on piety alone is to miss the mark. Social action *is* necessary. For the fulfillment of the commandments enshrined in the second table is a sign or proof of genuine piety. In the observance of these commandments lies the zeal for righteousness and integrity (I.8.50). There is a clear symbiotic relationship between these two dimensions. If the vertical provides the foundation for the social, the social validates the reality and genuineness of the vertical. For Calvin is convinced that "our life shall best conform to God's will and the prescription of the law when it is in every respect most fruitful for our brethren" (I.8.50). Marion Conditt aptly summarizes Calvin's twinning of these two obligations: "There is no service to God which denies to others what is their due, nor is there correct conduct outside of the commandment to love God."[19] This means that though important, the neighbor's welfare does not enjoy the status of ultimate good. The *summum bonum* is always God's glory. We must not offend God for the love of our neighbor (III.19.13).

In Calvin, we have a good example of what we would call today a reflective practitioner. Throughout his entire career we see him simultaneously involved intensely both in the practice of ministry and in reflection upon ministry. Because of this, an account of his socio-political ethics cannot be limited to his praxis alone; it must include his teaching also. Our analysis of his socio-political thought will focus on two areas: (1) the socio-political order, and (2) the socio-economic domain.

1.2.2 The socio-political order

For Calvin, reflection on the political order was a major preoccupation. Motivated by the requirements of his work in Geneva and influenced by the nature of his time, which seemed uncertain about the meaning and function of government, Calvin felt the need to articulate for his generation what he thought the nature and role of government to be.

Calvin's view on civil government is interspersed throughout his writings, but it receives a fuller treatment in Part IV, chapter 20 of the *Institutes*. In this sustained exposition, he discusses civil government under three main rubrics: the magistracy or governing leadership; the laws on instruments of governance; and the governed. For our purpose here, we will focus on the first and the third rubrics.

---

[19] Marion Conditt, *More Acceptable Than Sacrifice: Ethics and Election as Obedience to God's Will in the Theology of Calvin* (Basel: F. Reinhardt Kommissionsverlag, 1973), 34.

Both in structure and content, Calvin's treatment reveals a high view of the political order. Calvin not only accords pride of place to the magistracy, he grants that office the highest status. Magistrates are approved of God, receive their mandate from him, function as his representatives, and are invested with God's authority (IV.20.4). Civil government is thus a holy calling: "The most sacred and by far the most honorable of all callings in the whole life of mortal men" (IV.20.4). And magistrates enjoy this high honor regardless of the form of government under which they serve. Calvin, of course, expresses his preference for a system that combines aristocracy and democracy, in the belief that such a hybrid allows for greater freedom and hence of great happiness. But this notwithstanding, he sees no compelling reason to dispute the legitimacy of other forms. For him the appropriateness of any model must be judged by the prevailing circumstances, the nature of the environment, and, most of all, confidence in "divine providence [which] wisely arranges that various countries are governed by various kinds of government" (IV.20.8).

Based on this understanding, Calvin argues that the citizen's only appropriate response to government is willing acknowledgment and full obedience. Due recognition is given when the citizen considers government not a necessary evil to be grudgingly tolerated and shunned, but an entity that enjoys divine *imprimatur*, and that consequently deserves to be embraced and supported. As for obedience, recourse to any action designed to bring about political change is ruled out since to oppose "the ministers and representatives of God" is to resist God himself (IV.20.7). If change is to occur, the initiative must not come from the private citizen, but from the ruling powers themselves, or from lower ranking officials who have been granted the rights and obligation of resistance by prior constitutional provision. And such a deference is to be shown even to evil and corrupt rulers, for their entitlement to our obedience is not based on whether they obtained power in the right way, or govern well, but solely on the *fact* that they hold office. That fact alone is sufficient proof of divine endorsement.

> We are not only subject to the authority of princes who perform their offices toward us uprightly and faithfully as they ought, but also to the authority of all who, by *whatever means* have gotten control of affairs, even though they perform not a whit of the prince's office . . . Whoever they may be, they have their authority solely from him (IV.20.25), emphasis added)

If one asks Calvin his reason for considering the magistrate's conduct so totally beyond challenge, he offers at least a twofold rationale. First, the evil conduct of a mean ruler may well be divine chastisement "for one's own misdeeds" (IV.20.29). Second, the civil magistrates operate in the realm of the temporal kingdom with which the Christian citizen who is under the sway of the spiritual kingdom ought never to interfere, even though both kingdoms are under the rule of God.

At this point one may be tempted to sigh in despair and conclude that the whole political domain has been established for the sole benefit of the powers that be. And there would be some justification for this response. But Calvin does not see it that way. If God himself establishes government, he teaches, it is because government is *necessary to the public good*. To use it to private ends is to pervert the divine intention. For the law, which is the basis of all morality, never points to us but always to God and the other. To government God delegates and entrusts functions deemed as *vital* to the survival of humankind as are "bread, water, sun and air" (IV.20.3). And these functions are multifaceted. They are religious, economic, social, and ethical. As the servant of God, government is mandated to protect religion and "prevent idolatry, sacrilege against God's name, blasphemies against God's truth, and other public offenses against religion from abusing and spreading among the people" (IV.20.3). Further, government is obligated to maintain and safeguard public peace, private property, and social interaction as well as preserve honesty and modesty among people (IV.20.3). Moreover, it is especially the duty of government to dispense justice and righteousness to the weak and the oppressed. Calvin belabors this point further in his *Commentary on the Psalms* where he also interjects the important comment that the faithful discharge of this role and hence the "triumph of righteousness" is best realized "where rulers are free from avarice, ambition, and other vices."[20]

But at this juncture a fair question arises. Given Calvin's removal from the governed all power to hold governments accountable, what incentive do governments have to fulfill the lofty purpose he assigns to them? To this, Calvin responds in one word: God! When magistrates are aware that their calling and authority emanate from God, such knowledge should propel them to discharge their mandate with faithfulness, diligence, justice, courage, and integrity. It is to "hearten them to their task when they learn they are deputies of God to whom they must render account of the administration of their charge" (IV.20.6).

---

[20] Calvin, *Commentary on the Psalms*, on Ps. 82:3, quoted in David Little, "Economic Justice and the Grounds for a Theory of Progressive Taxation in Calvin's Thought," in Robert Stivers (ed.), *Reformed Faith and Economics* (New York: University Press), 73.

1.2.3 *The socio-economic order*

If Calvin could find good reasons to engage in political discourse, there was even more compelling justification for him to join the conversation on the socio-economic order. First, in his time, the economic field, just like the political realm, was in a state of flux, and thus needed the kind of creative thinking that his mental acumen could offer. Second, there was the need for clarity on many morally ambiguous issues that implicated not only the average citizen, but the clergy themselves. In addition, there were social issues that needed attention but could not be addressed without a clearer socio-economic understanding than was then prevalent.

As with his political thought, Calvin's ideas on the socio-economic domain are scattered throughout his writings. When one examines his thinking in this area, what seems to emerge as a main thrust is this: economic enterprise is legitimate, but the purpose of that activity is the common good.

In keeping with the thoroughgoing theocentrism that we saw earlier, Calvin grounds the economic domain firmly in God. For him, God is the possessor of all riches, and as sovereign owner, he dispenses material goods as he pleases, giving plenty to some and little to others. In this regard, economic fortune (good or bad) emanates from him. So "when we see one rich and another poor," we must recognize that it is God who so disposes, although "we cannot always see why [He] enriches one and leaves another in poverty."[21]

Based on this belief that material possession is the result of God's sovereign and distributive will, any unlawful dispossession is a perversion and cancellation of the divine dispensation. And for Calvin, this is anathema! For the good of society, the property owner alone is responsible to God for the management of his goods. And though the poor may be in need, they are not to violently capture what belongs to the rich.[22] But this affirmation of the recipients' exclusive rights does not mean that they are the *sole* beneficiaries of the divine gifts. In making the grants, the divine Bestower intends that the gifts be shared with others, particularly those in need. And, though voluntary, such sharing is not optional but a requirement that all recipients must fulfill lest they contravene the will of him who alone enjoys absolute right to all, and in so doing incur his wrath.

---

[21] John Calvin, *Sermons on Deuteronomy* (Sixteenth–Seventeenth Century Facsimile Editions) (Edinburgh: Banner of Truth Trust, 1987), 585, on Deut. 15:11–15.

[22] Calvin, *Sermons on Deuteronomy*, 866, on Deut. 24:19–22.

But divine endowment does *not* lead to human inactivity. Alongside the affirmation of the divine origin of economic fortune, Calvin extends unequivocal endorsement to the economic enterprise. This is evident from Calvin's views on many activities considered essential to economic life. For example, based on his perception of a clear link between God's activity and that of humans, he sees work as an activity endowed with the highest nobility and dignity. As such, it is to be pursued with diligence and honor, though not in a manner that displays a feverish pursuit of wealth.[23] And since work is the fulfillment of our vocation, which itself is directly assigned by God, this assessment applies to any activity—small or great. Similarly, believing that commerce and trade are the outworking of God's gifts and callings, Calvin sees them as legitimate pursuits. Indeed, they are necessary channels for the distribution of God's provision among humans, and concrete expressions of human interdependence. Calvin states,

> Those who usefully employ whatever God has committed to them are said to be engaged in trade (*negotiari*). The life of the godly is justly compared to trading, for they ought naturally to exchange and barter with each other, to maintain intercourse; and the industry with which each man discharges the office assigned to him, the calling itself, the power of acting properly, and other gifts, are reckoned to be so many kinds of merchandise, because the use and end that they have in view is to promote mutual intercourse among men.[24]

This strong belief in the propriety of commercial exchange explains, in part, Calvin's bold decision to break with the prevailing wisdom of his day and defend, with certain caveats, the legitimacy of lending money at interest, a view he expresses in his now famous response to his friend Sachinus, who had sought his teaching on the matter on behalf of an acquaintance.[25]

But as H.H. Eber has observed, this interest in economic progress is counterbalanced by a demonstrable commitment to social justice.[26] For Calvin, this means at least two things. First, a just economic order is

---

[23] Harkness, *Calvin*, 171.

[24] John Calvin, *Harmony of the Gospels, Opera Calvini*, 45:569, on Mt. 25:20, quoted in Sauer, *Faithful Ethics*, 221.

[25] The full text of Calvin's letter appears in Sauer, *Faithful Ethics*, 169–72, with critical comments.

[26] H.H. Eber, "Calvin's Concept of Property in View of the Introduction of the New Economic Order" in Wilhelm Neuser, *Calvin's Books*, 169–72.

one that is devoid of exploitation. Because of his high view of work, Calvin considers unemployment the most severe form of exploitation. Using the strongest language possible, he asserts that to deprive someone of work is tantamount to "cutting his throat."[27] Exploitation also occurs when employers reduce wages in response to a saturated labor market. To exploit the vulnerability of the poor in this way is cruel, callous, and fraudulent. Calvin would have had a serious problem with the modern practice of downsizing to improve the bottom line.

Second, a just economic system is one that is always mindful of the *common good*, and consequently refrains from acting in ways that undermine it. It is in keeping with this conviction that Calvin surrounds his approval of lending money at interest with a series of measures designed to keep this from degenerating into a socially harmful free-for-all. Interest was not to be charged to the poor who borrowed for consumptive purposes. And rates had to be set and monitored so as to avoid deleterious effects on the economy. Calvin's position on property reveals the same concern. While firmly believing that the state has a duty to guarantee the right to private property, he is insistent that it must not do so in a way that harms the interest of the collectivity. For, though sacred, ownership is not absolute; it is limited and conditional. In Schummer's apt words, for Calvin, possession is a "trust" that is to be managed and shared, not selfishly hogged.[28]

Third, in Calvin's view, a just economic order is one in which responsibility for the welfare of the other is assumed not by reason of charity but as a matter of obligation. His reasoning on this matter is stunning but clear. Calvin begins by asserting that in creating the world, God provides adequately for the needs of all. Were it not for sin, the divine intention regarding the satisfaction of the needs of all would be fulfilled. But despite this thwarting of his will, God still pursues his original goal. The uneven distribution of wealth that obtains in the post-Fall situation is not a cancellation of his will. True, God gives more to the rich than to the poor, but the excess of wealth that God places in the hands of the rich actually *belongs* to the poor and should go to them. In several texts Calvin stresses that God gives more to the rich *so that they may serve the poor.*[29] In keeping with this, Calvin makes the supply of the needs of the poor an essential criterion of the use of wealth. According to him, in

---

[27] Quoted in Schummer, "Aspect Méconnu, Oublié, Caché," 136.

[28] Calvin, *Sermons on Deuteronomy*, 833, on Deut. 24:1–4.

[29] John Calvin, *Commentary on 2 Thessalonians*, Calvin's Commentaries, vol. 12 (Wilmington, Del.: Associated Publishers and Authors, 1970), 2150.

helping the poor the rich satisfy one of the two laws of equity: the use of abundance to relieve those who are under economic pressure.[30] Neither should the poor succumb to a feeling of inferiority by receiving from the rich. For if the rich are God's servants in giving, so are the poor in receiving! The poor are God's ambassadors to the rich; the poor man collects from them what is his![31] The purpose of this economic sharing is equality. Commenting on 2 Corinthians 8:13, Calvin asserts: "God wants that there be this analogy and equality among us, that each one helps the needy as he is able so that some do not have great excess while others suffer."[32]

For Calvin, such sharing of resources is not optional—though not legally enforceable. To refuse to attend to the needs of the poor is no minor offense. Again resorting to the harshest language possible, Calvin says that such an omission is tantamount to theft, fraud, and murder. In a sermon on Matthew 3:9–10, Calvin states: "The Lord *commands* that the rich be not as *savage beasts to eat the poor . . . and suck their blood and life.*"[33] In his commentary on James 5:1–6, Calvin declares that such wrong will not go unpunished. For in response to such provocation God, who is the defender and protector of the poor, will not only bring about the destruction of the ill-gotten riches, but will also render judgment against the offenders.[34]

Calvin, of course, was no naïve idealist. He knew full well that given the depraved condition of the human heart, tough words alone would not bring about the ethos of human solidarity that he was advocating. It is for this reason that he endorses the intervention of the state to regulate economic exchange, curb the distorting effects of sin in the socioeconomic order, and thus enforce a fairer sharing of resources. This concern for the health of the collectivity has led André Biéler to label Calvin's social doctrine "social personalism"[35] or "personalist socialism." This is a perspective that seeks to strike a balance between safeguarding individual rights, on the one hand, and attending to the needs of the society as a whole, on the other.

---

[30] Calvin, *Sermons on Deuteronomy*, 865, on 24:19–22. The same point is made in his commentary on James. See note 34 below.

[31] Calvin, *Sermons on Deuteronomy*, 866–7, on Deut. 24:19–22.

[32] Cited in Schummer, "Un Aspect," 141–2.

[33] Cited in Schummer, "Un Aspect," 142 (emphasis added).

[34] *Commentary on James*, Calvin's Commentaries, vol. 12, 2580–1.

[35] Biéler, *Social Humanism*, 62.

2 Retrieving the usefulness of Calvin's socio-political ethics

Does the socio-political and the socio-economic construal that we have analyzed have any real pertinence for the here and now, or is it something endowed only with historical and inspirational significance? As I indicated in the introduction to this chapter, I stake my claim to the former judgment. Following Biéler's lead, I believe firmly that it is possible to retrieve from Calvin's ethical teaching insights that are valuable to the fashioning of a life-enhancing ethical stance for modern society in general and the Majority World in particular. I will now elaborate on this claim in this final section of this chapter.

2.1 Inspiration for socio-political engagement

It is no secret that the nonchalance and ambiguity displayed by the global church on the matter of socio-political engagement has been a major impediment to the fashioning of an ethical stance conducive to the enhancement of community life. Writing on the issue of women and politics in Africa, social scientist Hannah Kinoti highlights this problem of social indifference on the part of global evangelicalism as a whole and underscores its particular acuteness in the African context. "If evangelicals in general," Kinoti remarks, "have mislaid their social conscience temporarily, African evangelicals had been non-starters. Whereas 18th century revivals had results in socio-political action in the West, revivals in Africa have stifled that spirit."[36] Drawing on the analysis of the British theologian John W. Stott, Kinoti proceeds to attribute the ethical malaise to several factors. She draws attention to the church's lopsided and other-worldly orientation, its pessimistic attitude toward reformability of the world, its polemic against the "social" gospel, considered to be damaging to Christian orthodoxy, and the perceived futility of past reforming efforts.[37]

I am of the view that if these are the causes of the ethical lukewarmness, then Calvin can certainly help. I see in his ethics several elements that can help to combat it. One such element is what can be termed the *non-dichotomous* character of Calvin's praxis. Calvin, as we have seen, has no problem wedding together aspects of ministry that the modern Christian tends to keep apart. Latin American theologian Emilio Nunez has shown that in the aftermath of the modernist–fundamentalist controversy that

---

[36] Hannah W. Kinoti, "Evangelical Women and Politics in Africa," *Transformation*, II: 4 (October–December, 1994), 7.

[37] Kinoti, "Evangelical Women," 6.

raged in the United States in the first decade of the twentieth century, it took evangelicalism several decades, numerous forums, and vigorous debates before placing social responsibility on its agenda as an issue worthy of Christian concern.[38] In the heat of the debate, arguments centered around such matters as the legitimacy of diverting energy and resources from the care of "souls" to that of bodies, the relationship between evangelism and social action, and the ordering of priorities between these things. Reflecting retrospectively, Nunez states,

> From the Chicago Congress on Missions (1986) to the Consultation on Integral Transformation in Huampaní, Peru (1987), or from the interpretation of social responsibility as merely social assistance and development to the emphasis on social transformation, the road has been long, difficult, and somehow disturbing to some evangelical leaders around the world; but it has also been rewarding to many of us Third World evangelicals.[39]

But progress by no means signifies the completion of the task. For Nunez goes on to say, "After more than twenty years of wrestling . . . discrepancies still exist among us."[40]

Perhaps, if Calvin's ethics were given attention commensurate with the hearing that his theology has received among many of the participants to the debate, the progress reported by Nunez would have been greater, and the lingering discrepancies less pronounced. For as we have seen, the ethics of the Genevan churchman embraces without qualms the body *and* the soul; the spiritual *and* the social, the here and now, *and* the hereafter.

Another Calvinian feature that might help to invigorate involvement in the socio-political domain is the extension of social action to include *advocacy for systemic change*. This is an issue that modern-day Christians tend to shy away from. For many, the preferred approach is to focus on the salvation of the individual, with the hope that individual salvation will result in social change. This has its place, but its sufficiency is questionable. And Calvin seems to understand this. He saw clearly that if the permanence of the needed social provisions was to be ensured, social action had to go beyond mere social services. It had to embrace within its ambit structural and corporate change. In acting upon this

---

[38] William Taylor and Emilio Nunez, *Crisis and Hope in Latin America: An Evangelical Perspective* (Pasadena, Calif.: William Carey Library Pub., rev. ed. 1996), 407–33.

[39] Taylor and Nunez, *Crisis and Hope*, 431.

[40] Taylor and Nunez, *Crisis and Hope*, 432.

understanding, Calvin sought to accomplish not simply the temporary alleviation of needs, but the *elimination of their causes*. Here, Calvin's role as quasi-legislator and consultant on public policy proved critical. And in this he was clearly far ahead of his time. Recently, sociologist Lawrence Mamiya drew attention to the significance of just such a praxis for the transformation of socially stressed communities. Speaking from within the African American community, Mamiya argues that a firm knowledge of policy would prepare black clergy to nudge government into adopting "policy options that would lead to the empowerment of their people or bring healing to bruised and broken lives."[41] He went on to suggest that such a competency be included in the training of church leaders. In other words, Mamiya is suggesting that churches in the socio-economically deprived parts of the world need Calvinlike leaders.

Perhaps the most significant feature of Calvin's thought that bears mention in this connection is Calvin's insistence that *social concern finds its ground in God himself*. Although Calvin, as we have seen, does not believe that social concern should be elevated to the status of ultimate good, he is nonetheless clear that to be attentive to the needs of the neighbor *is* part of God's revealed will and a *demonstration* of genuine piety. For him, such an effort is not to be viewed as an abandonment of doctrinal orthodoxy or capitulation to misguided humanism. It is, instead, a *response* to an imperative that emanates from God himself. And for Calvin, such God-centeredness is not some contentless and vague pronouncement. It is rooted in Scripture. This explains why Calvin valiantly sought to buttress his ethical views by sound exegesis of the biblical text. Clearly, if one needed a compelling argument for the legitimacy of social action, and the compatibility of social engagement with evangelical commitment, Calvin, the theologian of divine sovereignty par excellence, provides it.

2.2 Basis for a prophetic critique of self-serving politics

Admittedly, Calvin's teaching on politics has much that can be seized upon to justify the status quo, stem the tide of change, and impede the pursuit of freedom. For example, his exclusive grounding of political legitimacy in God alone may be used by some to buttress their claim to political entitlement and create a feeling of inviolability. In recent times, President Robert Mugabe seems to illustrate this when, in response to

---

[41] Lawrence Mamiya, "A Black Church Challenge to and Perspective on Christianity and Civil Society" in Rodney Petersen (ed.), *Christianity and Civil Society* (Maryknoll, N.Y.: Orbis Books), 57.

mounting pressure to implement political change in his native Zimbabwe, he states that only God can remove him from power. Similarly, Calvin's virtual absolving of government of all accountability save to God himself can easily lead to political neglect and dereliction of duty. The claim that an awareness of the divine origin of the magistrate's power can serve as a good enough incentive to spur government to the faithful discharge of their duty is overly optimistic. While the claim *may* work in the case of those who acknowledge God, it seems to have little relevance to leaders who deny him. Moreover, the preclusion of resistance on the part of the private citizen except in cases where government usurps divine authority can generate in some an attitude of resignation and indifference to the political process. Lastly, the granting of divine legitimacy to any political *fait accompli, regardless* of how it came about, can undermine the democratic process, encourage the employment of illegitimate means to gain political office, and threaten political stability.

But while these features may have a debilitating effect on an ethical platform, others can have quite the opposite result. I select three for special mention. First, Calvin's elevation of politics to the status of divinely sanctioned vocation delivers it from the stigma of *inherent* unholiness and, in so doing, makes it a calling that, in principle, is worthy of being pursued by non-Christians and Christians alike. In Majority World contexts where the moral devaluation of the political domain tends to encourage the adoption of an apolitical stance and an attitude of disengagement, such a change of outlook is significant.

Second, besides this rehabilitating feature and its potential benefits, Calvin's view of the purpose of the political sphere is also pertinent. As we have seen, Calvin belabors the point that the purpose of civil government is the pursuit of the public good, not private gain. If God deemed it necessary to establish the political order, it was to entrust it with functions considered vital to the well-being of public life. This being the case, the neglect of the public good by any government casts doubt on its very *raison d'être* and legitimacy. Again, in contexts where the political balance tends to tip on the side of self-serving pursuits, such a teaching is a necessary prophetic witness which *may* exert a corrective influence.

The third socially redeeming element of Calvin's political teaching is his subordination of all temporal power to the authority of God. By means of this doctrine Calvin declares all earthly power derivative and limited, and thus *incapable* of being legitimately absolutized. Ghanaian missiologist Kwame Bediako sees clearly the potential that this concept holds for the transformation of politics on the African continent. In an article entitled "De-sacralization and Democratization," Bediako notes that the entrenchment in Africa of a one-party system that considers multi-party

politics antithetical to the African cultural ethos is a formidable obstacle to
the establishment of democratic rule on the continent. Exploring the phenomenon further, Bediako finds that the state of affairs is based, in part,
on an idea of power that views holders of political office not just as secular leaders but as religious figures endowed with "mystical credentials"
derived from the past—a past that includes departed ancestors. Leaders
who are conscious of their connection with these revered ancestors tend
to consider opposition to their rule an affront to the ancestors themselves.
This equation of the authority of the living and the dead sacralizes human
power and leaves the door open to manipulative and self-serving politics.
Because the ancestors are still considered essential to the well-being of the
community, all a leader who feels threatened has to do to avert opposition
is to stress his identity with the ancestors. Bediako rightly sees that if
change is to occur, a new concept of human power, one that relativizes all
human authority, including that of bygone ancestors, needs to replace the
traditional understanding. For when it is understood that "all human
authority is *delegated* [and] that its source is divine," it will be realized that
it is "not an arbitrary power which can be capriciously exercized without
moral blame"[42]—and, I would add, without moral challenge.

Bediako, of course, did not reference Calvin in his piece but it is clear
that his view resonates perfectly with that of the Reformer. Both he and
Calvin insist on the need to de-absolutize all earthly powers, and in so
doing expose them to legitimate prophetic critique. On their view, government has no legitimate ground to bar the church from engaging in
prophetic activity as it tends to do in many Majority World contexts.
Conversely, nor can the church claim to be a faithful witness if it abdi-
cates its prophetic role, again as it tends to do in many Majority World
contexts! Such a witness is essential to a robust ethical stance. It is
through this kind of "political evangelism"[43] that the church keeps constantly before the political powers their reason for being, namely, that *by
vocation and calling, they are the servants of God, called to pursue the public
good, not their own self-interest.*

2.3 Relativization of self-interest and promotion of an ethos of other regard

The persistence of an ever-widening gap between the "haves" and the
"have-nots" is one of the most vexing realities of our world. This

[42] Kwame Bediako, "De-sacralization and Democratization: Some Theological
Reflections on the Role of Christianity in Nation-building in Modern Africa,"
Transformation, 12:1 (1995), 9.
[43] Bediako, "De-sacralization," 9.

perplexing disparity rears its ugly head both within nations and among nations. At the heart of this nagging problem is the issue of how economic life should be ordered. And on this, opinions widely vary. While some take the view that greater economic equality accrues when government holds the reins of economic life, others contend that that ideal is best fulfilled when the helm is placed in private hands.

Although these positions were not as sharply drawn in Calvin's time as they are today, he was by no means oblivious to the broader question that inspires them. Because of this, as we saw in section 2, Calvin's social thought accords pride of place to economic justice. In my view, it contains insights that are useful to any modern ethical construal that seeks to be sensitive to economic justice.

In his book *The Social Humanism of Calvin*, André Biéler offers an interpretation of Calvin's economic thought that seems to situate him between statism or collectivism and a free enterprise model. According to Biéler, while "Calvin's emphasis on personal responsibility would never have led him to ask the state to be the exclusive animator of economy, [his] awareness of the ambiguity of man's nature . . . would never have inclined him to believe that society can reach a harmonious economic activity through the simple play of individual interests."[44]

Besides being an apt summary of Calvin's position on the ordering of economic life, this statement of Biéler's, in my view, encapsulates the pertinence of Calvin's economic ethic for our time. Of significance is the theme of personal empowerment for participation in economic life, which Calvin so clearly highlights in his writings. The note of personal responsibility to which Biéler draws attention is based on this emphasis. That a person *can* and *ought* to play a prominent role in economic life is buttressed by the theological conviction that *whatever* vocation she receives emanates from God and therefore ought to be exercised with diligence, satisfaction, and single-minded devotion. Because of this, Calvin abhors vocational restlessness. Personal responsibility is further strengthened by the understanding that the labor exerted in the fulfillment of one's vocational calling (whatever it is) is a sacred activity by virtue of the fact that it is the emulation of God himself and the enjoyment of a gift he has given.

This twin view of vocation and work has great relevance for the parts of the Majority World where the legacy of slavery and colonialism has led to a devaluation of both. For newly independent countries steeped in the process of nation building, for example, Calvin's idea of vocation can be a strong corrective to a lingering classist notion that holds certain

---

[44] Biéler, *Social Humanism*, 62.

callings as inferior to others and consequently thinks that these can only be pursued nonchalantly and with a sense of resignation. The Calvinist concept of the worthiness and equal status of all vocations can help break this inhibiting elitism inherited from the past, unleash enormous energy for individual initiative, and encourage excellence in *all* professional pursuits. As for Calvin's high view of work, it provides a strong rebuttal of the colonial notion that work is a punishment to be endured by the "inferior" for the sole benefit of the "superior."

But if Calvin's economic thought encourages the release of individual energy in the conduct of economic activity, it also emphasizes two bedrock principles that can have enormous bearing on our common life. The first principle is that the *economic enterprise must be mindful of the common good*. While self-interest must be served, it is *not* the absolute aim of economic efforts. The well-being of the community is. Indeed, it is not enough that economics should *not hurt* the common good; it must also *serve* and *enhance* it. Wherever there are economic systems that make profitability the *summum bonum* of economic activity, Calvin's advocacy on behalf of the common good *will* remain relevant. The current oil crisis is an apt illustration of this point.

Early in 2008, in search of a solution to the problem of exorbitant gas prices, the U.S. Congress conducted a series of hearings with the top executives of the main oil companies. From the line of questioning, it appears that the goal of the investigation was to determine whether the unprecedented increases in the cost of this vital commodity could be attributed to price gouging and speculative practice. The executives came well prepared, and for all their efforts the interrogators could not get them to acknowledge any illegal practices. But what the oilmen did acknowledge, with some reluctance, was the huge profit that their companies were making in the midst of the crisis and the mega salaries that they were collecting. When, in frustration, a lawman asked the oil executives if they did not have any qualms of conscience, knowing the havoc the crisis was wreaking in the economy at large and the pain it was causing to millions of their fellow citizens, with straight faces they responded that the profit they were making was generated by the *standard rate of return on capital investment*. Now everyone knew that a slight reduction in the percentage of the profit margin would have alleviated the crisis and relieved the public's pain. But this was not to happen because in stark contrast to Calvin's view of communal mindfulness, private gain took precedence over the common good.

This illustration is not from a Majority World context, but it is relevant to the case being made here for at least two reasons. First, the repercussions that the oil crisis spawned were much more severe in certain parts of the Majority World than in the United States. Not only was the price of gas much higher in these countries, but the crisis contributed to a severe food shortage for several of them. The millions who suffered from the shortage would have been grateful if the congressmen had been successful in their effort at price reductions! Second, it is worth noting that when the congressmen could not find a legal breakthrough for their investigation, they resorted to an ethical argument of a Calvinist sort. They appealed to conscience in their polemic for the common good. Here is the point. If Calvin's ethic of the primacy of common good could be appealed to as a useful tool in a context with a fairly good system of checks and balances, its usefulness takes on even greater importance in places where these protective measures are all but nonexistent. Indeed, in these contexts such an ethical polemic may be *all* the defense there is. If it is not made, the common good remains defenseless.

The second principle concerns resource-sharing based on a position of mutual responsibility. While economic activity is legitimate and is to be conducted with zeal and joy, its fruit, as we have seen, is never for the enjoyment of the individual alone. What Calvin did in the political sphere, he repeated in the economic domain: he *de-absolutized self-interest*! Because both vocation and work emanate from God, what results from them belongs to God. And since it is his will that *all* human needs be met, what he gives must be used with moderation and temperance to allow for the maximum level of sharing and generosity toward the needy.

In a world where extreme poverty and extravagant opulence coexist so comfortably that much of humanity seems to have fallen into ethical slumber, Calvin's emphasis on resource sharing can play the important role of conscience arouser. To a stance of social indifference inspired by a philosophy of excessive individualism, he counterposes an ethic of other-regard grounded in our shared humanity and the demand of neighbor-love. In recent times this Calvinist plea for the assumption of mutual responsibility has found a clear echo in the ideas of Majority World thinkers who are concerned about the plight of the poor. In Latin America, the group known as the Latin American Theological Fraternity leads the charge,[45] pressing for a vibrant ethic of social responsibility. In

---

[45] Chief among the Fraternity theologians are thinkers such as René Padilla of Argentina, Emilio Nunez of Guatemala, the late Orlando Costas of Puerto Rico, and Samuel Escobar of Peru. Though representative of all of them, the ideas presented in this paragraph are from Escobar's lecture to the 1974 Lausanne Congress of World Evangelization, entitled "Evangelism and Man's Search for Freedom, Justice and Fulfillment" in J.D. Douglas (ed.), *Let the Earth Hear His Voice* (Minneapolis, Minn.: World Wide Publications, 1975), 303–26.

characteristic Calvinist fashion, the Fraternity underscores the incongruousness of the gross disparity separating the "haves" and the "have-nots," chastises the consumerism that fuels it, and calls for the espousal of a simple lifestyle on the part of the well-to-do as a concrete step designed to reduce it. Besides forestalling the danger of social indifference resulting from a moribund conscience, such an alternative lifestyle would model for the world an ethos of other-regard in accordance with God's ideal for life in community.

3 Conclusion

Professor du Plessis' caution against dogmatizing and parroting Calvin's social ethics for our time is worth heeding. There are many features of his social thought that were only relevant in sixteenth-century Genevan society and which, therefore, must be left there. It goes without saying, for example, that in a world that encourages a tolerant stance vis-à-vis the sociological reality of religious plurality, any view that espouses theological purgation by means of legal enforcement is out of place. The same is true of any effort to promote personal morality by legal means. Commitment to religious liberty and freedom of conscience places these beyond the pale of the law. But, as we've seen throughout our analysis, there are elements in Calvin's extensive social teaching that do not suffer from such fatal deficiencies, and hence could be transferred to our times with less lukewarmness and timidity than is often shown. For instance, from Calvin we should learn that while the modality of the church's engagement with the socio-political order will depend on a given context, the *principle* and indeed the *necessity* of that engagement should not be in question. Also, of equal significance is the clear insight that while the political order and the economic order can make incontrovertible claims to legitimacy, they must never be allowed to lose sight of the divinely established purpose for their existence, namely, the service of the common good, not the enhancement of self-interest. These principles will prove useful anytime and anywhere—particularly in Majority World contexts.

As I write the concluding words to this essay, the U.S. financial system has experienced a mighty shakeup. This event, in turn, threatens to throw the world economy into a crisis of unprecedented magnitude. In the view of most analysts, the massive crash, which was prompted by the insolvency of several giant financial institutions, was caused by a careless pursuit of private gain, which was oblivious to the common good, combined with ineffective oversight on the part of the state whose role is to rein in economic greed and thereby protect the collectivity. Early estimates place the cost of repairing the damage at a whopping $700,000,000,000—a burden to be borne by the public purse! *Perhaps* a page taken from Calvin's politico-socio-economic ethics *might* help avert this calamity.

13

"A Pearl and a Leaven": John Calvin's Critical Two-Kingdoms Eschatology[1]

John Bolt

This chapter is a summary of and challenge to a contemporary interpretation of Calvin's eschatology. I will not be providing a comprehensive overview of Calvin's eschatological views, including the reign of Christ, the intermediate state and soul sleep, bodily resurrection, the final judgment, and so forth. For such broader treatment readers are encouraged to consult the literature provided in the notes. My focus is more narrow: Does the trend of recent scholarship do full justice to Calvin's own intentions and concerns? There is a conventional template for scholarly discussions of Calvin's eschatology that I shall describe and document in part but not pursue in detail.[2] After an initial brief survey of the direction

---

[1] I want to express my thanks to Calvin Theological Seminary student David Salverda for his assistance in getting material ready for me and in helping prepare this chapter for publication.

[2] The full-length study remains H. Quistorp, *Calvin's Doctrine of the Last Things*, tr. Harold Knight (London: Lutterworth; Richmond, Va.: John Knox, 1955). Partial treatments include: Willem Balke, *Calvin and the Anabaptist Radicals*, tr. Willem Heynen (Grand Rapids: Eerdmans, 1981), 295–300; Wilhelm Niesel, *The Theology of John Calvin* (Philadelphia: Westminster Press, 1956), who discusses eschatological themes in bits and pieces but has no distinct section on it; Thomas Torrance, *Kingdom and Church* (Edinburgh: Oliver & Boyd, 1956), 90–164; François Wendel, *Calvin: Origins and Development of his Religious Thought* (New York: Harper & Row, 1950), 284–90. Among the numerous essays, I have especially found the following to be helpful: Wilhelm Balke, "Some Characteristics of Calvin's Eschatology," in *Christian Hope in Context*, vol. 1, eds. A. van Egmond and D. van Keulen (Zoetermeer: Meinema, 2001),

of this scholarship, I will develop a counter-thesis to the generally prevailing tangent. While not disputing that Calvin's theology provides rich resources for a strong this-worldly (*Diesseits*), the-kingdom-is-already emphasis, I shall argue that the formulation of this emphasis in recent scholarship potentially misrepresents Calvin and also that *in our context* it is important to accent the equally strong two-kingdoms, other-worldly (*Jenseits*), not-yet dimension of Calvin's eschatology. To make this point I shall make use of the favorite metaphor of another Calvinist: Herman Bavinck's application of our Lord's parables on the pearl of great price and the leaven in Matthew 13.[3]

1 Is Calvin's eschatology adequate?

The template usually begins with some acknowledgment that Calvin's theology seems to lack a robust eschatology. Thus David Holwerda begins his article on eschatology and history in Calvin with these words: "Calvin has never been famous for his eschatology."[4] Then follows the author's exploration of some important eschatological angle or theme that he judges has hitherto been inadequately appreciated and utilized by Calvin scholars, themes that include Calvin's view of

---

(cont.) 30–64; I. John Hesselink, "The Millennium in the Reformed Tradition," *Reformed Review*, 52:2 (1999), 97–125; Jan Hoek, "Towards a Revitalization of Calvinistic Eschatology," *In die Skriflig*, 37:1 (2003): 95–113; David Holwerda, "Eschatology and History: A Look at Calvin's Eschatological Vision," in David Holwerda (ed.), *Exploring the Heritage of John Calvin* (Grand Rapids: Baker Academic, 1976), 110–39; Richard A. Muller, "Christ and the Eschaton: Calvin and Moltmann on the Duration of the Munus Regium," *Harvard Theological Review*, 74:1 (January 1981), 31–59; P.F. Theron, "The Kingdom of God and the Theology of Calvin," *In die Skriflig*, 35:2 (2001), 207–13; Van Wyk, "John Calvin on the Kingdom of God and Eschatology," *In die Skriflig*, 35:2 (2001), 191–205; C. Vander Kooi, "De Spanning van het 'reeds' en het 'nog niet' bij Calvijn, Kuyper, en Berkouwer," in M.E. Brinkman (ed.), *100 Jaar Theologie: Aspecten van een eeuw theologie in de Gereformeerde Kerken in Nederland* (Kampen: Kok, 1982), 248–82.

[3] Among the numerous places where Bavinck uses this double image, see John Bolt (ed.), *Essays on Religion, Science and Society*, trs. Harry Boonstra and Gerrit Sheeres (Grand Rapids: Baker Academic, 2008), 141.

[4] Holwerda, "Eschatology and History," 110; cf. Balke, "Characteristics of Calvin's Eschatology": "Calvin has been frequently accused of lacking interest in eschatology," 32.

history,[5] the kingdom of God,[6] the millennium,[7] corporate selfhood and *meditatio vitae futurae*,[8] and a closer look beyond the *Institutes* to the Commentaries.[9]

What exactly is being referred to in these complaints about Calvin's alleged inadequate eschatology? It is important to raise this because key historical periods of eschatological fervor, notably the Puritan tradition in England, did track from Calvin's legacy[10] and certain aspects of Calvin's eschatology are well known and have been explored by scholars. Already in 1901 Martin Schulze produced a monograph on Calvin's *meditatio vitae futurae* in *Institutes*, III.9, a work in which he explores at some length the parallels and differences between Calvin and Plato, particularly comparisons with Plato's *Phaedo*.[11] In addition, Quistorp's study appeared in German in 1941[12] before its English translation publication in 1955. Then, consider the discussions about Calvin's first theological treatise, *Psychopannychia*. In the Author's Preface to his study of Calvin's eschatology, Quistorp expresses his indebtedness to the inspiration of a lecture by Paul Althaus on the last things and to the "meetings of a Society for Dogmatics held in the house of Prof. D. Karl Barth in Bonn during the winter term of 1934–5." Quistorp adds that the subject for this seminar was "Calvin's eschatological writing *Psychopannychia*; unfortunately this theological seminary in the home of my revered

---

[5] Holwerda, "Eschatology and History."

[6] Hoek, "Towards a Revitalization of Calvinistic Eschatology"; and Torrance, *Kingdom and Church.*

[7] Hesselink, "The Millennium in the Reformed Tradition."

[8] Raymond Kemp Anderson, "Corporate Selfhood and *Meditatio Vitae Futurae*: How necessary is Eschatology for Christian Ethics?" *Journal of the Society of Christian Ethics*, 23:1 (2003), 21–46.

[9] Balke, "Characteristics of Calvin's Eschatology."

[10] See, *inter alia*, Iain Murray, *Puritan Hope: A Study in Revival and the Interpretation of Prophecy* (London: Banner of Truth Trust, 1971); Peter Toon, *Puritans, the Millennium and the Future of Israel: Puritan Eschatology, 1600 to 1660* (London: James Clarke, 1971); Michael Walzer, *The Revolution of the Saint* (Cambridge: Harvard University Press, 1965); David Little, *Religion, Order, and Law: A Study in Pre-Revolutionary England* (Chicago, University of Chicago Press, 1984).

[11] Martin Schulze, *Meditatio futurae vitae; ihr Begriff und ihre herrschende Stellung im System Calvins. Ein Beitrag zum Verstandnis von dessen Institutio, Studien zur Geschichte der Theologie und der Kirche*; Bd. 6, Heft 4 (Leipzig: Dieterich, 1901).

[12] Heinrich Quistorp, *Die letzten Dinge im Zeugnis Calvins: Calvins Eschatologie* (Gütersloh: Bertelsmann, 1941); this was a dissertation done at Halle.

teacher had to be broken up on account of the untimely suspension of his Bonn professorship by the National Socialist régime."[13] Barth and the students in his seminar were availing themselves of the recently published *Corpus Reformatorum* critical edition of *Psychopannychia*, prepared by Walther Zimmerli.[14] The *Psychopannychia* was first translated into English in 1581 and, as Timothy George has shown, is a rich source for key themes in Calvin's theology, especially his eschatology.[15]

And yet here are a few of the probes of concern about Calvin's eschatology. J.H. Van Wyk wonders more broadly "whether eschatology had not been the stepchild of the Reformation of the sixteenth century" and also whether eschatology was all that important for the Reformers and for Calvin in particular.[16] Van Wyk indicates his appreciation for the anti-speculative character of Calvin's eschatology, its Christocentricity, its emphasis on the physical resurrection, and its inclusion of a cosmic dimension, though the latter is, he says, "underexposed."[17] What he finds fault with is "a dualistic anthropology influenced by Platonism," a failure "to develop the Kingdom of God as a central theme," and a slight tendency to spiritualizing.[18] Heinrich Quistorp also suggests that Calvin "is less interested in the fulfillment of the church as society than in the salvation of its individual members" and speaks of language that is "characteristic of the individualizing tendency in the eschatology of Calvin which necessarily coheres with the spiritualizing tendency." Jan Hoek also takes note of "a spiritualizing and individualizing tendency"[19] in Calvin's eschatology though he is fair to point out that "this tendency is counterbalanced by his obedience to the Scriptural testimony of the resurrection of the body and the renewal of the cosmos."[20] Clark Pinnock's summary

[13] Quistorp, *Calvin's Doctrine of the Last Things*, 9–10.
[14] John Calvin, *Psychopannychia*, ed. Walther Zimmerli (Leipzig: A. Deichert, 1932).
[15] Timothy George, "Calvin's *Psychopannychia*: Another Look," in *In honor of John Calvin, 1509–64*, ed. E.J. Furcha (Montreal: McGill University Press, 1987), 297–329.
[16] Van Wyk, "John Calvin on the Kingdom of God and Eschatology," 193–4.
[17] Van Wyk, "John Calvin on the Kingdom of God and Eschatology," 201–2.
[18] Van Wyk, "John Calvin on the Kingdom of God and Eschatology," 202–3.
[19] Quistorp, *Calvin's Doctrine of the Last Things*, 180–1.
[20] Hoek, "Towards a Revitalization of Calvinistic Eschatology," 99–100; Hoek cites Calvin interpreters who argue for the spiritualizing and/or individualizing tendency, Balke, *Calvin and the Anabaptist Radicals*, 298; Velema, *Ethiek en Pelgrimage* (Amsterdam: Bolland, 1974), 35–5.

serves as a useful statement of the perceived problem: "The conservative Reformation, as we have noted, did not recover biblical eschatology in its fullness, and tended to lose the gains it made. Hope for the
coming of the kingdom became eclipsed in Protestant orthodoxy by an
almost exclusive concentration on the assurance of personal salvation
and what happened at death."[21]

2 Modern preoccupations

What, then, is the problem? When scholars fault Calvin for his alleged
eschatological anemia, for what they call the spiritualizing and individualizing character of his eschatology, and note a lack, which they want to
remedy, what they seem to have in mind is Calvin's perceived inadequacy with respect to *modern*, especially twentieth-century, concerns
about eschatology. More particularly, the concern is with eschatology and
ethics, and to specify the point more sharply, with *social ethics*. Here we
need to go back to the seminal challenges brought against liberal
Kulturprotestantismus by, among others, Albert Schweitzer[22] and Johannes
Weiss.[23] With these fundamental calls for reorientation, for an end to the
domestication of Jesus and a call to take his eschatological, even apocalyptic, message seriously, eschatology became the new arena for a theological call to arms. Leading the charge was Karl Barth with his statement
in the second edition of his *Römerbrief* that "if Christianity be not
altogether thoroughgoing eschatology, there remains in it no relationship
with Christ. Spirit which does not at every moment point from death to
the new life is not the Holy Spirit."[24] As James Orr had predicted in his

---

[21] Clark Pinnock, "Eschatological Hopes in the Protestant Tradition," in
Frederick Greenspahn (ed.), *The Human Condition in Jewish and Christian
Traditions* (Denver: KTAV Publishing House, 1986), 242–3.

[22] Albert Schweitzer, *The Quest of the Historical Jesus* (Minneapolis: Fortress
Press, 2001); this is the first complete English edition, ed. John Bowden, trs.
W. Montgomery, Susan Cupitt, and John Bowden.

[23] Johannes Weiss, *Jesus' Proclamation of the Kingdom of God*, tr. and ed. and with
an introduction by Richard Hyde Hiers and David Larrimore Holland
(Philadelphia, Fortress Press,1971).

[24] Karl Barth, *The Epistle to the Romans*, tr. Edwyn C. Hoskins (Oxford and New
York: Oxford University Press, 1933; rpt. 1972), 314. Hoskins' translation is a
rather tame rendering of Barth's almost violent German: "*Christentum, das
nicht ganz und gar und restlos Eschatologie ist, hat mit Christus ganz und gar und
restlos nicht zu tun.*"

Progress of Dogma,[25] the scramble for an eschatological Christianity was on, particularly for an eschatological ethics.[26]

It is the quest for a more eschatological, that is to say, more historical and *diesseitig* Calvin, a Calvin that provides theological grounding for a this-worldly social ethic, that has fueled the dissatisfaction with Calvin and some Calvin scholarship. After David Holwerda's opening comment, "Calvin has never been famous for his eschatology," he observes that "political and economic historians have frequently emphasized Calvin's revolutionary understanding of history."[27] One need not make a full-blown case for Calvin the "revolutionary,"[28] to seek and legitimately

---

[25] In the conclusion to his *Progress of Dogma* (New York: A.C. Armstrong; London: Hodder and Stoughton, 1901), James Orr judges that eschatology, particularly its ethical application to concrete life in society, would be *the* doctrinal issue of the twentieth century. According to Orr, "the lines of essential doctrine are by this time well and established" so that the church's task now is "to bring in the Kingdom of God among men. I look to the twentieth century to be an era of Christian ethic even more than of Christian theology. With God on our side, history behind us, and the unchanging needs of the human heart to appeal to, we need tremble for the future of neither," 351–2.

[26] In addition to Weiss, also see Amos Niven Wilder, *Eschatology and Ethics in the Teaching of Jesus* (New York: Harper, 1950); Richard H. Hiers, *Jesus and Ethics: Four Interpretations* (Philadelphia: Westminster Press, 1968); Wolfhart Pannenberg, *Theology and the Kingdom of God* (Philadelphia: Westminster Press, 1969); Herman Ridderbos, *The Coming of the Kingdom* (Phillipsburg, N.J.: Presbyterian & Reformed Pub. Co., 1975); Carl Braaten, *Eschatology and Ethics* (Minneapolis, Augsburg, 1974); Jürgen Moltmann, *Theology of Hope*, tr. James W. Leitch (New York: Harper and Row, 1967); Wolfhart Pannenberg, *Ethics*, tr. Keith Crim (Philadelphia: Westminster John Knox, 1981; London: Search Press, 1999); Douglas James Schuurman, *Creation, Eschaton, and Ethics: The Ethical Significance of the Creation–Eschaton Relation in the Thought of Emil Brunner and Jürgen Moltmann* (New York: P. Lang, 1991); Philip LeMasters, *Discipleship for all Believers: Christian Ethics and the Kingdom of God* (Scottdale, Pa.: Herald Press, 1992).

[27] Holwerda, "Eschatology and History," 110; Herman Bavinck makes a similar claim in "The Influence of the Protestant Reformation on the Moral and Religious Condition of Communities and Nations," *Proceedings of the Fifth General Council Toronto 1892 of the Alliance of the Reformed Churches holding the Presbyterian System* (London: Publication Committee of the Presbyterian Church of England, 1892), 48–55.

[28] Though this is frequently done, for example, W. Fred Graham, *The Constructive Revolutionary: John Calvin and his Socio-Economic Impact* (Lansing: Michigan State University Press, 1987).

find in Calvin sources for a more dynamic and future-oriented purposive view of history. Rather than repeat or summarize the large body of writing that makes this point, let me cite just one additional commentator on Calvin's eschatology in its context. In his work on the eschatology of the Reformation T.F. Torrance defines Calvin's views in contrast with Luther's "two-kingdoms" doctrine. Torrance notes that though it is not true to say that "Luther had no sense of the new creation," he did not adequately propose "a positive connexion between the two kingdoms in history, no *tertium comparitionis* which faith may discern here and now in this world."[29] Stated differently: "Luther did not give sufficient attention to the corporeal embodiment of the Word here and now within the world, an embodiment which already spans the distinction between the two kingdoms as a *tertium datur*."[30] For Luther, the "apocalyptic strife of the Kingdom of God" is understood in terms of a struggle that creates anxiety of faith for the believer. Christ's victory is more "a consolation in *Anfechtung* than an actual anticipation of the final victory of the Son of Man."[31] According to Torrance, the influence of Martin Butzer, especially his *De Regno Christi*,[32] is important for understanding how Calvin rethought the doctrine of the kingdom of Christ through the person of the Mediator and his resurrection and ascension. Thus, the kingdom of God is here *now*, especially in the church as the new humanity.[33] Therefore, in addition to consolation in times of struggle and suffering, Calvin also emphasized the reality of the new creation as a *present* reality. Salvation is restoration of lost order, the restoration of the image of God, the renewal of creation.[34] This gave impetus to a vibrant action of gospel outreach and concrete social transformation.[35] The dissatisfaction we alluded to earlier is thus a conviction that the elements in Calvin's eschatology that underscore the present reality of the kingdom of God in human history have not received their proper due.

---

[29] Torrance, "Eschatology of the Reformation," 52, 45.

[30] Torrance, "Eschatology of the Reformation," 48.

[31] Torrance, "Eschatology of the Reformation," 52.

[32] See Wilhelm Pauck (ed.), *Melanchthon and Bucer, The Library of Christian Classics*, vol. 19 (Philadelphia, Westminster Press, 1969).

[33] Torrance, "Eschatology of the Reformation," 60.

[34] See Ronald S. Wallace, *Calvin's Doctrine of the Christian Life* (Edinburgh: Oliver & Boyd, 1959), Part III, "The Restoration of True Order"; Lucien J. Richard, *The Spirituality of John Calvin* (Atlanta: John Knox Press, 1974), ch. IV, C: "Sanctification as the Restoration of God's Image in Man and His World: The Concept of Order and the Spiritual Life."

[35] Torrance, "Eschatology of the Reformation," 61–2.

The trajectory of this scholarship then seeks to compensate by emphasizing a Calvin who is not a closet other-worldly Platonist[36] but one whose interests are *diessietig*, whose eschatology is linked to history, who underscores resurrection, ascension, and victory as Christ's action for and gift to the church. Appeal is made to such passages in Calvin as his commentary on John 13:31: "Now the Son of Man has been glorified, and God has been glorified in him."

> . . . for in the cross of Christ, as in a magnificent theater, the inestimable goodness of God is displayed before the whole world. In all the creatures, indeed, both high and low, the glory of God shines, but nowhere has it shone more brightly than in the cross, in which there has been an astonishing change of things, the condemnation of all men has been manifested, sin has been blotted out, salvation has been restored to men; and, in short, the whole world has been renewed, and everything restored to good order.

Similarly, Calvin's commentary on John 12:31: "Now is the judgment of this world; now the ruler of this world will be driven out."

> Now is the judgment of this world. The Lord now, as if he had already succeeded in the contest, boasts of having obtained a victory not only over fear, but over death; for he describes, in lofty terms, the advantage of his death, which might have struck his disciples with consternation. Some view the word, judgment (*krisis*) as denoting reformation, and others, as denoting condemnation. I rather agree with the former who explain it to mean, that the world must be restored to a proper order; for the Hebrew word *mishpat*, which is translated judgment, means a well-ordered state. Now we know, that out of Christ there is nothing but confusion in the world; and though Christ had already begun to erect the kingdom of God, yet his death was the commencement of a well-regulated condition, and the full restoration of the world.

Even the *meditatio vitae futurae*, properly understood, we are repeatedly told, must not be taken to suggest approval of world-flight.[37] In itself this

---

36 As argued by Martin Schulze, *Meditatio futurae vitae*.

37 Holwerda, "Eschatology and History," 113–21; Van Wyk, "John Calvin on the Kingdom of God," 196–97; Wallace, *Calvin's Doctrine of the Christian Life*, 87–93; *contra* M. Schulze, *Meditatio futurae vitae*. This was already understood by P. Lobstein, *Das Ethik Calvins in Ihren Gründzugen entworfen* (Strasbourg: C.F. Schmidt, 1877), 110–12; cited by Anderson, "Corporate Selfhood," 26.

is not a controversial claim; its truth is apparent immediately from a quick reading of *Institutes*, III.9.[38] Though the language of *contemptio mundi* jars with modern readers, Calvin insists that "contempt of the present life" must never "engender a hatred of it or ingratitude against God" (III.9.3). Rather it is a "perverse love of this life" that leads us "to the desire for a better one." In sum: "Therefore, if the earthly life be compared with the heavenly, it is doubtless to be at once despised and trampled underfoot. Of course it is never to be hated *except in so far as it holds us subject to sin*; although not even hatred of that condition may ever properly *be turned against life itself*" (III.9.4; emphasis added). Believers are to use *and* enjoy(!) the earthly goods given to us by our Creator, but never to forget that we are pilgrims on the way to our homeland.[39] "By his word the Lord lays down this measure when he teaches that the present life is for his people as a pilgrimage on which they are hastening toward the Heavenly Kingdom" (III.10.1). Anderson has provided a helpful set of examples in which Calvin uses the *meditatio vitae futurae* as a guide for pilgrims making concrete decisions in the world.[40] To take just one,

> Finally, let your whole life correspond to your profession. Shew that the gospel of our Lord Jesus Christ is a light to your path, that you err not like the children of darkness. And forasmuch as the world is now so corrupt and perverse, be so much the more vigilant not to prick yourselves among the thorns. The time of our pilgrimage is short, so that if we reflect on that immortal glory to which God invites us, we shall have no occasion to faith by the way. On the other hand, if we meditate on the inestimable goodness which our indulgent Heavenly Father has shewn us, and the precious treasures of grace which in every form he has shed on us so abundantly, we shall be base indeed if we are not touched by his love, so as to forget or despise whatever belongs to the world, to break all the ties which hold us back from him and disentangle ourselves of every obstacle that clogs our march.[41]

---

[38] John Calvin, *Institutes of the Christian Religion*, ed. John T. McNeill, tr. Ford Lewis Battles (Philadelphia: Westminster Press, 1960 (1559)).

[39] On pilgrimage, see W.H. Velema, *Ethiek en Pelgrimage: Over de Bijbelse Vreemdelingschap* (Amsterdam: Bolland, 1974²).

[40] Anderson, "Corporate Selfhood," 38–9.

[41] John Calvin, "Letter to the Brethren of Poitou," 3 September 1554, in Henry Beveridge and Jules Bonnet (eds.), *Selected Works of John Calvin: Tracts and Letters*, vol. 6, Letters, part 3 (1554–1558), tr. Robert Gilchrist (Grand Rapids: Baker Academic, 1983), 70–1.

Meditation on the future life is simply part of the gospel call to follow our Lord; it is to live in the power of his resurrection. "To conclude in a word: if believers' eyes are turned to the power of the resurrection, in their hearts the cross of Christ will at last triumph over the devil, flesh, sin and wicked men" (III.9.6). Niesel has it exactly right when he observes: "The ethics of Calvin are not negativist; they are rather determined by the fact that we have a living Lord who was crucified and rose again and who will come again as our Savior. In the strictest sense they stem from the principle of the imitation of Christ."[42]

3 This world or the next?

I do not quarrel with the basic *content* of the scholarship that wants to accent the positive, creation-affirming side of Calvin's eschatology. This emphasis is true to Calvin and it is an important part of his theological vision; many other passages from Calvin's oeuvre could be provided in addition to the citations above from his *Commentary on the Gospel of John*.[43] Calvin does indeed think of the renewal that is the fruit of Christ's work as cosmic, involving the whole creation. Salvation is the restoration of lost order,[44] a restoration that had already taken place in Christ, "especially in His death and resurrection."[45] For the purposes of this chapter, I shall simply affirm the conclusions of this trajectory and stipulate that Calvin's eschatological vision is indeed cosmic, that the "renewal manifesting itself in the body of Christ is the renewal that embraces the whole creation . . . The destiny of the church cannot be divorced from the destiny of the world."[46] Or, to once again quote David Holwerda, "The history of salvation which becomes visible in the church contains within it the meaning of the history of the world. And the

---

[42] Niesel, *Theology of Calvin*, 151.

[43] For a more complete portrait, see Holwerda, "Eschatology and History"; Torrance, "The Eschatology of Hope: John Calvin," in Thomas F. Torrance, *Kingdom and Church* (Edinburgh: Oliver & Boyd, 1956); Hoek, "Toward a Revitalization of Calvinist Eschatology."

[44] See note 34 above.

[45] Holwerda, "Eschatology and History," 135; Holwerda points to Calvin's Commentaries, on Lk. 17:20; Amos 9:13; Mt. 6:10; Is. 11:6; Eph. 1:10.

[46] Holwerda, "Eschatology and History," 135; the evidence Holwerda puts forth includes a close reading of the *meditatio vitae futurae* section in *Institutes*, III.9, Calvin's exegesis of John. 12:31 and 13:31, his strong Christocentrism, Calvin's interpretation of biblical prophecy in passages such as Daniel 7:27

renewal manifesting itself in the body of Christ is the renewal that embraces the whole creation."[47]

But, having said that, have we said enough? Is this accent on the historical, on the immanent, *as it has been understood and proclaimed in the twentieth century*, really true to Calvin? And is it the accent that the church needs to hear today? On both questions I dissent from the trajectory of scholarship briefly summarized above. Rather than treating Calvin's *jenseitig* accents as regrettable lapses that need to be balanced by strong affirmations of the history-changing power of "kingdom action" by believers, I will argue the reverse. Directly put, I do not think that David Willis' characteristic statement about Calvin's "otherworldliness" is entirely helpful: "It is accurate to categorize Calvin's ethic as 'other-worldly,' but only if one recognizes that his concentration on the other world is for the purpose of providing an impetus for Christian life in this world."[48]

While this is an accurate description of twentieth-century interest in eschatology, I do not believe it correctly describes Calvin's concerns, at least not without important qualification. Instead, I propose a somewhat contrary thesis,

> Calvin's world- and history-affirming eschatology must be clearly distinguished from and seen as a critique of all attempts to immanentize (and historicize)[49] the kingdom of God on earth, including many twentieth-century appropriations of Calvin's own eschatology.

I shall defend this thesis by briefly discussing the immanentist leanings of twentieth-century eschatological ethics, locating Calvin's position in the larger historical-narrative frame of historicizing eschatology, and considering Calvin's two-kingdoms doctrine within his

---

(cont.) and Matthew 24:7, and his discussion of the Antichrist. Holwerda concludes that "the church and its activity is an essential part of the eschatological movement of history from Advent to Return" ("Eschatology and History," 133).

[47] Holwerda, "Eschatology and History," 135.

[48] E. David Willis, *Calvin's Catholic Christology* (Leiden: Brill, 1966), 143.

[49] I take this language from Eric Voegelin, *The New Science of Politics: An Introduction* (Chicago: University of Chicago Press, 1952). "Historicizing" or "immanentizing" the eschaton takes place when the Christian understanding of history's fulfillment *beyond* history is exchanged for a progressivist fulfillment *within* history. The meaning of history is then sought not outside history but within history itself. (See *The New Science of Politics*, ch. IV.)

convictions about the kingly rule of Christ (*munus regium*). I shall conclude by using Herman Bavinck's "pearl and leaven" imagery to summarize the implications of Calvin's eschatology for the Christian life today.

4 The trajectory of theologies of hope

No one knowledgeable in theological developments of the late twentieth century could, *anno domini* 2008, read Thomas Torrance's 1956 essay, "The Eschatology of Hope: John Calvin,"[50] without immediately bringing to mind Jürgen Moltmann's epochal work, *Theology of Hope*,[51] a work that represents its own trajectory in the history of Christian thought. A brief comparison of Torrance's and Moltmann's treatment is instructive. Both authors point to the *missionary* character of hope, in Calvin's case a hope that can be spoken of as "a wish that the kingdom of Christ should flourish everywhere."[52] Torrance cites Calvin using language that might sound surprising to some when Calvin observes that it is "a work of immense difficulty to establish the heavenly reign of God upon earth."[53] Torrance then comments that for Calvin, the church as a covenant community, participating in Christ's death, resurrection and ascension, is compelled by "an inner necessity: to a threefold action: (1) Gathering the lost and fallen into the church; (2) bearing a public face through Word and sacrament along with godly life; (3) working for the unity of Christ's body."[54] We shall consider shortly how Calvin works this out concretely in a discussion of his two-kingdoms doctrine, but first take a brief look at Moltmann's understanding of the missionary character of a theology of hope.

As a truly twentieth-century theologian, Moltmann is a convicted adherent of the Barthian dictum that all theology must be about eschatology,

> There is therefore only one real problem in Christian theology, which its own object forces upon it and which it in turn forces on mankind and on

---

[50] In Torrance, *Kingdom and Church*, 90–164.

[51] Jürgen Moltmann, *Theology of Hope*, tr. James W. Leitch (New York: Harper and Row, 1967).

[52] Calvin, "Letter to Nicholas Radziwill" (13 February 1555) in Beveridge and Bonnet, *Selected Works*, 134.

[53] Calvin, "Letter to Nicholas Radziwill," 135.

[54] Torrance, "Eschatology of Hope," 163–4.

human thought: the problem of the future . . . A proper theology would therefore have to be constructed in the light of its future goal. Eschatology should not be its end, but its beginning.[55]

Christian theology *is* a theology of *hope*. Christian hope is based on the fulfilled promises of God in Christ: "The God who reveals himself in Jesus must be thought of as the God of the Old Testament, as the God of the exodus and the promise, as the God with 'future as his essential nature,'" as the one who "is declared by Israel's history of promise."[56] The resurrection of Jesus Christ is therefore the great new act of God, in fulfillment of his promises, an eschatological event that serves "as an analogy of what is to come to all . . . a foreshadowing and anticipation of the future."[57] Stated differently,

> The Christian hope for the future comes of observing a specific, unique event—that of the resurrection and appearing of Jesus Christ. The hopeful theological mind, however, can observe this event only in seeking to span the future horizon projected by this event. Hence to recognize the resurrection of Christ means to recognize in this even the future of God for the world and the future which man finds in this God and his acts.[58]

It is in this light that Moltmann begins to speak of the "missionary" dimension of a theology of hope. It is first of all the *missio* of Jesus, it is about the *intention* of God in the mission of Jesus, a *missio* that "becomes intelligible only by the *promissio*." The future of Jesus, "in the light of which he can be recognized as what he is, is illuminated in advance by

> *the promise of the righteousness of God,*
> *the promise of life as a result of resurrection* from the dead,
> and *the promise of the kingdom of God* in a new totality of being."[59]

For Moltmann, this kingdom must be seen and experienced under the concealment of the cross (*tectum sub cruce*). Thus "the coming lordship of God takes place here in the suffering of the Christians, who because of their hope cannot be conformed to the world, but are drawn by the mission and love of Christ into discipleship and conformity to his sufferings."

---

[55] Moltmann, *Theology of Hope*, 16.
[56] Moltmann, *Theology of Hope*, 141.
[57] Moltmann, *Theology of Hope*, 180–1.
[58] Moltmann, *Theology of Hope*, 194.
[59] Moltmann, *Theology of Hope*, 203.

However, Moltmann is concerned to point out that "this way of taking into consideration the cross and resurrection does not mean that the 'kingdom of God' is spiritualized and made into a thing of the beyond, but it becomes this-worldly and becomes the antithesis and contradiction of a godless and god-forsaken world."[60] Moltmann spells out concretely what this means,

> If the promise of the kingdom of God shows us a universal eschatological future horizon spanning all things—'that God may be all in all'—then it is impossible for the man of hope to adopt an attitude of religious and cultic resignation from the world. On the contrary, he is compelled to accept the world in all meekness, subject as it is to death and the powers of annihilation, and to guide all things toward their new being. He becomes homeless with the homeless, for the sake of the peace of God. He becomes rightless with the rightless, for the sake of the divine right that is coming.[61]

The "man of hope" accepts the promise of the kingdom, which includes all things, "excluding nothing, but embracing in hope everything wherein God will be all in all. The *pro-missio* of the kingdom is the ground of the *missio* of love to the world."[62]

Moltmann develops this further in his *The Crucified God*,[63] where modern "speculative christologies of the atonement" are faulted for their "lack of eschatology."[64] By contrast, Moltmann attempts to join "historical and eschatological method" in a "reciprocal relationship" and see the historical Jesus, his trial and his death in terms of "eschatological anticipation" where "the last must come first, the future precedes the past, the end reveals the beginning and objective time-relationships are reversed."[65] Christology—who Jesus is and what he does—must be interpreted as "in the service of the eschatology of God who is coming and his righteousness that makes all things

---

[60] Moltmann, *Theology of Hope*, 222; Moltmann's universalization of "god-forsakenness" as a category by which to describe the world is reminiscent of Gnostic notions that the world is an alien place.

[61] Moltmann, *Theology of Hope*, 224.

[62] Moltmann, *Theology of Hope*, 224.

[63] Jürgen Moltmann, *The Crucified God: The Cross of Christ as the Foundation and Criticism of Christian Theology*, translated by R.A. Wilson and John Bowden (London: SCM Press, 1974).

[64] Moltmann, *Crucified God*, 92.

[65] Moltmann, *Crucified God*, 113.

new."[66] Here the new kingdom of God, the kingdom of righteousness and love, enters the world. "Through his death the risen Christ introduces the coming kingdom of God into the godless present by means of representative suffering."[67] Jesus' death on the cross is given a Trinitarian significance by Moltmann; the death of Christ is a "death in God."[68] Moltmann judges that this is the only possible answer to an atheism that declares the "death of God,"

> The only way past protest atheism is through a theology of the cross which understands God as the suffering God in the suffering Christ and which cries out with the godforsaken God "my God, why have you forsaken me?" For this theology, God and suffering are no longer contradictions, as in theism and atheism, but God's being is in suffering and the suffering is in God's being.[69]

The death of Christ is a dialectical event in the inner Trinitarian life of God, it is the means by which God becomes "the great companion—the fellow sufferer, who understands."[70] Thus, all evil, "even Auschwitz is taken up into God himself."[71] The practical consequence is *liberation* from the vicious cycles of death in personal repression and alienation, poverty, political oppression, and the exploitation of nature. The liberation called for includes socialism, democracy, emancipation, and peace with nature.[72]

Moltmann's understanding of "mission" is shaped by an eschatological kingdom vision that begins with a "godless" and "god-forsaken" world needing the "embrace" of God's love and leading to liberation; the mission of God's people is to join those who suffer and to stand with them. Calvin, on the other hand, understands mission to be a matter of bringing the word of reconciling grace that calls sinners under divine judgment to experience the forgiveness of God earned at the cross. Moltmann's cross is the sign of solidarity in suffering;[73] Calvin's cross represents the divine judgment on human sin, atones for it, and in the power of the resurrection saves us.[74]

---

[66] Moltmann, *Crucified God*, 180.

[67] Moltmann, *Crucified God*, 185.

[68] Moltmann, *Crucified God*, 207.

[69] Moltmann, *Crucified God*, 227.

[70] Moltmann, *Crucified God*, 255; Moltmann is quoting A.N. Whitehead here.

[71] Moltmann, *Crucified God*, 278.

[72] Moltmann, *Crucified God*, 325–8.

[73] This is the whole purpose of, especially, his *The Crucified God*.

[74] Recall our earlier citation: "To conclude in a word: if believers' eyes are turned to the power of the resurrection, in their hearts the cross of Christ will at last triumph over the devil, flesh, sin and wicked men" (III.9.6).

5 Calvin and messianic eschatology: the two kingdoms

I have taken this little excursion into Moltmann's eschatology in order to present Calvin in sharper relief. With Moltmann in mind, it is hard to present Calvin faithfully as a "revolutionary" thinker whose joining of history and eschatology provides a vision for establishing the kingdom of Christ on earth. Calvin is an Augustinian on this score while Moltmann's eschatology of hope is part of a tradition of challenge to Augustine. Instead of seeing the kingdom of God as a spiritual reality manifested primarily in the church, as Augustine did, Moltmann joins a long line of theologians of messianic eschatology or historicizing eschatology that was present in the early church, repudiated by Augustine,[75] but revived by the twelfth-century Calabrian Abbot, Joachim of Fiore (c. 1135–1202).[76] Moltmann acknowledges his link to Joachim in an essay comparing Joachim and Thomas Aquinas as representatives of "messianic" and "transcendental" eschatologies respectively.[77] Joachim's thought undoubtedly had a formative influence on Moltmann, especially in the notion of a "Trinitarian history." As Moltmann notes: "Joachim was the first, but not the only one, to see Trinity and eschatology together eschatologically in such a way that the history of the kingdom has a trinitarian determination and the Trinity is thought of in the realm of its own glory as the consummation of its own trinitarian history."[78] Exploring this "conversation" between Joachim and Thomas leads Moltmann to a position that, he says, embraces both chiliasm and

---

[75] Augustine knew the messianic millenarian dreams of some in the early church—admitting he once shared them—but upon considered reflection, at the time he wrote the *City of God*, he judged them to be "ridiculous fancies" (*City of God*, xx, 7), a judgment shared by Calvin who spoke of them as "Jewish vanity," a matter of "stupidly imagining such a perfection as can never be found in a community of men" (*Institutes*, IV.20.1, 2).

[76] Among the volumes of literature that have been written about Joachim and his tangents, I have found the following especially helpful: Norman Cohn, *The Pursuit of the Millennium* (1957; 1970); Bernard McGinn, *Visions of the End: Apocalyptic Traditions in the M. A.* (1979); Marjorie Reeves, *Joachim of Fiore and the Prophetic Future* (1976); Eric Voegelin, *The New Science of Politics* (Chicago and London: The University of Chicago Press, 1952).

[77] Jürgen Moltmann, "Christian Hope—Messianic or Transcendent: A Theological Conversation with Joachim of Fiore and Thomas Aquinas," in *History and the Triune God: Contributions to Trinitarian History* (New York: Crossroad, 1992), 91–109.

[78] Moltmann, "Christian Hope," 104.

(transcendental) eschatology: "no chiliasm without eschatology; no eschatology without chiliasm . . . Christian hope is messianic hope against a horizon of eschatological expectation."[79]

Placing Moltmann in a line of thinkers, including Joachim, the radical Anabaptists, the Fifth Monarchy men, secular utopians such as Saint-Simon and Karl Marx, and twentieth-century theologies of liberation, helps us understand Calvin better.[80] Whatever we do with the world- and history-affirming statements that figure so prominently in recent scholarship, it is clear that Calvin cannot be thought of as a "revolutionary" in the historicizing and immanentizing tradition of Joachim. Calvin strongly opposes this tradition, believing it the greatest confusion to think of the kingdom of Christ in non-spiritual, earthly, forms.[81] It was, he declared, crucial to distinguish two kingdoms, one spiritual "whereby the conscience is instructed in piety and reverencing God," the other political "whereby man is educated for the duties of humanity and citizenship that must be maintained among men" (III.19.15). The distinction is very important for Calvin since he wishes to avoid the serious mistake of "misapplying to the political order the gospel teaching on spiritual freedom." The distinction is as basic for Calvin as that of body and soul:

> For some, on hearing that liberty is promised in the gospel, a liberty which acknowledges no king and no magistrate among men, but looks to Christ alone, think that they can receive no benefit from their liberty so long as they see any power placed over them. Accordingly, they think that nothing will be safe until the whole world is changed into a new form, when there will be neither courts, nor laws, nor magistrates, nor anything of the kind to interfere, as they suppose, with their liberty.
>
> But if it is the will of God that while we aspire to true piety we are pilgrims upon the earth, and if such pilgrimage stands in need of such aids, those who take them away from man rob him of his humanity. As to their allegation that there ought to be such perfection in the Church of God that

---

[79] Moltmann, "Christian Hope," 109.

[80] Of the voluminous literature on political messianism, J.L. Talmon's two-volume treatment is particularly illuminating: Jacob Leib Talmon, *The Origins of Totalitarian Democracy* (New York: Praeger, 1960); Jacob Leib Talmon, *Political Messianism : The Romantic Phase* (London : Secker & Warburg, 1960).

[81] For a helpful treatment of Calvin's doctrine of the two-kingdoms, see David Van Drunen, "The Two Kingdoms: A Reassessment of the Transformationist Calvin," *Calvin Theological Journal* 40 (2005), 248–66. I am indebted to Van Drunen for his extended conversation on this topic and recommend his article as a solid complement to what I am attempting in this chapter.

her guidance should suffice for law, they stupidly imagine her to be such
as she never can be found in the community of men. For while the inso-
lence of the wicked is so great, and their iniquity so stubborn, that it can
scarcely be curbed by any severity of laws, what do we expect would be
done by those whom force can scarcely repress from doing ill, were they
to see perfect impunity for their wickedness? (IV.20.1, 2)

It is in the very nature of pilgrimage that one seeks a "better" place and
Calvin explicitly directs our attention there in a discussion of the kingly
office of Christ(!),

Now with regard to the special application of this to each one of us—the
same "eternity" ought to inspire us to hope for blessed immortality. For
we see that whatever is earthly is of the world and of time and is indeed
fleeting. Therefore Christ, to lift our hope to heaven, declares that his
"kingship is not of this world" (John 18:36). In short, when any one of us
hears that Christ's kingship is spiritual, aroused by this word let him
attain to the hope of a better life; and since it is now protected by Christ's
hand, let him await the full fruit of this grace in the age to come. (II.15.3)

For Calvin, Christ's kingdom is spiritual: "We have said that we can perceive the force and usefulness of Christ's kingship only when we recognize it to be spiritual . . . the happiness promised us in Christ does not
consist in outward advantages—such as leading a joyous and peaceful
life, having rich possessions, being safe from all harm, and abounding
with delights such as the flesh commonly longs after. No, our happiness
belongs to the heavenly life!" Calvin does speak of the benefits of
Christ's kingdom, and for this life: "For since it is not earthly or carnal
and hence subject to corruption, but spiritual, it lifts us up even to eternal life" (II.15.4). It is patience and endurance in our pilgrim life of suffering that Calvin accents, not a history-grabbing, world-transforming
revolutionary program for action.

It is worth noting that Calvin here is in full agreement with representatives of the Augustinian tradition, such as Thomas Aquinas, when he says:
"Nevertheless we are not to look forward to a state wherein man is to possess the Holy Ghost more perfectly that he has possessed it hithertofore . . .
[i.e., before the consummation]."[82] Even Jonathan Edwards, celebrated and
condemned for his "postmillennial optimism," nonetheless refuses to grant
the possibility of perfection for the redeemed. Here is his claim at the conclusion of *Dissertation Concerning the End for Which God Created the World*,

---

[82] Thomas Aquinas, *Summa Theologia*, I–II, q. 106, art. 4, resp.

> 'Tis no solid objection against God's aiming at an infinitely perfect union
> of the creature with himself, that the particular time will never come when
> it can be said, the union is now infinitely perfect . . . God, in glorifying the
> saints in heaven with eternal felicity, aims to satisfy his infinite grace or
> benevolence, by the bestowment of a good infinitely valuable, because
> eternal: and yet there will never come the moment, when it can be said
> that now this infinitely valuable good has been actually bestowed.[83]

The Augustinian tradition categorically repudiates all historicizing and
immanentizing of the eschaton because it is convinced that our human
destiny is not exhausted in this world. There are eternal benefits available
now to Christian pilgrims: a freedom in the Spirit that liberates the conscience and a conviction about Christ's kingship that sustains us in times
of trouble and suffering. The other government is political, "whereby man
is educated for the duties of humanity and citizenship that must be maintained among men." According to Calvin, it is crucial that these two governments be kept distinct, "that we not misapply to the political order the
gospel teaching on spiritual freedom" (III.19.15). What Calvin says in
Institutes, III.19 about the misapplication of Christian liberty he reiterates
more generally in *Institutes*, IV.20 with respect to the magistracy. To those
who wish to have ecclesiastical polity serve as the rule for the *res publica*,
Calvin thunderously objects: "But they stupidly imagine such a perfection
as can never be found in a community of men" (IV.20.2). The principle is
clear: gospel categories are not to be applied to the arena of law, politics,
and statecraft. This is the fundamental objection of the Augustinian tradition more generally to the millenarian and Joachimist alternative: it is
eschatologically premature; it immanentizes the eschaton and gives our
universal human history an eternal weight of glory that it does not
deserve and cannot possibly bear. Political messianism always disap-
points and frustrates those who place their hope in it. Furthermore, hope
thus conceived cannot give birth to genuine liberty; instead, tyranny is its
fruit as the history of political messianism clearly demonstrates.

6 Conclusion: a pearl and a leaven

This chapter has been less of a direct and complete exposition of Calvin's
eschatology than an attempt to provide a frame for it. As I indicated

---

[83] Jonathan Edwards, *Dissertation Concerning the End for which God Created the
World*, in *The Works of Jonathan Edwards*, vol. 8, *Ethical Writings* (New Haven
and London: Yale University Press, 1989), 536.

earlier, I do not have a scholarly beef with those who more recently accent the historical–eschatological and dynamic elements in Calvin's thought. I quarrel with some of the application that in my judgment ignores Calvin's own clear insistence that the kingdom of Christ is spiritual and that it is a mistake to apply gospel and eschatological categories to this-worldly realities. Some of the citations taken from Calvin inadvertently contribute to this misunderstanding and misuse because they are incomplete. Consider, for example, a favorite passage we considered earlier, Calvin's commentary on John 12:31, where Calvin says the following,

> Now we know, that out of Christ there is nothing but confusion in the world; and though Christ had already begun to erect the kingdom of God, yet his death was the commencement of a well-regulated condition, and the full restoration of the world.

On its own, this seems like a strong affirmation of a this-worldly, history-transforming statement. However, Calvin immediately adds a sentence that should have warned anyone tempted to read him in that way:

> Yet it must also be observed, that this proper arrangement cannot be established in the world, until the kingdom of Satan be first destroyed, until the flesh, and everything opposed to the righteousness of God, be reduced to nothing.

The *telos* of history cannot be found within history itself; it is transcendent and comes only with the consummation.

It remains now to sketch briefly why this challenge to much of the revisionist reading of Calvin is so important. For Augustine and those who follow his path,[84] including Calvin, this world is always on the short side of the consummation and characterized by a radical antithesis between the City of God and the City of this World. Christians are therefore pilgrims, citizens of two kingdoms, and this duality is an essential part of their ecclesiology and their eschatology. Augustinian and Calvinist Christians resist all forms of monism, including gospel monism, that imply a righteousness possible for this age that is reserved for the age to come.

It is important to honor the concerns of those who have accented Calvin's *diesseitig* statements. Apprehensions about "individualizing"

---

[84] Here I want to put in a word of praise and recommendation for Jean Bethke Elshtain's wonderful book on Augustine, *Augustine and the Limits of Politics* (Notre Dame, Ind.: University of Notre Dame Press, 1995).

and "spiritualizing" arise from fears that Christians will be indifferent to the brokenness of this world, uncaring about the suffering and the needy. This is a legitimate concern. My challenge in this chapter will undoubtedly be received by some as a capitulation to the status quo, an unduly conservative response to a hurting world.[85] My pre-emptive response is twofold.

First, it is my considered judgment that the church today is in less danger of being other-worldly than it is of being too worldly. Social concerns such as poverty and climate change are ever before us; evangelizing the lost not as much. In the summer of 2008, my own denomination, the Christian Reformed Church, put a great deal of energy and money in a "Sea-to-Sea" bicycle event to raise awareness for poverty. I honor the concern but wonder if this is the church's primary task; why not a similar event to raise up 100 new missionaries a year, especially to the Muslim world? We ought to be concerned if our attention to this-worldly problems and solutions begins to command a more prominent place in our hearts than the world's lost. Calvin's understanding of the spiritual kingship of Christ serves as an impetus to gather his sheep into the fold; it was never intended as a motivator for social amelioration.

But didn't Calvin work for the improvement of Geneva? Doesn't the Reformed tradition place a high value on the office of the diaconate? Shouldn't Christians be an influence for good in society? Of course. To

---

[85] This is a fairly safe prediction. As proof I would call attention to the response by Timothy Palmer to David Van Drunen's essay on the two kingdoms in Calvin (see note 81 above): "Calvin the Transformationalist and the Kingship of Christ," *Pro Rege* XXXV/3 (March 2007): 31–8. Palmer claims that the two-kingdoms doctrine is a vestige of nature–grace dualism and leads to a conservative politics. He takes the transformational Calvin for granted: "It goes without saying that Calvin was a transformationalist." The problem with this claim is that it fails to distance itself from the enormous baggage that the term "transformational" carries with it, baggage intimately associated with the political messianism discussed in this chapter. Though I was unable to address the point in this chapter, my critique of many contemporary readings of Calvin applies to non-specialists as well, notably to those such as Nicholas Wolterstorff, who appropriate Calvin and the Calvinist tradition for a social ethic of world transformation, see Nicholas Wolterstorff, *Until Justice and Peace Embrace* (Grand Rapids: Eerdmans, 1984). For a thoughtful critique of this line of thinking, see William D. Dennison, "Dutch Neo-Calvinism and the Roots for Transformation: An Introductory Essay," *Journal of the Evangelical Theological Society*, 42 (June 1999), 271–91, and the extensive literature cited there.

clarify this and provide the second part of my pre-emptive response, I call on the testimony of my own favorite Calvinist, Herman Bavinck. Bavinck was a contemporary of Abraham Kuyper and knew very well the urgency and the pitfalls of aggressive cultural engagement by Christians. The urgency came in response to the assault on cherished freedoms such as the right of parents to determine the educational direction of their own children. But, though he himself served with distinction a significant term in the First Chamber of the Dutch Parliament, Bavinck also knew well the seductions of power. In a discussion of the pattern among his fellow Dutch Reformed in the nineteenth century to escape from public life, a pattern he resists, he also notes the danger of the opposite tendency,

> While these nineteenth century Christians [pietists] forgot the world for themselves, we run the danger of losing ourselves in the world. Nowadays we are out to convert the whole world, *to conquer all areas of life for Christ*. But we often neglect to ask whether we ourselves are truly converted and whether we belong to Christ in life and in death. For this is indeed what life boils down to. We may not banish this question from our personal or church life under the label of pietism or methodism. What does it profit a man if he gain the whole world, *even for Christian principles*, if he loses his own soul?[86]

How, then, does Bavinck the committed neo-Calvinist, committed to a vision of Christian discipleship that includes public obedience, integrate this with his concern to make sure that we keep first things first?

The answer is found in Bavinck's favorite joining of two images of the kingdom of God taken from our Lord's parables—the pearl of great price (treasure) and the leaven. Bavinck's point is always that the kingdom of God must be seen as *both* a pearl (or treasure) *and* a leaven. Furthermore, it is a treasure or pearl first and foremost; the leavening role is *secondary*. Picking up from the previous lengthy citation, here is what he says about pietism in his essay on the "Catholicity of Christianity and the Church,"

> Without a doubt, there is a glorious truth to be found in Pietism and all the religious movements akin to it. Jesus himself indeed calls us to the one thing that is necessary; namely that we seek the kingdom of heaven above

---

[86] H. Bavinck, *The Certainty of Faith*, tr. Harry der Nederlanden (St. Catharines, Ont.: Paideia, 1980), 94. The italicized phrases, which are my emphasis, are thinly veiled references to the Kuyperian Calvinists.

all . . . Faith appears to be great, indeed, when a person renounces all and shuts himself up in isolation. But even greater, it seems to me, is the faith of the person who, while keeping the kingdom of heaven as a treasure, at the same time brings it out into the world as a leaven, certain that He who is for us is greater than he who is against us and that He is able to preserve us from evil even in the midst of the world.[87]

My pre-emptive response, therefore, to concerns that refusing to grant eschatological ultimacy to any social or political movement or program implies a conservative satisfaction with the status quo, is to reply with Bavinck: "The kingdom of heaven may be a treasure and a pearl of great price, but it is also a mustard seed and a leaven."[88] Those who have heard the gospel, believe it, and seek to honor their Lord, will be a force for good in their societies; they will do good, seek justice and love mercy, while walking humbly with their God.

What they will not do is confuse the good deeds of neighbor love, the cup of cold water, the loaf of bread, the cloak for warmth, with the gospel itself. The gospel creates a new spiritual community of those who are forgiven in Christ and joined to him in the power of the Holy Spirit. Here Bavinck is as clear and emphatic as Calvin was,

> Even if Christianity had resulted in nothing else than this spiritual and holy community, even if it had not brought about any modification in earthly relationships, even if, for instance, it had done nothing for the abolition of slavery, it would still be and remain something of everlasting worth. *The significance of the Gospel does not depend on its influence on culture, its usefulness for life today; it is a treasure in itself, a pearl of great value, even if it might not be a leaven.*[89]

But we do not have to choose between the treasure of the gospel or doing good. When we have our priorities straight, we are *free* to do good.[90] As Bavinck then adds,

[87] Herman Bavinck, "The Catholicity of Christianity and the Church," tr. J. Bolt, *Calvin Theological Journal*, 27:2 (1992), 248.

[88] Bavinck, "Catholicity," 236.

[89] Bavinck in Bolt, *Essays*, 141 (emphasis added).

[90] It is very important to remember that Calvin's treatment of the two kingdoms is first dealt with in the chapter on "Christian Liberty" (*Institutes*, III.9). It is liberating to realize that our "doing good" cannot and need not save us; that knowledge is crucial to prevent us from giving greater significance to our good works than they deserve. Politics, for example, is always penultimate, never ultimate in the way that it is in political messianism.

But, although the worth of Christianity is certainly not only and exclusively, and not even in the first place determined by its influence on civilization, it nevertheless cannot be denied that it indeed exerts such influence. *The kingdom of heaven is not only a pearl, but is a leaven as well.* Whoever seeks it is offered all kinds of other things. Godliness has a promise for the future, but also for life today. In keeping God's commandments there is great reward. Christianity in its long and rich history has borne much valuable fruit for all of society in all its relationships, in spite of the unfaithfulness of its confessors.[91]

I see no need to improve on that vision of the Christian life. It is true to Calvin and to the gospel of our Lord Jesus Christ. I also believe that it is a needed corrective for the church today.

---

[91] Bavinck in Bolt, *Essays*, 11 (emphasis added).

14

Calvin and Religions

Veli-Matti Kärkkäinen

1 First words: Calvin's view of religions in his context

The uncompromising statement from Luther's *Large Catechism* illustrates the generally shared mindset toward religions of Protestant Reformers: "For all outside of Christianity, whether heathen, Turks, Jews, or false Christians and hypocrites . . . abide in eternal wrath and damnation. For they have not the Lord Christ, and, besides, are not illumined and favored by any gifts of the Holy Ghost."[1] Luther's right hand, Philipp Melanchthon, similarly contended: "It is certainly true that outside the Church . . . there is no forgiveness of sins, grace, or salvation, as among the Turks, Jews, and heathen."[2] John Calvin, in the main, concurred with his Lutheran colleagues and with them shared serious doubts about his Reformed colleague Ulrich Zwingli's allegedly more open-minded attitude as presented in his *Exposition of the Christian Faith to the Christian King* (1531, Francis I of France). Luther accused Zwingli of becoming a "full-blown heathen." What really annoyed Luther was the teaching in that book that in heaven,

---

[1] Martin Luther, *The Large Catechism*, Part First: Ten Commandments, First Commandment, trs. F. Bente and W.H.T. Dau (St. Louis: Concordia, 1921); <www.ccel.org/ccel/luther/large_cat/files/large_catechism.html#Heading 13>. For a brief consideration of the views of religions and the theology of religions among the Protestant Reformers, including Calvin, see Veli-Matti Kärkkäinen, *An Introduction to the Theology of Religions: Biblical, Historical, and Contemporary Perspectives* (Downers Grove: InterVarsity Press, 2003), 71–7, 85–7.

[2] Philipp Melanchthon, *On Christian Doctrine* (New York: Oxford University Press, 1965), 212.

You will see in the same fellowship all holy, godly, wise, brave, honorable people, the redeemed and the Redeemer, Adam, Abel, Enoch, Noah, Abraham, Isaac, Jacob, Judah, Moses, Joshua . . . also Isaiah and the Virgin Mother of God of whom he prophesied, David . . . and Paul; Hercules, Thesus, Socrates, Aristides, Antigonus, Numa, Camillus, the Catos and Scipios and all your ancestors who have departed in the faith . . .[3]

What is also similar between Luther and Calvin is that neither one of them had any meaningful experience of, or contact with, other living religions. As Samuel Zwemer puts it, "Calvin's knowledge of the pagan nations was taken from the Bible and classical literature. There is no proof that he had ever come in touch with the newly discovered world of Asian and African paganism."[4]

It goes without saying that Calvin, in common with other Protestant Reformers, did not present any systematic consideration of Christianity's relation to other religions. To Calvin's—and Luther's—credit we have to grant, however, that he "lived in the sixteenth century, not in the nineteenth. We cannot expect of him a world-view and world vision like that of William Carey. But he was not blind or deaf to the heathen world and its needs."[5]

Because of the dearth of any formal theology of religions in the teaching of the Geneva Reformer, the current attempt to reconstruct his views of religions needs to be acknowledged as just that, a reconstruction. The issue of the theology of religions is a question Calvin himself never had to face, and as such his "answer" is open to more than one interpretation. Let me state openly and clearly how I attempt to do this after-the-fact theological construal. First, I will assess as carefully as I can Calvin's views of religion or religiosity and how they may help us better reconstruct his judgment of living religions that he knew about. Second, I will attempt to discern main ideas in Calvin's understanding of the "knowledge of God the Creator," with regard to its universality and limits. Third, I will turn my attention to the uncompromising judgment of religions and gods in the Geneva Reformer's thought.

---

[3] Martin Luther, *Word and Sacrament IV*, in *Luther's Works*, vol. 38, ed. Martin E. Lehmann (Philadelphia: Fortress Press, 1971), 290.
[4] Samuel Marinus Zwemer, "Calvinism and the Missionary Enterprise," *Theology Today*, 7: 2 (1950), 208. Similarly, Jan Slomp, "Calvin and the Turks," in *Christian–Muslim Encounters*, eds. Yvonne Y. Haddad and Wadi Z. Haddad (Gainesville, Fla.: University Press of Florida, 1995), 138.
[5] Zwemer, "Calvinism and the Missionary Enterprise," 207.

Thereafter, fourth, I am ready to explain the necessity of the Mediator, the Christ. Fifth, before my conclusions, I will offer a brief case study by zooming in on the question of Calvin's assessment of Islam as a religion. While Calvin probably never had much contact with Muslims, his writings—espec-ially those of an exegetical nature—make reference to Islam and its religious views. I will end this chapter with reflections on Calvin's legacy to contemporary evangelicalism.

2 The value of religion(s)

While the most natural way of beginning the inquiry into Calvin's theology of religions might appear to be his well-known insistence on the existence of the sense of the divine among all men and women, all people having been created in the image of God, I will turn first to his view of religion(s) and religiosity, which in my assessment plays a foundational role in his embedded theology of religions. The famous opening lines of Calvin's *Institutes*[6] may have much to do with the reconstrual of his theology of religions in that the Reformer understands the knowledge of God and the knowledge of human beings to be mutually conditioned—of course, not equal since the former precedes and informs the latter—but nevertheless mutual:

> Our wisdom, in so far as it ought to be deemed and solid Wisdom, consists almost entirely of two parts: the knowledge of God and of ourselves. But as these are connected together by many ties, it is not easy to determine which of the two precedes and gives birth to the other. For, in the first place, no man can survey himself without forthwith turning his thoughts towards the God in whom he lives and moves; because it is perfectly obvious, that the endowments which we possess cannot possibly be from ourselves; nay, that our very being is nothing else than subsistence in God alone. (I.1.1)

The significance of this statement lies in the observation that if the knowledge of the human person is a constitutive part of the knowledge of God, then religiosity as part of human nature and life cannot be ignored. In other words, if Calvin claims, as he does, that in order to know God one must turn to the human being, then the role of religiosity

---

[6] References to John Calvin, *The Institutes of the Christian Religion*, tr. Henry Beveridge (Grand Rapids: Christian Classics Ethereal Library, <www.ccel.org>, 2002) will be given in the main text (e.g. I.1.1).

as a constitutive part of humanity has to be taken into consideration when speaking of God.[7]

This indeed is something Calvin categorically states: "For, properly speaking, we cannot say that God is known where there is no religion or piety" (I.2.1).[8] Therefore, it is no wonder that religion is everywhere in the world because *sensus divinitatis* (the sense of the divine)—which for Calvin is a matter without dispute (I.3.1)—has been implanted so deeply in the hearts of men and women and manifests itself and is being mediated by religions.

> Certainly, if there is any quarter where it may be supposed that God is unknown, the most likely for such an instance to exist is among the dullest tribes farthest removed from civilisation. But, as a heathen tells us, there is no nation so barbarous, no race so brutish, as not to be imbued with the conviction that there is a God. Even those who, in other respects, seem to differ least from the lower animals, constantly retain some sense of religion; so thoroughly has this common conviction possessed the mind, so firmly is it stamped on the breasts of all men. Since, then, there never has been, from the very first, any quarter of the globe, any city, any household even, without religion, this amounts to a tacit confession, that a sense of Deity is inscribed on every heart. (I.3.1)

It seems to me that the sense of the divine among religions and religious ideas is but part of the wonderful providence of the good God celebrated by Calvin in the opening lines of his *Institutes* when he speaks of "those blessings which unceasingly distil to us from heaven, [and] are like streams conducting us to the fountain" (I.1.1). Somewhat ironically, for Calvin, even the existence of idolatry is a tribute to the necessity and power of religion as the mediator of the sense of the divine,

> Nay, even idolatry is ample evidence of this fact. For we know how reluctant man is to lower himself, in order to set other creatures above him.

---

[7] Building on the long history of tradition, in contemporary theology the Roman Catholic K. Rahner and Protestant W. Pannenberg have argued forcefully for the theological significance of religiosity as constitutive of humanity.

[8] Interpreting Calvin's use of the term "piety" along the lines of Schleiermacher's Liberal theology and his turn to the subjectivistic "feelings of absolute dependence" (as some historical theologians have done) is in my understanding a mistaken road. That discussion, however, falls outside my key concerns in this chapter and thus I do not engage it.

Therefore, when he chooses to worship wood and stone rather than be thought to have no God, it is evident how very strong this impression of a Deity must be; since it is more difficult to obliterate it from the mind of man, than to break down the feelings of his nature,—these certainly being broken down, when, in opposition to his natural haughtiness, he spontaneously humbles himself before the meanest object as an act of reverence to God. (I.3.1)

Commenting on Acts 8:27, which speaks of the Ethiopian Eunuch who came to worship in Jerusalem, Calvin grants that "the name of the true God was spread far abroad" and that there were seemingly "some worshippers in far countries," whether in the East or among Romans and beyond. There were places with "some smell of the knowledge of the true God," as he puts it.[9]

Lest some may draw from the existence of false ideas among religions the conclusion that therefore religions per se are evil, Calvin states the opposite: "It is most absurd, therefore, to maintain, as some do, that religion was devised by the cunning and craft of a few individuals, as a means of keeping the body of the people in due subjection, while there was nothing which those very individuals, while teaching others to worship God, less believed than the existence of a God" (I.3.2). So convinced is the Reformer of the role of the religions in God's world that he boldly argues this as a self-evident fact even among non-Christian writers such as Plato,

> For it is the very thing which Plato meant (in *Phæd. et Theact.*) when he taught, as he often does, that the chief good of the soul consists in resemblance to God; i.e., when, by means of knowing him, she is wholly transformed into him. Thus Gryllus, also, in Plutarch (*lib. guod bruta anim. ratione utantur*), reasons most skilfully, when he affirms that, if once religion is banished from the lives of men, they not only in no respect excel, but are, in many respects, much more wretched than the brutes, since, being exposed to so many forms of evil, they continually drag on a troubled and restless existence: that the only thing, therefore, which makes them superior is the worship of God, through which alone they aspire to immortality. (I.3.3)

---

[9] John Calvin, *Commentary on the Acts of the Apostles*, vol. 1, in *Calvin's Commentaries*, complete from the Calvin Translation Society (Grand Rapids: Christian Classics Ethereal Library, <www.ccel.org>, on Acts 8:27. (Hereafter all references to Calvin's commentaries will be from this edition.)

This is, of course, not to say that therefore the sense of the divine is generally well cultivated and properly discerned; indeed, the contrary is the case.[10] Yet the corruption of the knowledge of God in religions does not make void the role of religions. The "seed of religion" is implanted in all human beings even in their corrupted nature.[11] Richard Plantinga accurately summarizes Calvin's assessment of religions,

> What are the implications of Calvin's position? First of all, religion is no arbitrary invention or construction; even those who deny God feel an inkling of divine fear or terror. Second, atheism is not really possible because the sense of divinity cannot be destroyed; it lies deep within us in the marrow of our bones. This is a doctrine we learn, Calvin says, not in school but in the womb.[12]

Having established the role of religion as the mediator of the sense of the Divine, which points to the potential of reaching to the saving knowledge of God that can only come from the self-revelation in Christ, let me now highlight the importance of Calvin's idea of the knowledge of God as the Creator.

3 The knowledge of God the Creator: its universality and limits[13]

As routinely mentioned—following Calvin's way of titling the first two books of his *Institutes*—the knowledge of God has two facets, namely,

---

[10] See, for example, *Institutes*, I.4.1 among many other similar passages (this one with reference to Rom. 1:22): "But though experience testifies that a seed of religion is divinely sown in all, scarcely one in a hundred is found who cherishes it in his heart, and not one in whom it grows to maturity so far is it from yielding fruit in its season. Moreover, while some lose themselves in superstitious observances, and others, of set purpose, wickedly revolt from God, the result is that, in regard to the true knowledge of him, all are so degenerate, that in no part of the world can genuine godliness be found."

[11] John Calvin, *Commentary on the Gospel of John*, vol. 1, in *Calvin's Commentaries*, on Jn.1:5: "The light which still dwells in corrupt nature consists chiefly of two parts; for, first, all men naturally possess some seed of religion; and, secondly, the distinction between good and evil is engraven on their consciences."

[12] Richard J. Plantinga, "God So Loved the World: Theological Reflections on Religious Plurality in the History of Christianity," *Calvin Theological Journal*, 39:2 (2004), 284.

[13] The question of the knowledge of God in Calvin's theology is a huge topic. Since that is covered in this volume elsewhere, I will not attempt any kind of

the knowledge of God as Creator and as Redeemer. In this section, I will establish the presence of the former in Calvin's theology, based on the creative and providential works of God. However one may theologically connect this with the traditional notions of "natural knowledge of God" and "general revelation,"[14] it is axiomatic for Calvin that some kind of "preliminary" knowledge of God exists, deeply embedded in the structure of the human being.

> My meaning is: we must be persuaded not only that as he once formed the world, so he sustains it by his boundless power, governs it by his wisdom, preserves it by his goodness, in particular, rules the human race with justice and Judgment, bears with them in mercy, shields them by his protection; but also that not a particle of light, or wisdom, or justice, or power, or rectitude, or genuine truth, will anywhere be found, which does not flow from him, and of which he is not the cause; in this way we must learn to expect and ask all things from him, and thankfully ascribe to him whatever we receive. (I.2.1)[15]

So evident is this knowledge of God that Calvin agrees with some philosophers of old who had called the human person "a *microcosm* (*miniature world*) . . . [and] the human race . . . a bright mirror of the

---

(cont.) comprehensive treatment of that. I focus solely on those aspects of the topic that have direct bearing on Calvin's theology of religions. The standard source is Edward A. Dowey, Jr., *The Knowledge of God in Calvin's Theology* (Grand Rapids: Eerdmans, rev. ed.1994).

[14] As is well known among students of Calvin's theology, the distinction between the two types of the knowledge of God in his thinking does not follow neatly the standard theological divide between general and special revelation. The knowledge of God the Creator goes beyond the limits of the traditional understanding of general revelation. For a reliable discussion, see Dowey, *Knowledge of God*, especially chapter 2.

[15] Similarly, for example, *Institutes*, I.5.1: "Since the perfection of blessedness consists in the knowledge of God, he has been pleased, in order that none might be excluded from the means of obtaining felicity, not only to deposit in our minds that seed of religion of which we have already spoken, but so to manifest his perfections in the whole structure of the universe, and daily place himself in our view, that we cannot open our eyes without being compelled to behold him. His essence, indeed, is incomprehensible, utterly transcending all human thought; but on each of his works his glory is engraven in characters so bright, so distinct, and so illustrious, that none, however dull and illiterate, can plead ignorance as their excuse."

Creator's works." Indeed, adds Calvin, "infants hanging on their mothers' breasts have tongues eloquent enough to proclaim his glory without the aid of other orators" (I.5.3). Commenting on Acts 14:17, Calvin even goes as far as to say that "God hath, indeed, revealed himself to all mankind by his word since [from] the beginning."[16] While this kind of general knowledge of God does not suffice for salvific knowledge of God per se, it surely is the fountain of "piety, out of which religion springs." Piety for Calvin is nothing less than "that union of reverence and love to God which the knowledge of his benefits inspires" (I.2.1).

Parallel to his argument concerning religions, Calvin ironically argues for the certainty of the general knowledge of God on the basis of the miserable condition of humanity: "For as there exists in man something like a world of misery, and ever since we were stript of the divine attire our naked shame discloses an immense series of disgraceful properties[,] every man, being stung by the consciousness of his own unhappiness, in this way necessarily obtains at least some knowledge of God" (I.1.1).

In fairness to Calvin, we have to set the record straight: having first established the value of religions as the mediators of the sense of the divine and the existence of a general knowledge of God on the basis of the fact that God is the Creator and Preserver of the world, we may not imagine that that is enough for humanity to know about God. It is one thing for Calvin to establish firmly the universal knowledge of God the Creator and another thing to ascertain the proper usage of that kind of knowledge of God. Here Calvin gives an uncompromising judgment,

> Those, therefore, who, in considering this question, propose to inquire what the essence of God is, only delude us with frigid speculations,—it being much more our interest to know what kind of being God is, and what things are agreeable to his nature. For, of what use is it to join Epicures in acknowledging some God who has cast off the care of the world, and only delights himself in ease? What avails it, in short, to know a God with whom we have nothing to do? The effect of our knowledge rather ought to be, *first*, to teach us reverence and fear; and, *secondly*, to induce us, under its guidance and teaching, to ask every good thing from him, and, when it is received, ascribe it to him. For how can the idea of God enter your mind without instantly giving rise to the thought, that since you are his workmanship, you are bound, by the very law of creation, to submit to his authority? (I.2.2)

---

[16] Calvin, *Commentary on Acts*, vol. 2, on Acts 14:17.

A similar kind of uncompromising statement can be found in the beginning of the discussion on the need for Scripture, special revelation, to complement and correct what is lacking in the knowledge of God as Creator,

> Therefore, though the effulgence which is presented to every eye, both in the heavens and on the earth, leaves the ingratitude of man without excuse, since God, in order to bring the whole human race under the same condemnation, holds forth to all, without exception, a mirror of his Deity in his works, another and better help must be given to guide us properly to God as a Creator. (I.6.1)

A number of other passages can be easily found to the same effect.[17]

To underline his point, Calvin makes a distinction between the mere "knowing" of God and "fearing" God. Commenting on Joshua 4:24, he says that the difference between the Israelites and the other nations was that "the nations may know [Yahweh] but that Israel alone may 'fear thy God.'" Only this "special knowledge," as Calvin puts it, makes the difference.[18] At the same time—while judging quite harshly the inadequacy of the general knowledge of God among the pagans—Calvin is pastorally mindful of the need of evangelists to try to find a common point between the audience and the "full gospel" presentation. He finds a biblical precedent in Paul's and Barnabas' missionary experience in Lystra, as recorded in Acts 14.

> There is no express mention made indeed of the Word, because they spake to the Gentiles . . . We know that the order of teaching doth require that we begin with things which are better known. Seeing that Paul and Barnabas spake to the Gentiles, they should have in vain essayed to bring them unto Christ. Therefore, it was expedient for them to begin with some other point, which was not so far separate from common sense, [perception] that after that was confessed they might afterward pass over unto Christ. The minds of the men of Lystra were possessed with that error, that there be more gods than one. Paul and Barnabas show, on the contrary, that there is but one Creator of the world.[19]

---

[17] See further the rest of *Institutes*, I.6.1; and also I.4.2; I.5.1; I.5.12–15.
[18] Calvin, *Commentary on Joshua*, on Josh. 4:24.
[19] Calvin, *Commentary on Acts*, vol. 2, on Acts 14:15. A similar strategy was followed by Paul in his speech in Athens.

4 The judgment on religions and their gods

Since the purpose of this essay is to give a preliminary assessment of Calvin's implicit and unthematic theology of religions, it will do no good to mount evidence on one side of the issue, whether a negative or positive attitude to other religions, but rather to make an effort to take stock of the whole evidence. If the acknowledgment of the value of religion as the mediator of the knowledge of God, the universality of the *sensus divinitatis*, as well as the knowledge of God as the Creator—albeit truncated and limited—embedded in the structure of the human being having been created in the image of God and provided for by the same Creator, all point to a more tolerant and accepting spirit with regard to religions, there are also several key orientations in Calvin's theology that bespeak judgment on religions. The first has to do with what Calvin saw as the mainstream biblical way, namely, an uncompromising judgment of the gods of the nations vis-à-vis the acknowledgment of and humble submission to the one and only true God. The following lengthier summary statement offers a testimony to this judgment.

> First, then, let the reader observe that the Scripture, in order to direct us to the true God, distinctly excludes and rejects all the gods of the heathen, because religion was universally adulterated in almost every age. It is true, indeed, that the name of one God was everywhere known and celebrated. For those who worshipped a multitude of gods, whenever they spoke the genuine language of nature, simply used the name god, as if they had thought one god sufficient. And this is shrewdly noticed by Justin Martyr, who, to the same effect, wrote a treatise, entitled, *On the Monarchy of God*, in which he shows, by a great variety of evidence, that the unity of God is engraven on the hearts of all. Tertullian also proves the same thing from the common forms of speech. But as all, without exception, have in the vanity of their minds rushed or been dragged into lying fictions, these impressions, as to the unity of God, whatever they may have naturally been, have had no further effect than to render men inexcusable. The wisest plainly discover the vague wanderings of their minds when they express a wish for any kind of Deity, and thus offer up their prayers to unknown gods. And then, in imagining a manifold nature in God, though their ideas concerning Jupiter, Mercury, Venus, Minerva, and others, were not so absurd as those of the rude vulgar, they were by no means free from the delusions of the devil. We have elsewhere observed, that however subtle the evasions devised by philosophers, they cannot do away with the charge of rebellion, in that all of them have corrupted the truth of God. For this reason, Habakkuk (2:20), after condemning all idols,

orders men to seek God in his temple, that the faithful may acknowledge none but Him, who has manifested himself in his word. (I.10.3)

Calvin states categorically that the Bible's "exclusive definition . . . annihilates every deity" created by men and women for their own purposes whether that god be the sun worshipped by the Persians or the stars venerated by many nations or even the wisdom loved by the Greeks (I.11.1).[20] The biblical God is a jealous God who does not tolerate other deities (I.12.1). What makes the idol an idol is that it is a human invention rather than something appointed by God.[21]

5 The necessity of the Mediator

Along with judgment of religions and their gods, Calvin also balances his otherwise affirmative standpoint toward religiosity by arguing forcefully for the need of Christ, the mediator of true knowledge of God and salvation.

> The whole human race having been undone in the person of Adam . . . is so far from availing us, that it rather turns to our greater disgrace, until God, who does not acknowledge man when defiled and corrupted by sin as his own work, appears as a Redeemer in the person of his only begotten Son. Since our fall from life unto death, all that knowledge of God the Creator . . . would be useless, were it not followed up by faith, holding forth God to us as a Father in Christ . . . Wherefore, we must conclude with Paul, "After that in the wisdom of God the world by wisdom knew not God, it pleased God by the foolishness of preaching to save them that believe," (1 Cor. 1:21) . . . Therefore, although the preaching of the cross is not in accordance with human wisdom, we must, however, humbly

[20] *Institutes*, I.11.2–3 lists a number of familiar biblical passages to support this claim. Commenting on Josh. 2:11, Calvin commends to the reader Rahab's decisive shift from serving idols to serving the God of the Bible: "For it is perfectly clear that when heaven and earth are declared subject to the God of Israel, there is a repudiation of all the pagan fictions by which the majesty, and power, and glory of God are portioned out among different deities." Calvin, *Commentary on Joshua*, on Josh. 2:11. In *Institutes*, I.11.8 Calvin offers interesting speculations into the origins of idols, for example, entertaining the possibility of relation to the custom of honoring the dead among many nations.
[21] Calvin, *Commentary on Acts*, vol. 1, on Acts 7:41.

embrace it if we would return to God our Maker, from whom we are estranged, that he may again become our Father. It is certain that after the fall of our first parent, no knowledge of God without a Mediator was effectual to salvation. Christ speaks not of his own age merely, but embraces all ages, when he says "This is life eternal that they might know thee the only true God, and Jesus Christ, whom thou hast sent," (John 17:3). (II.6.1)

Even the chosen people of God in the Old Testament could not be saved without the Mediator (II.6.2) and, therefore, the ultimate purpose of prophecies in the old covenant is to turn the eyes of the Jews to Christ (II.6.4). Whether Jews or Gentiles, the way of salvation is the same,

> For though in old time there were many who boasted that they worshipped the Supreme Deity, the Maker of heaven and earth, yet as they had no Mediator, it was impossible for them truly to enjoy the mercy of God, so as to feel persuaded that he was their Father. Not holding the head, that is, Christ, their knowledge of God was evanescent; and hence they at length fell away to gross and foul superstitions betraying their ignorance, just as the Turks in the present day, who, though proclaiming, with full throat, that the Creator of heaven and earth is their God, yet by their rejection of Christ, substitute an idol in his place. (II.6.4)

Calvin's view of double predestination undoubtedly plays into his theology of religions.[22] According to the Catholic Francis Sullivan,

> It is clear that for Calvin the mere fact that the newly discovered peoples had not, until now, had a chance to hear the gospel preached is a manifest sign that all their ancestors were among the reprobate, for if God had willed their salvation, he would have made it possible for them to come to the knowledge of the truth, and thus to faith in Christ, without which there was no possibility of their salvation. Even now, when they have a chance to hear the gospel, it is God's intention, with regard to those whom he has predestined to damnation, that it should blind them and make them all the more guilty.[23]

Calvin did not acknowledge the possibility of the second chance, as his comments on the disputed passage of 1 Peter 3:19 reveal: "Moreover, the

---

[22] For a definition of double predestination, see *Institutes*, III.21.5.

[23] Francis A. Sullivan, *Salvation Outside the Church?* (New York: Paulist Press, 1992), 78.

strange notion of those who think that unbelievers as to the coming of Christ, were after his death freed from their sin, needs no long refutation; for it is an indubitable doctrine of Scripture, that we obtain not salvation in Christ except by faith; then there is no hope left for those who continue to death unbelieving."[24]

At the same time, Calvin was not totally dogmatic about how much knowledge of Christ the person needs to have to be saved. Commenting on Acts 10:5, he grants that Cornelius did not seem to have any knowledge of the Savior, yet as a recipient of the gifts of the Spirit, this Gentile can be compared to the Old Testament saints who were exercising faith in Christ whom they did not yet know.[25]

In order to make my discussion more focused, I will next offer a brief consideration of Calvin's views of a particular religion, Islam. While both he and Luther probably had no first-hand contact with Muslims, he offered scattered remarks on that religion.

6 Calvin on Islam

While there are several studies on Luther's views of Muslims[26]—whom he most often calls, similarly to Calvin, the "Turks"—there is little research on Calvin in this respect.[27] Both Calvin and Luther often lump Muslims together with the "Papists" (Catholics of the time), and sometimes even with others who in their outlook were heretical, such as the Anabaptists.[28] It is thus not often easy to make a distinction between Calvin's more general pejorative remarks on various kinds of opponents and Muslims in particular.

As mentioned above, Calvin most probably had very little, if any, first-hand contact with Muslims. His writings do not contain any direct

[24] Calvin, *Commentaries on Catholic Epistles*, on 1 Pet. 3:19.

[25] Calvin, *Commentary on Acts*, vol. 1, on Acts 10:5.

[26] For a brief overview, see Egil Grislis, "Luther and the Turks," *The Muslim World*, 64 (July 1974), 180–93, and (October 1974), 275–91.

[27] The main critical study is that offered by Slomp, "Calvin and the Turks," 126–42. A massive study (which unfortunately is not accessible to most English-speaking readers) about the attitudes of the Reformers of Zurich is Victor Segesvary, *L'Islam et la Réforme* (Lausanne: Éd. L'Age d'Homme, 1978).

[28] In some cases, even Jews are included: "This delusion of Satan is equally common among Papists, Turks, Jews, and other nations" (Calvin, *Commentary on Psalms*, vol. 1, on Ps. 32:1).

citations from the Qur'an.[29] However, historically, his times were of course influenced by the Turkish Empire. The Turkish emperor Sulayman I, sometimes called "The Magnificent," was Calvin's contemporary. Calvin's keen interest in political developments (to which there is also testimony in his introductory letter to the King of France in the *Institutes*), made him well aware of the affairs of the Muslim world. From Calvin's "footnote" remarks on Daniel 3:21, it has been gleaned that he might have met members of the Turkish delegation that disembarked in Marseilles in 1534 on the way to meet the king.[30]

There is no doubt that Calvin was concerned about the Turks' military and religious power over Europe. In his commentary on Jeremiah 13:21, which speaks of the threat of Assyrians and Babylonians, Calvin makes this pointed remark,

> The case was similar to that of the Turks at this day, were they to pass over to these parts and exercise their authority; for it might be asked the French kings and their counsellors, "Whose fault is it that the Turks come to us so easily? It is because ye have prepared for them the way by sea, because ye have bribed them, and your ports have been opened to them; and yet they have wilfully exercised the greatest cruelty towards your subjects. All these things have proceeded from yourselves; ye are therefore the authors of all these evils."[31]

---

[29] Slomp, "Calvin and the Turks," 135. Slomp lists three references to the term "Qur'an" (for which Calvin uses the French translation "Alcuran") in Calvin's writings. One example is in his commentary on John 16:14 to be cited below; the other two are in the sermons on Job 33 and 2 Tim. 1:6–8.

[30] So Slomp, "Calvin and the Turks," 127. Daniel 3:21 (RSV) speaks of men who "were bound in their mantles, their tunics, their hats and their other garments." Calvin adds this remark: "We know that the Orientals then wore turbans as they do now, for they wrap up the head; and though we do not see many of them, yet we know the Turkish dress; then the general name is added" (*Commentary on Daniel*, vol. 1, on Dan. 3:21).

[31] Calvin, *Commentary on Jeremiah–Lamentations*, vol. 2, on Jer. 13:21. It is instructive to note that in his *Commentary on Isaiah* (vol. 3), on Is. 36:20, Calvin surmises that God has indeed raised "the Turks . . . haughtily against us," and that whatever prosperity there is among them, that is also not something the Turks could have produced on their own. Calvin sees here a parallel between what happened in Israelite history when the Lord raised opponents to the People of God and his own times with regard to the church. Similarly to biblical times, the same Lord is also going to destroy those whom he has used against his own people.

Similarly, Calvin was greatly distressed by the threat of Muslim forces to the safety of the church: "My readers now understand, that all the sects by which the Church has been lessened from the beginning, have been so many streams of revolt which began to draw away the water from the right course, but that the sect of Mahomet was like a violent bursting forth of water, that took away about the half of the Church by its violence."[32]

Calvin did not spare any words in condemning the Muslim faith and their rejection of and replacement of Christ for idols have already been quoted (see page 277, II.6.4).[33] His exposition of the Paraclete passage of John 14:25 lumps together Mohammed, Pope, Anabaptists, and Libertines and condemns their interpretations of "new revelations" after the coming of Christ and the Holy Spirit.[34] In his commentary on Acts 22:14, he even accuses Muslims (and Papists!) of inventing "a new God."[35] John 16:14 names both Mohammed and the Pope as Anti-Christ.[36] In the same context, Calvin juxtaposes Islam and Christianity, one being built on the foundation of the Qur'an, the other on the Word of God.[37]

---

[32] Calvin, *Commentaries on Philippians, Colossians and Thessalonians*, on 2 Thess. 2:3.

[33] Similarly, for example, Calvin, *Catholic Epistles*, on 1 Pet. 1:3: "Hence they who form their ideas of God in his naked majesty apart from Christ, have an idol instead of the true God, as the case is with the Jews and the Turks." So also his comments on 1 Pet. 1:21. Yet another example can be found in Calvin, *Catholic Epistles*, on 1 Jn. 2:22: "It hence follows, that Turks, Jews, and such as are like them, have a mere idol and not the true God. For by whatever titles they may honor the God whom they worship, still, as they reject him without whom they cannot come to God, and in whom God has really manifested himself to us, what have they but some creature or fiction of their own?"

[34] Calvin, *Commentary on the Gospel of John*, vol. 2, on Jn. 14:25.

[35] Calvin, *Commentary on Acts*, vol. 2, on Acts 22:14. Interestingly enough, in this passage Calvin uses the term Muhametistae instead of Turks.

[36] Calvin, *Commentary on the Gospel of John*, vol. 2, on Jn. 16:14.

[37] Calvin, *Commentary on the Gospel of John*, vol. 2, on Jn. 16:14: "Mahomet asserts that, without his Alcoran, men always remain children. Thus, by a false pretense of the Spirit, the world was bewitched to depart from the simple purity of Christ; for, as soon as the Spirit is separated from the word of Christ, the door is open to all kinds of delusions and impostures. A similar method of deceiving has been attempted, in the present age, by many fanatics. The written doctrine appeared to them to be literal, and, therefore, they chose to contrive a new theology that would consist of revelations."

In the light of these and similar fears of Islamic threat, and judgments of Islamic faith by Calvin, it is interesting that commonalities between the two religions have been suggested. According to Zwemer,

> Islam indeed . . . is the Calvinism of the Orient. It, too, was a call to acknowledge the sovereignty of God's will. "There is no god but Allah." . . . Calvinism and Islam had much in common. Both are opposed to compromise and all half-measures. Both were a trumpet-call in hard times for hard men, for intellects that could pierce to the roots of things where truth and lies part company. Intolerance is sometimes a virtue. The very essence and life of all great religious movements is the sense of authority; of an external, supernatural framework or pattern to which all must be made comformable.[38]

Zwemer is not alone in his opinion. Jan Slomp likewise argues that there are similarities between the teachings of Calvinism and the Qur'anic message, similarities such as the teaching on the sovereignty and glory of God. Too bad, Slomp laments, that Calvin never took time to study the Qur'an, which was available to him through his friend Oporinus.[39] What about evangelizing Muslims? "Were a Turk to offer himself for baptism, we would not at once perform the rite without receiving a confession which was satisfactory to the Church" (IV.16.24).

7 Last words: Calvin's legacy and prospects

There is a tendency in contemporary reflection on the theology of religions to try to find positive and affirming elements in every theologian's and theological movement's heritage. Often this leads to a somewhat uncritical and unbalanced reading of the evidence in favor of a more tolerant attitude toward other religions. While this kind of "twisting the evidence" may need to be tolerated for the time being as a way of balancing the overly negative assessments of the past, in a longer perspective it is hardly able to redeem its promises.

Our discussion has revealed that on religions and religiosity, there are two kinds of material in Calvin's writings. On the one hand, he affirms the significance and necessity of religion(s) as the mediator of the sense of the divine (which may or may not lead to the true knowledge and fear of God). This is a path that contemporary evangelicals

---

[38] Zwemer, "Calvinism and the Missionary Enterprise," 212–13.
[39] Slomp, "Calvin and the Turks," 138.

would do well to follow.[40] On the other hand, religions as they now appear, apart from the revelation of God, have distorted the knowledge of God and are under God's judgment.[41] Thus, there is a need for divine intervention. Contemporary evangelicalism by and large agrees.[42]

Bluntly put: neither Calvin nor Luther—nor even the somewhat more open-minded Zwingli—ever endorsed other religions as in any way salvific, or their scriptures as divine revelations. In keeping with the mindset of the times, as well as the tradition of the church, other religions were held to be vastly inferior to the Christian faith and by any account were incapable of mediating saving knowledge of God. Furthermore, Calvin's remarks about persons and beliefs in other religions (in his case, remarks limited to the Muslim faith) were often pejorative and harsh—but no different from the opinions of other Reformers.

It is understandable, therefore, that Calvin never saw a need to construct any kind of biblical or systematic theology of religions. He commented on other religions and their relation to Christianity only occasionally and without any conscious effort to put them in a perspective. That said, it is significant that with hindsight one can see indications of an embedded, unthematic contribution to what we nowadays call the theology of religions. While Calvin did not develop these ideas with the theology of religions in mind, their potential should be investigated and reflected upon by contemporary evangelicals. Let me mention the most important tasks in this regard. In gleaning from, and summarizing the main insights of Calvin, there are three questions in particular that need to be asked:

---

[40] For an overview and assessment of the state of evangelical reflections on religions and the theology of religions, see Veli-Matti Kärkkäinen, "Evangelical Theology and the Religions," in Timothy Larsen and Daniel J. Treier (eds.), *Cambridge Companion to Evangelical Theology* (Cambridge: Cambridge University Press, 2007), 199–212.

[41] One of the few reflections on the pros and cons among religions from a theological perspective among evangelicals is Clark H. Pinnock, *A Wideness in God's Mercy: The Finality of Jesus Christ in a World of Religions* (Grand Rapids: Zondervan, 1992), chs. 3 and 4 respectively.

[42] For a representative discussion, see Douglas R. Geivett and W. Gary Phillips, "A Particularist View: An Evidentialist Approach," in D.L. Ockholm and T.R. Phillips (eds.), *More Than One Way? Four Views on Salvation in a Pluralistic World* (Grand Rapids: Zondervan, 1995), 211–45, 259–70.

- First, what is an evangelical assessment of the value of religions as mediators of the knowledge of God?[43]

- Second, what is an evangelical assessment of the value and limits of the existence of the sense of the divine in the human being?

  As this has everything to do with theological anthropology, that should occupy the minds of contemporary evangelicals.

- Third, how could evangelicals think of the role of the universal nature of the knowledge of God as Creator and Provider and of its relation to the knowledge of God as Savior?

  As is well known, evangelical theology of religions to date has majored on the question of the possibility of salvation and left the theological reflection on the knowledge of God as Creator to others.

---

[43] Some contemporary evangelicals have engaged living religions and the religiosity of the world and offered theological reflections based on those observations: Gerald R. McDermott, *Can Evangelicals Learn from World Religions? Jesus, Revelation and Religious Traditions* (Downers Grove, Ill.: InterVarsity Press, 2000); Winfried Corduan, *A Tapestry of Faiths: The Common Threads Between Christianity and World Religions* (Downers Grove, Ill.: InterVarsity Press, 2002); Timothy C. Tennent, *Christianity at the Religious Roundtable: Evangelicalism in Conversation with Hinduism, Buddhism, and Islam* (Grand Rapids: Baker Academic, 2002).